mother panic
GOTHAM A.D.

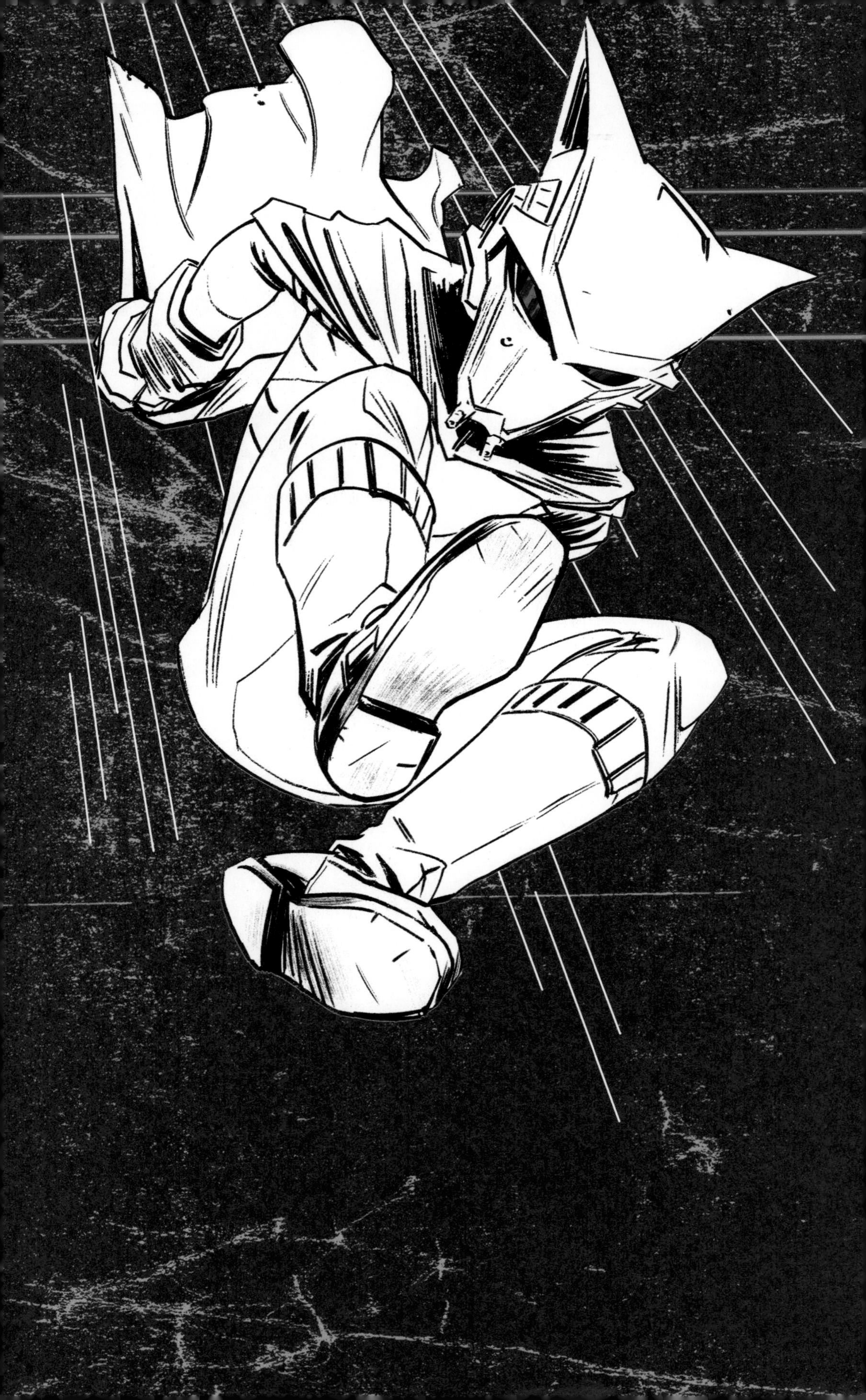

mother panic
GOTHAM A.D.

JODY HOUSER
Writer

IBRAHIM MOUSTAFA
Artist

JORDAN BOYD
with MARISSA LOUISE
Colorists

JOHN WORKMAN
Letterer

TOMMY LEE EDWARDS
Collection Cover Art and Original Series Covers

GERARD WAY
DC's Young Animal Curator

MOTHER PANIC created by **GERARD WAY**,
JODY HOUSER and **TOMMY LEE EDWARDS**

MOLLY MAHAN Editor – Original Series
JEB WOODARD Group Editor – Collected Editions
SCOTT NYBAKKEN Editor – Collected Edition
STEVE COOK Design Director – Books
MEGEN BELLERSEN Publication Design

BOB HARRAS Senior VP – Editor-in-Chief, DC Comics
MARK DOYLE Executive Editor, Vertigo & Black Label

DAN DiDIO Publisher
JIM LEE Publisher & Chief Creative Officer
AMIT DESAI Executive VP – Business & Marketing Strategy, Direct to Consumer
& Global Franchise Management
BOBBIE CHASE VP & Executive Editor, Young Reader & Talent Development
MARK CHIARELLO Senior VP – Art, Design & Collected Editions
JOHN CUNNINGHAM Senior VP – Sales & Trade Marketing
BRIAR DARDEN VP – Business Affairs
ANNE DePIES Senior VP – Business Strategy, Finance & Administration
DON FALLETTI VP – Manufacturing Operations
LAWRENCE GANEM VP – Editorial Administration & Talent Relations
ALISON GILL Senior VP – Manufacturing & Operations
JASON GREENBERG VP – Business Strategy & Finance
HANK KANALZ Senior VP – Editorial Strategy & Administration
JAY KOGAN Senior VP – Legal Affairs
NICK J. NAPOLITANO VP – Manufacturing Administration
LISETTE OSTERLOH VP – Digital Marketing & Events
EDDIE SCANNELL VP – Consumer Marketing
COURTNEY SIMMONS Senior VP – Publicity & Communications
JIM (SKI) SOKOLOWSKI VP – Comic Book Specialty Sales & Trade Marketing
NANCY SPEARS VP – Mass, Book, Digital Sales & Trade Marketing
MICHELE R. WELLS VP – Content Strategy

MOTHER PANIC: GOTHAM A.D.

DC Comics
2900 West Alameda Avenue
Burbank, CA 91505
Printed by LSC Communications, Kendallville, IN, USA.
10/5/18. First Printing.
ISBN: 978-1-4012-8100-7

Library of Congress Cataloging-in-Publication Data is available.

FSC
www.fsc.org

MIX
Paper from
responsible sources
FSC® C132124

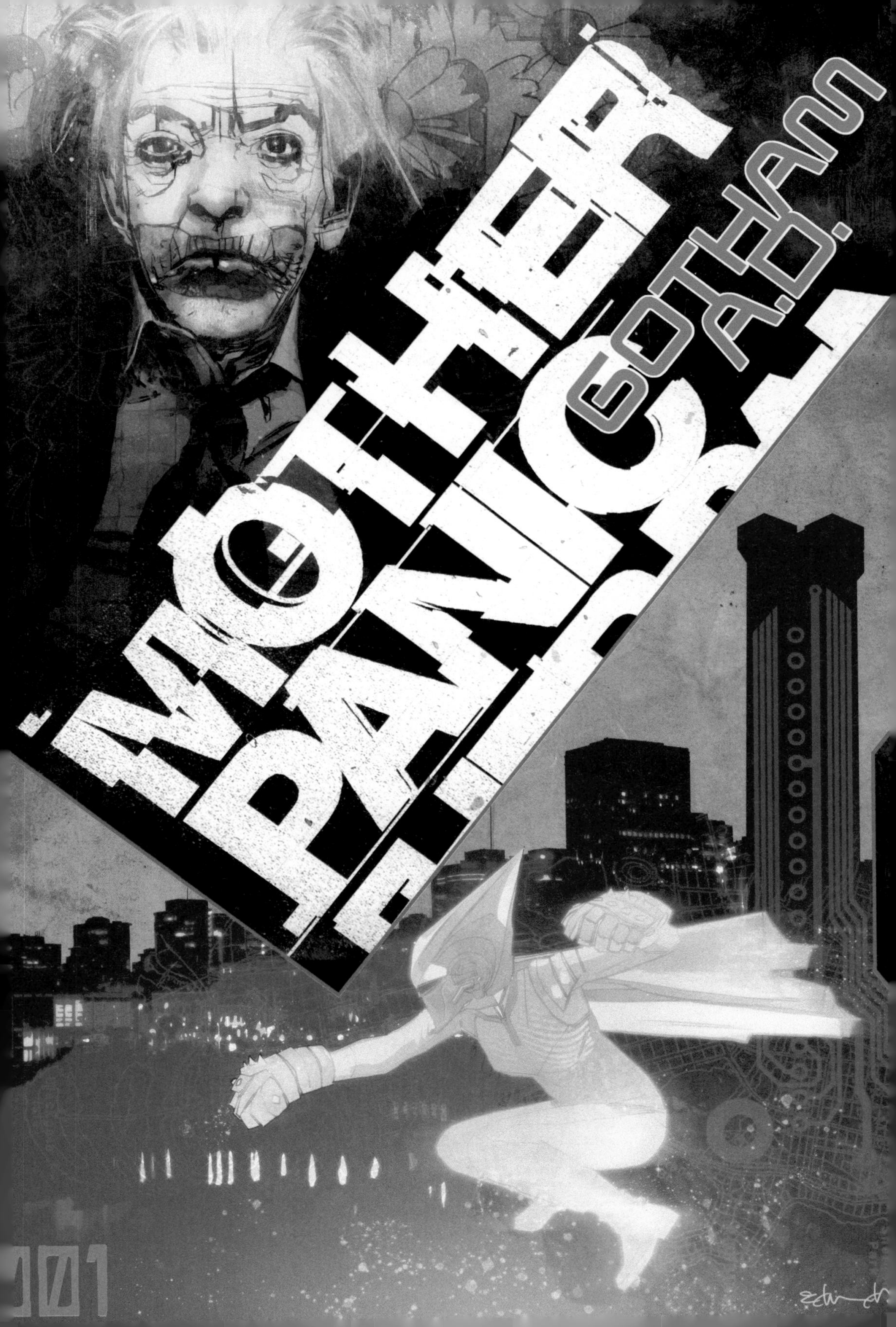
MOTHER
PANIC
GOTHAM A.D.
001

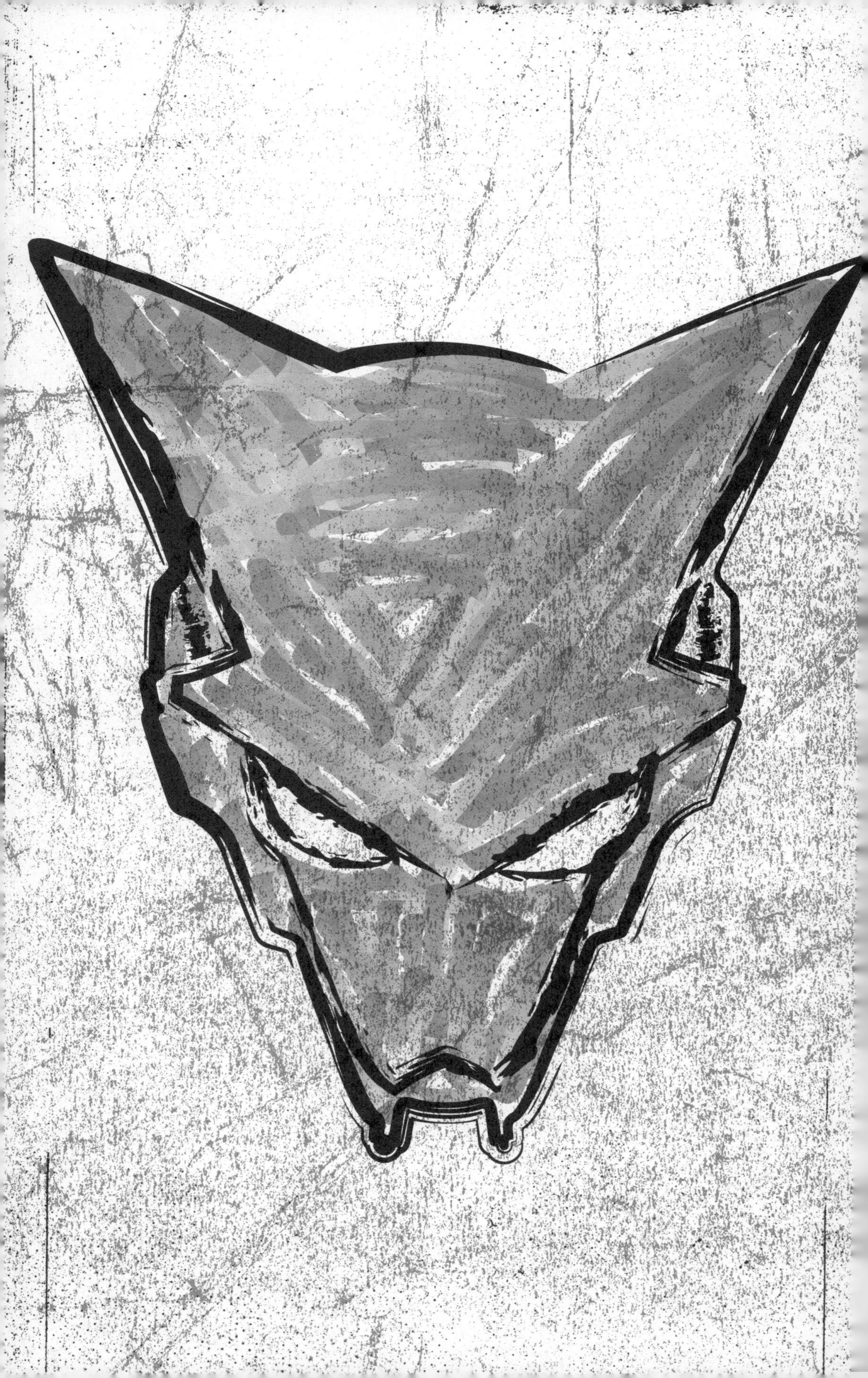

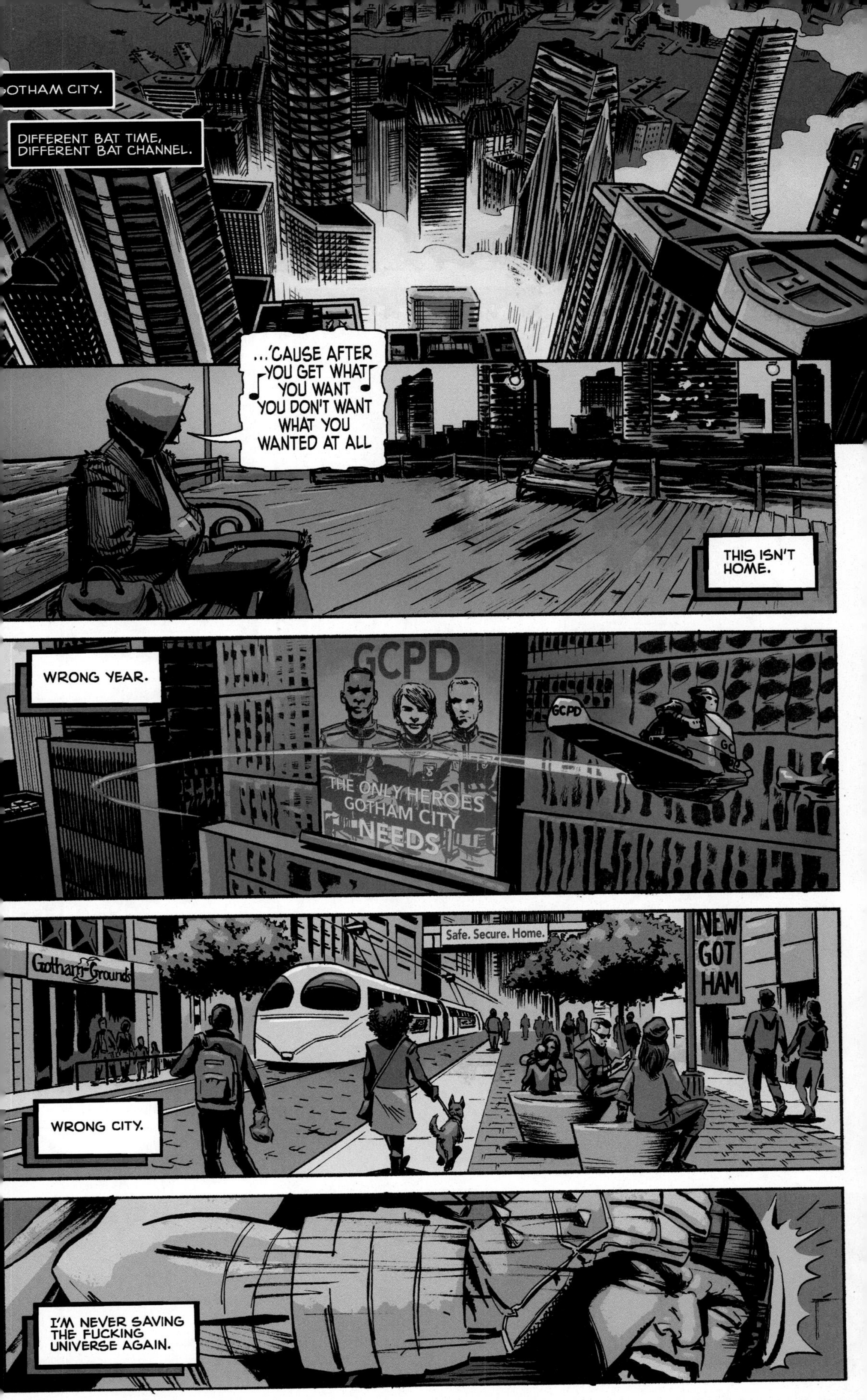
GOTHAM CITY.
DIFFERENT BAT TIME, DIFFERENT BAT CHANNEL.
...'CAUSE AFTER YOU GET WHAT YOU WANT YOU DON'T WANT WHAT YOU WANTED AT ALL
THIS ISN'T HOME.
WRONG YEAR.
GCPD
THE ONLY HEROES GOTHAM CITY NEEDS
GCPD
WRONG CITY.
Gotham Grounds
Safe. Secure. Home.
NEW GOT HAM
I'M NEVER SAVING THE FUCKING UNIVERSE AGAIN.

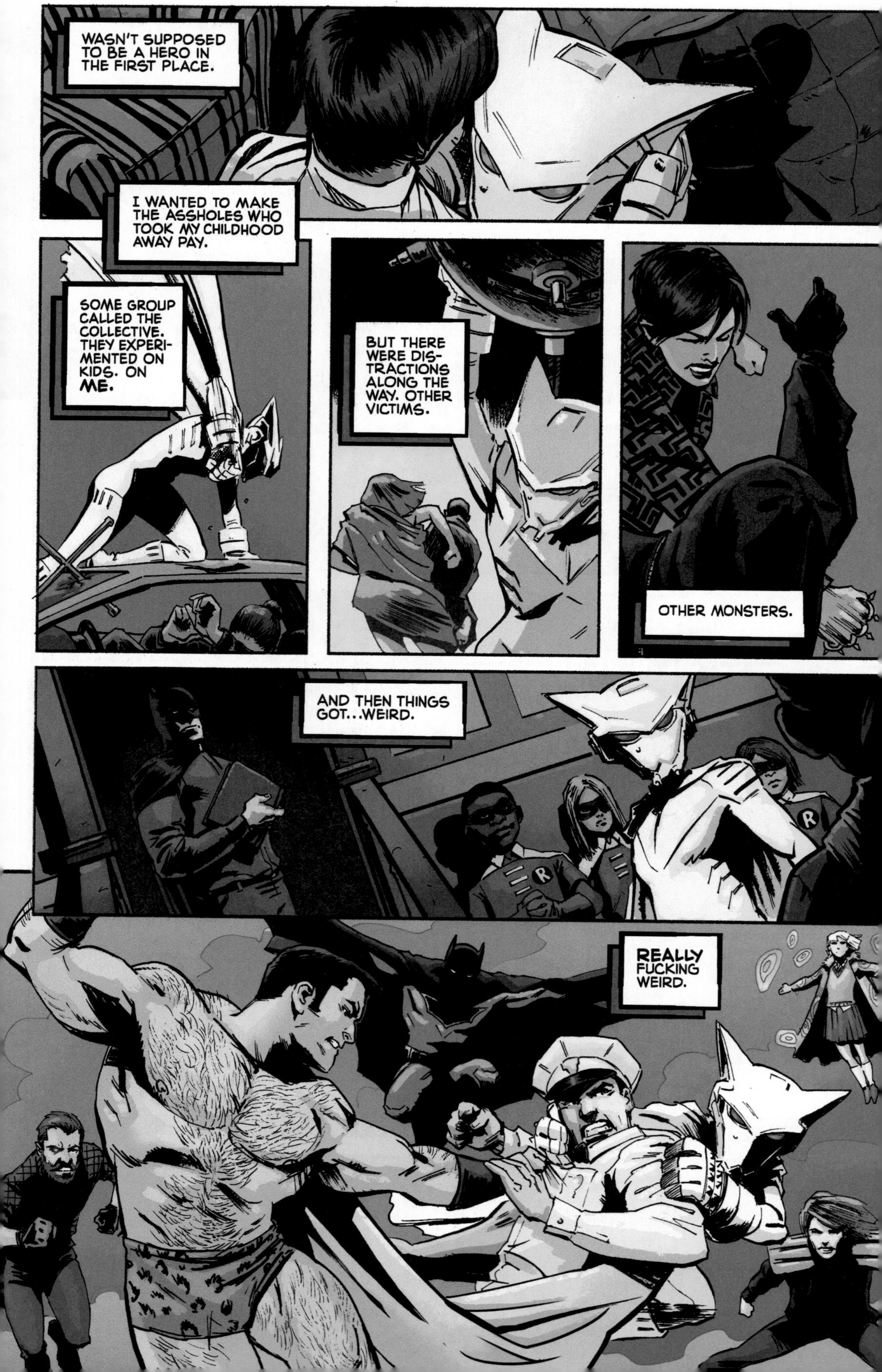
WASN'T SUPPOSED TO BE A HERO IN THE FIRST PLACE.
I WANTED TO MAKE THE ASSHOLES WHO TOOK MY CHILDHOOD AWAY PAY.
SOME GROUP CALLED THE COLLECTIVE. THEY EXPERIMENTED ON KIDS. ON ME.
BUT THERE WERE DISTRACTIONS ALONG THE WAY. OTHER VICTIMS.
OTHER MONSTERS.
AND THEN THINGS GOT...WEIRD.
REALLY FUCKING WEIRD.

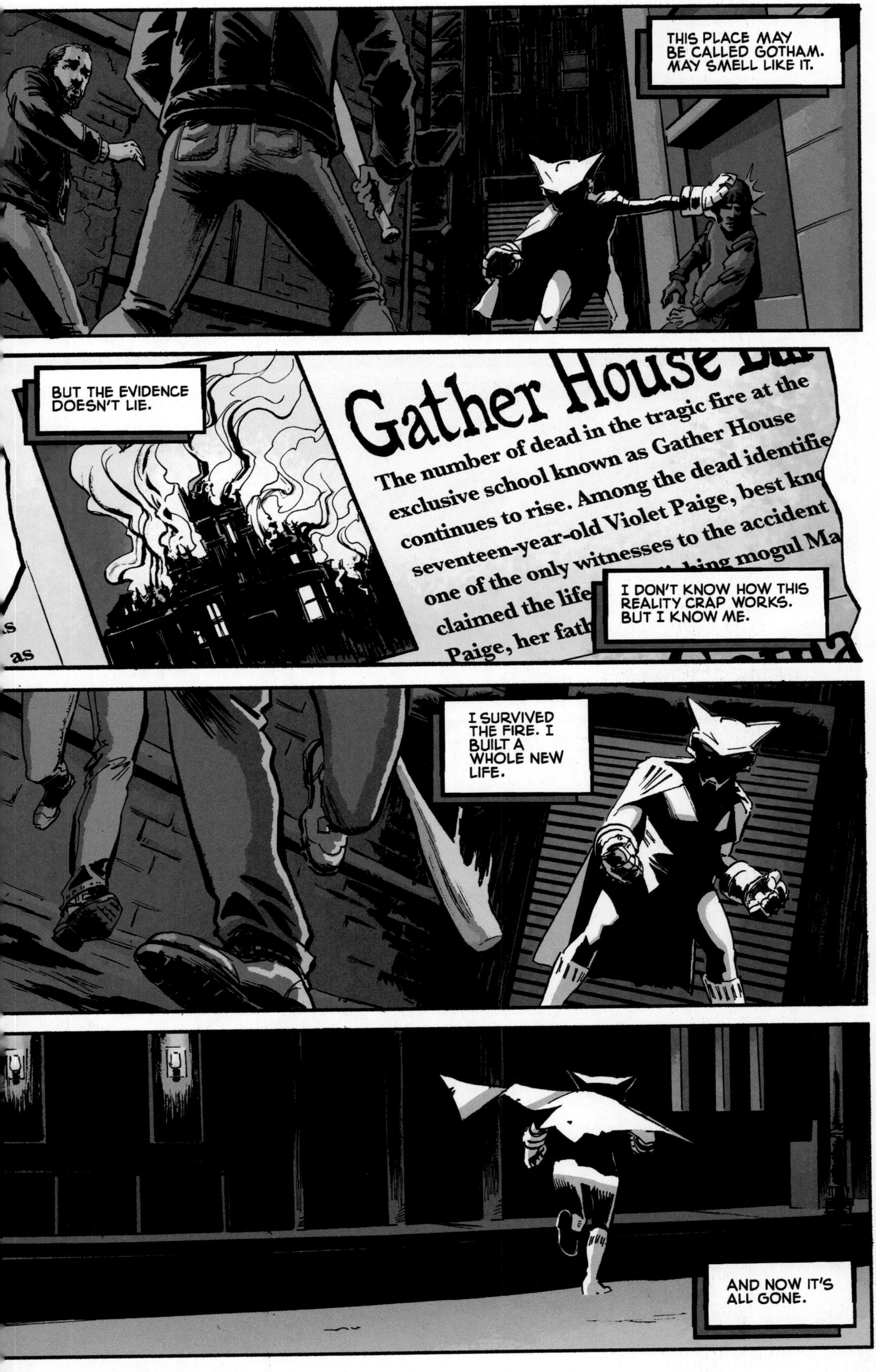
THIS PLACE MAY BE CALLED GOTHAM. MAY SMELL LIKE IT.
BUT THE EVIDENCE DOESN'T LIE.
Gather House
The number of dead in the tragic fire at the
exclusive school known as Gather House
continues to rise. Among the dead identifie
seventeen-year-old Violet Paige, best kno
one of the only witnesses to the accident
claimed the life
Paige, her fath
I DON'T KNOW HOW THIS REALITY CRAP WORKS. BUT I KNOW ME.
I SURVIVED THE FIRE. I BUILT A WHOLE NEW LIFE.
AND NOW IT'S ALL GONE.

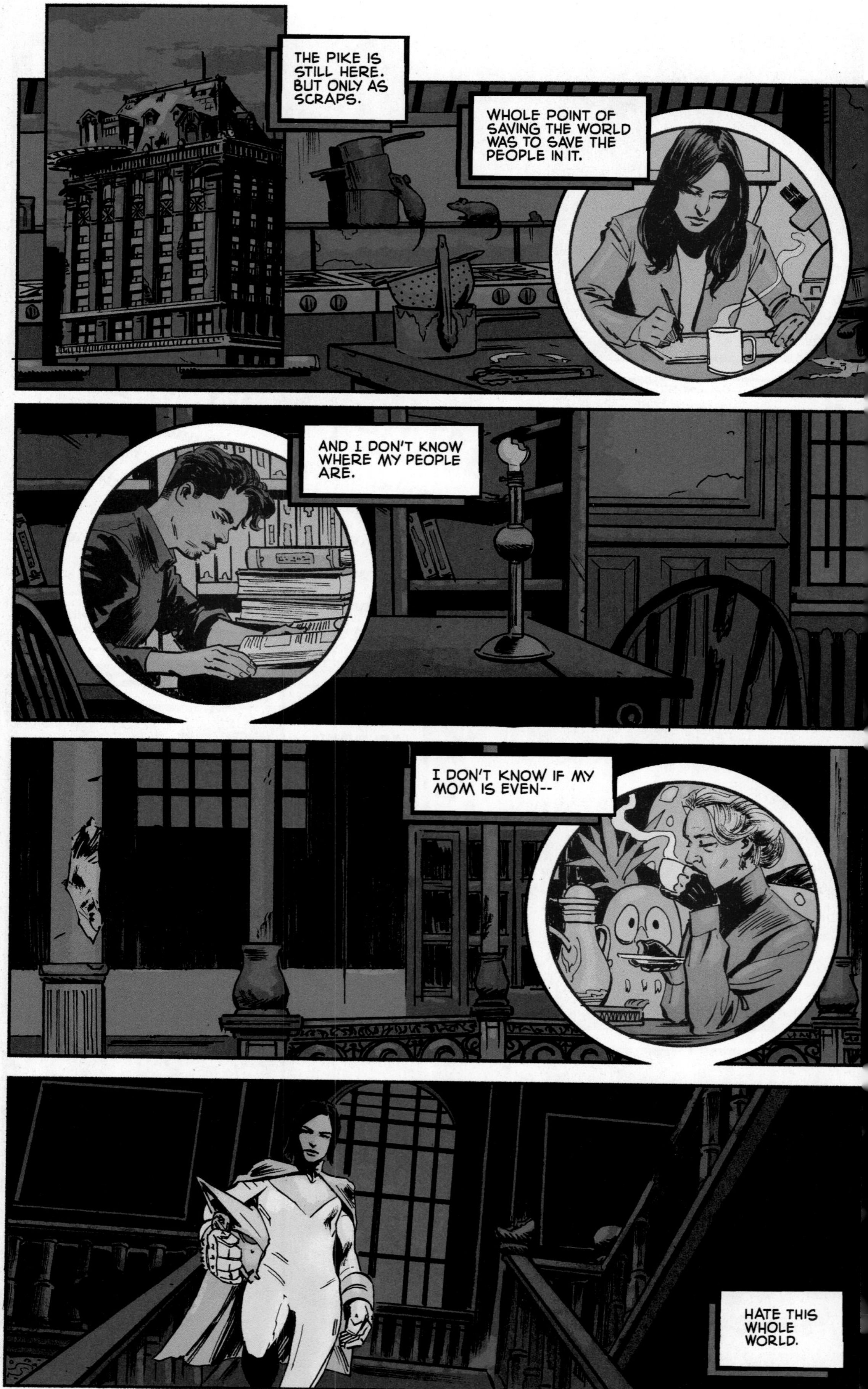
THE PIKE IS STILL HERE. BUT ONLY AS SCRAPS.
WHOLE POINT OF SAVING THE WORLD WAS TO SAVE THE PEOPLE IN IT.
AND I DON'T KNOW WHERE MY PEOPLE ARE.
I DON'T KNOW IF MY MOM IS EVEN--
HATE THIS WHOLE WORLD.

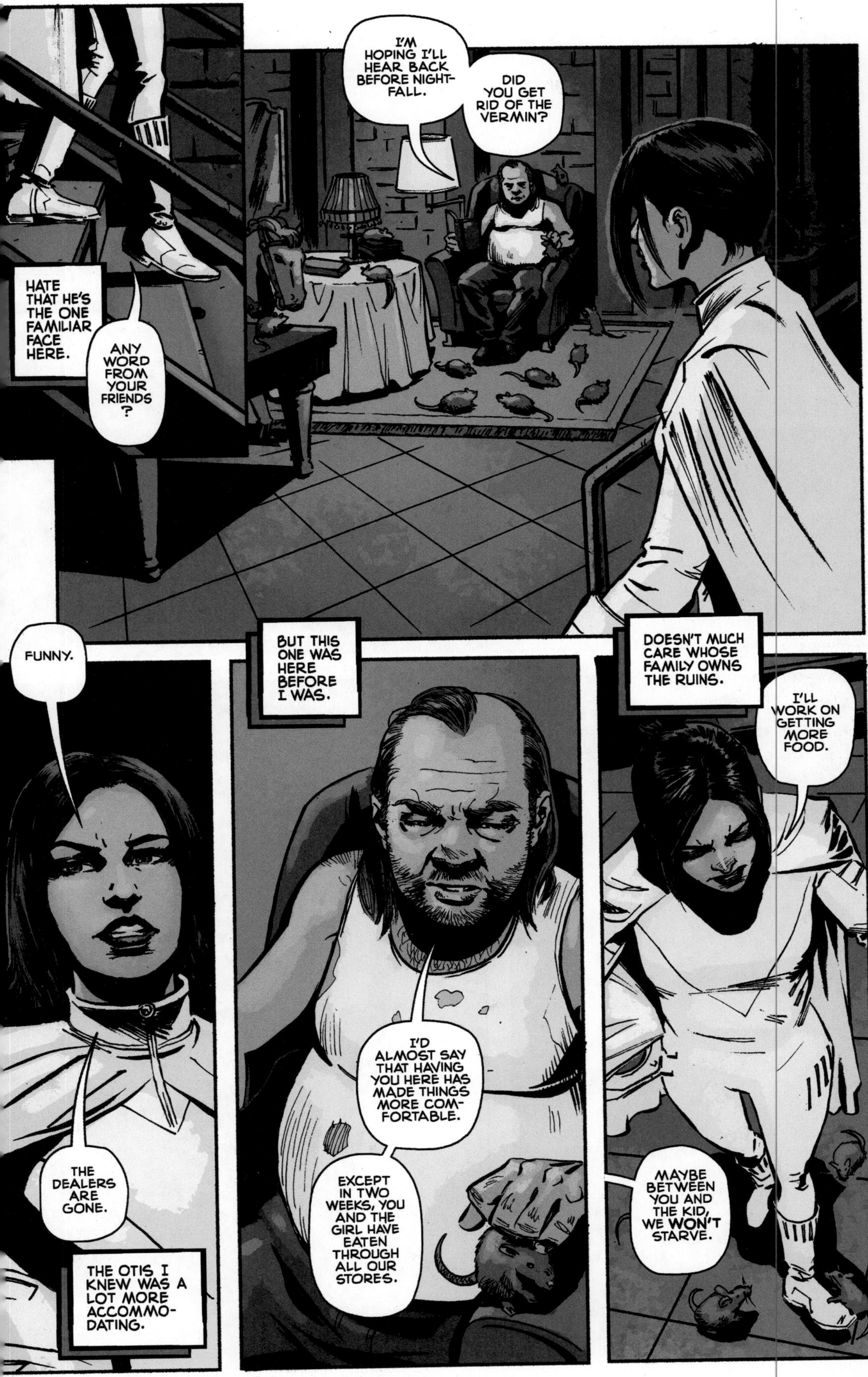
HATE THAT HE'S THE ONE FAMILIAR FACE HERE.
ANY WORD FROM YOUR FRIENDS?
I'M HOPING I'LL HEAR BACK BEFORE NIGHT-FALL.
DID YOU GET RID OF THE VERMIN?
FUNNY.
THE DEALERS ARE GONE.
THE OTIS I KNEW WAS A LOT MORE ACCOMMO-DATING.
BUT THIS ONE WAS HERE BEFORE I WAS.
I'D ALMOST SAY THAT HAVING YOU HERE HAS MADE THINGS MORE COM-FORTABLE.
EXCEPT IN TWO WEEKS, YOU AND THE GIRL HAVE EATEN THROUGH ALL OUR STORES.
DOESN'T MUCH CARE WHOSE FAMILY OWNS THE RUINS.
I'LL WORK ON GETTING MORE FOOD.
MAYBE BETWEEN YOU AND THE KID, WE WON'T STARVE.

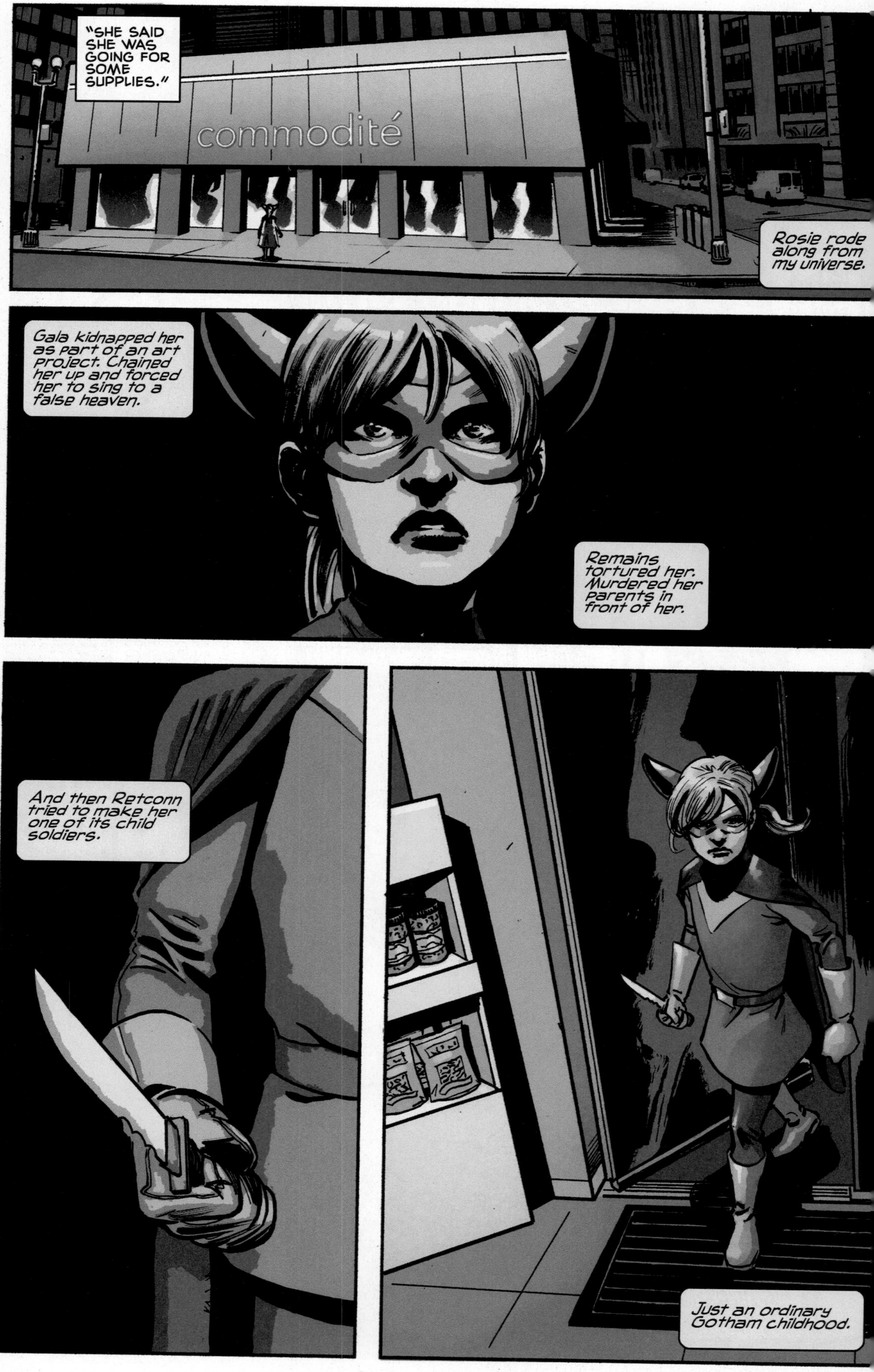
"SHE SAID SHE WAS GOING FOR SOME SUPPLIES."
commodité
Rosie rode along from my universe.
Gala kidnapped her as part of an art project. Chained her up and forced her to sing to a false heaven.
Remains tortured her. Murdered her parents in front of her.
And then Retconn tried to make her one of its child soldiers.
Just an ordinary Gotham childhood.

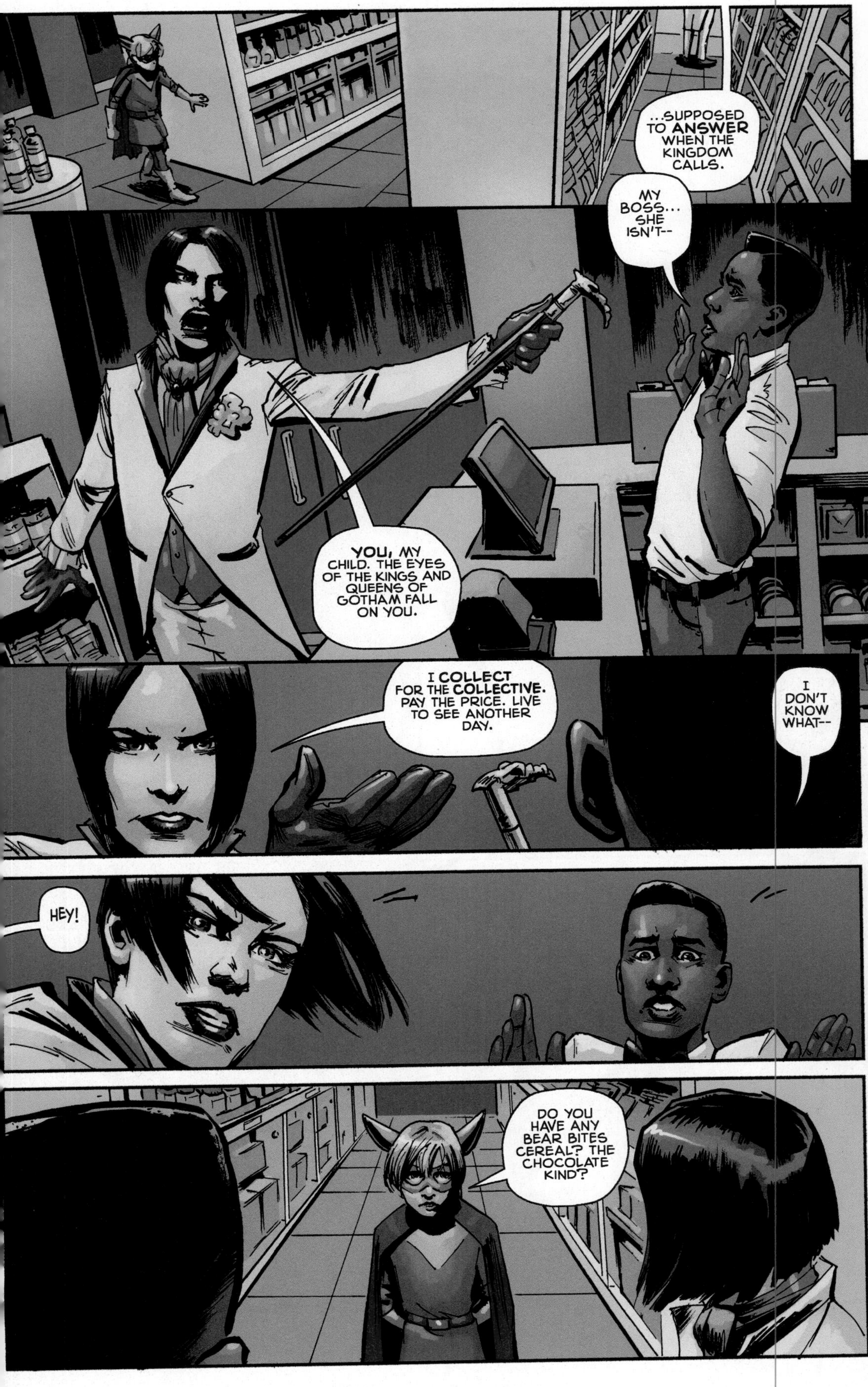
...SUPPOSED TO ANSWER WHEN THE KINGDOM CALLS.
MY BOSS... SHE ISN'T--
YOU, MY CHILD. THE EYES OF THE KINGS AND QUEENS OF GOTHAM FALL ON YOU.
I COLLECT FOR THE COLLECTIVE. PAY THE PRICE. LIVE TO SEE ANOTHER DAY.
I DON'T KNOW WHAT--
HEY!
DO YOU HAVE ANY BEAR BITES CEREAL? THE CHOCOLATE KIND?

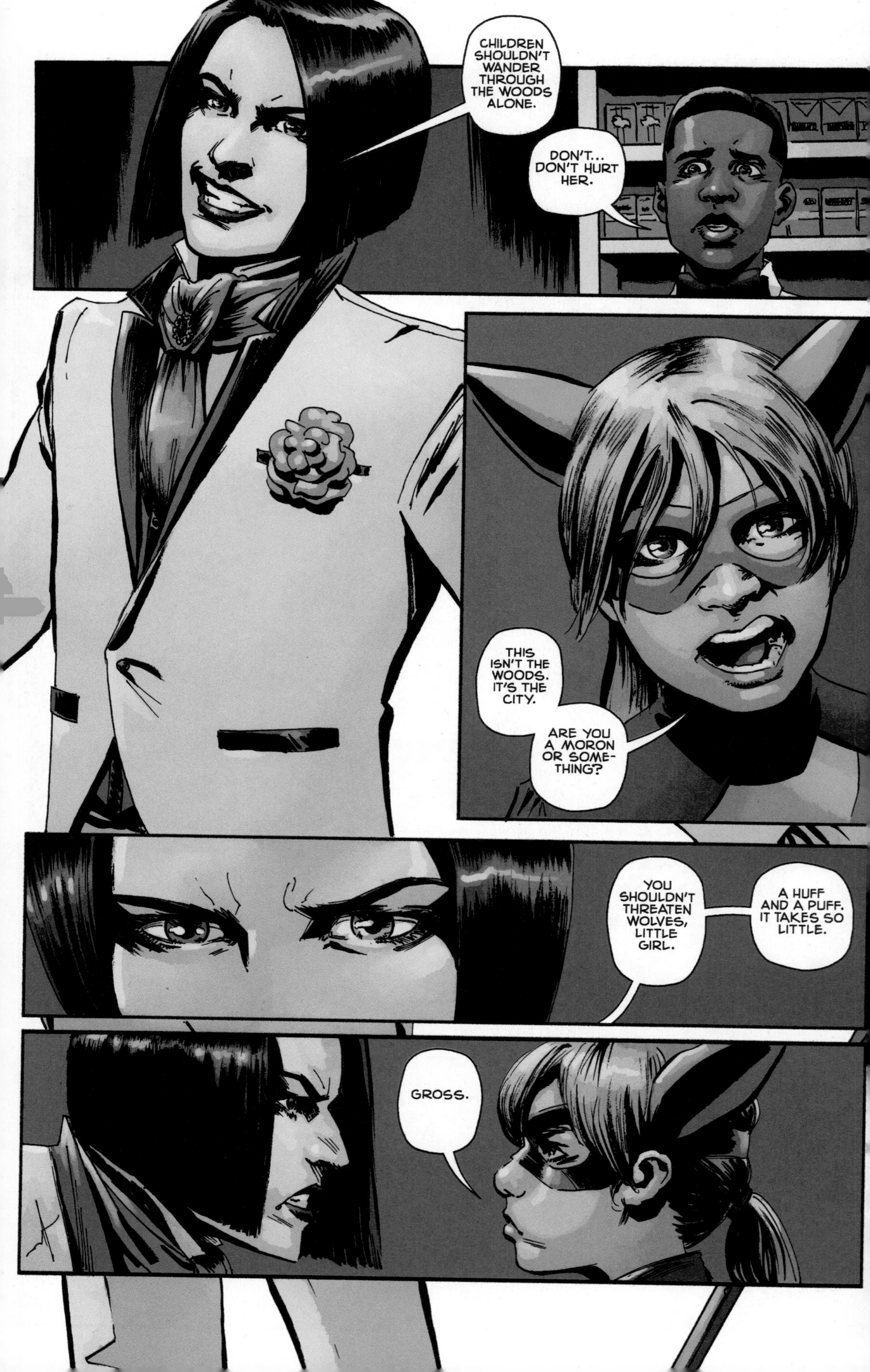
CHILDREN SHOULDN'T WANDER THROUGH THE WOODS ALONE.
DON'T... DON'T HURT HER.
THIS ISN'T THE WOODS. IT'S THE CITY.
ARE YOU A MORON OR SOME-THING?
YOU SHOULDN'T THREATEN WOLVES, LITTLE GIRL.
A HUFF AND A PUFF. IT TAKES SO LITTLE.
GROSS.

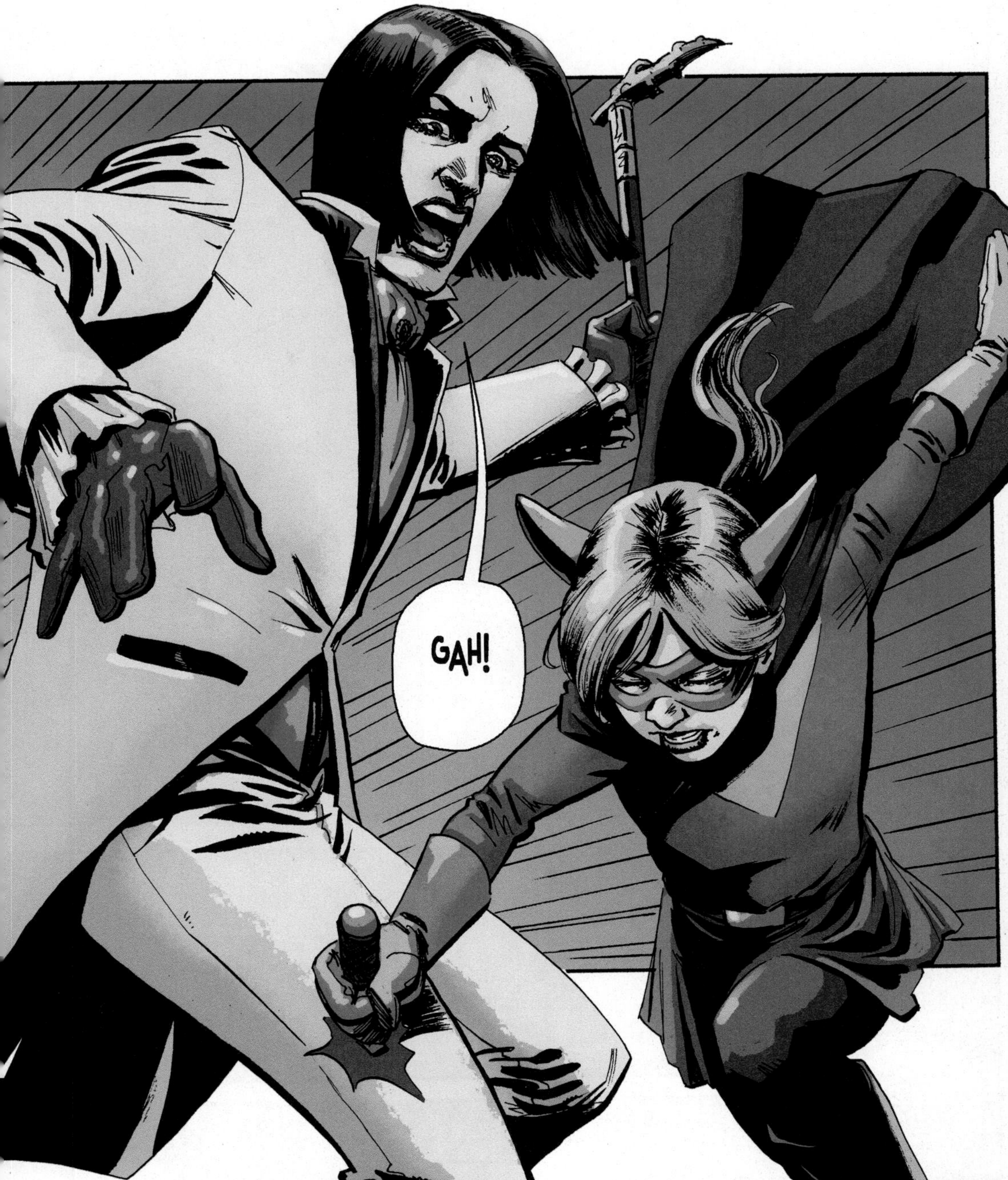
GAH!

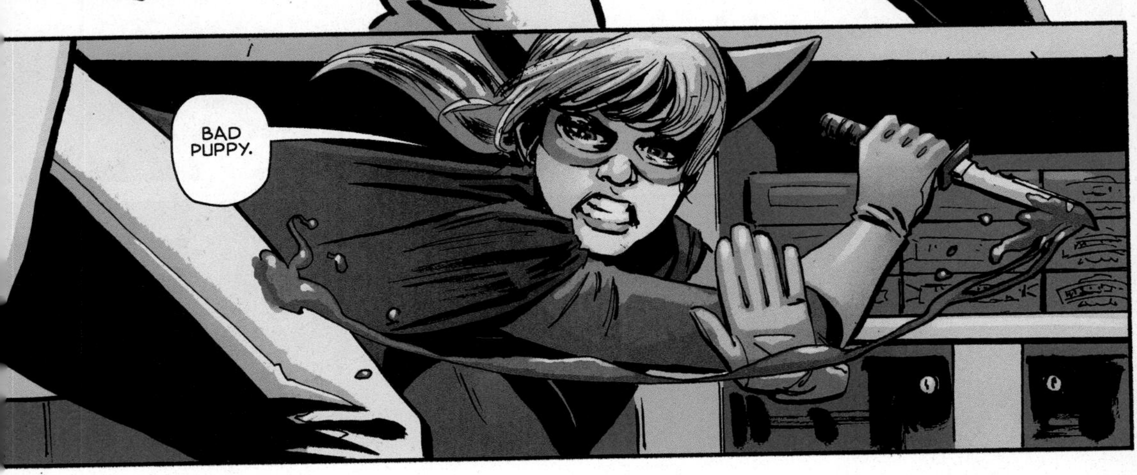
BAD PUPPY.

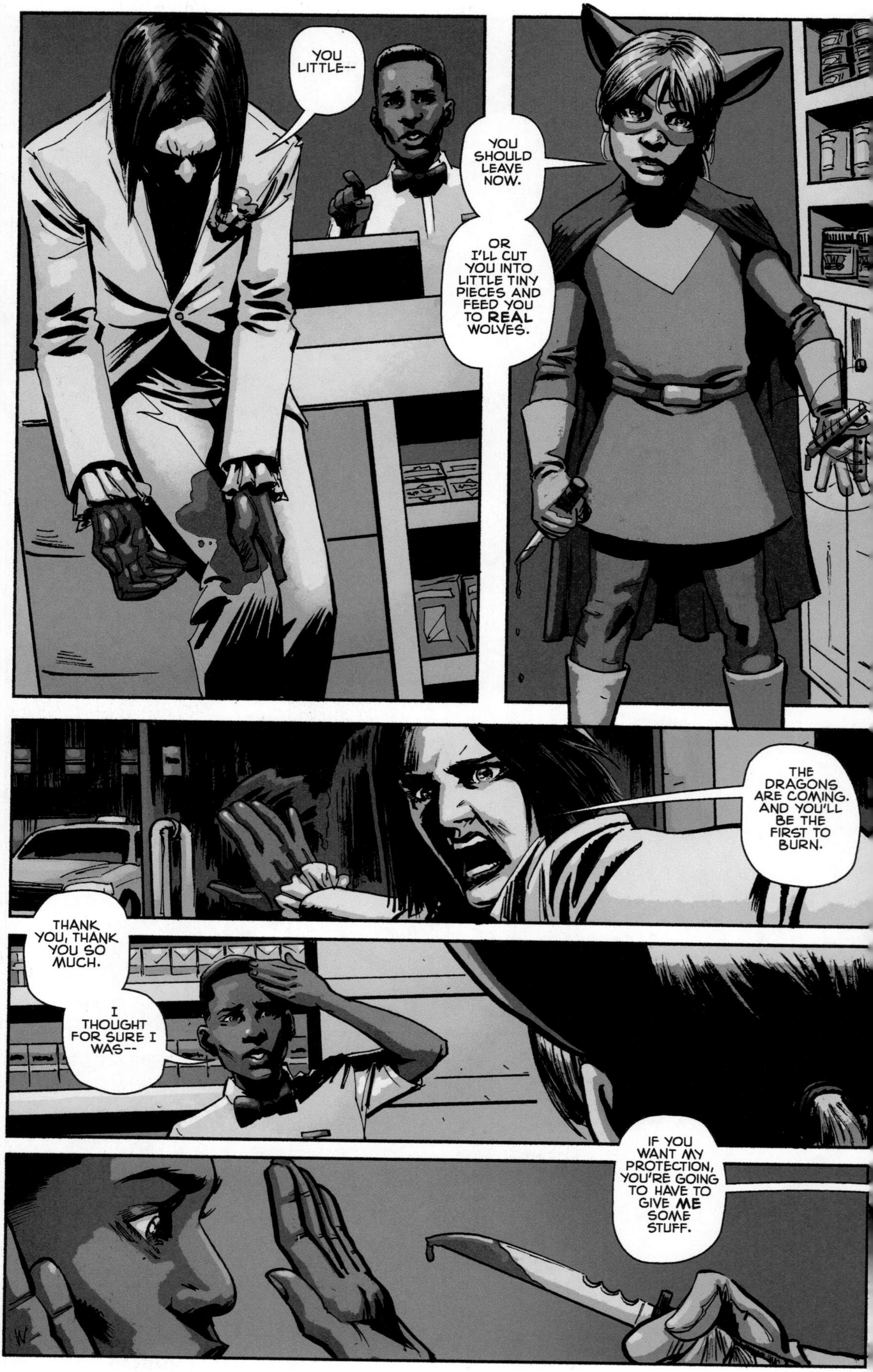

YOU LITTLE--
YOU SHOULD LEAVE NOW.
OR I'LL CUT YOU INTO LITTLE TINY PIECES AND FEED YOU TO REAL WOLVES.
THE DRAGONS ARE COMING. AND YOU'LL BE THE FIRST TO BURN.
THANK YOU, THANK YOU SO MUCH.
I THOUGHT FOR SURE I WAS--
IF YOU WANT MY PROTECTION, YOU'RE GOING TO HAVE TO GIVE ME SOME STUFF.

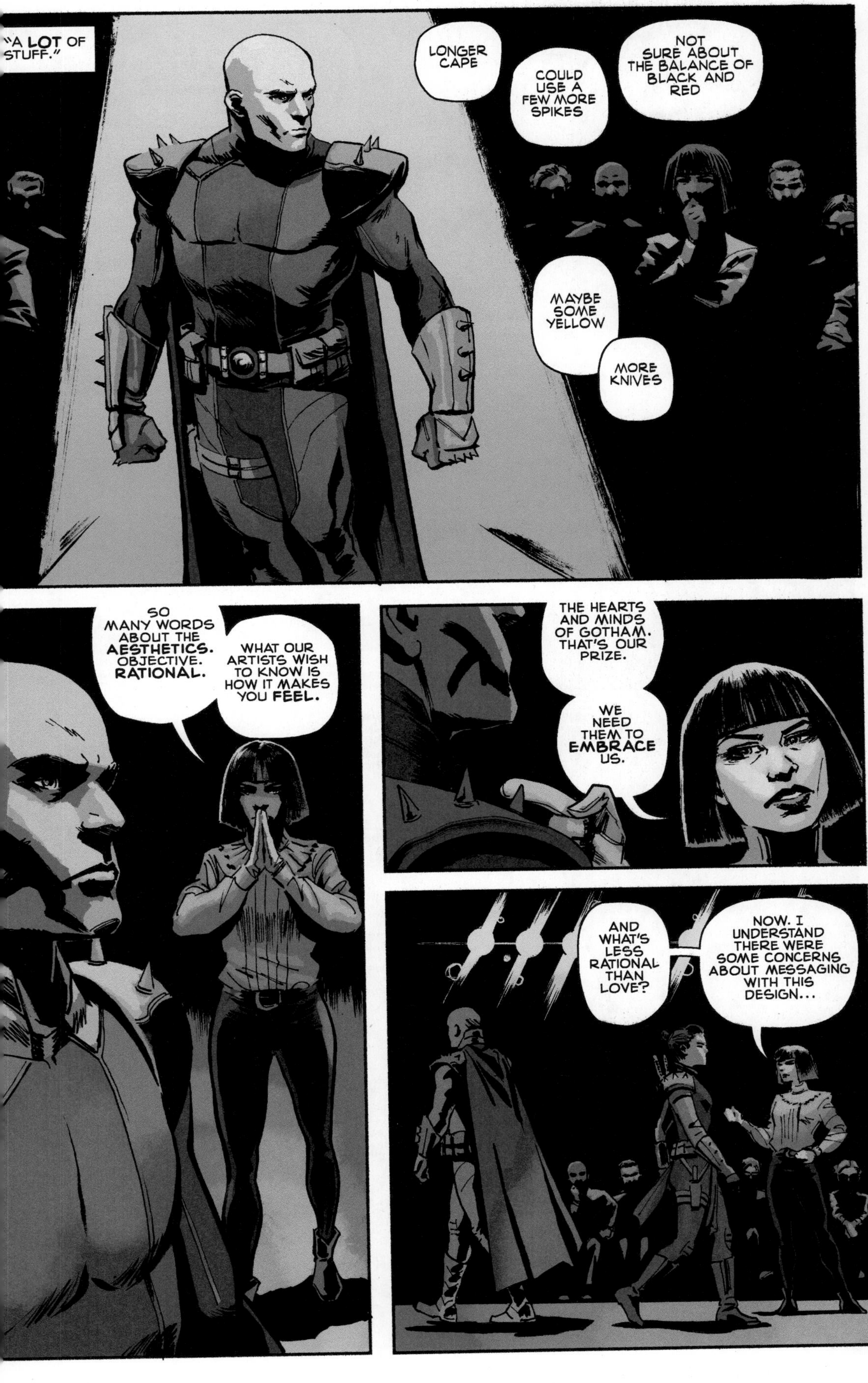
"A **LOT** OF STUFF."
LONGER CAPE
COULD USE A FEW MORE SPIKES
NOT SURE ABOUT THE BALANCE OF BLACK AND RED
MAYBE SOME YELLOW
MORE KNIVES
SO MANY WORDS ABOUT THE **AESTHETICS**. OBJECTIVE. **RATIONAL**.
WHAT OUR ARTISTS WISH TO KNOW IS HOW IT MAKES YOU **FEEL**.
THE HEARTS AND MINDS OF GOTHAM. THAT'S OUR PRIZE.
WE NEED THEM TO **EMBRACE** US.
AND WHAT'S LESS RATIONAL THAN LOVE?
NOW. I UNDERSTAND THERE WERE SOME CONCERNS ABOUT MESSAGING WITH THIS DESIGN...

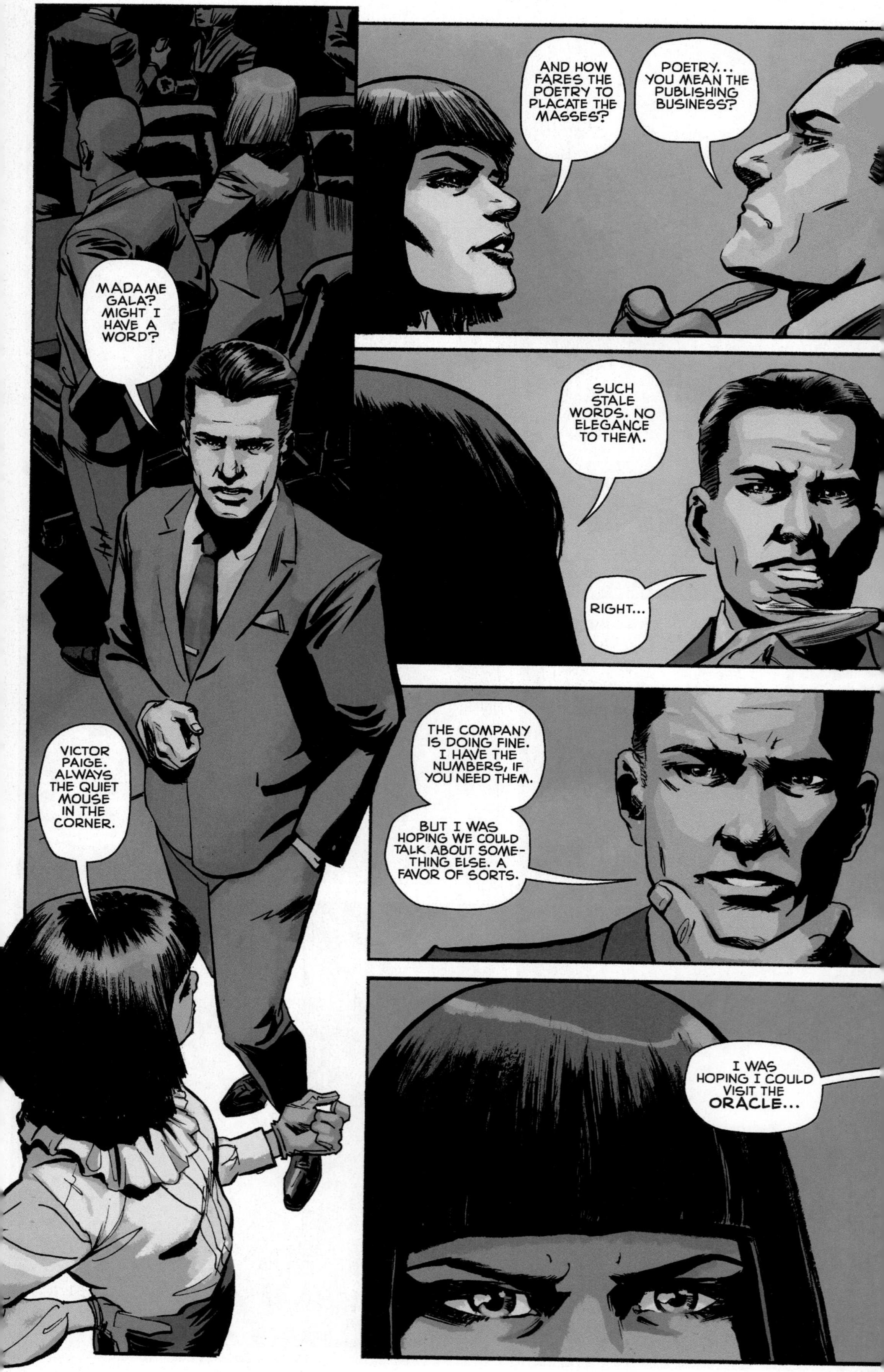
MADAME GALA? MIGHT I HAVE A WORD?
VICTOR PAIGE. ALWAYS THE QUIET MOUSE IN THE CORNER.
AND HOW FARES THE POETRY TO PLACATE THE MASSES?
POETRY... YOU MEAN THE PUBLISHING BUSINESS?
SUCH STALE WORDS. NO ELEGANCE TO THEM.
RIGHT...
THE COMPANY IS DOING FINE. I HAVE THE NUMBERS, IF YOU NEED THEM.
BUT I WAS HOPING WE COULD TALK ABOUT SOMETHING ELSE. A FAVOR OF SORTS.
I WAS HOPING I COULD VISIT THE ORACLE...

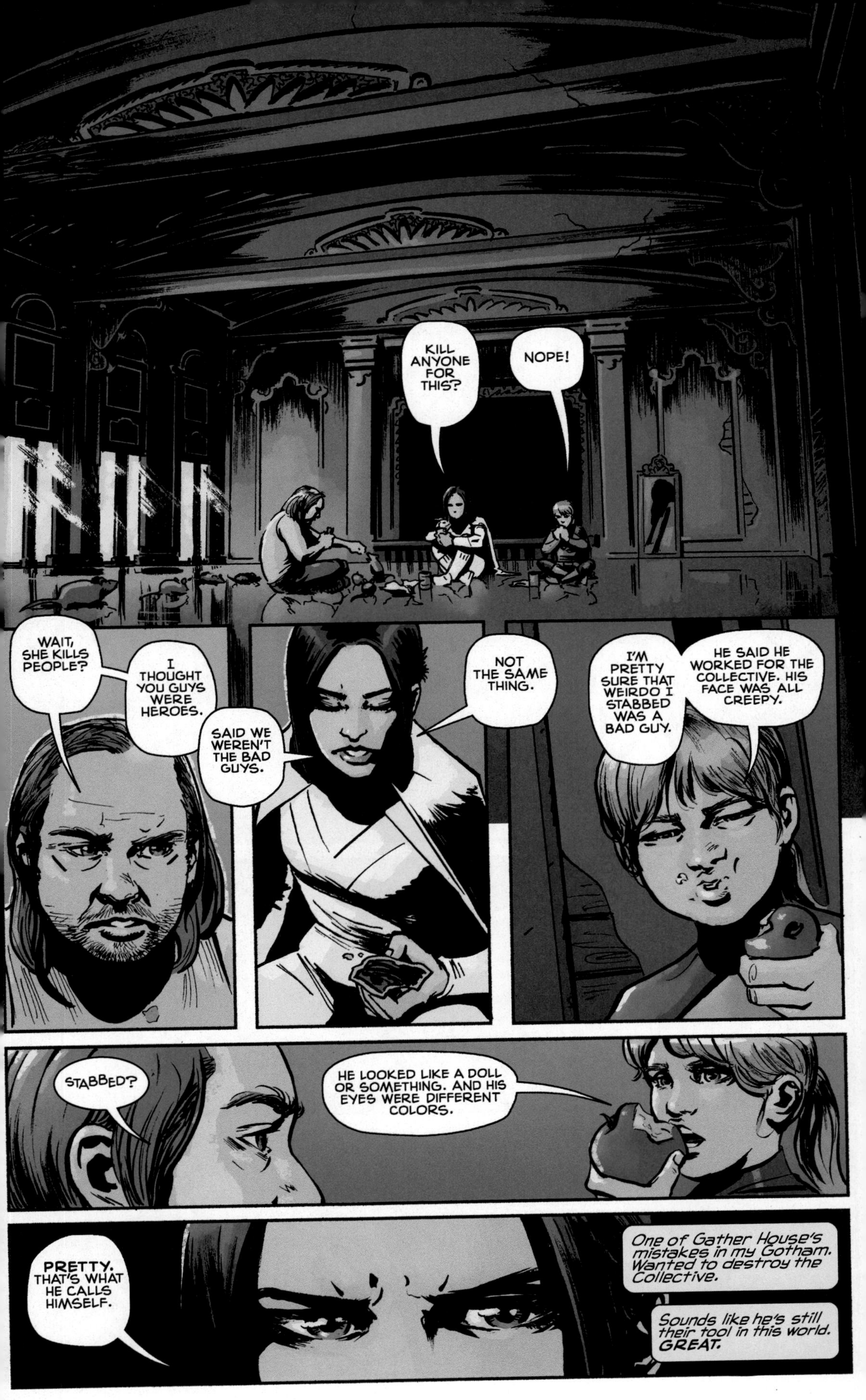
KILL ANYONE FOR THIS?
NOPE!
WAIT, SHE KILLS PEOPLE?
I THOUGHT YOU GUYS WERE HEROES.
SAID WE WEREN'T THE BAD GUYS.
NOT THE SAME THING.
I'M PRETTY SURE THAT WEIRDO I STABBED WAS A BAD GUY.
HE SAID HE WORKED FOR THE COLLECTIVE. HIS FACE WAS ALL CREEPY.
STABBED?
HE LOOKED LIKE A DOLL OR SOMETHING. AND HIS EYES WERE DIFFERENT COLORS.
PRETTY. THAT'S WHAT HE CALLS HIMSELF.
One of Gather House's mistakes in my Gotham. Wanted to destroy the Collective.
Sounds like he's still their tool in this world. GREAT.

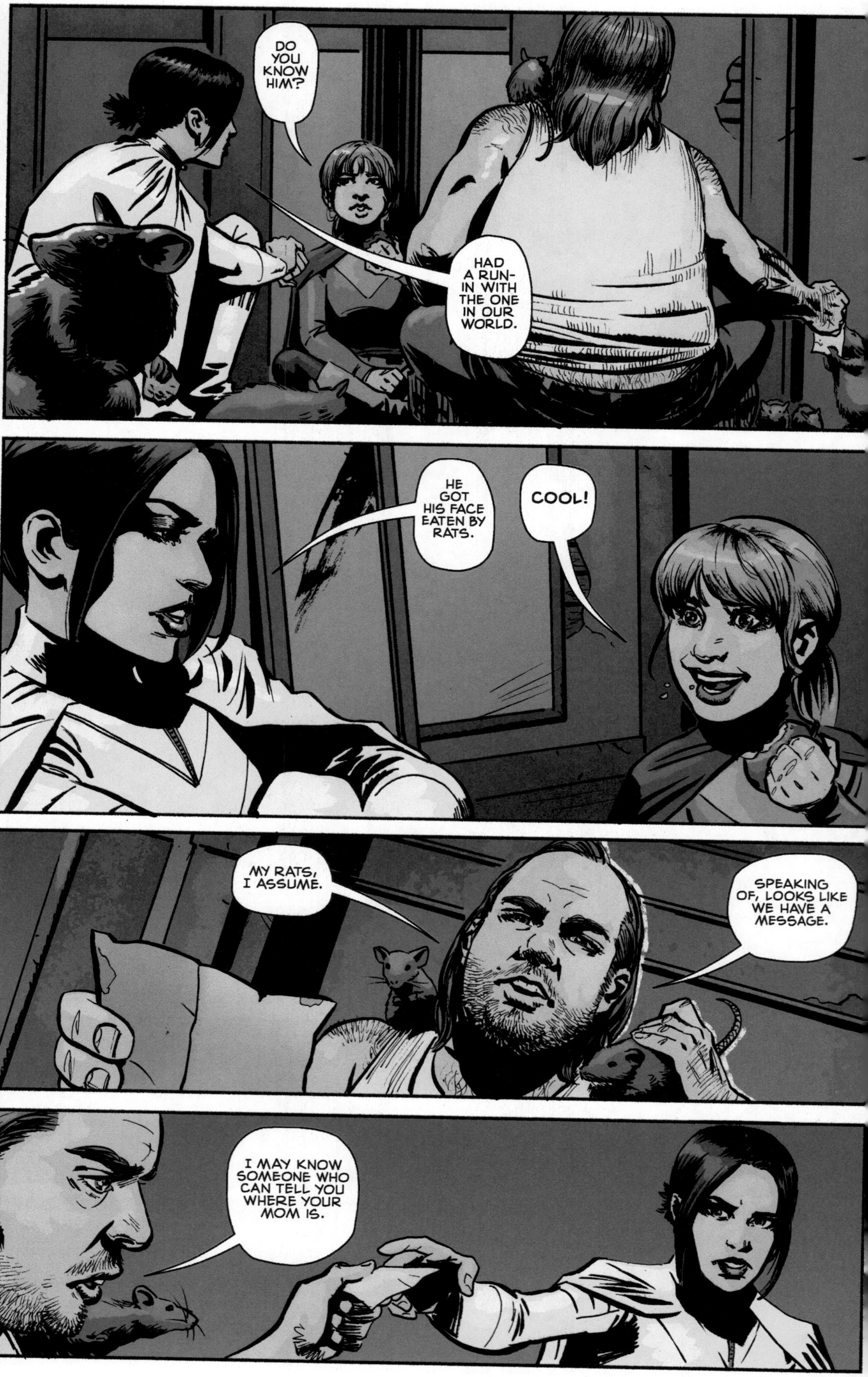
DO YOU KNOW HIM?
HAD A RUN-IN WITH THE ONE IN OUR WORLD.
HE GOT HIS FACE EATEN BY RATS.
COOL!
MY RATS, I ASSUME.
SPEAKING OF, LOOKS LIKE WE HAVE A MESSAGE.
I MAY KNOW SOMEONE WHO CAN TELL YOU WHERE YOUR MOM IS.

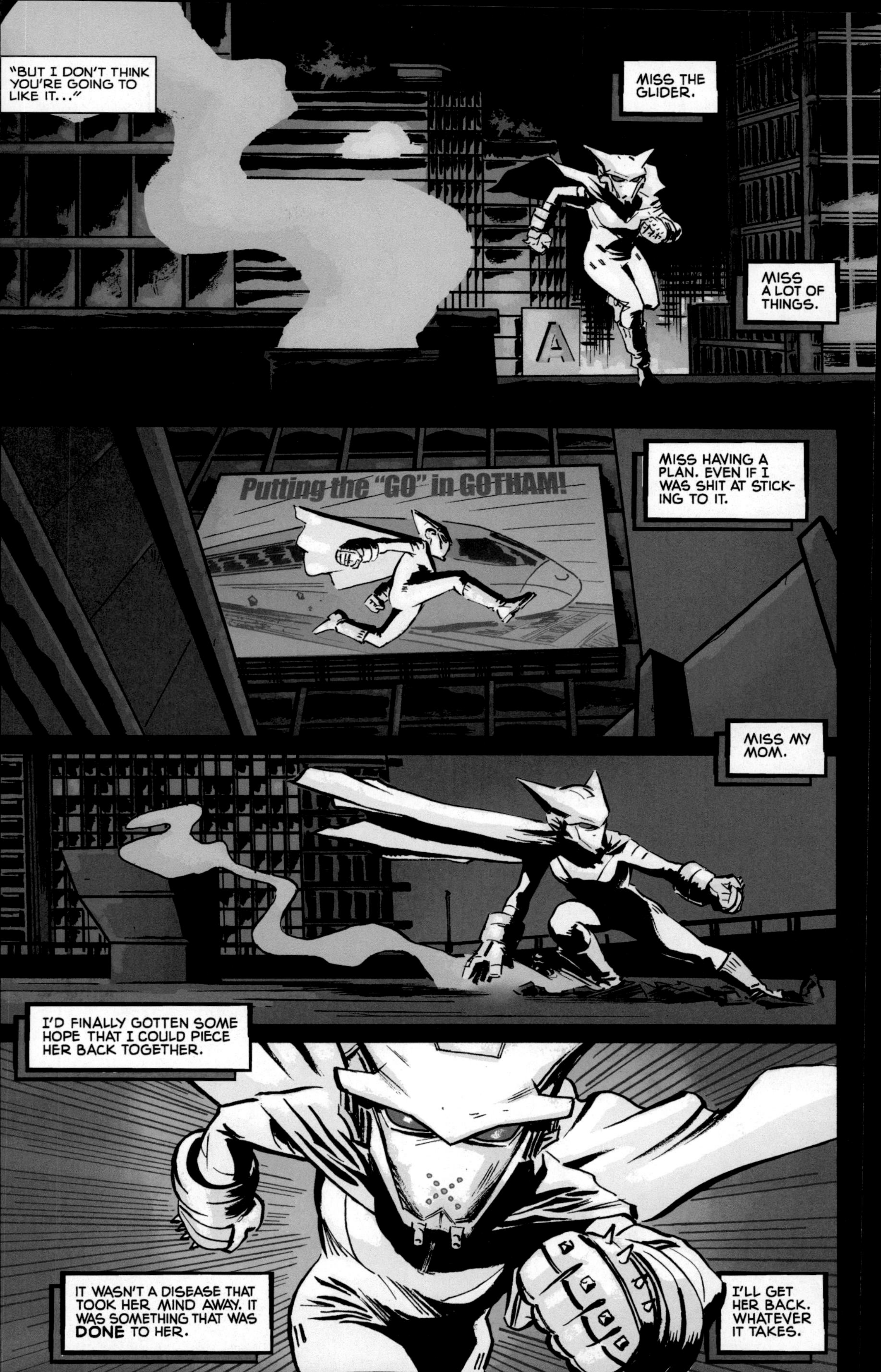
"BUT I DON'T THINK YOU'RE GOING TO LIKE IT..."
MISS THE GLIDER.
MISS A LOT OF THINGS.
Putting the "GO" in GOTHAM!
MISS HAVING A PLAN. EVEN IF I WAS SHIT AT STICKING TO IT.
MISS MY MOM.
I'D FINALLY GOTTEN SOME HOPE THAT I COULD PIECE HER BACK TOGETHER.
IT WASN'T A DISEASE THAT TOOK HER MIND AWAY. IT WAS SOMETHING THAT WAS **DONE** TO HER.
I'LL GET HER BACK. WHATEVER IT TAKES.

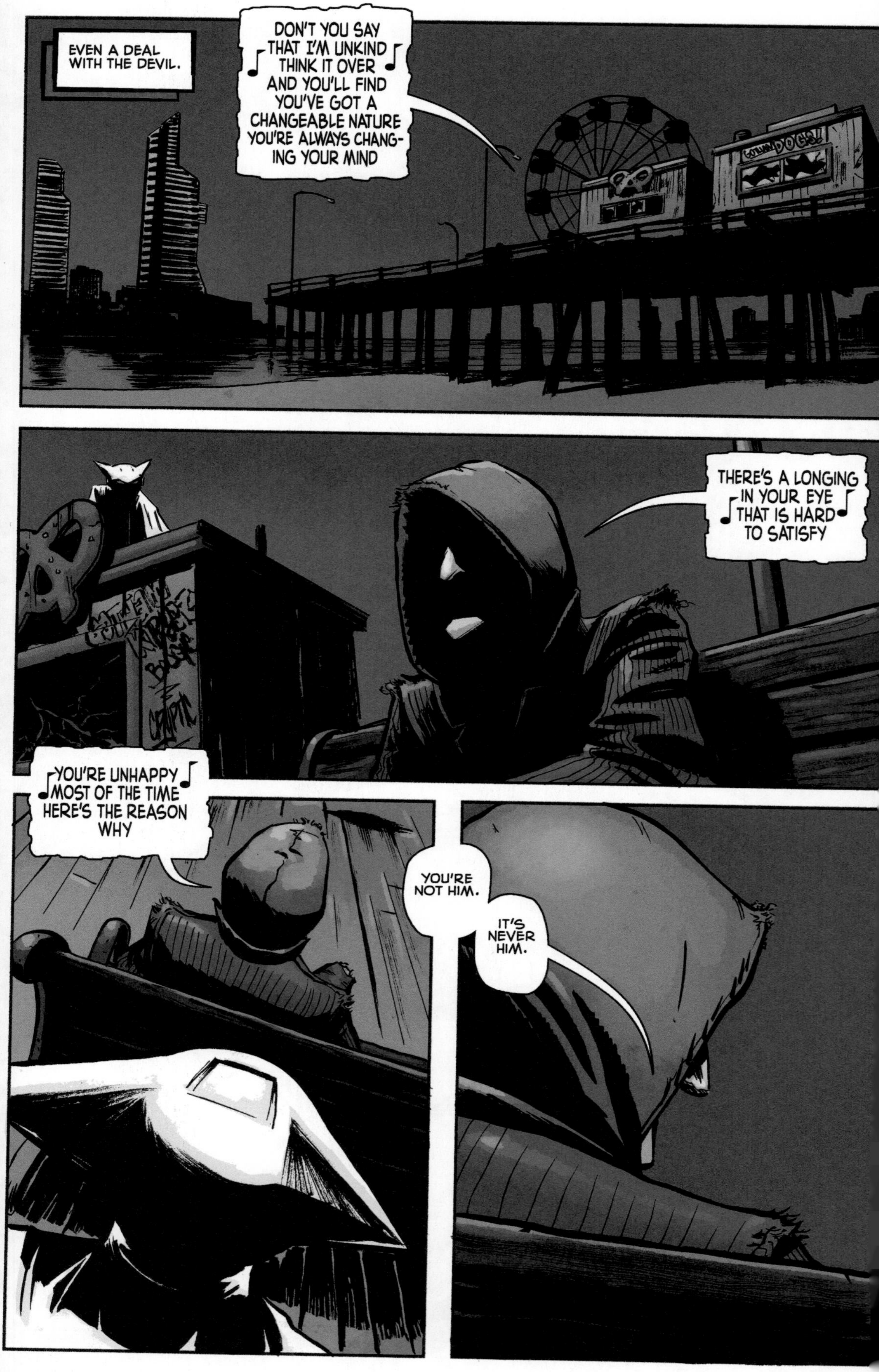
EVEN A DEAL WITH THE DEVIL.
DON'T YOU SAY THAT I'M UNKIND THINK IT OVER AND YOU'LL FIND YOU'VE GOT A CHANGEABLE NATURE YOU'RE ALWAYS CHANGING YOUR MIND
THERE'S A LONGING IN YOUR EYE THAT IS HARD TO SATISFY
YOU'RE UNHAPPY MOST OF THE TIME HERE'S THE REASON WHY
YOU'RE NOT HIM.
IT'S NEVER HIM.

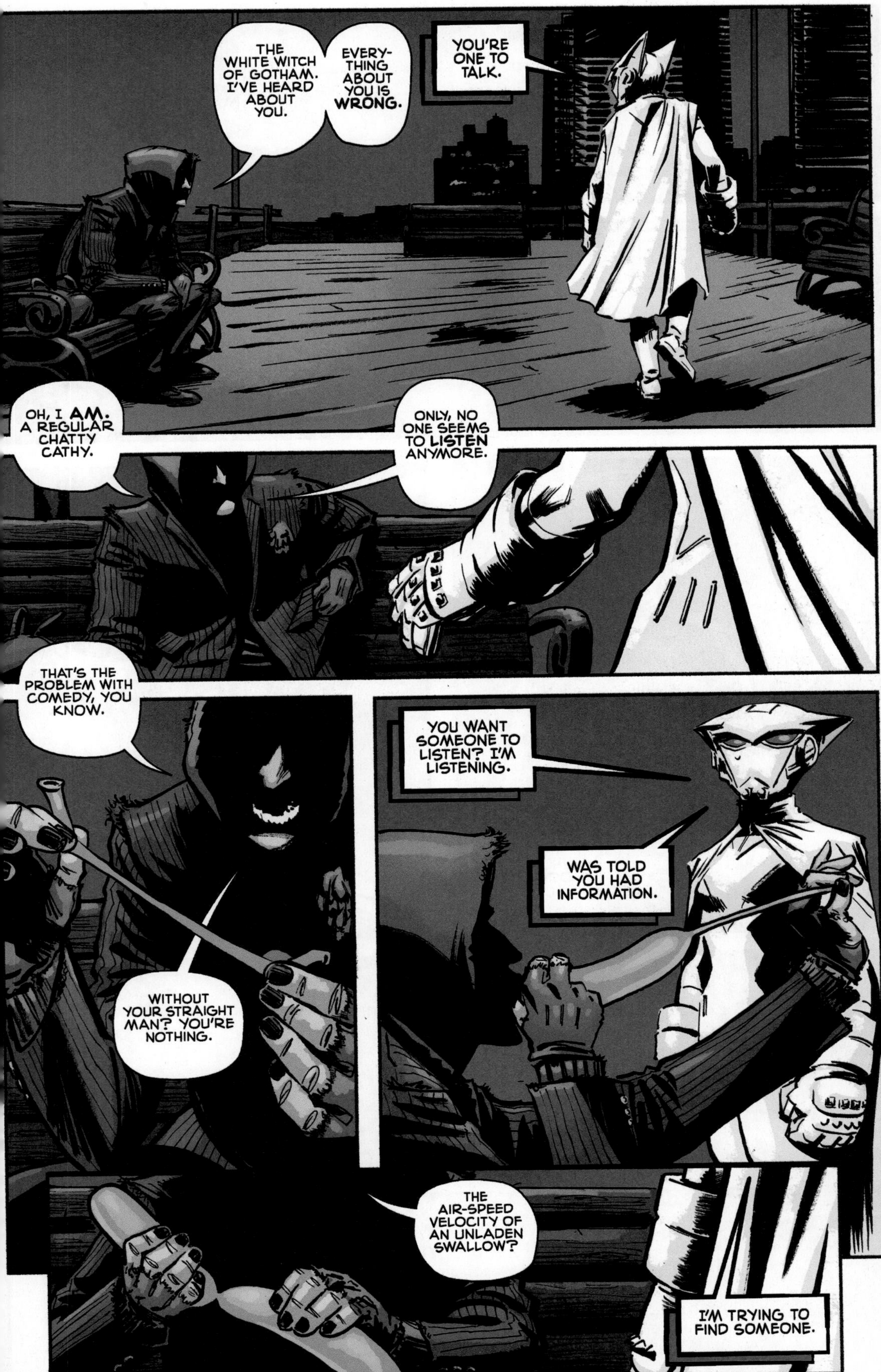
THE WHITE WITCH OF GOTHAM. I'VE HEARD ABOUT YOU.
EVERY-THING ABOUT YOU IS WRONG.
YOU'RE ONE TO TALK.
OH, I AM. A REGULAR CHATTY CATHY.
ONLY, NO ONE SEEMS TO LISTEN ANYMORE.
THAT'S THE PROBLEM WITH COMEDY, YOU KNOW.
WITHOUT YOUR STRAIGHT MAN? YOU'RE NOTHING.
YOU WANT SOMEONE TO LISTEN? I'M LISTENING.
WAS TOLD YOU HAD INFORMATION.
THE AIR-SPEED VELOCITY OF AN UNLADEN SWALLOW?
I'M TRYING TO FIND SOMEONE.

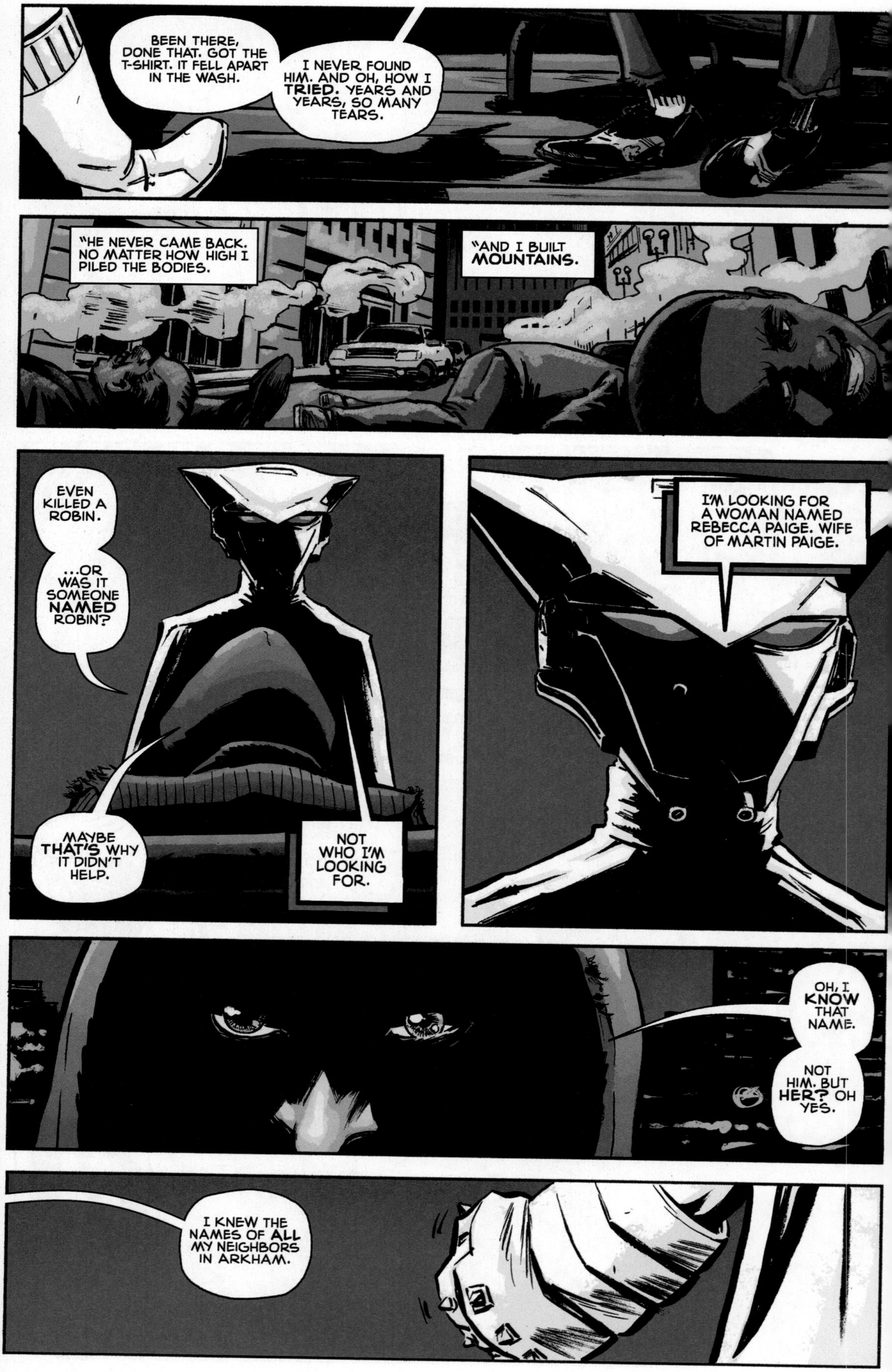
BEEN THERE, DONE THAT. GOT THE T-SHIRT. IT FELL APART IN THE WASH.
I NEVER FOUND HIM. AND OH, HOW I TRIED. YEARS AND YEARS, SO MANY TEARS.
"HE NEVER CAME BACK. NO MATTER HOW HIGH I PILED THE BODIES.
"AND I BUILT MOUNTAINS.
EVEN KILLED A ROBIN.
...OR WAS IT SOMEONE NAMED ROBIN?
MAYBE THAT'S WHY IT DIDN'T HELP.
NOT WHO I'M LOOKING FOR.
I'M LOOKING FOR A WOMAN NAMED REBECCA PAIGE. WIFE OF MARTIN PAIGE.
OH, I KNOW THAT NAME.
NOT HIM. BUT HER? OH YES.
I KNEW THE NAMES OF ALL MY NEIGHBORS IN ARKHAM.

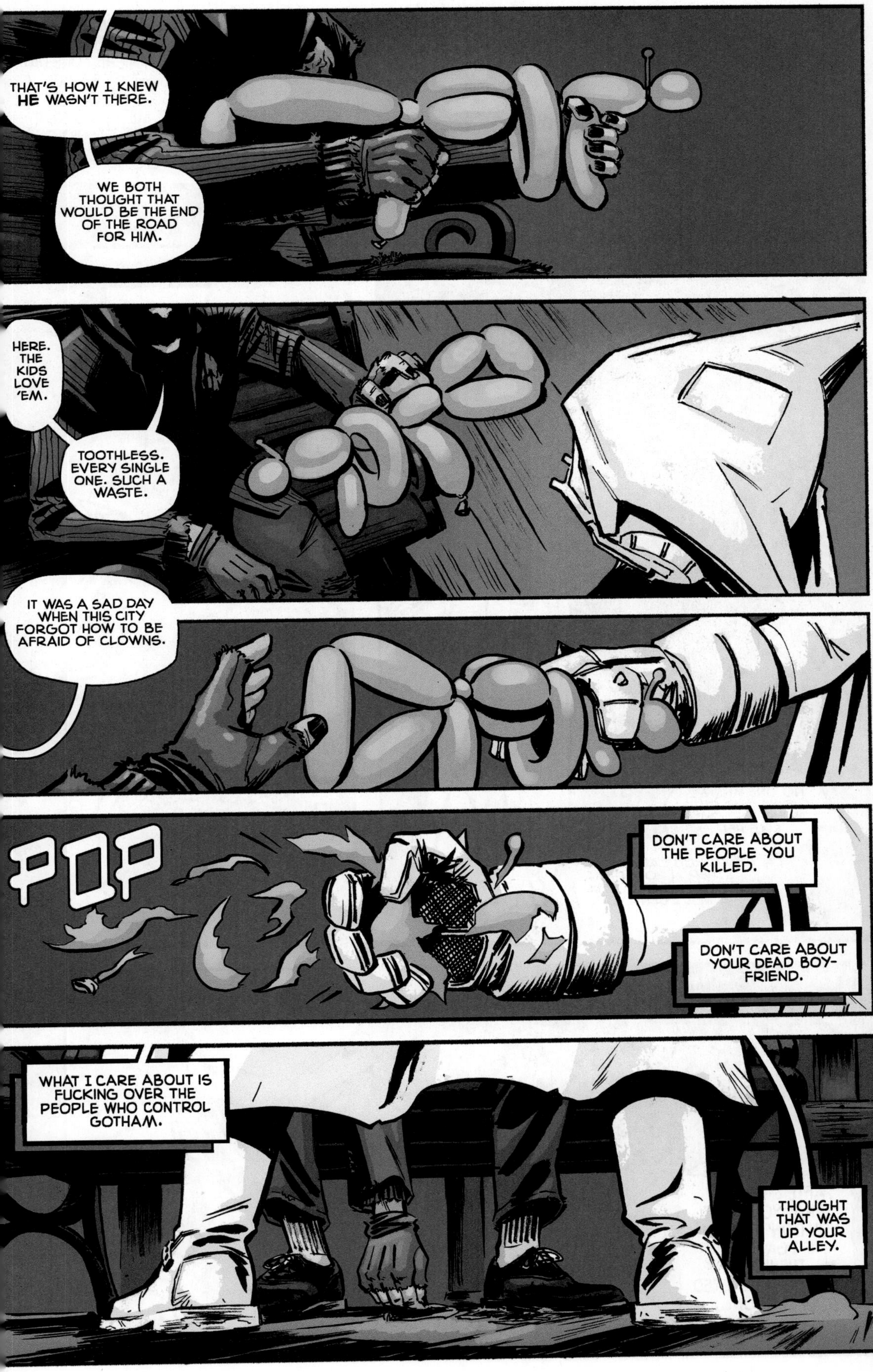
THAT'S HOW I KNEW HE WASN'T THERE.
WE BOTH THOUGHT THAT WOULD BE THE END OF THE ROAD FOR HIM.
HERE. THE KIDS LOVE 'EM.
TOOTHLESS. EVERY SINGLE ONE. SUCH A WASTE.
IT WAS A SAD DAY WHEN THIS CITY FORGOT HOW TO BE AFRAID OF CLOWNS.
POP
DON'T CARE ABOUT THE PEOPLE YOU KILLED.
DON'T CARE ABOUT YOUR DEAD BOY-FRIEND.
WHAT I CARE ABOUT IS FUCKING OVER THE PEOPLE WHO CONTROL GOTHAM.
THOUGHT THAT WAS UP YOUR ALLEY.

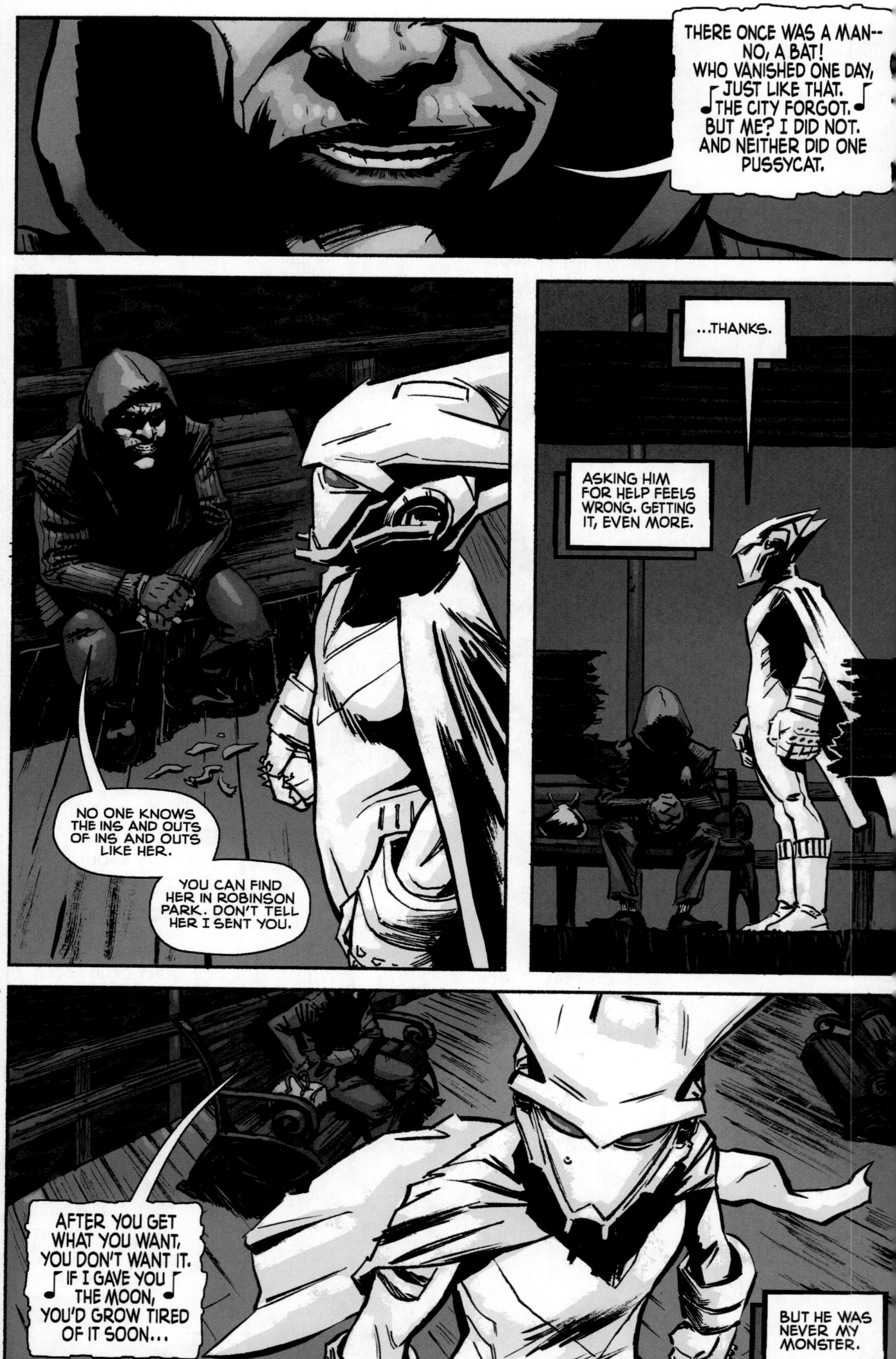
THERE ONCE WAS A MAN-- NO, A BAT! WHO VANISHED ONE DAY, JUST LIKE THAT. THE CITY FORGOT. BUT ME? I DID NOT. AND NEITHER DID ONE PUSSYCAT.
NO ONE KNOWS THE INS AND OUTS OF INS AND OUTS LIKE HER.
YOU CAN FIND HER IN ROBINSON PARK. DON'T TELL HER I SENT YOU.
...THANKS.
ASKING HIM FOR HELP FEELS WRONG. GETTING IT, EVEN MORE.
AFTER YOU GET WHAT YOU WANT, YOU DON'T WANT IT. IF I GAVE YOU THE MOON, YOU'D GROW TIRED OF IT SOON...
BUT HE WAS NEVER MY MONSTER.

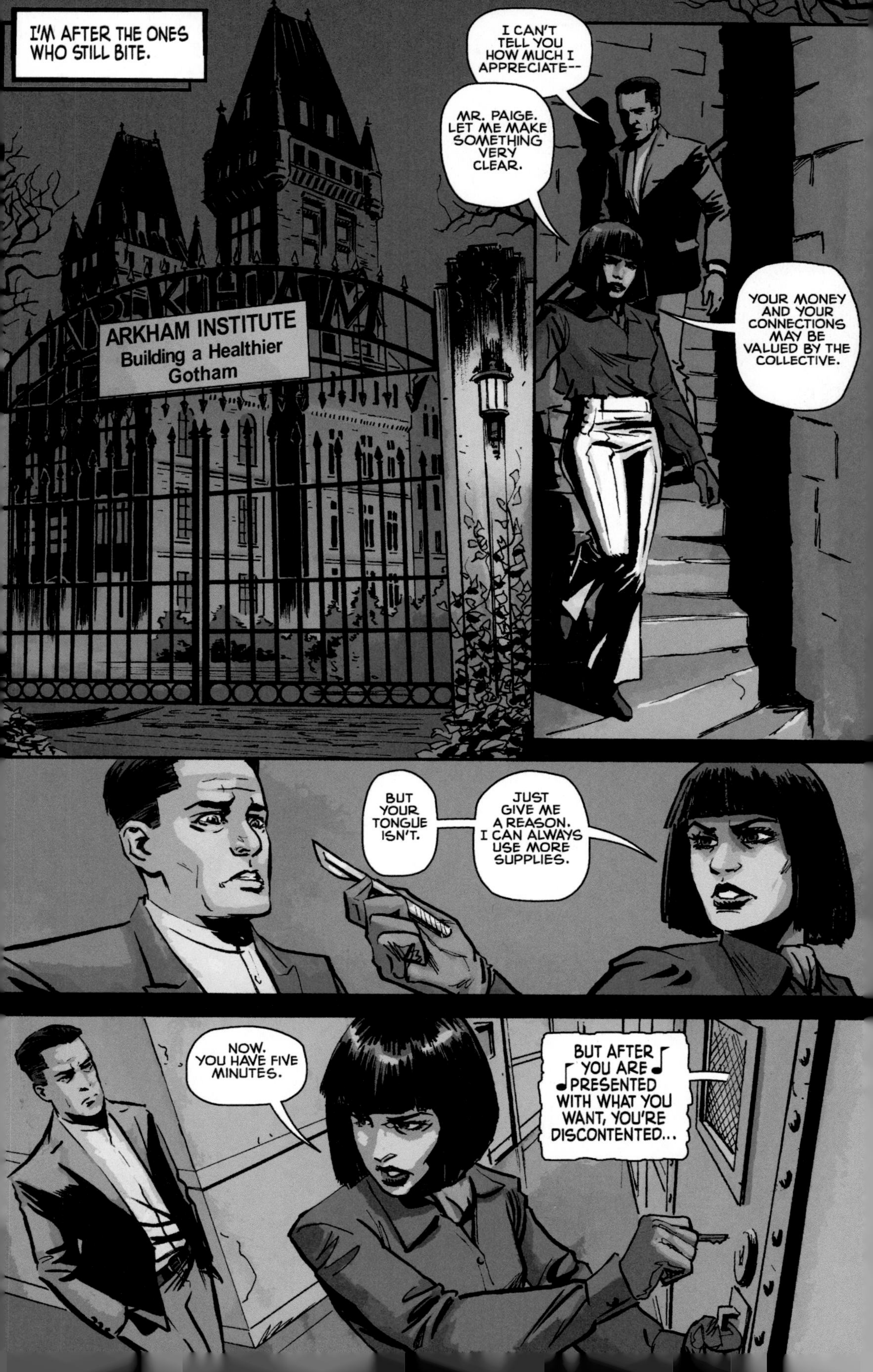
I'M AFTER THE ONES WHO STILL BITE.
ARKHAM INSTITUTE Building a Healthier Gotham
I CAN'T TELL YOU HOW MUCH I APPRECIATE--
MR. PAIGE. LET ME MAKE SOMETHING VERY CLEAR.
YOUR MONEY AND YOUR CONNECTIONS MAY BE VALUED BY THE COLLECTIVE.
BUT YOUR TONGUE ISN'T.
JUST GIVE ME A REASON. I CAN ALWAYS USE MORE SUPPLIES.
NOW. YOU HAVE FIVE MINUTES.
BUT AFTER YOU ARE PRESENTED WITH WHAT YOU WANT, YOU'RE DISCONTENTED...

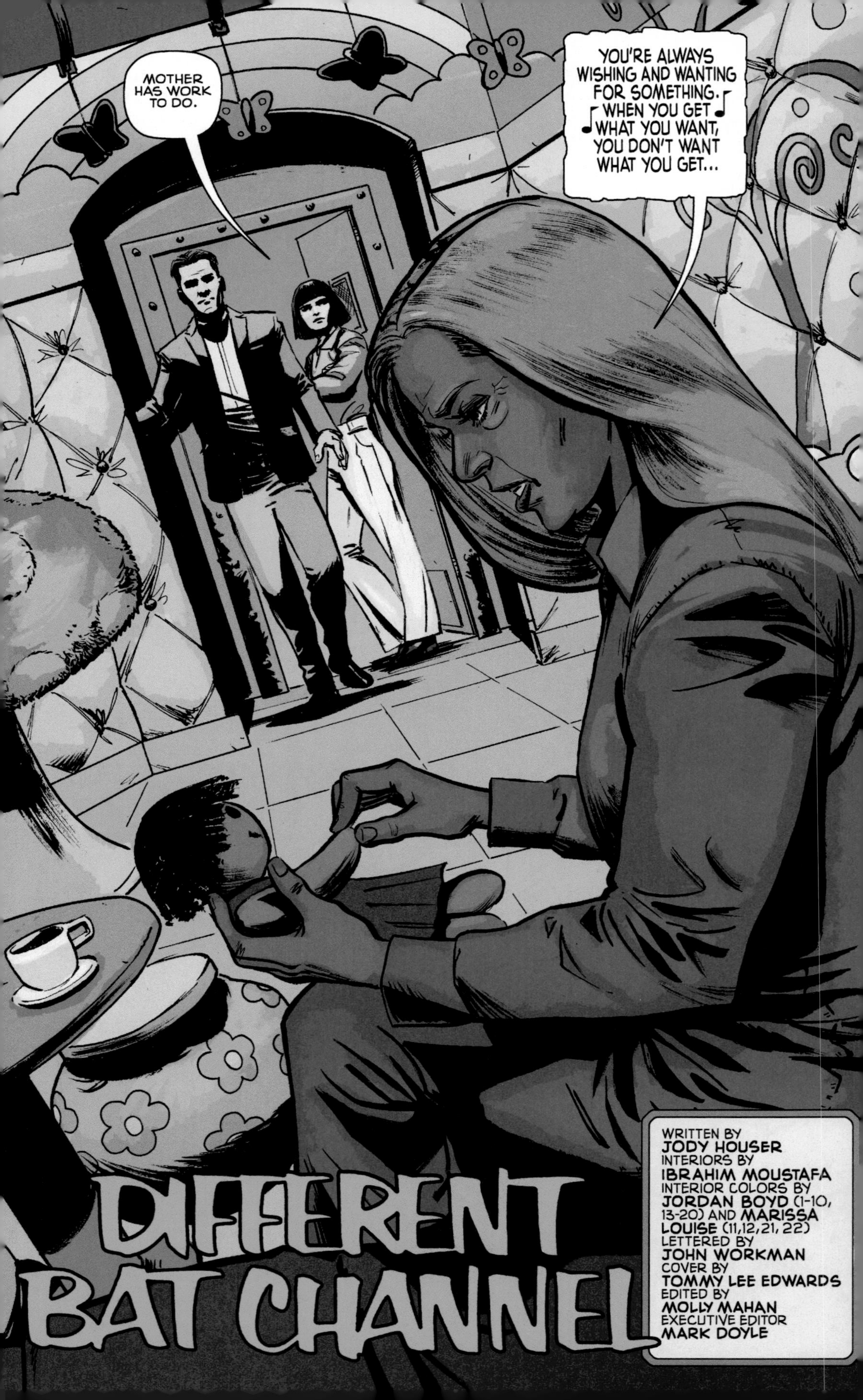
MOTHER HAS WORK TO DO.
YOU'RE ALWAYS WISHING AND WANTING FOR SOMETHING. ♪ WHEN YOU GET ♪ WHAT YOU WANT, YOU DON'T WANT WHAT YOU GET...
DIFFERENT BAT CHANNEL
WRITTEN BY JODY HOUSER
INTERIORS BY IBRAHIM MOUSTAFA
INTERIOR COLORS BY JORDAN BOYD (1-10, 13-20) AND MARISSA LOUISE (11,12, 21, 22)
LETTERED BY JOHN WORKMAN
COVER BY TOMMY LEE EDWARDS
EDITED BY MOLLY MAHAN
EXECUTIVE EDITOR MARK DOYLE

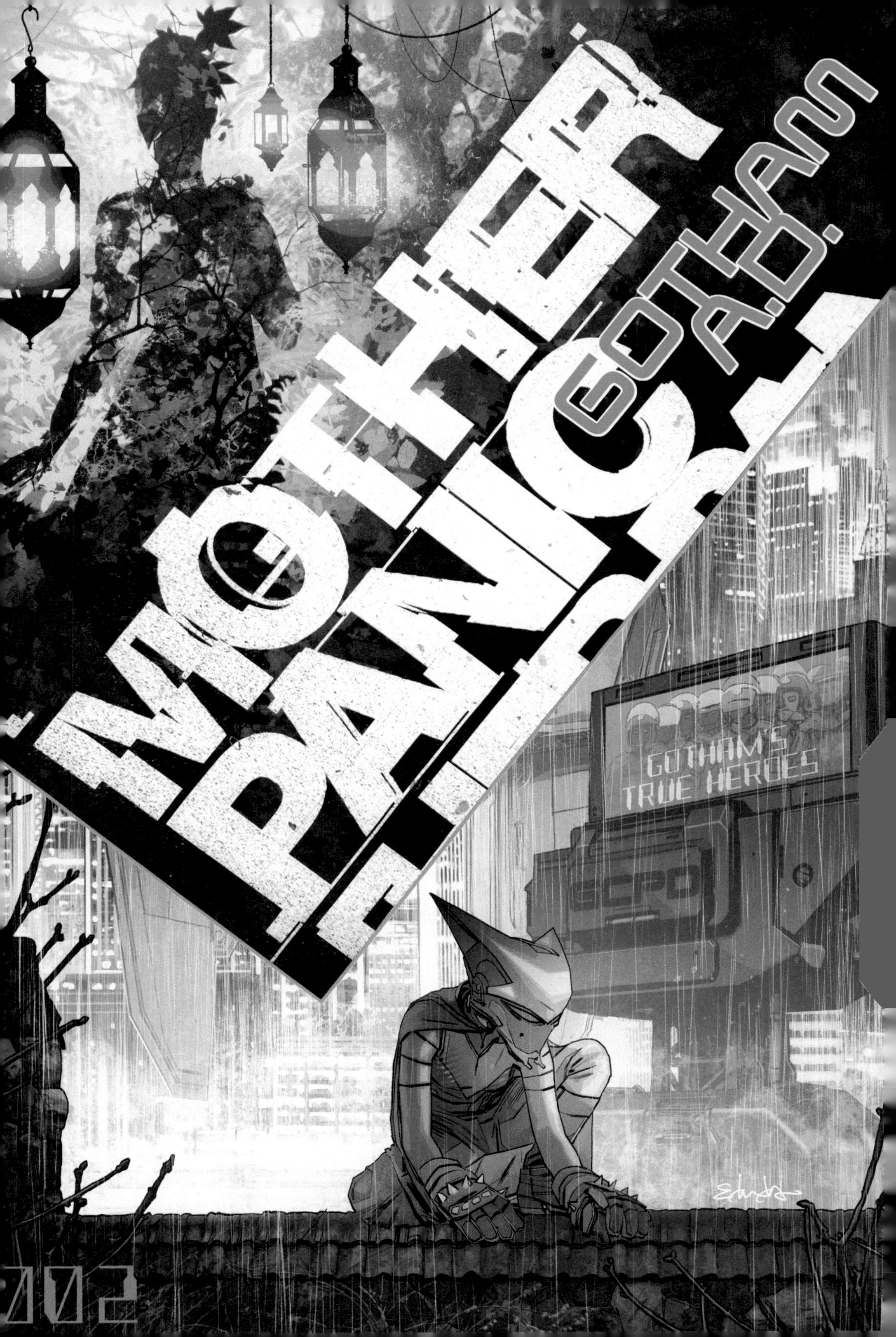
MOTHER PANIC
GOTHAM A.D.
GOTHAM'S TRUE HEROES
GCPD
002

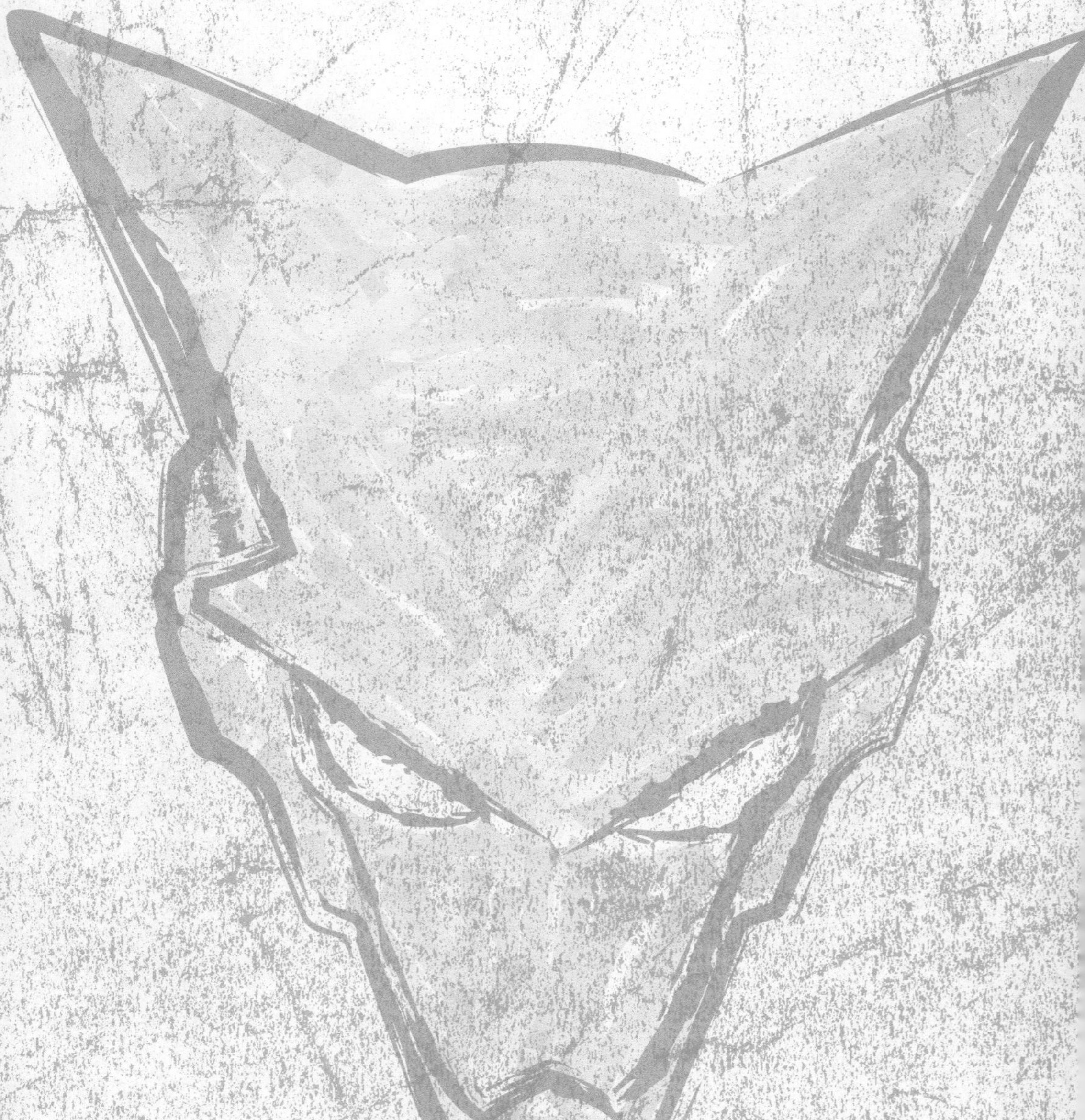

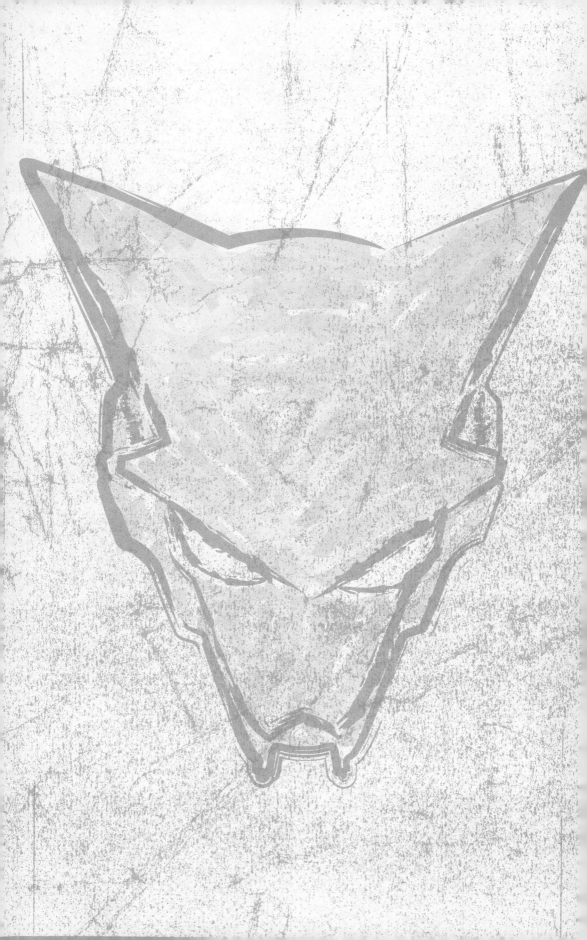

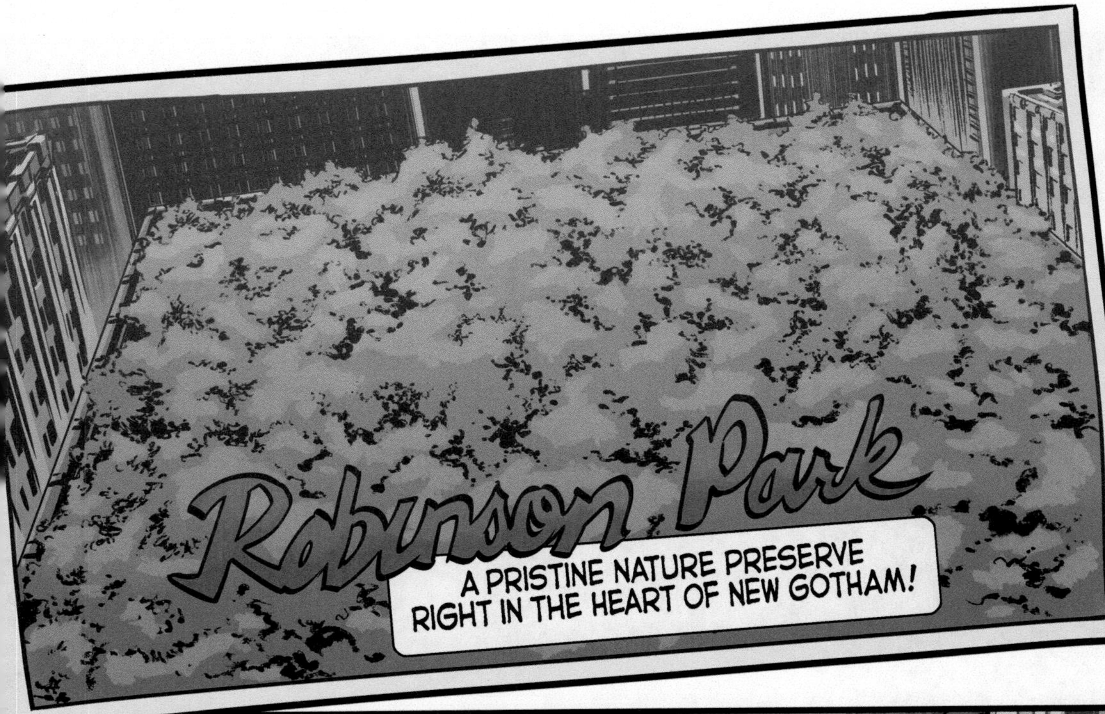
Robinson Park
A PRISTINE NATURE PRESERVE RIGHT IN THE HEART OF NEW GOTHAM!

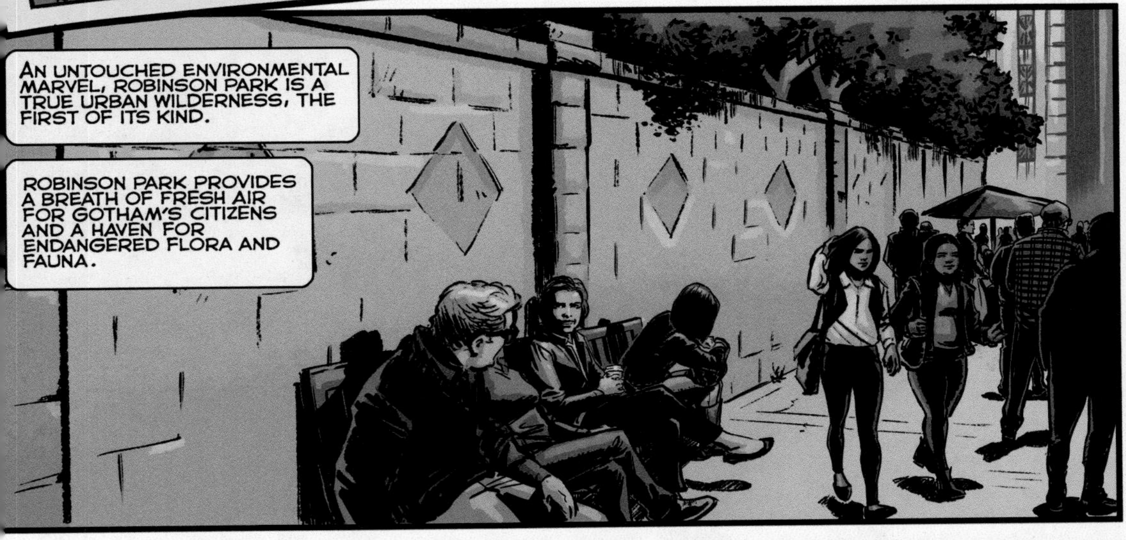
AN UNTOUCHED ENVIRONMENTAL MARVEL, ROBINSON PARK IS A TRUE URBAN WILDERNESS, THE FIRST OF ITS KIND.
ROBINSON PARK PROVIDES A BREATH OF FRESH AIR FOR GOTHAM'S CITIZENS AND A HAVEN FOR ENDANGERED FLORA AND FAUNA.

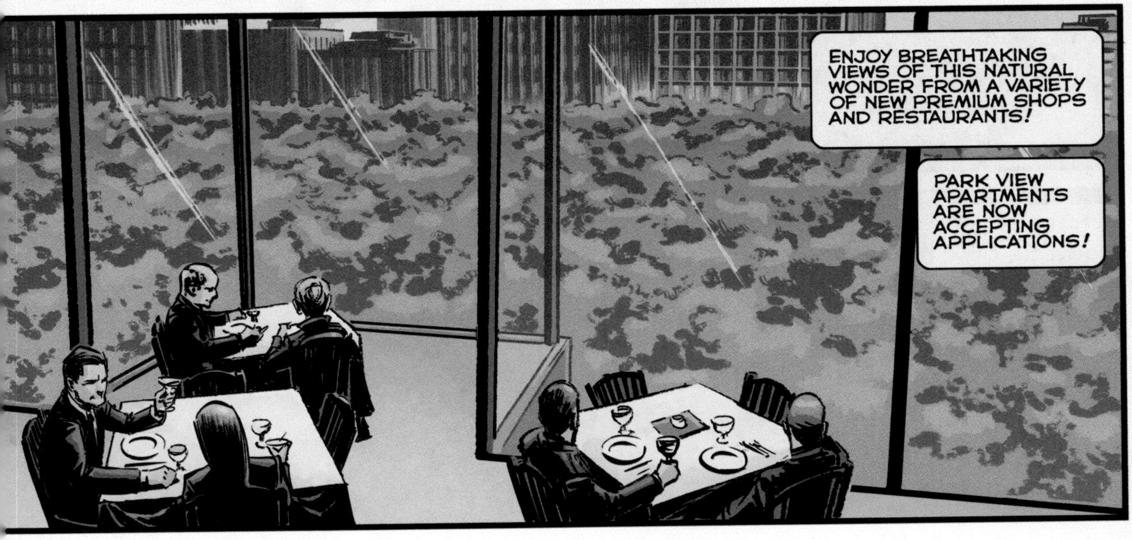
ENJOY BREATHTAKING VIEWS OF THIS NATURAL WONDER FROM A VARIETY OF NEW PREMIUM SHOPS AND RESTAURANTS!
PARK VIEW APARTMENTS ARE NOW ACCEPTING APPLICATIONS!

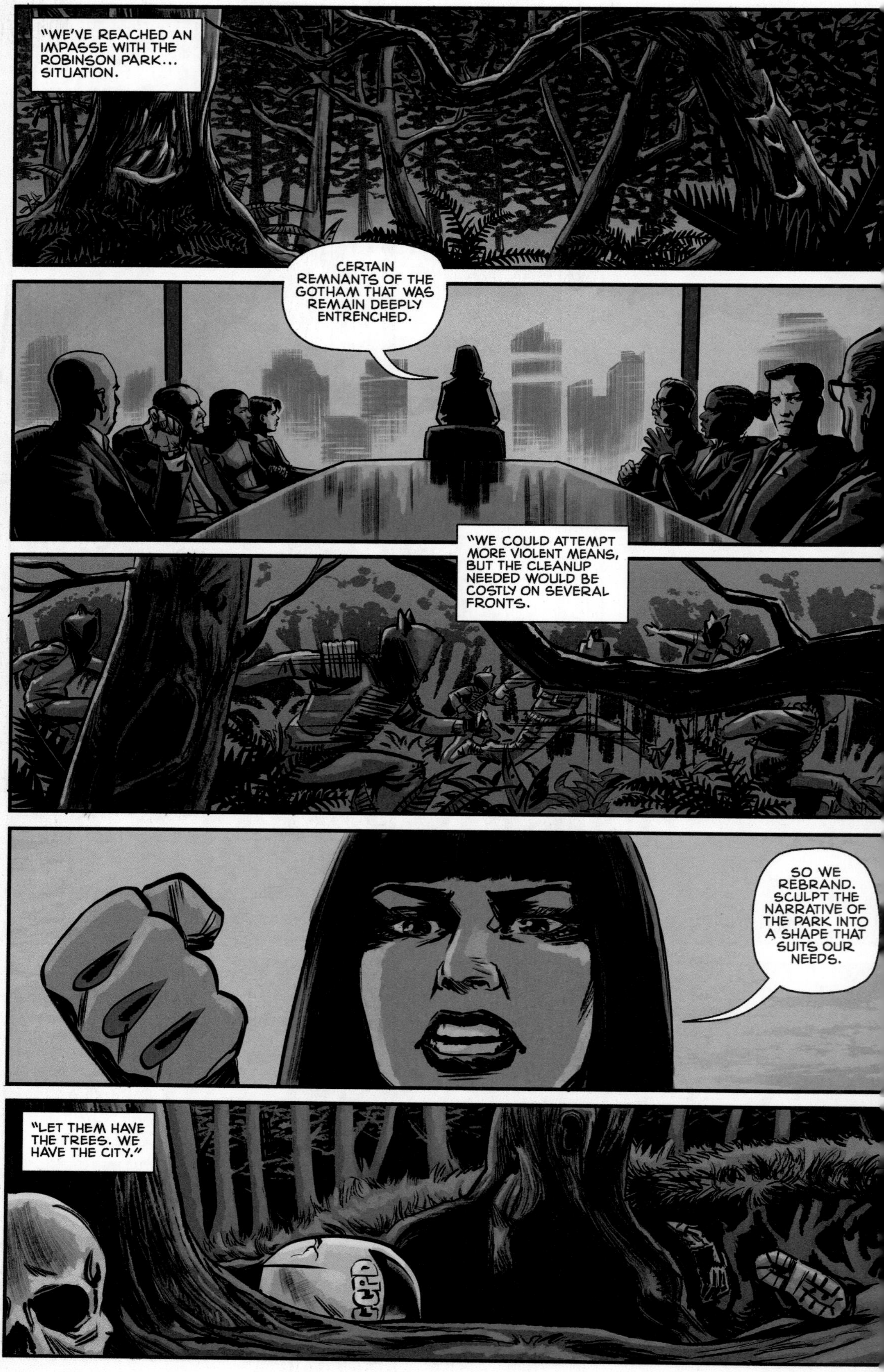
"WE'VE REACHED AN IMPASSE WITH THE ROBINSON PARK... SITUATION.
CERTAIN REMNANTS OF THE GOTHAM THAT WAS REMAIN DEEPLY ENTRENCHED.
"WE COULD ATTEMPT MORE VIOLENT MEANS, BUT THE CLEANUP NEEDED WOULD BE COSTLY ON SEVERAL FRONTS.
SO WE REBRAND. SCULPT THE NARRATIVE OF THE PARK INTO A SHAPE THAT SUITS OUR NEEDS.
"LET THEM HAVE THE TREES. WE HAVE THE CITY."
GCPD

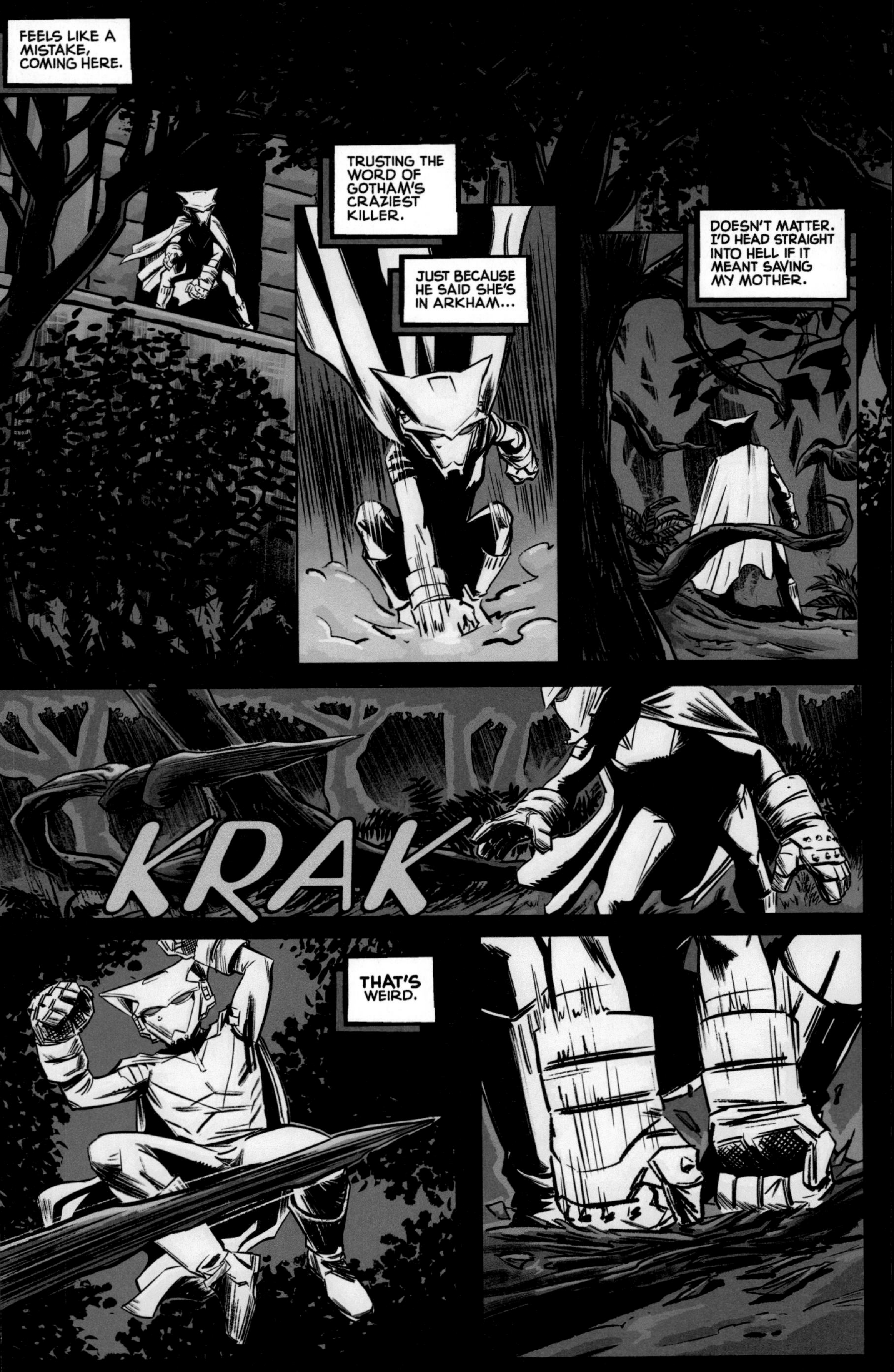
FEELS LIKE A MISTAKE, COMING HERE.
TRUSTING THE WORD OF GOTHAM'S CRAZIEST KILLER.
JUST BECAUSE HE SAID SHE'S IN ARKHAM...
DOESN'T MATTER. I'D HEAD STRAIGHT INTO HELL IF IT MEANT SAVING MY MOTHER.
KRAK
THAT'S WEIRD.

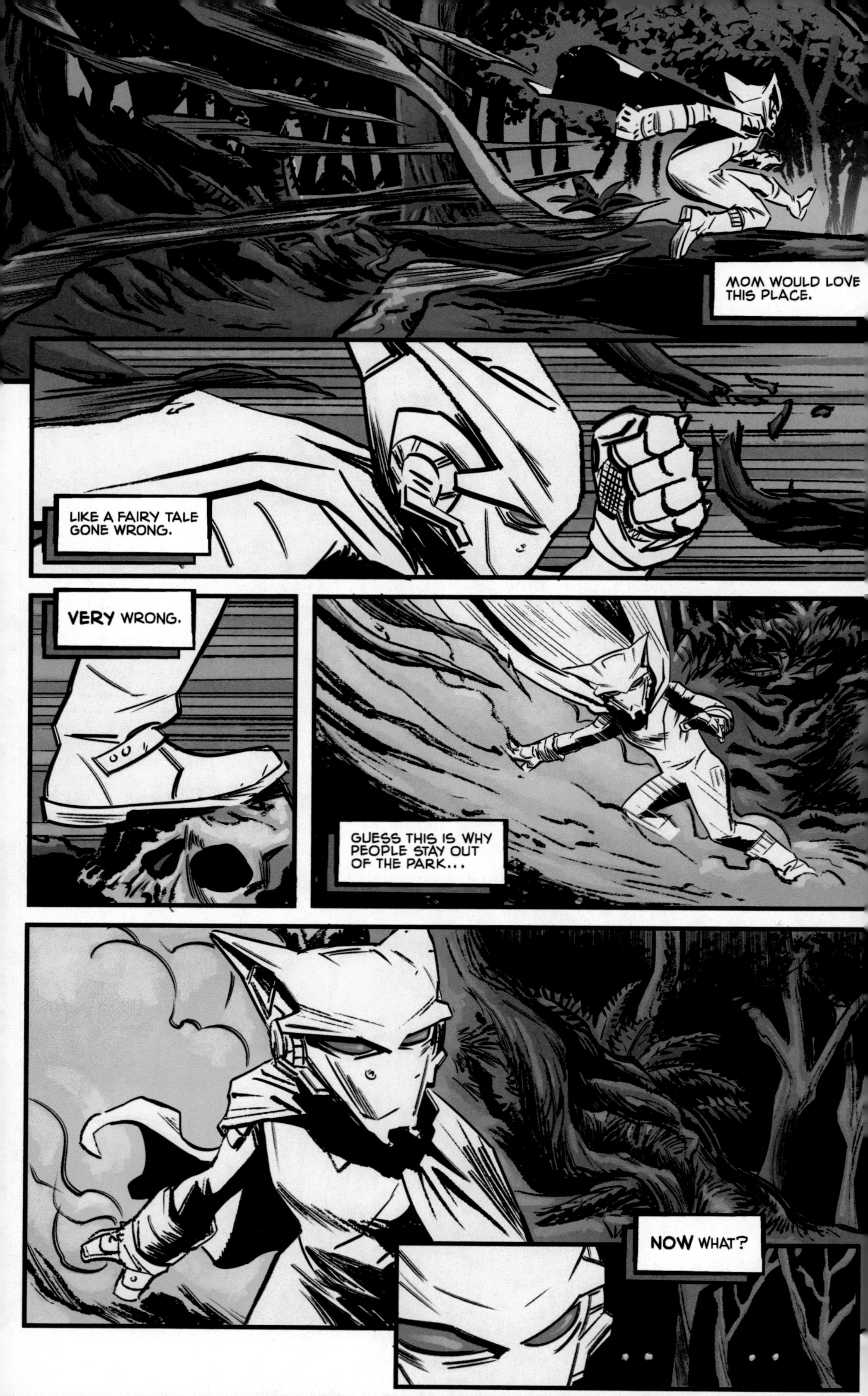
MOM WOULD LOVE THIS PLACE.
LIKE A FAIRY TALE GONE WRONG.
VERY WRONG.
GUESS THIS IS WHY PEOPLE STAY OUT OF THE PARK...
NOW WHAT?

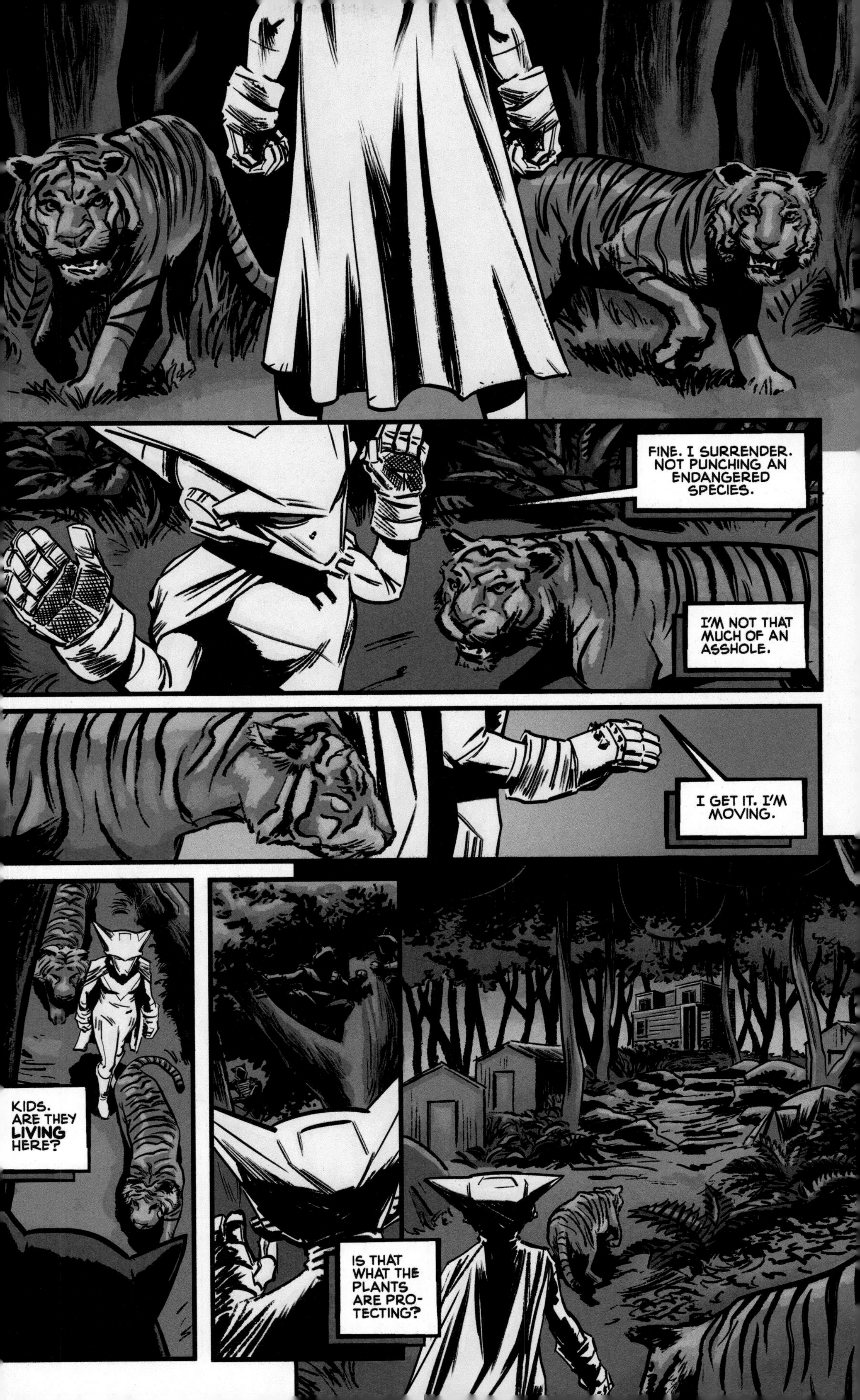
FINE. I SURRENDER. NOT PUNCHING AN ENDANGERED SPECIES.
I'M NOT THAT MUCH OF AN ASSHOLE.
I GET IT. I'M MOVING.
KIDS. ARE THEY **LIVING** HERE?
IS THAT WHAT THE PLANTS ARE PRO-TECTING?

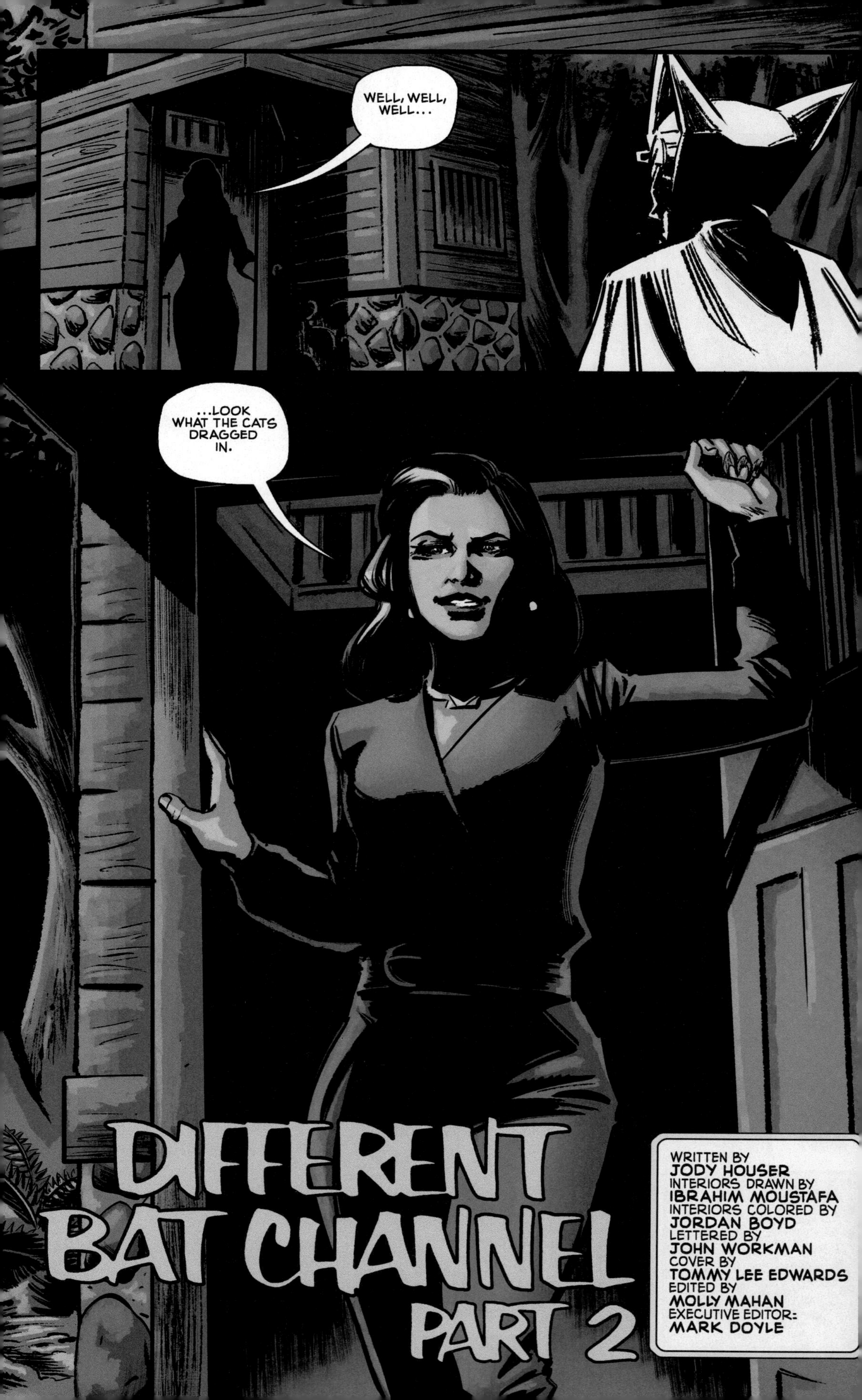
WELL, WELL, WELL...
...LOOK WHAT THE CATS DRAGGED IN.
DIFFERENT BAT CHANNEL PART 2
WRITTEN BY JODY HOUSER
INTERIORS DRAWN BY IBRAHIM MOUSTAFA
INTERIORS COLORED BY JORDAN BOYD
LETTERED BY JOHN WORKMAN
COVER BY TOMMY LEE EDWARDS
EDITED BY MOLLY MAHAN
EXECUTIVE EDITOR: MARK DOYLE

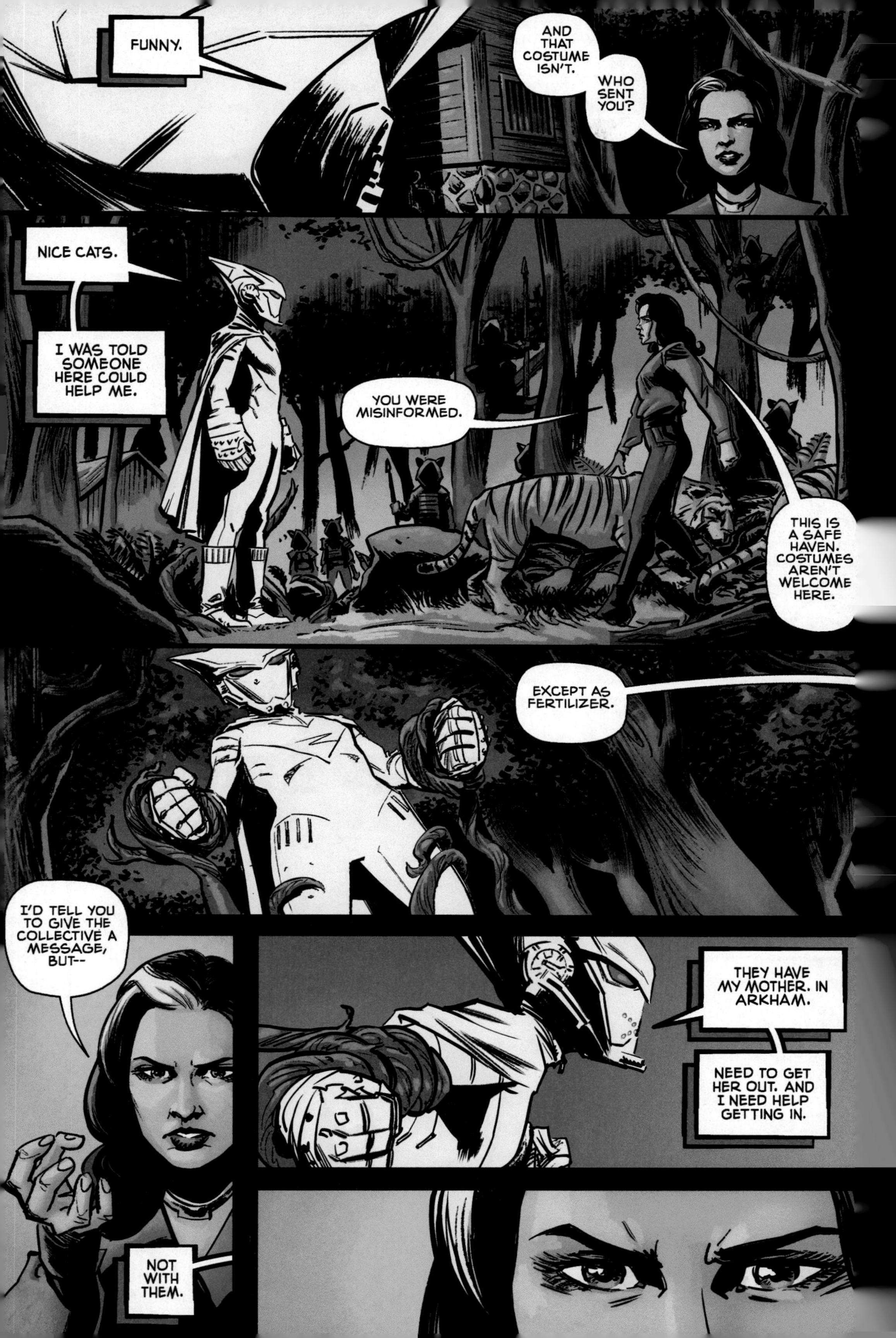
FUNNY.
AND THAT COSTUME ISN'T.
WHO SENT YOU?
NICE CATS.
I WAS TOLD SOMEONE HERE COULD HELP ME.
YOU WERE MISINFORMED.
THIS IS A SAFE HAVEN. COSTUMES AREN'T WELCOME HERE.
EXCEPT AS FERTILIZER.
I'D TELL YOU TO GIVE THE COLLECTIVE A MESSAGE, BUT--
THEY HAVE MY MOTHER. IN ARKHAM.
NEED TO GET HER OUT. AND I NEED HELP GETTING IN.
NOT WITH THEM.

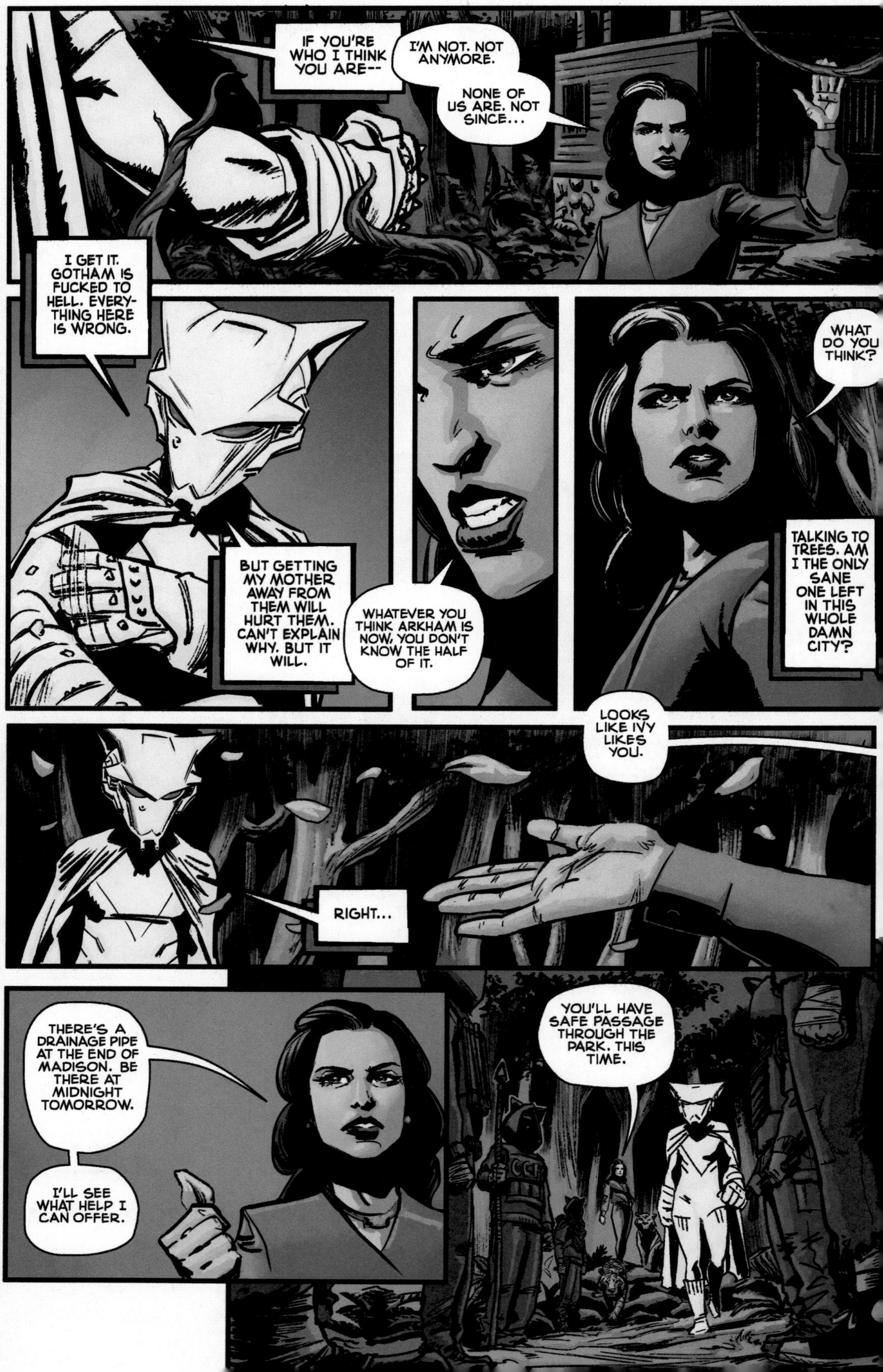
IF YOU'RE WHO I THINK YOU ARE--
I'M NOT. NOT ANYMORE.
NONE OF US ARE. NOT SINCE...
I GET IT. GOTHAM IS FUCKED TO HELL. EVERY-THING HERE IS WRONG.
BUT GETTING MY MOTHER AWAY FROM THEM WILL HURT THEM. CAN'T EXPLAIN WHY. BUT IT WILL.
WHATEVER YOU THINK ARKHAM IS NOW, YOU DON'T KNOW THE HALF OF IT.
WHAT DO YOU THINK?
TALKING TO TREES. AM I THE ONLY SANE ONE LEFT IN THIS WHOLE DAMN CITY?
LOOKS LIKE IVY LIKES YOU.
RIGHT...
THERE'S A DRAINAGE PIPE AT THE END OF MADISON. BE THERE AT MIDNIGHT TOMORROW.
I'LL SEE WHAT HELP I CAN OFFER.
YOU'LL HAVE SAFE PASSAGE THROUGH THE PARK. THIS TIME.

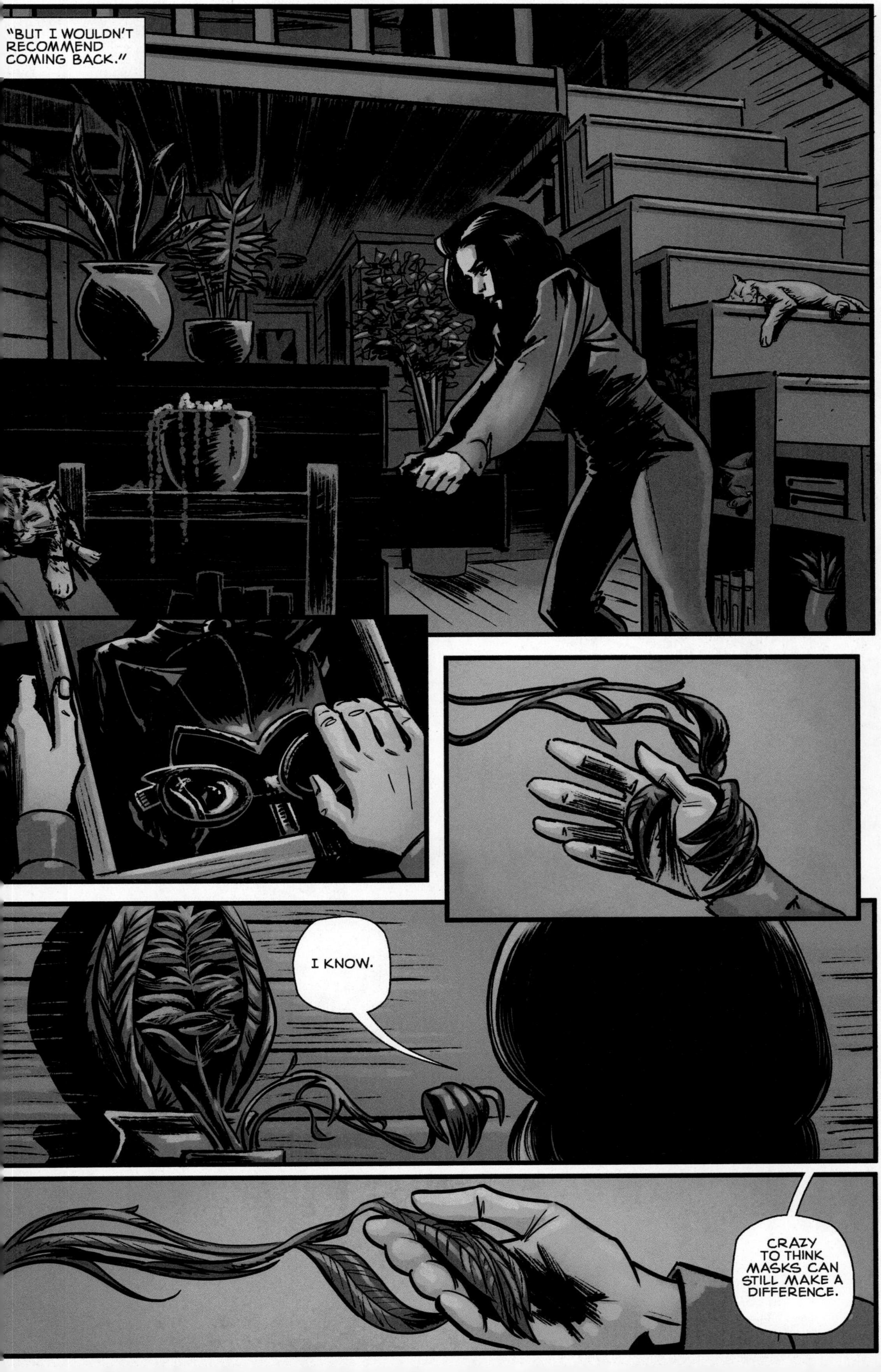
"BUT I WOULDN'T RECOMMEND COMING BACK."
I KNOW.
CRAZY TO THINK MASKS CAN STILL MAKE A DIFFERENCE.

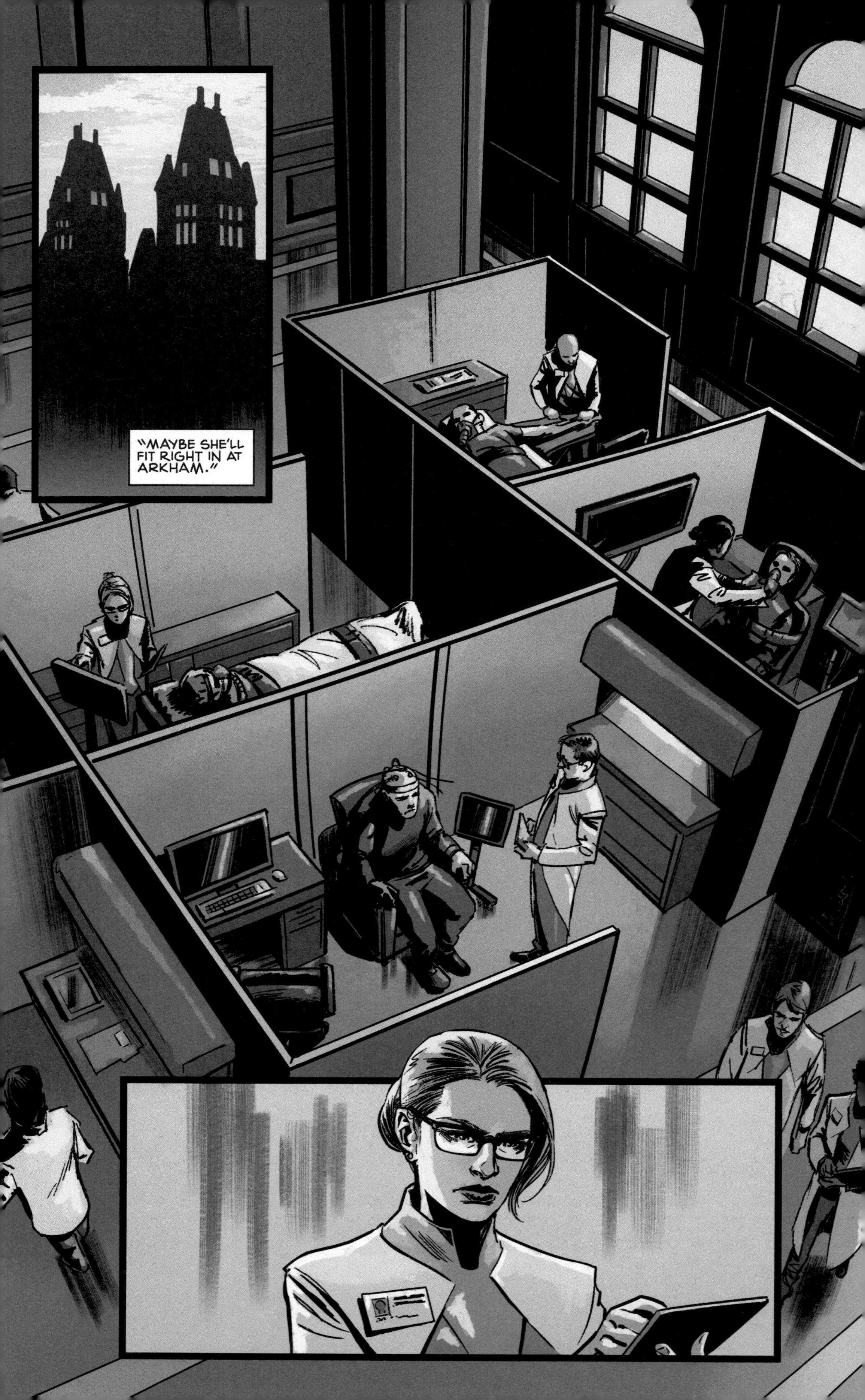
"MAYBE SHE'LL FIT RIGHT IN AT ARKHAM."

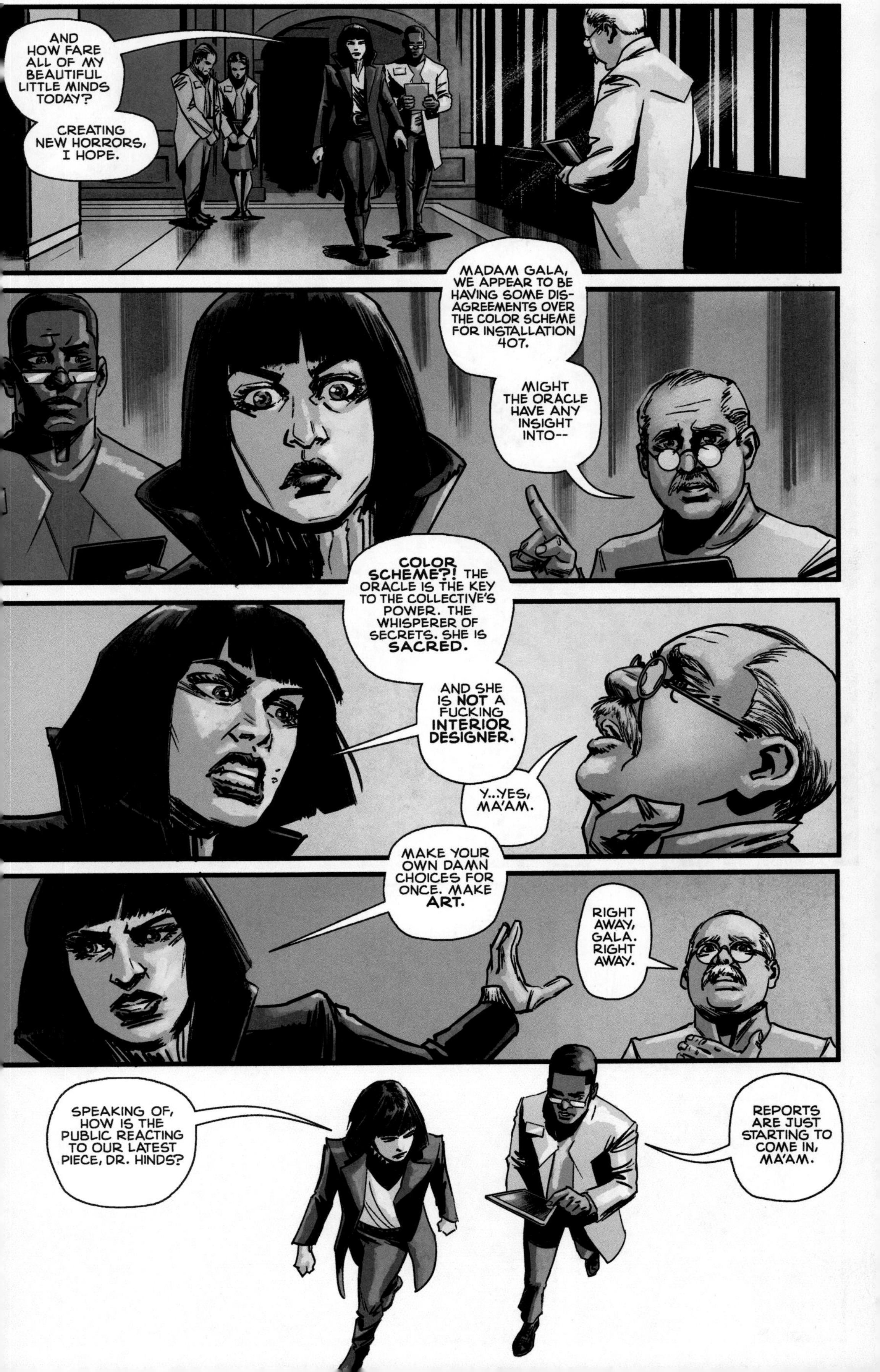
AND HOW FARE ALL OF MY BEAUTIFUL LITTLE MINDS TODAY?
CREATING NEW HORRORS, I HOPE.
MADAM GALA, WE APPEAR TO BE HAVING SOME DIS-AGREEMENTS OVER THE COLOR SCHEME FOR INSTALLATION 407.
MIGHT THE ORACLE HAVE ANY INSIGHT INTO--
COLOR SCHEME?! THE ORACLE IS THE KEY TO THE COLLECTIVE'S POWER. THE WHISPERER OF SECRETS. SHE IS **SACRED.**
AND SHE IS **NOT** A FUCKING **INTERIOR DESIGNER.**
Y...YES, MA'AM.
MAKE YOUR OWN DAMN CHOICES FOR ONCE. MAKE **ART.**
RIGHT AWAY, GALA. RIGHT AWAY.
SPEAKING OF, HOW IS THE PUBLIC REACTING TO OUR LATEST PIECE, DR. HINDS?
REPORTS ARE JUST STARTING TO COME IN, MA'AM.

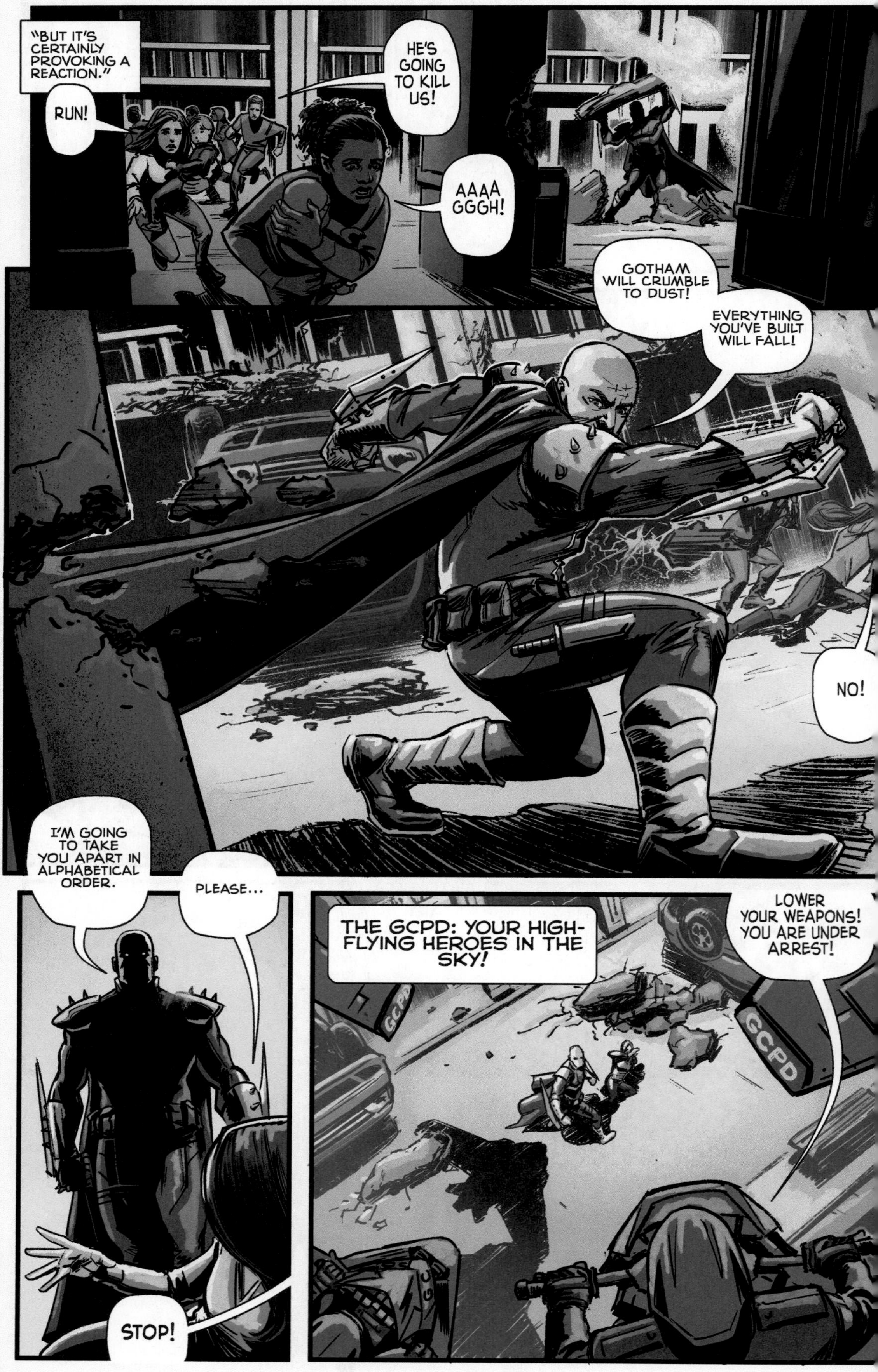
"BUT IT'S CERTAINLY PROVOKING A REACTION."
RUN!
HE'S GOING TO KILL US!
AAAA GGGH!
GOTHAM WILL CRUMBLE TO DUST!
EVERYTHING YOU'VE BUILT WILL FALL!
NO!
I'M GOING TO TAKE YOU APART IN ALPHABETICAL ORDER.
PLEASE...
STOP!
THE GCPD: YOUR HIGH-FLYING HEROES IN THE SKY!
LOWER YOUR WEAPONS! YOU ARE UNDER ARREST!
GCPD
GCPD

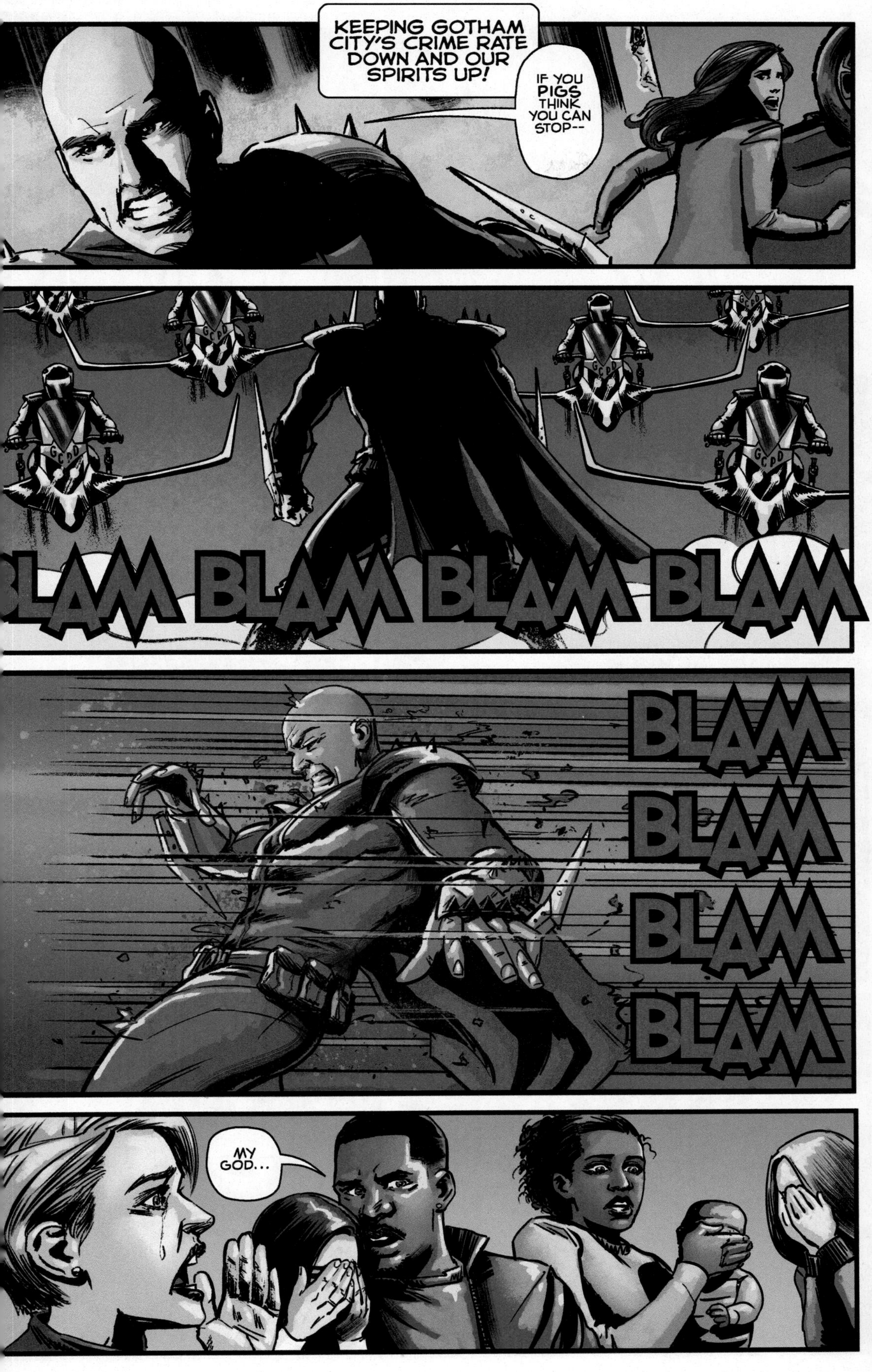
KEEPING GOTHAM CITY'S CRIME RATE DOWN AND OUR SPIRITS UP!
IF YOU PIGS THINK YOU CAN STOP--
GCPD
BLAM BLAM BLAM BLAM
BLAM BLAM BLAM BLAM
MY GOD...

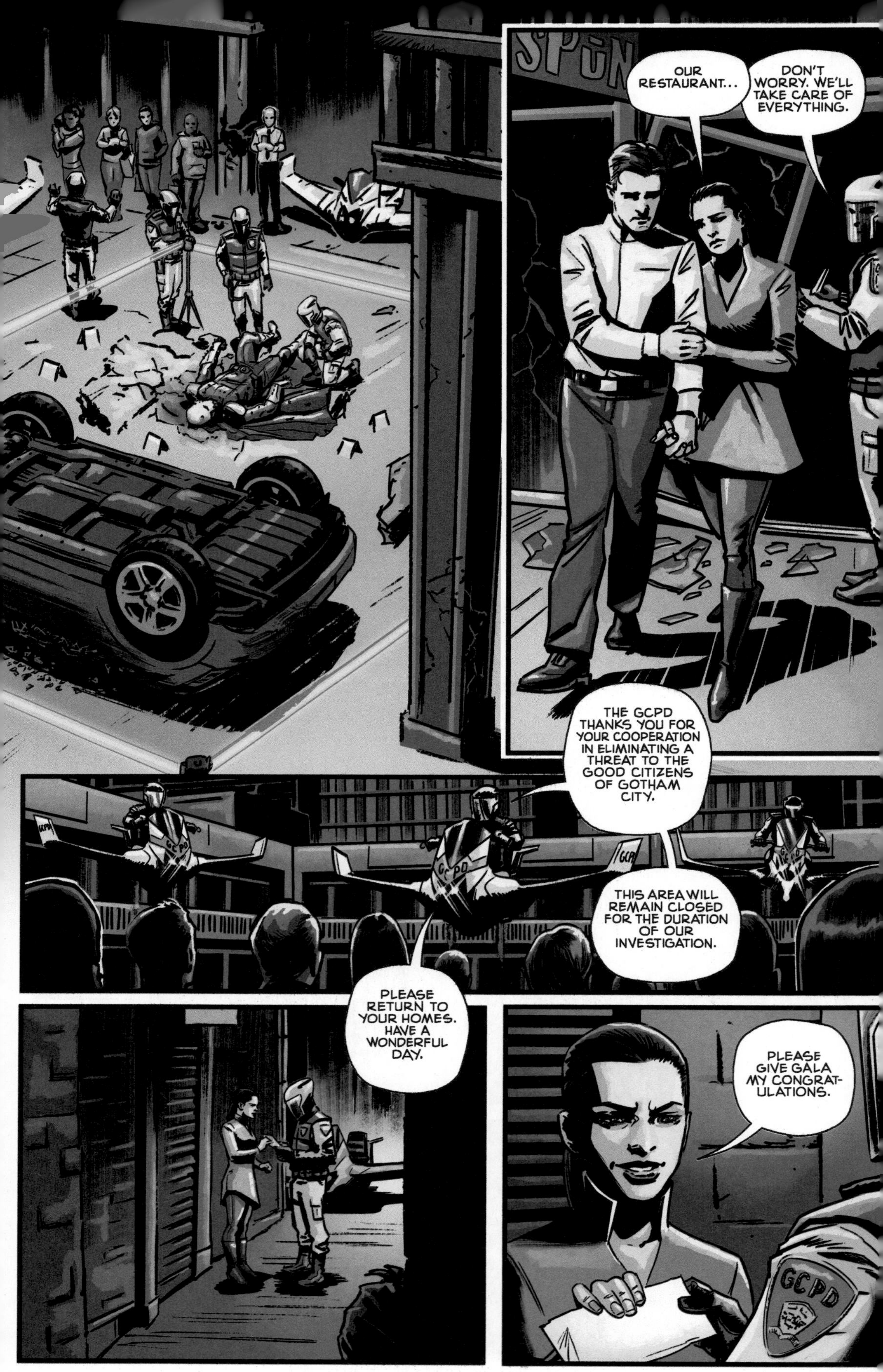
OUR RESTAURANT...
DON'T WORRY. WE'LL TAKE CARE OF EVERYTHING.
THE GCPD THANKS YOU FOR YOUR COOPERATION IN ELIMINATING A THREAT TO THE GOOD CITIZENS OF GOTHAM CITY.
THIS AREA WILL REMAIN CLOSED FOR THE DURATION OF OUR INVESTIGATION.
PLEASE RETURN TO YOUR HOMES. HAVE A WONDERFUL DAY.
PLEASE GIVE GALA MY CONGRATULATIONS.

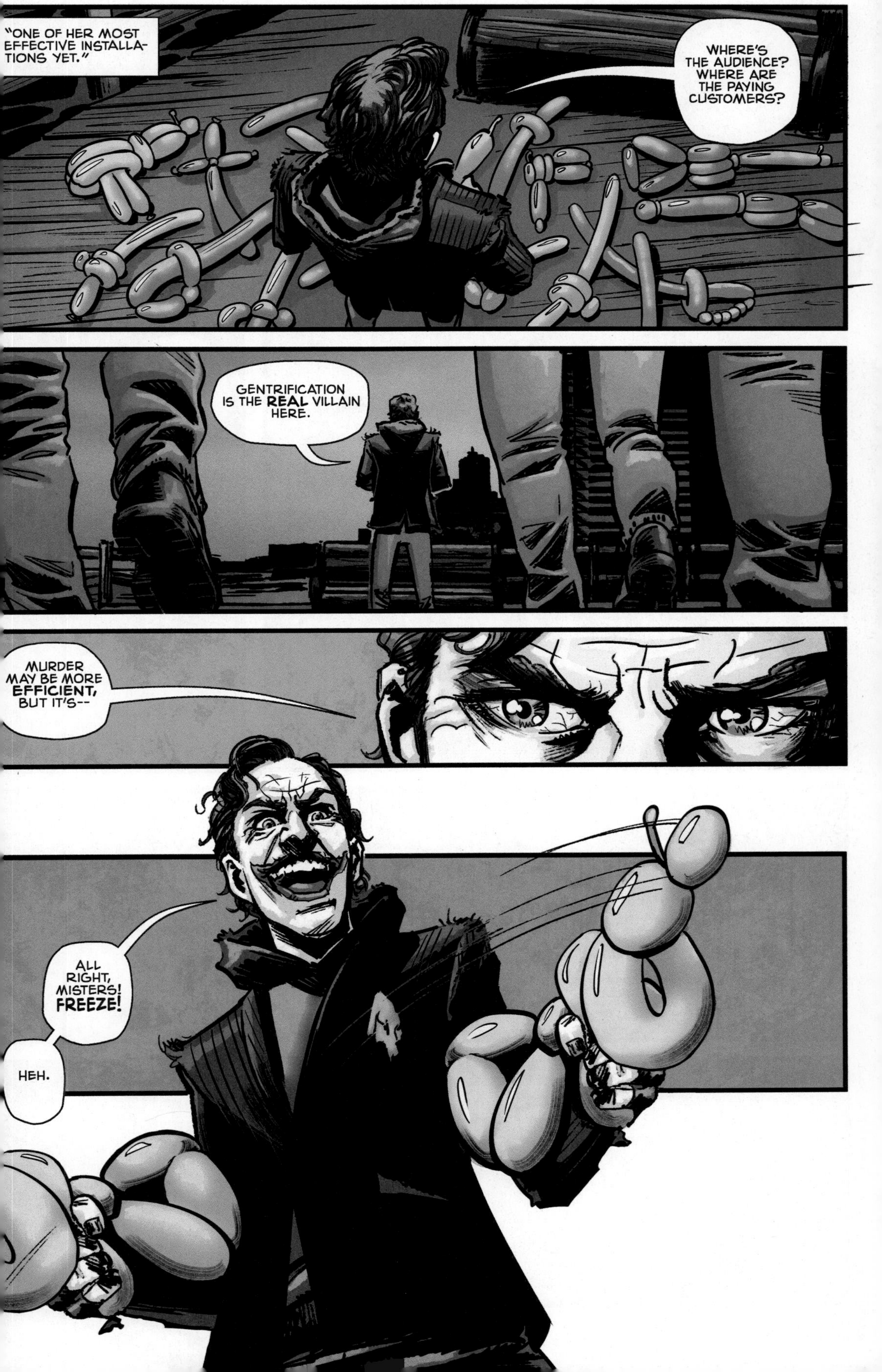
"ONE OF HER MOST EFFECTIVE INSTALLATIONS YET."
WHERE'S THE AUDIENCE? WHERE ARE THE PAYING CUSTOMERS?
GENTRIFICATION IS THE **REAL** VILLAIN HERE.
MURDER MAY BE MORE **EFFICIENT,** BUT IT'S--
ALL RIGHT, MISTERS! **FREEZE!**
HEH.

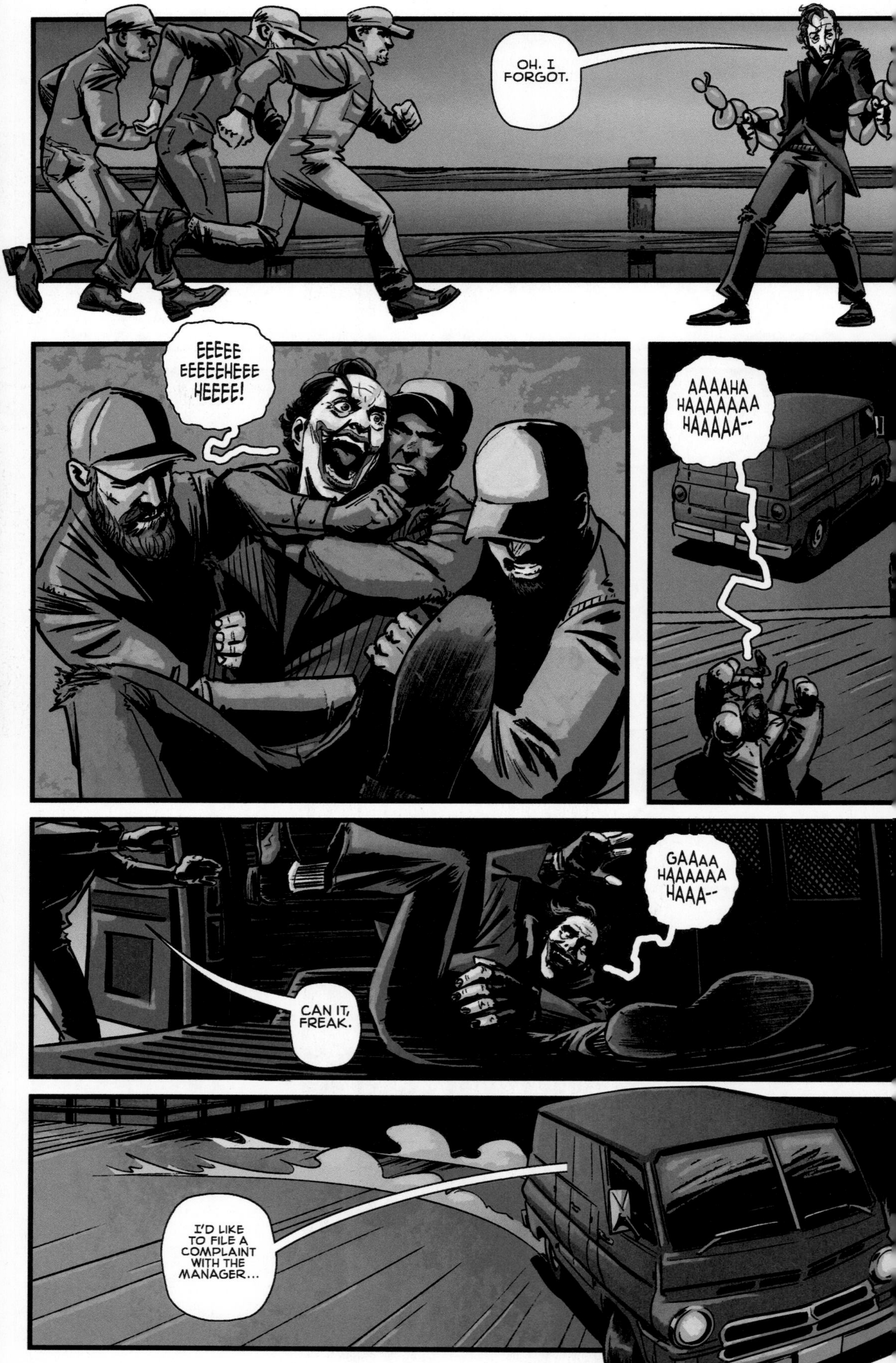

OH. I FORGOT.
EEEEE EEEEEHEEE HEEEE!
AAAAHA HAAAAAAA HAAAAA--
GAAAA HAAAAAA HAAA--
CAN IT, FREAK.
I'D LIKE TO FILE A COMPLAINT WITH THE MANAGER...

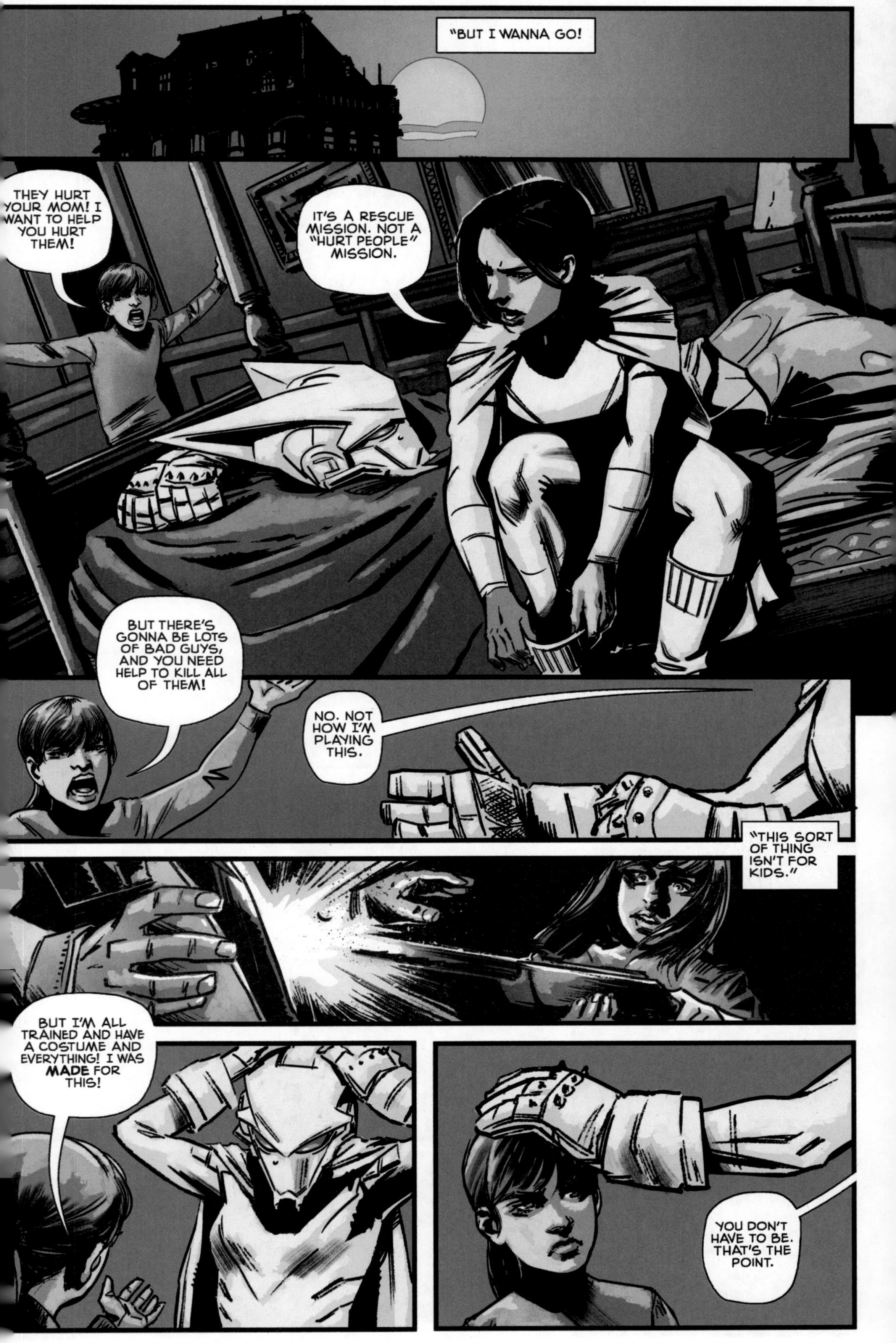
"BUT I WANNA GO!
THEY HURT YOUR MOM! I WANT TO HELP YOU HURT THEM!
IT'S A RESCUE MISSION. NOT A "HURT PEOPLE" MISSION.
BUT THERE'S GONNA BE LOTS OF BAD GUYS, AND YOU NEED HELP TO KILL ALL OF THEM!
NO. NOT HOW I'M PLAYING THIS.
"THIS SORT OF THING ISN'T FOR KIDS."
BUT I'M ALL TRAINED AND HAVE A COSTUME AND EVERYTHING! I WAS MADE FOR THIS!
YOU DON'T HAVE TO BE. THAT'S THE POINT.

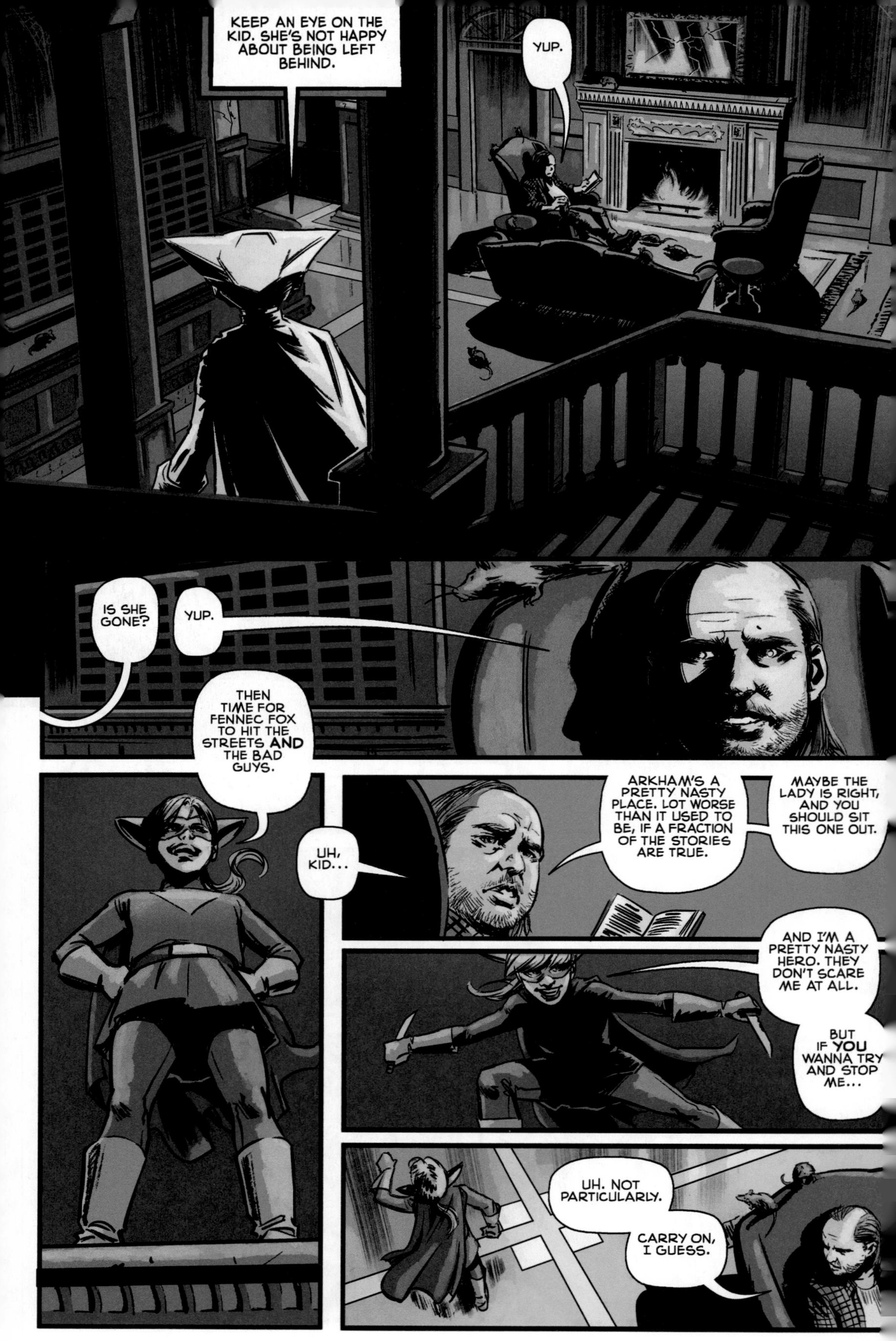
KEEP AN EYE ON THE KID. SHE'S NOT HAPPY ABOUT BEING LEFT BEHIND.
YUP.
IS SHE GONE?
YUP.
THEN TIME FOR FENNEC FOX TO HIT THE STREETS AND THE BAD GUYS.
UH, KID...
ARKHAM'S A PRETTY NASTY PLACE. LOT WORSE THAN IT USED TO BE, IF A FRACTION OF THE STORIES ARE TRUE.
MAYBE THE LADY IS RIGHT, AND YOU SHOULD SIT THIS ONE OUT.
AND I'M A PRETTY NASTY HERO. THEY DON'T SCARE ME AT ALL.
BUT IF YOU WANNA TRY AND STOP ME...
UH. NOT PARTICULARLY.
CARRY ON, I GUESS.

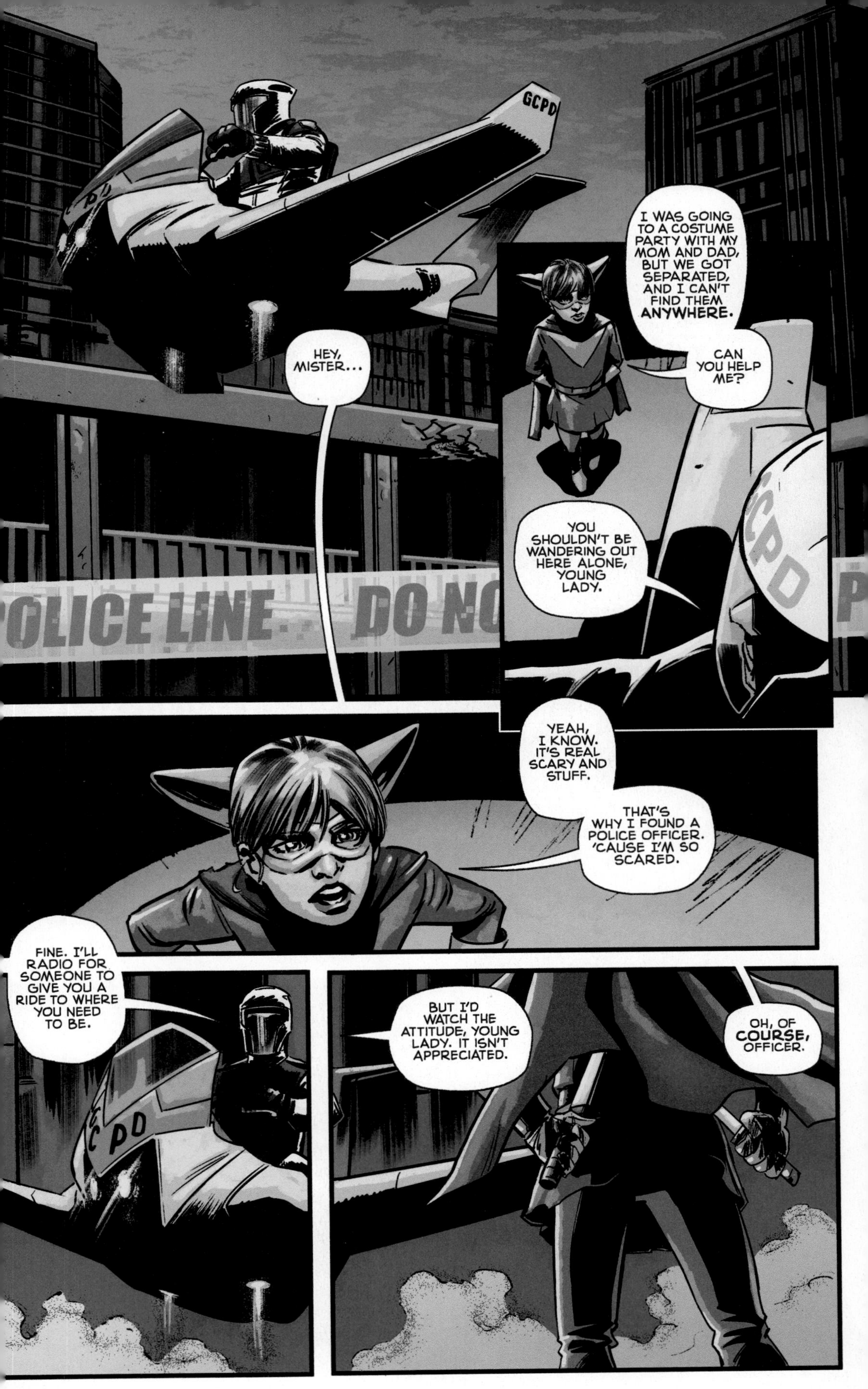
GCPD
HEY, MISTER...
I WAS GOING TO A COSTUME PARTY WITH MY MOM AND DAD, BUT WE GOT SEPARATED, AND I CAN'T FIND THEM **ANYWHERE.**
CAN YOU HELP ME?
YOU SHOULDN'T BE WANDERING OUT HERE ALONE, YOUNG LADY.
POLICE LINE DO NO
GCPD
YEAH, I KNOW. IT'S REAL SCARY AND STUFF.
THAT'S WHY I FOUND A POLICE OFFICER. 'CAUSE I'M SO SCARED.
FINE. I'LL RADIO FOR SOMEONE TO GIVE YOU A RIDE TO WHERE YOU NEED TO BE.
GCPD
BUT I'D WATCH THE ATTITUDE, YOUNG LADY. IT ISN'T APPRECIATED.
OH, OF **COURSE,** OFFICER.

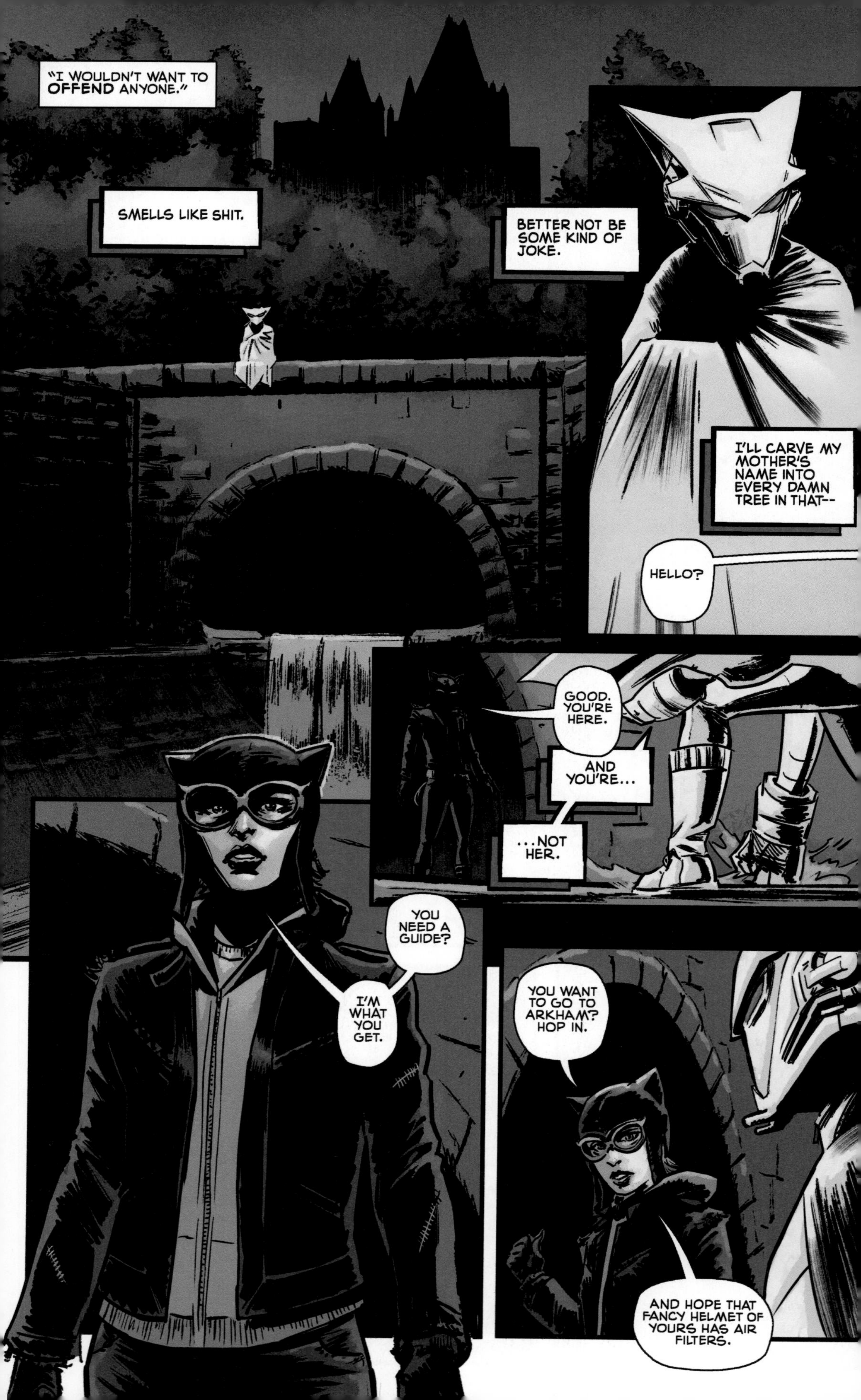

"I WOULDN'T WANT TO OFFEND ANYONE."
SMELLS LIKE SHIT.
BETTER NOT BE SOME KIND OF JOKE.
I'LL CARVE MY MOTHER'S NAME INTO EVERY DAMN TREE IN THAT--
HELLO?
GOOD. YOU'RE HERE.
AND YOU'RE...
...NOT HER.
YOU NEED A GUIDE?
I'M WHAT YOU GET.
YOU WANT TO GO TO ARKHAM? HOP IN.
AND HOPE THAT FANCY HELMET OF YOURS HAS AIR FILTERS.

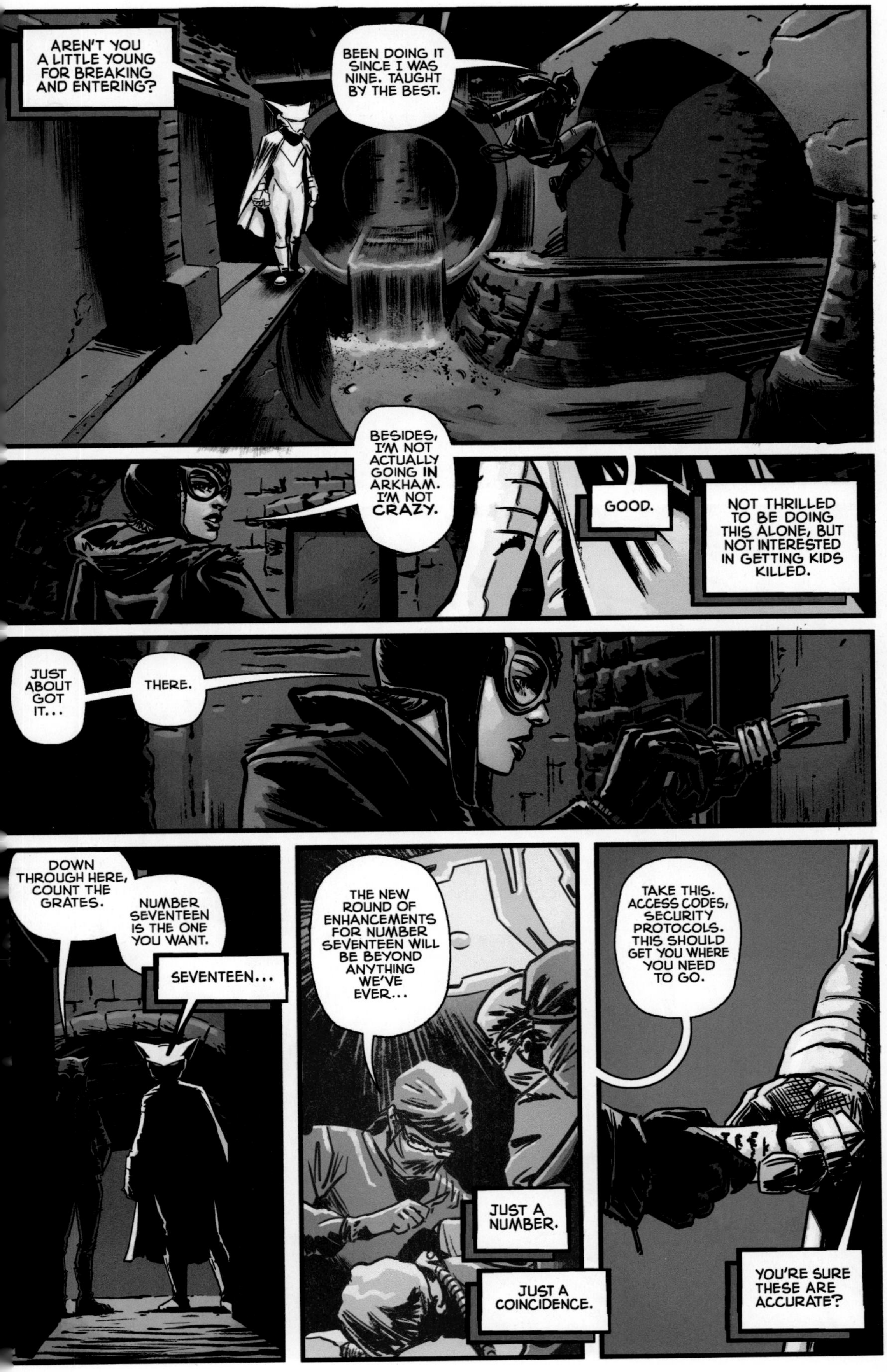
AREN'T YOU A LITTLE YOUNG FOR BREAKING AND ENTERING?
BEEN DOING IT SINCE I WAS NINE. TAUGHT BY THE BEST.
BESIDES, I'M NOT ACTUALLY GOING IN ARKHAM. I'M NOT CRAZY.
GOOD.
NOT THRILLED TO BE DOING THIS ALONE, BUT NOT INTERESTED IN GETTING KIDS KILLED.
JUST ABOUT GOT IT...
THERE.
DOWN THROUGH HERE, COUNT THE GRATES.
NUMBER SEVENTEEN IS THE ONE YOU WANT.
SEVENTEEN...
THE NEW ROUND OF ENHANCEMENTS FOR NUMBER SEVENTEEN WILL BE BEYOND ANYTHING WE'VE EVER...
JUST A NUMBER.
JUST A COINCIDENCE.
TAKE THIS. ACCESS CODES, SECURITY PROTOCOLS. THIS SHOULD GET YOU WHERE YOU NEED TO GO.
YOU'RE SURE THESE ARE ACCURATE?

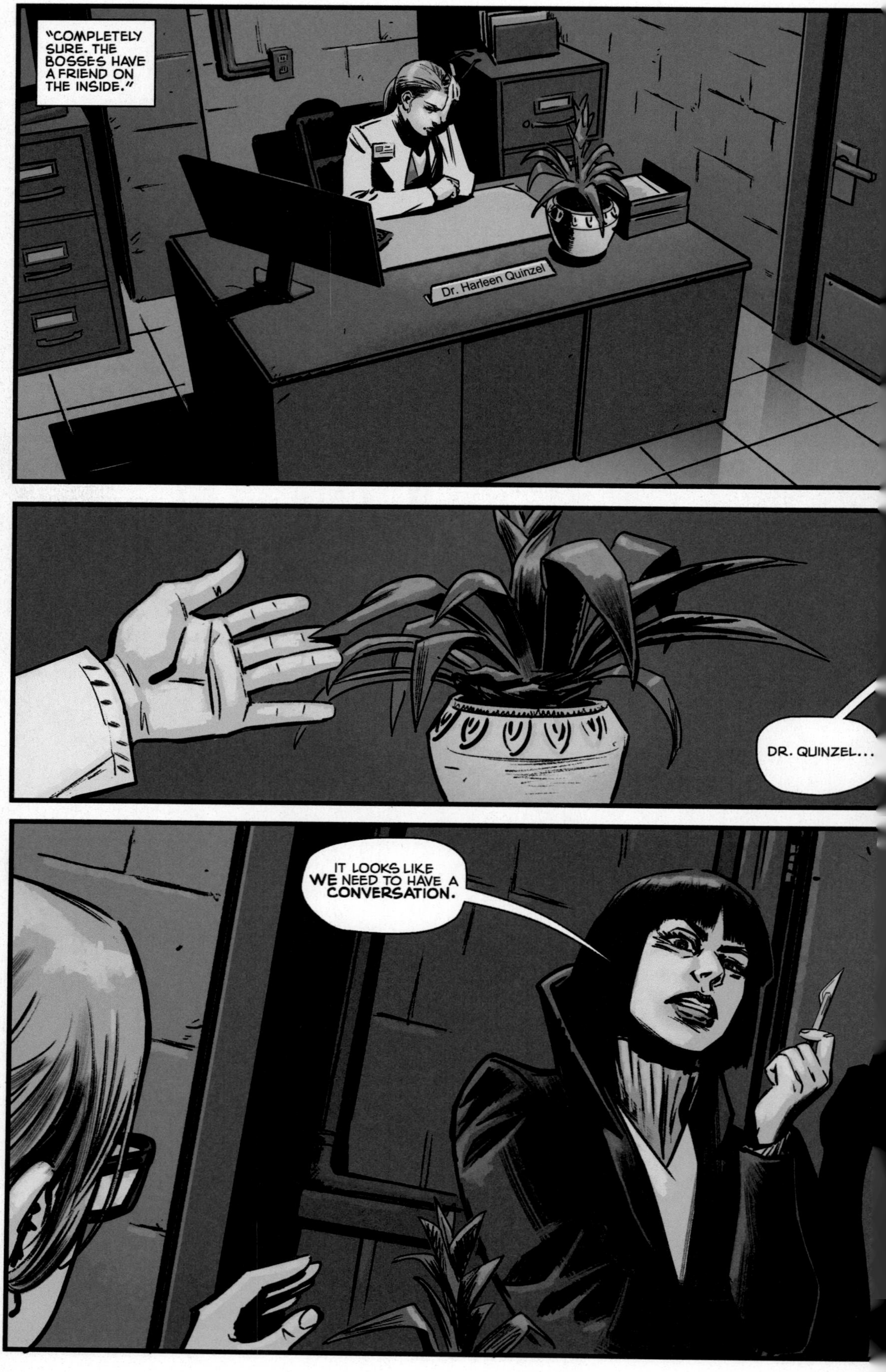
"COMPLETELY SURE. THE BOSSES HAVE A FRIEND ON THE INSIDE."
Dr. Harleen Quinzel
DR. QUINZEL...
IT LOOKS LIKE WE NEED TO HAVE A CONVERSATION.

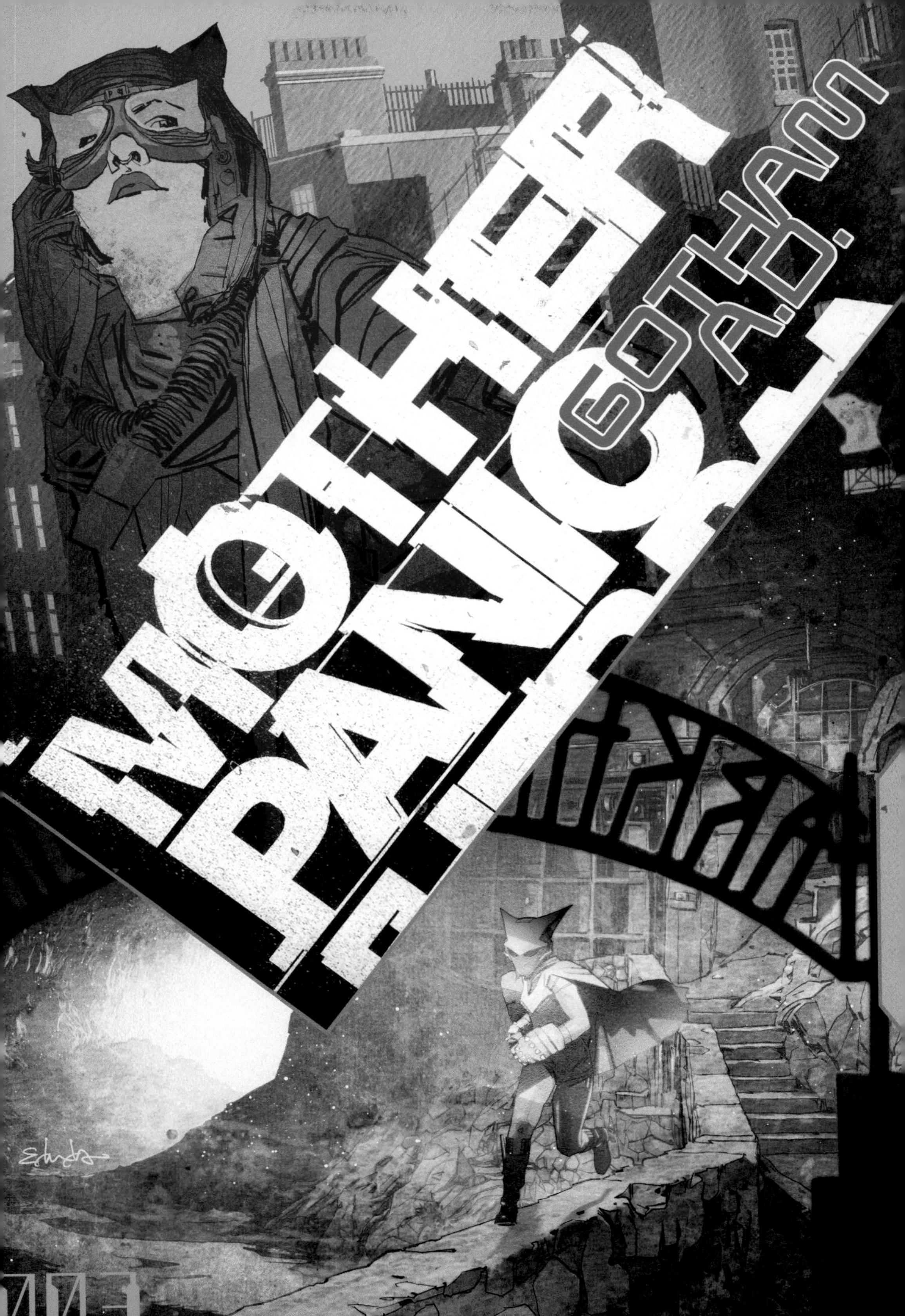
MOTHER PANIC
GOTHAM A.D.

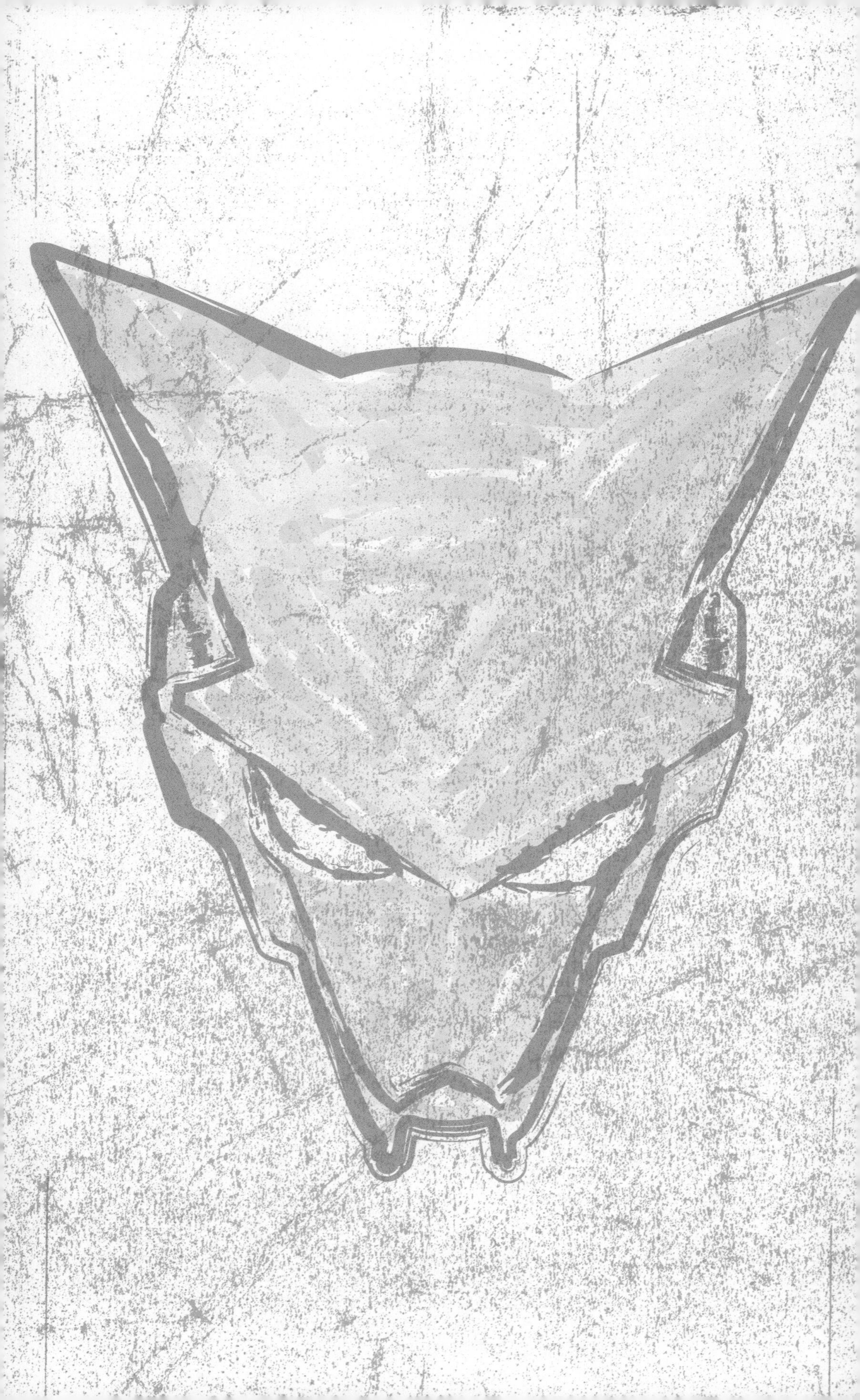

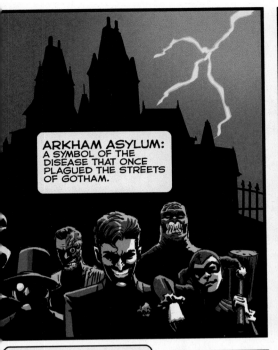

ARKHAM ASYLUM: A SYMBOL OF THE DISEASE THAT ONCE PLAGUED THE STREETS OF GOTHAM.

A FESTERING WOUND IN THE HEART OF THE CITY, SPILLING THE DERANGED AND THE DANGEROUS INTO OUR STREETS.

BUT THAT NIGHTMARE IS NOW BEHIND US.

THE NEW ARKHAM INSTITUTE INCORPORATES THE LATEST INNOVATIONS IN TECHNOLOGY AND THERAPY FOR A HOLISTIC APPROACH TO HEALING.

OUR PRACTITIONERS ARE DEDICATED TO PROVIDING A CALM AND CARING ATMOSPHERE FOR ALL OUR PATIENTS.

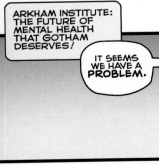

ARKHAM INSTITUTE: THE FUTURE OF MENTAL HEALTH THAT GOTHAM DESERVES!

IT SEEMS WE HAVE A PROBLEM.

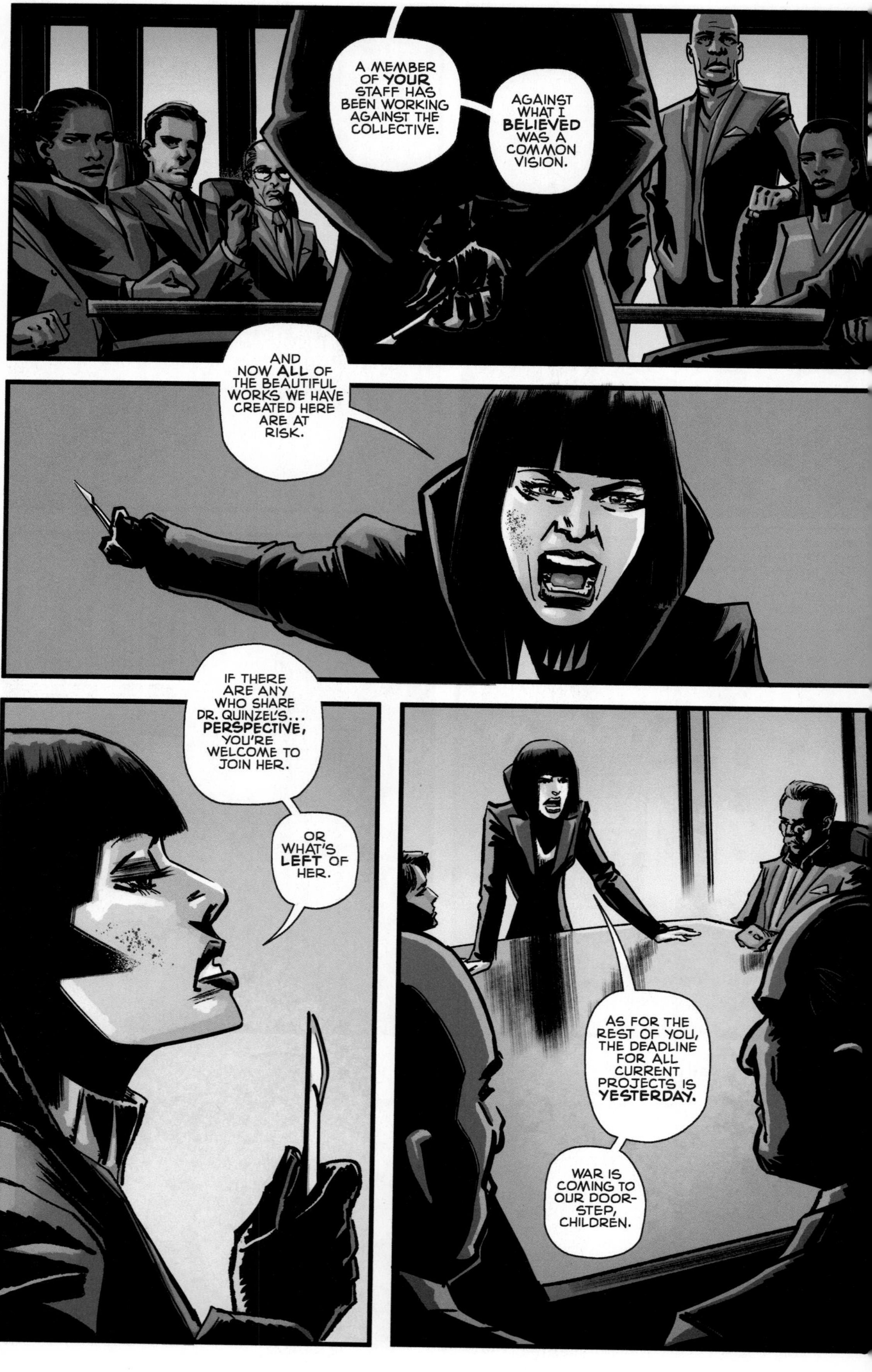
A MEMBER OF YOUR STAFF HAS BEEN WORKING AGAINST THE COLLECTIVE.
AGAINST WHAT I BELIEVED WAS A COMMON VISION.
AND NOW ALL OF THE BEAUTIFUL WORKS WE HAVE CREATED HERE ARE AT RISK.
IF THERE ARE ANY WHO SHARE DR. QUINZEL'S... PERSPECTIVE, YOU'RE WELCOME TO JOIN HER.
OR WHAT'S LEFT OF HER.
AS FOR THE REST OF YOU, THE DEADLINE FOR ALL CURRENT PROJECTS IS YESTERDAY.
WAR IS COMING TO OUR DOOR-STEP, CHILDREN.

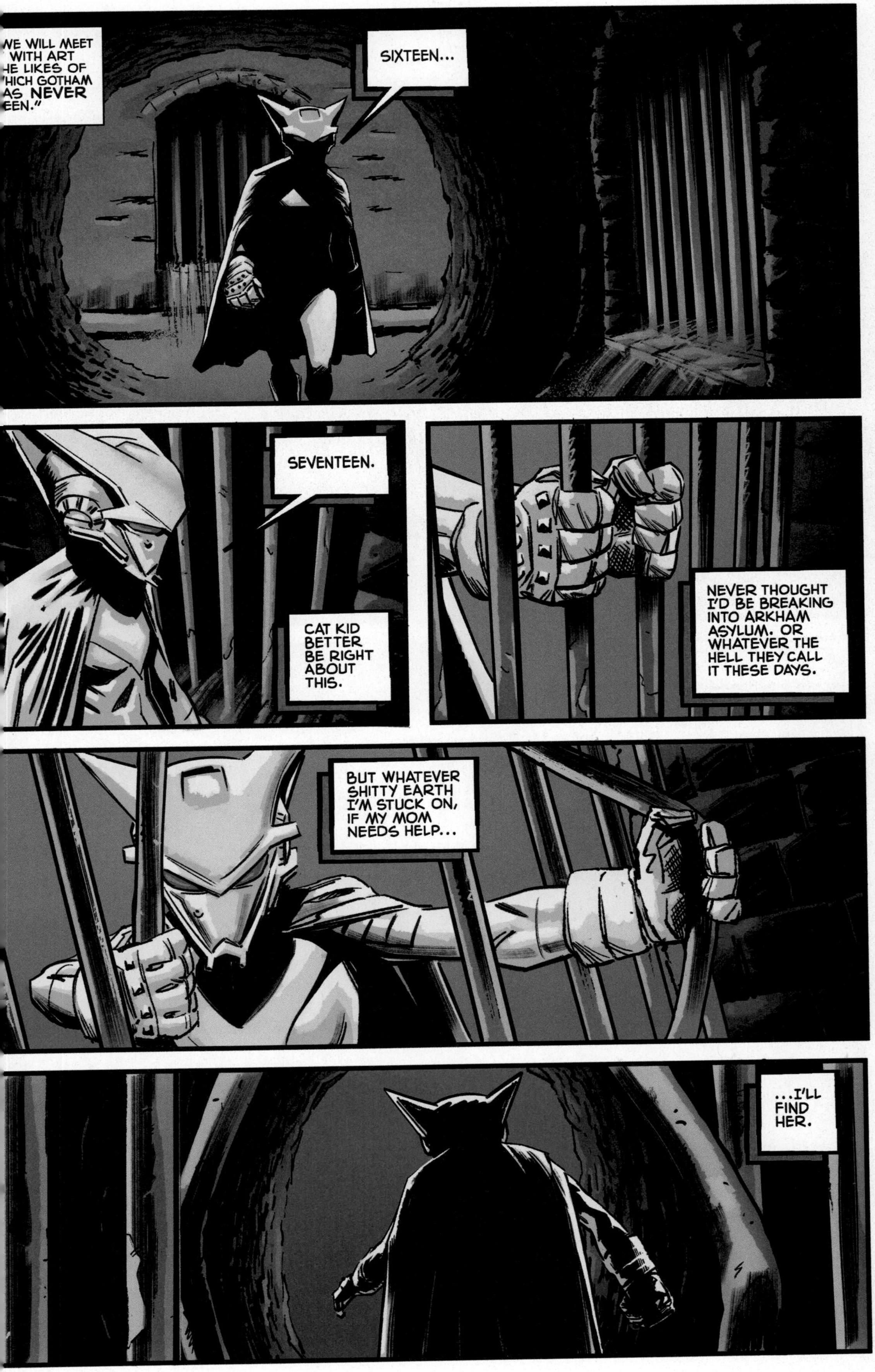
WE WILL MEET WITH ART HE LIKES OF HICH GOTHAM AS NEVER EEN."
SIXTEEN...
SEVENTEEN.
CAT KID BETTER BE RIGHT ABOUT THIS.
NEVER THOUGHT I'D BE BREAKING INTO ARKHAM ASYLUM. OR WHATEVER THE HELL THEY CALL IT THESE DAYS.
BUT WHATEVER SHITTY EARTH I'M STUCK ON, IF MY MOM NEEDS HELP...
...I'LL FIND HER.

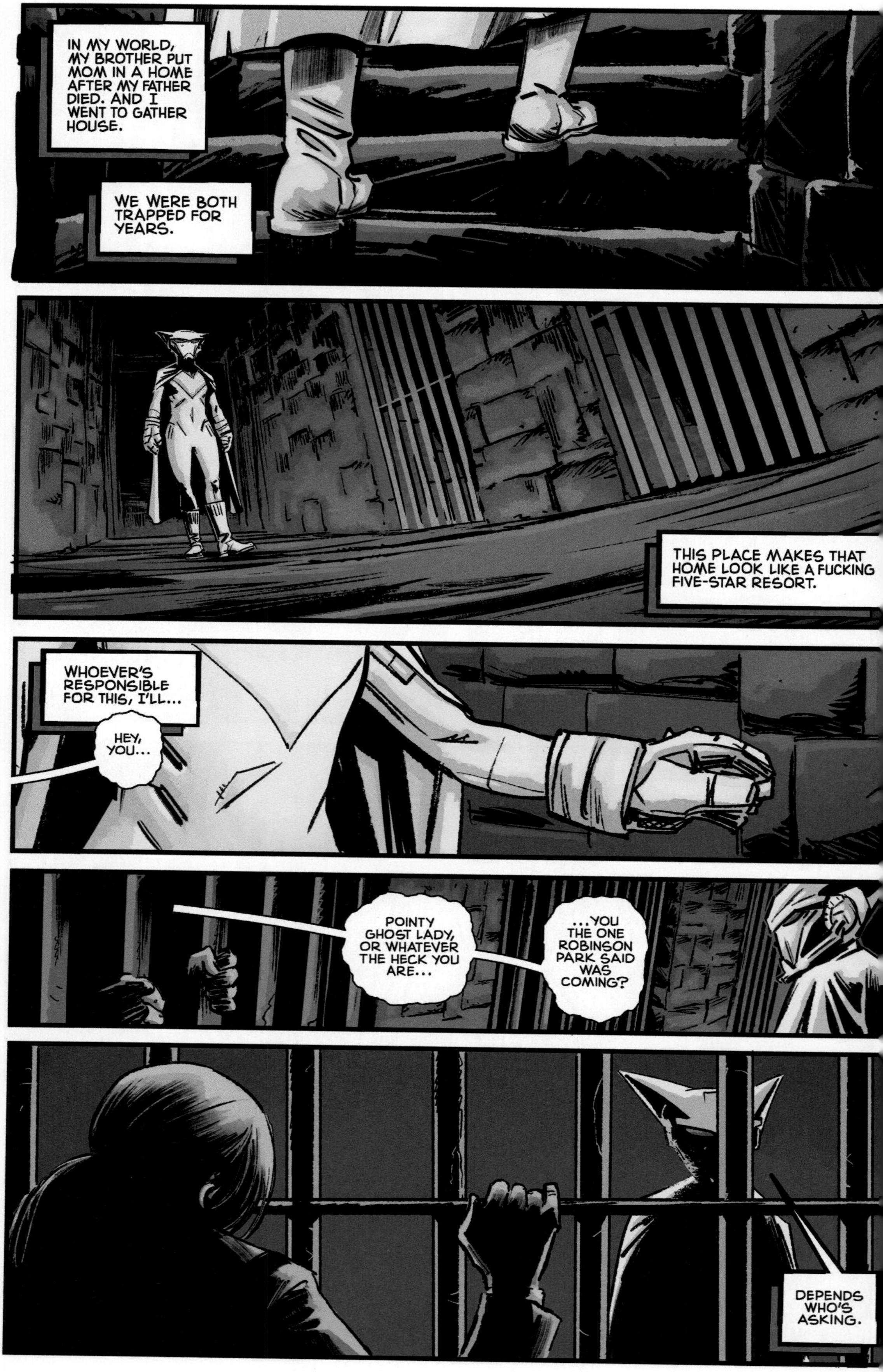
IN MY WORLD, MY BROTHER PUT MOM IN A HOME AFTER MY FATHER DIED. AND I WENT TO GATHER HOUSE.
WE WERE BOTH TRAPPED FOR YEARS.
THIS PLACE MAKES THAT HOME LOOK LIKE A FUCKING FIVE-STAR RESORT.
WHOEVER'S RESPONSIBLE FOR THIS, I'LL...
HEY, YOU...
POINTY GHOST LADY, OR WHATEVER THE HECK YOU ARE...
...YOU THE ONE ROBINSON PARK SAID WAS COMING?
DEPENDS WHO'S ASKING.

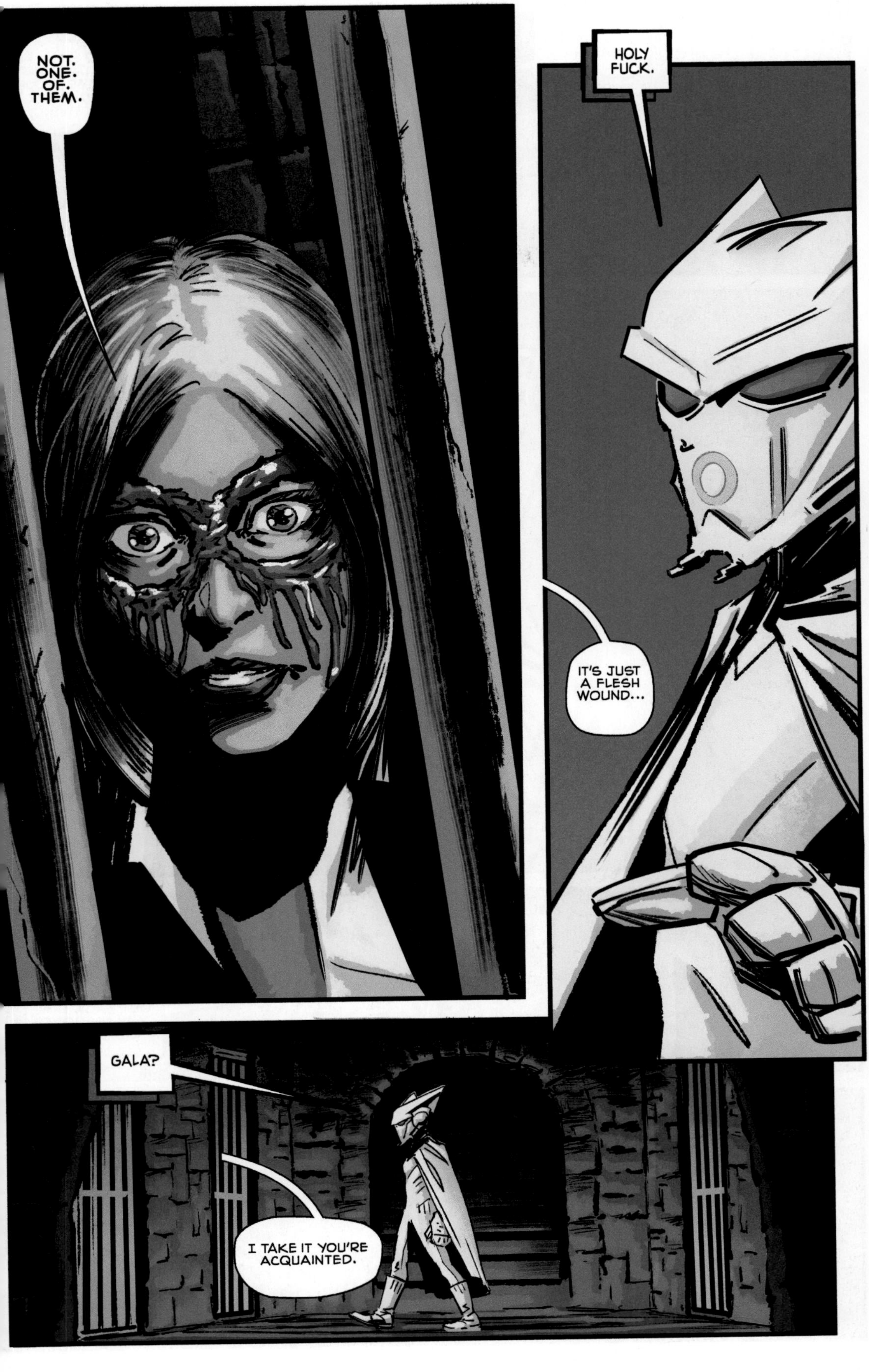
NOT. ONE. OF. THEM.
HOLY FUCK.
IT'S JUST A FLESH WOUND...
GALA?
I TAKE IT YOU'RE ACQUAINTED.

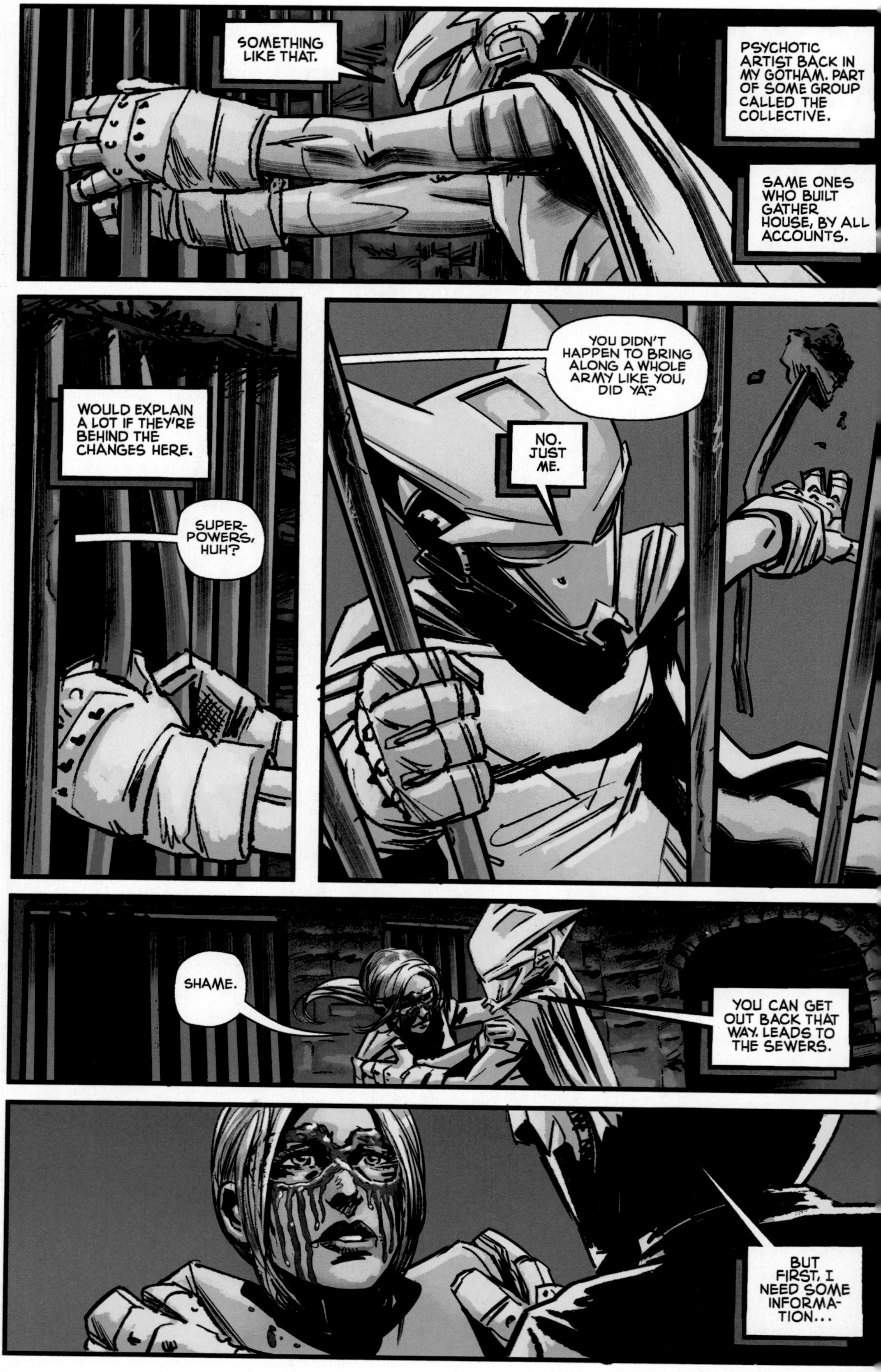

SOMETHING LIKE THAT.
PSYCHOTIC ARTIST BACK IN MY GOTHAM. PART OF SOME GROUP CALLED THE COLLECTIVE.
SAME ONES WHO BUILT GATHER HOUSE, BY ALL ACCOUNTS.
WOULD EXPLAIN A LOT IF THEY'RE BEHIND THE CHANGES HERE.
SUPER-POWERS, HUH?
YOU DIDN'T HAPPEN TO BRING ALONG A WHOLE ARMY LIKE YOU, DID YA?
NO. JUST ME.
SHAME.
YOU CAN GET OUT BACK THAT WAY. LEADS TO THE SEWERS.
BUT FIRST, I NEED SOME INFORMA-TION...

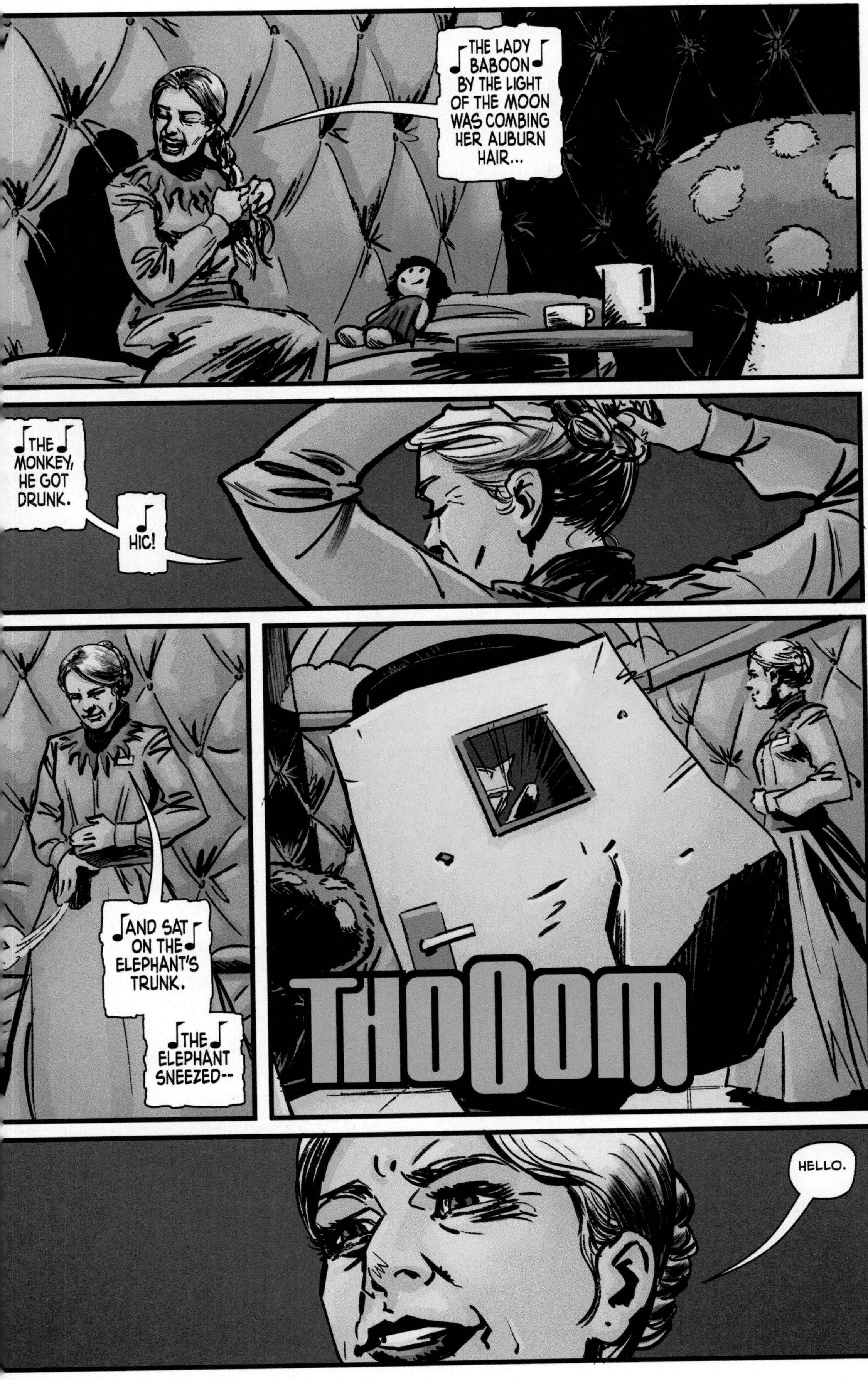
THE LADY BABOON BY THE LIGHT OF THE MOON WAS COMBING HER AUBURN HAIR...
THE MONKEY, HE GOT DRUNK.
HIC!
AND SAT ON THE ELEPHANT'S TRUNK.
THE ELEPHANT SNEEZED--
THOOOM
HELLO.

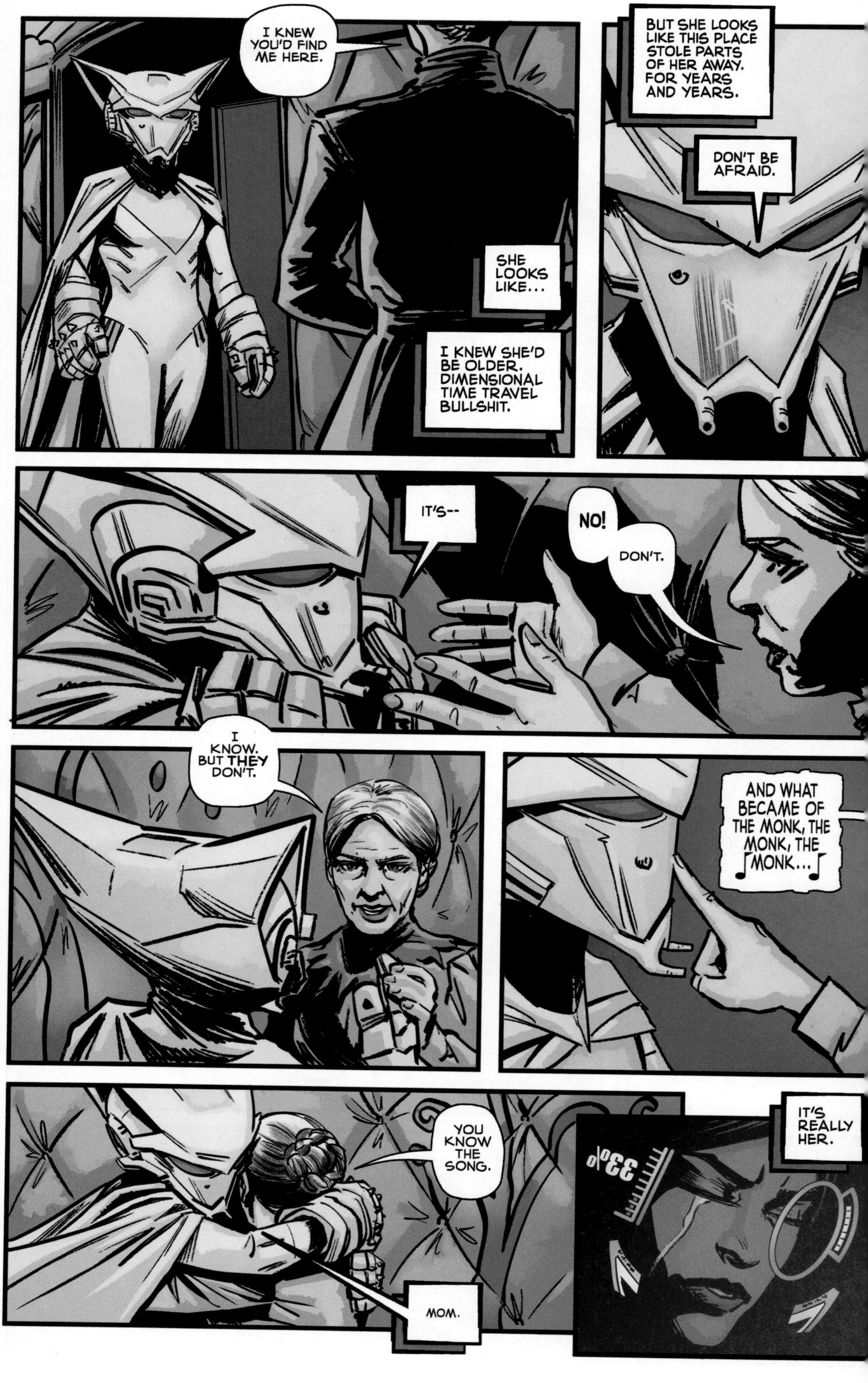
I KNEW YOU'D FIND ME HERE.
SHE LOOKS LIKE...
I KNEW SHE'D BE OLDER. DIMENSIONAL TIME TRAVEL BULLSHIT.
BUT SHE LOOKS LIKE THIS PLACE STOLE PARTS OF HER AWAY. FOR YEARS AND YEARS.
DON'T BE AFRAID.
IT'S--
NO!
DON'T.
I KNOW. BUT THEY DON'T.
AND WHAT BECAME OF THE MONK, THE MONK, THE MONK...
YOU KNOW THE SONG.
MOM.
IT'S REALLY HER.
33%

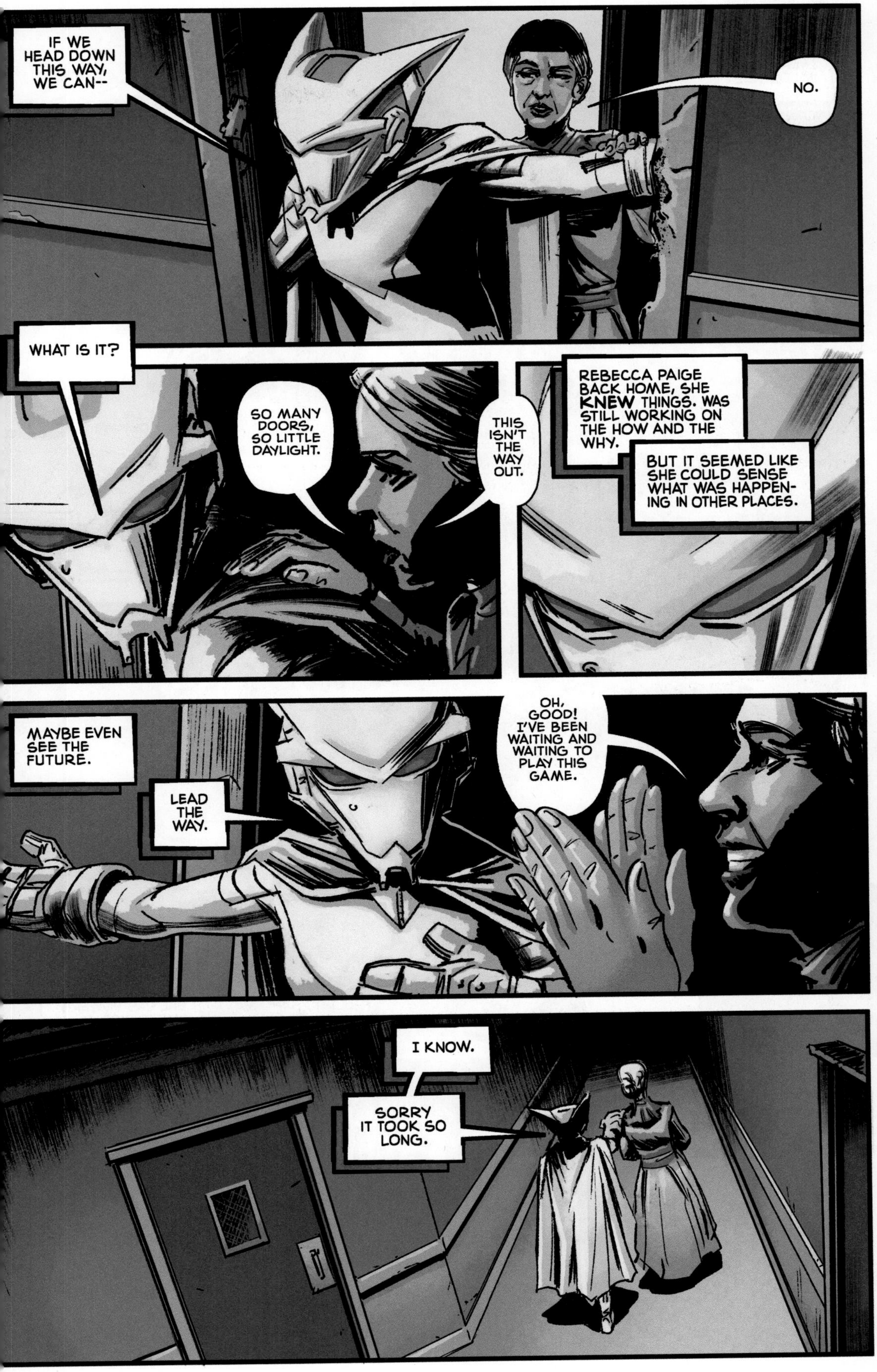
IF WE HEAD DOWN THIS WAY, WE CAN--
NO.
WHAT IS IT?
SO MANY DOORS, SO LITTLE DAYLIGHT.
THIS ISN'T THE WAY OUT.
REBECCA PAIGE BACK HOME, SHE KNEW THINGS. WAS STILL WORKING ON THE HOW AND THE WHY.
BUT IT SEEMED LIKE SHE COULD SENSE WHAT WAS HAPPENING IN OTHER PLACES.
MAYBE EVEN SEE THE FUTURE.
LEAD THE WAY.
OH, GOOD! I'VE BEEN WAITING AND WAITING TO PLAY THIS GAME.
I KNOW.
SORRY IT TOOK SO LONG.

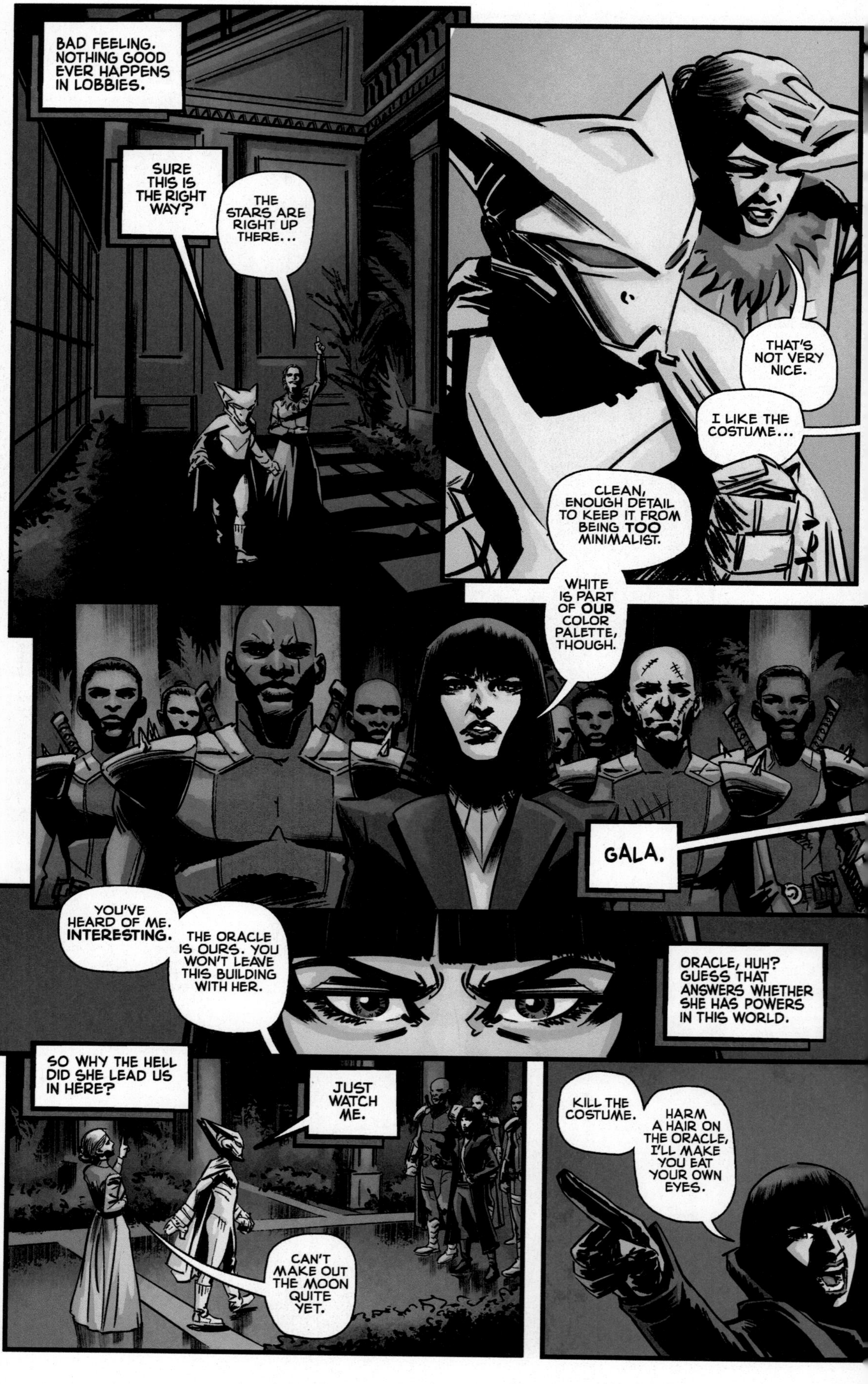
BAD FEELING. NOTHING GOOD EVER HAPPENS IN LOBBIES.
SURE THIS IS THE RIGHT WAY?
THE STARS ARE RIGHT UP THERE...
THAT'S NOT VERY NICE.
I LIKE THE COSTUME...
CLEAN, ENOUGH DETAIL TO KEEP IT FROM BEING **TOO** MINIMALIST.
WHITE IS PART OF **OUR** COLOR PALETTE, THOUGH.
GALA.
YOU'VE HEARD OF ME. **INTERESTING.**
THE ORACLE IS OURS. YOU WON'T LEAVE THIS BUILDING WITH HER.
ORACLE, HUH? GUESS THAT ANSWERS WHETHER SHE HAS POWERS IN THIS WORLD.
SO WHY THE HELL DID SHE LEAD US IN HERE?
JUST WATCH ME.
CAN'T MAKE OUT THE MOON QUITE YET.
KILL THE COSTUME.
HARM A HAIR ON THE ORACLE, I'LL MAKE YOU EAT YOUR OWN EYES.

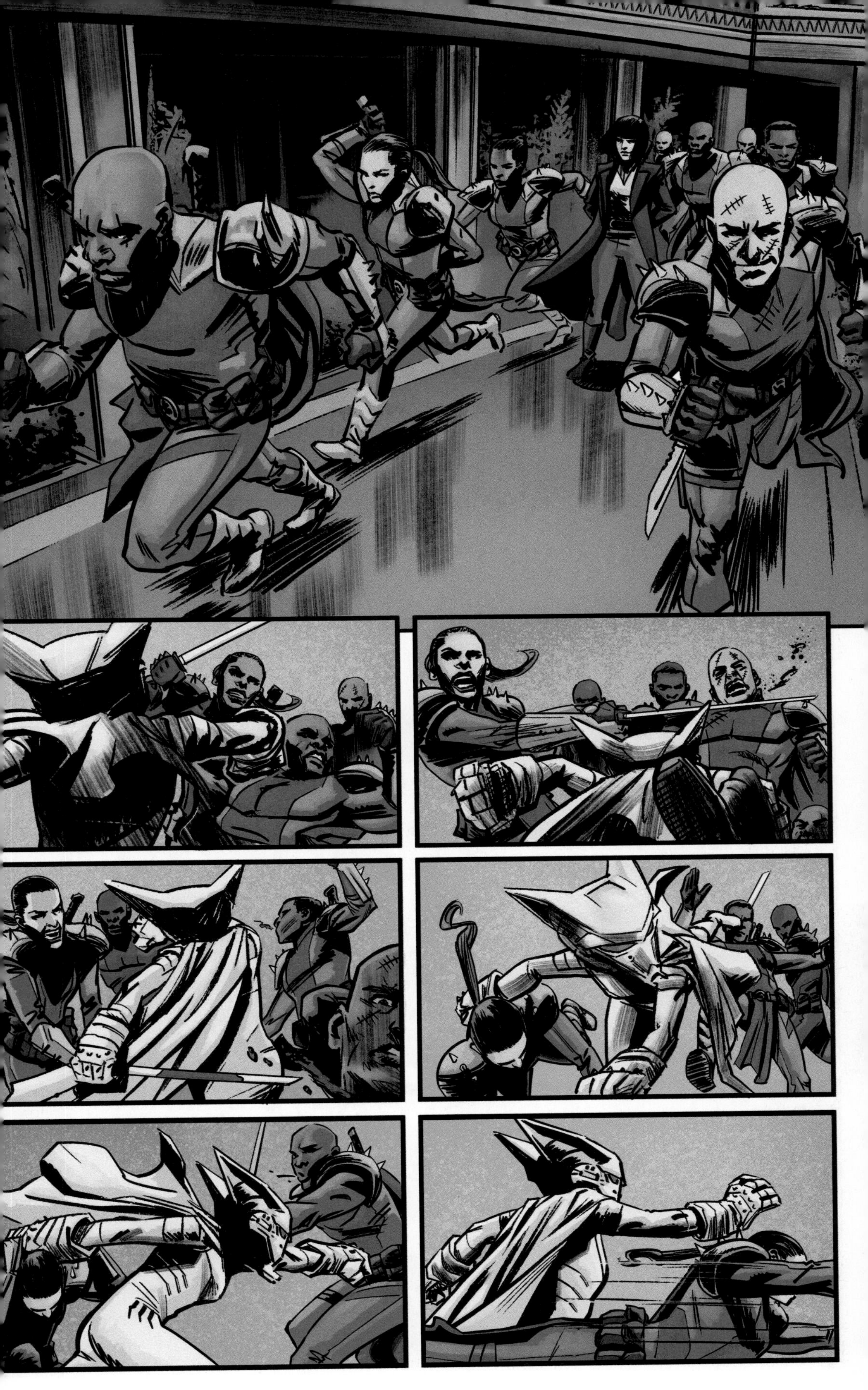

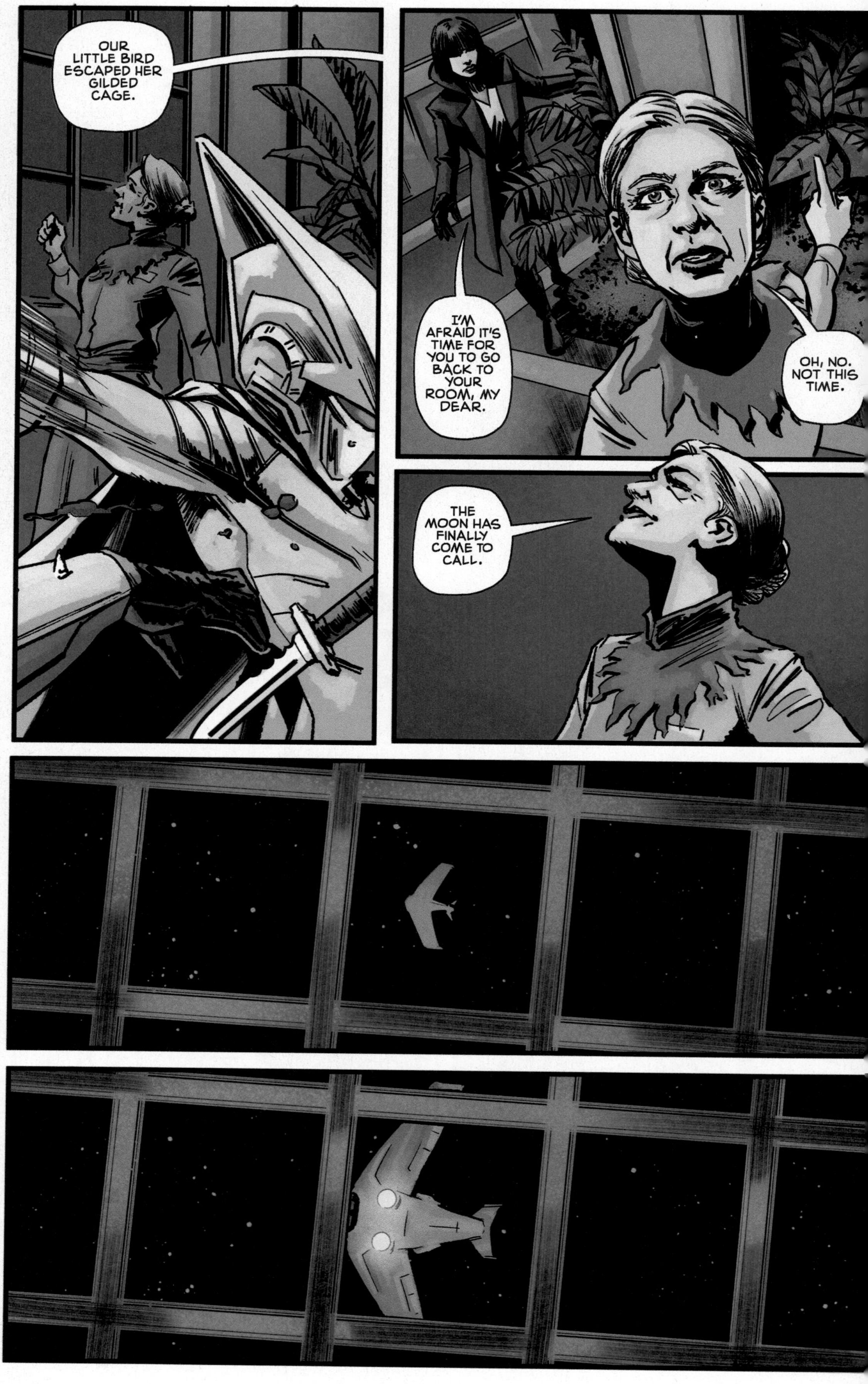
OUR LITTLE BIRD ESCAPED HER GILDED CAGE.
I'M AFRAID IT'S TIME FOR YOU TO GO BACK TO YOUR ROOM, MY DEAR.
OH, NO. NOT THIS TIME.
THE MOON HAS FINALLY COME TO CALL.

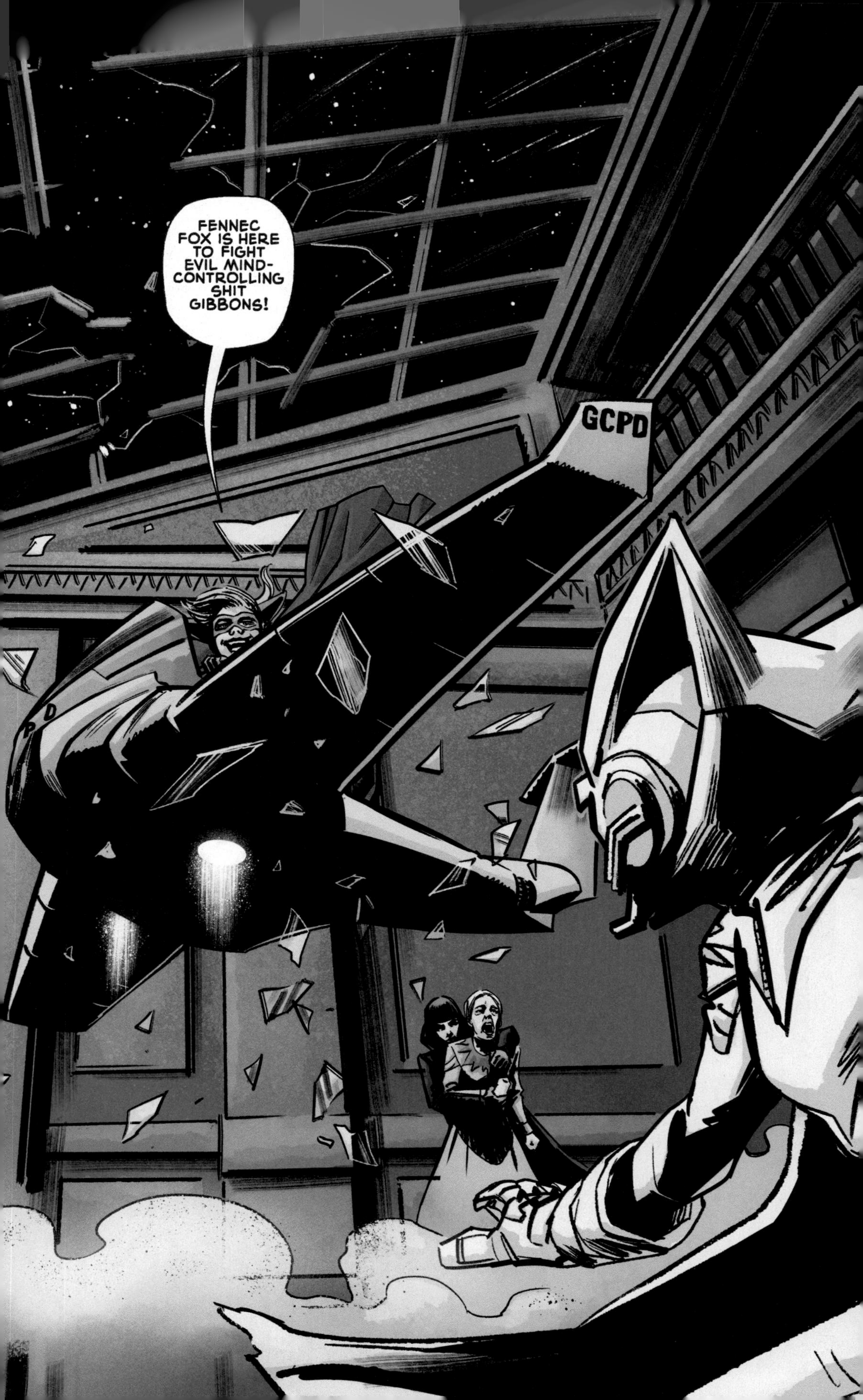
FENNEC FOX IS HERE TO FIGHT EVIL MIND-CONTROLLING SHIT GIBBONS!
GCPD

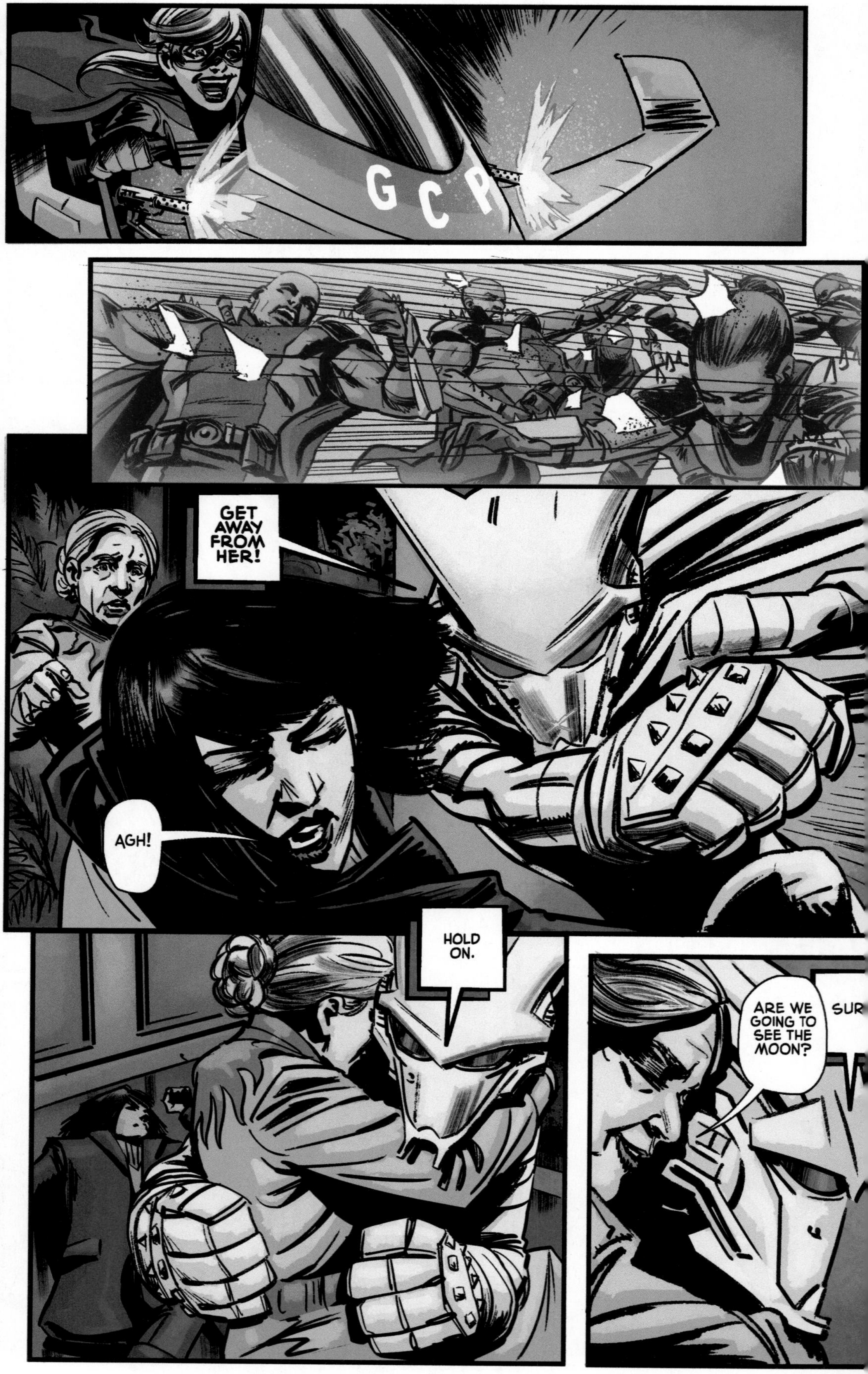
GCP
GET AWAY FROM HER!
AGH!
HOLD ON.
ARE WE GOING TO SEE THE MOON?
SUR

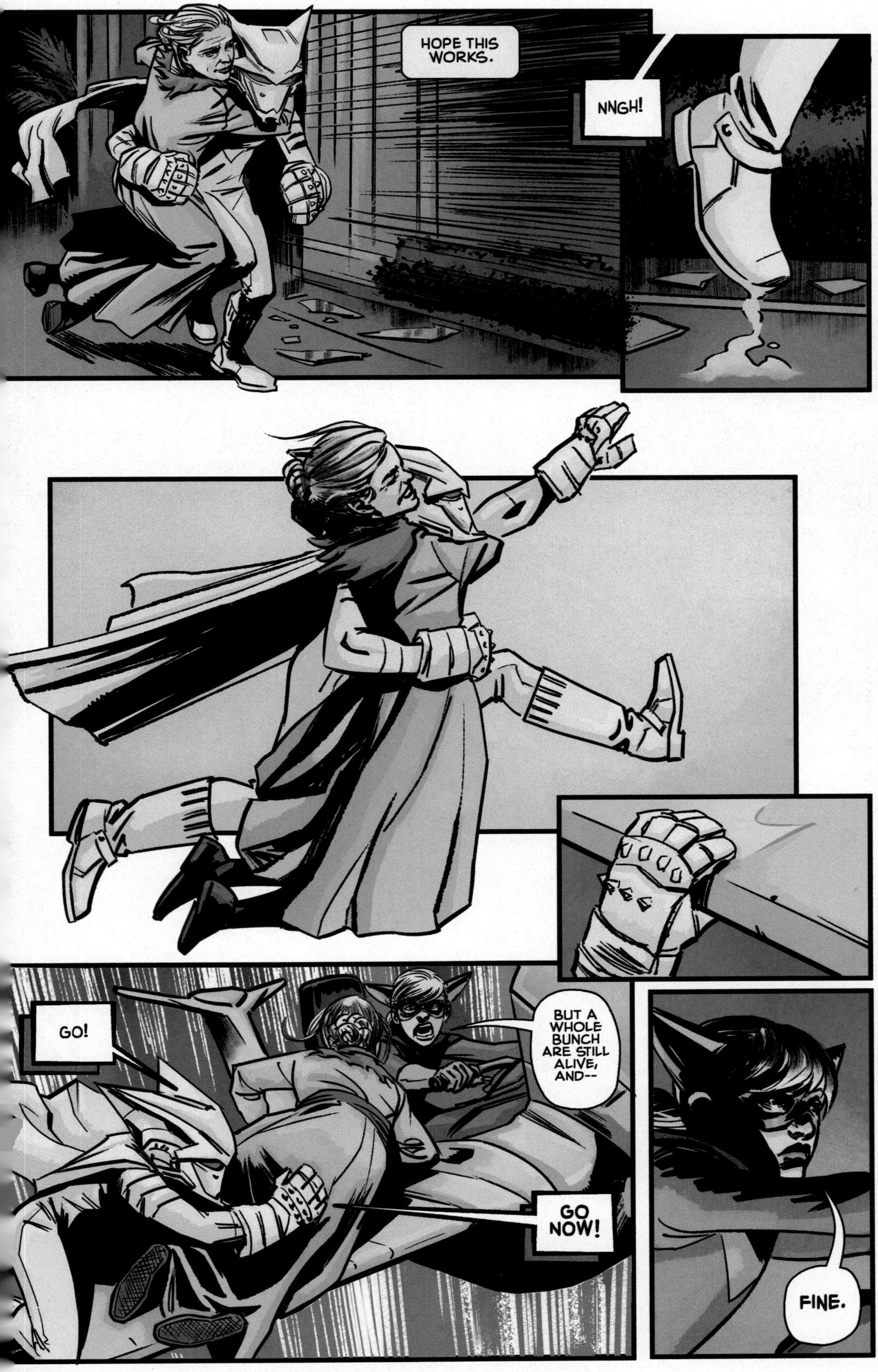
HOPE THIS WORKS.
NNGH!
GO!
BUT A WHOLE BUNCH ARE STILL ALIVE, AND--
GO NOW!
FINE.

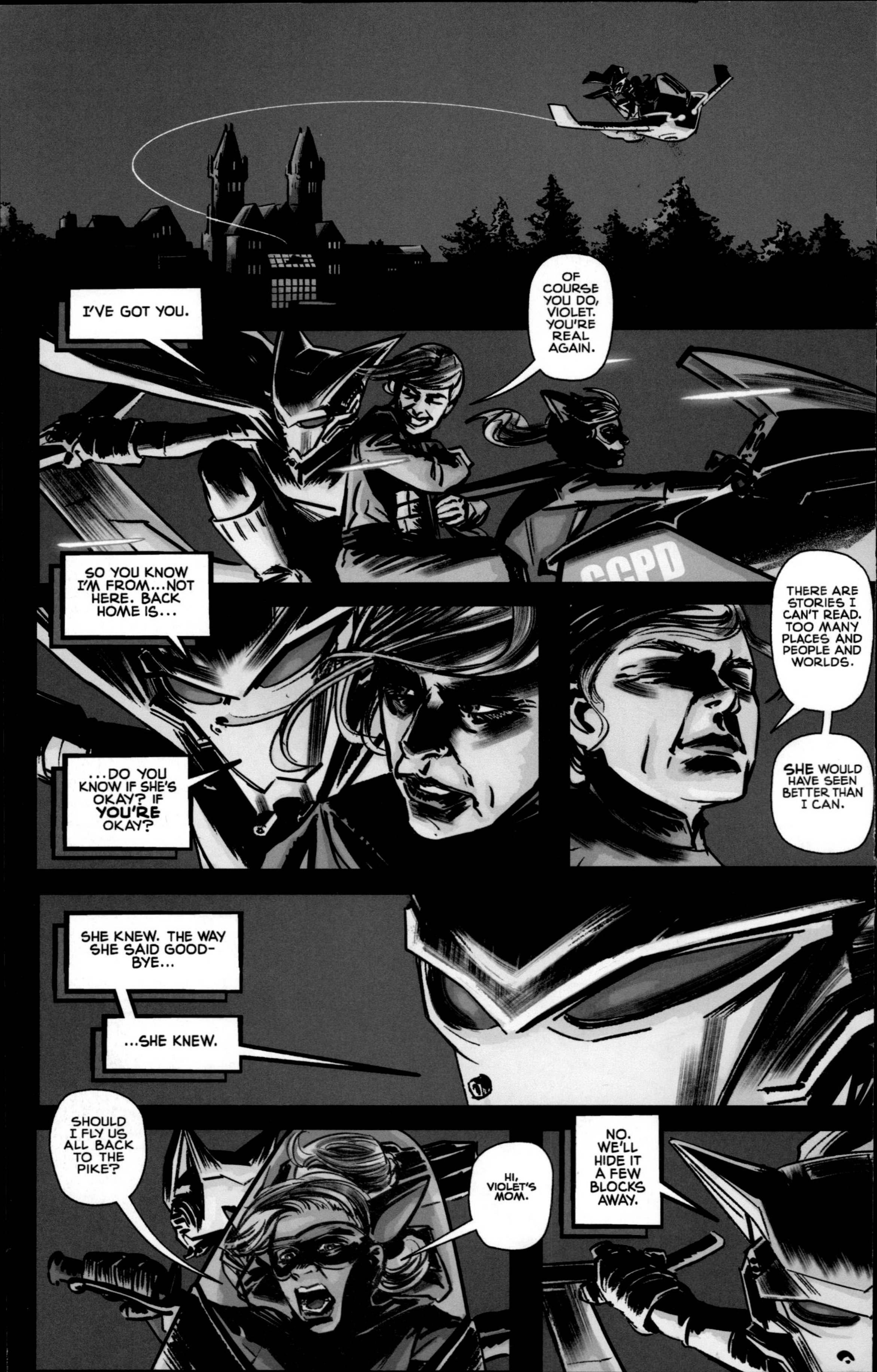
I'VE GOT YOU.
OF COURSE YOU DO, VIOLET. YOU'RE REAL AGAIN.
GCPD
SO YOU KNOW I'M FROM...NOT HERE. BACK HOME IS...
...DO YOU KNOW IF SHE'S OKAY? IF YOU'RE OKAY?
THERE ARE STORIES I CAN'T READ. TOO MANY PLACES AND PEOPLE AND WORLDS.
SHE WOULD HAVE SEEN BETTER THAN I CAN.
SHE KNEW. THE WAY SHE SAID GOOD-BYE...
...SHE KNEW.
SHOULD I FLY US ALL BACK TO THE PIKE?
HI, VIOLET'S MOM.
NO. WE'LL HIDE IT A FEW BLOCKS AWAY.

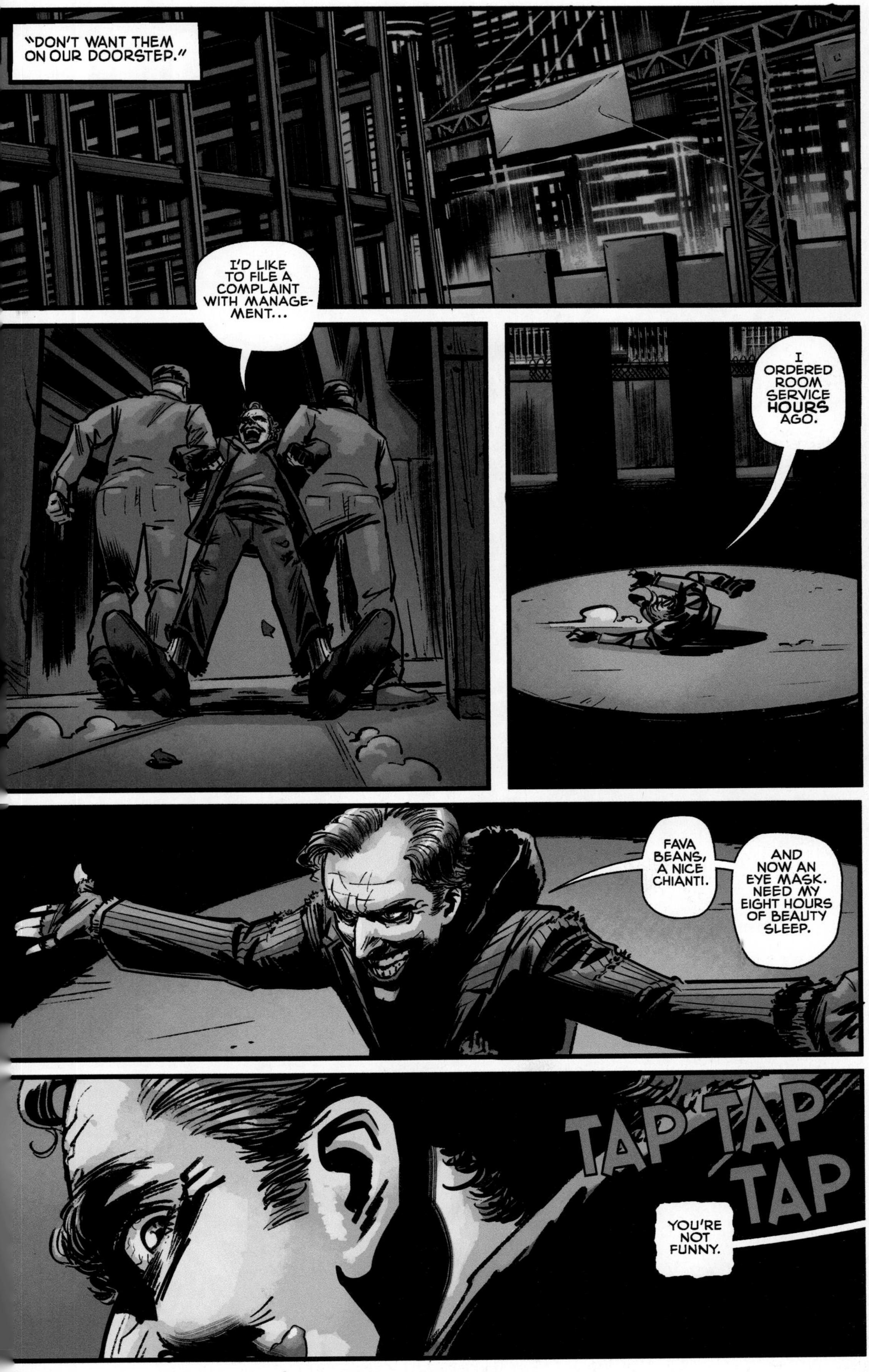
"DON'T WANT THEM ON OUR DOORSTEP."
I'D LIKE TO FILE A COMPLAINT WITH MANAGE-MENT...
I ORDERED ROOM SERVICE HOURS AGO.
FAVA BEANS, A NICE CHIANTI.
AND NOW AN EYE MASK. NEED MY EIGHT HOURS OF BEAUTY SLEEP.
TAP TAP TAP
YOU'RE NOT FUNNY.

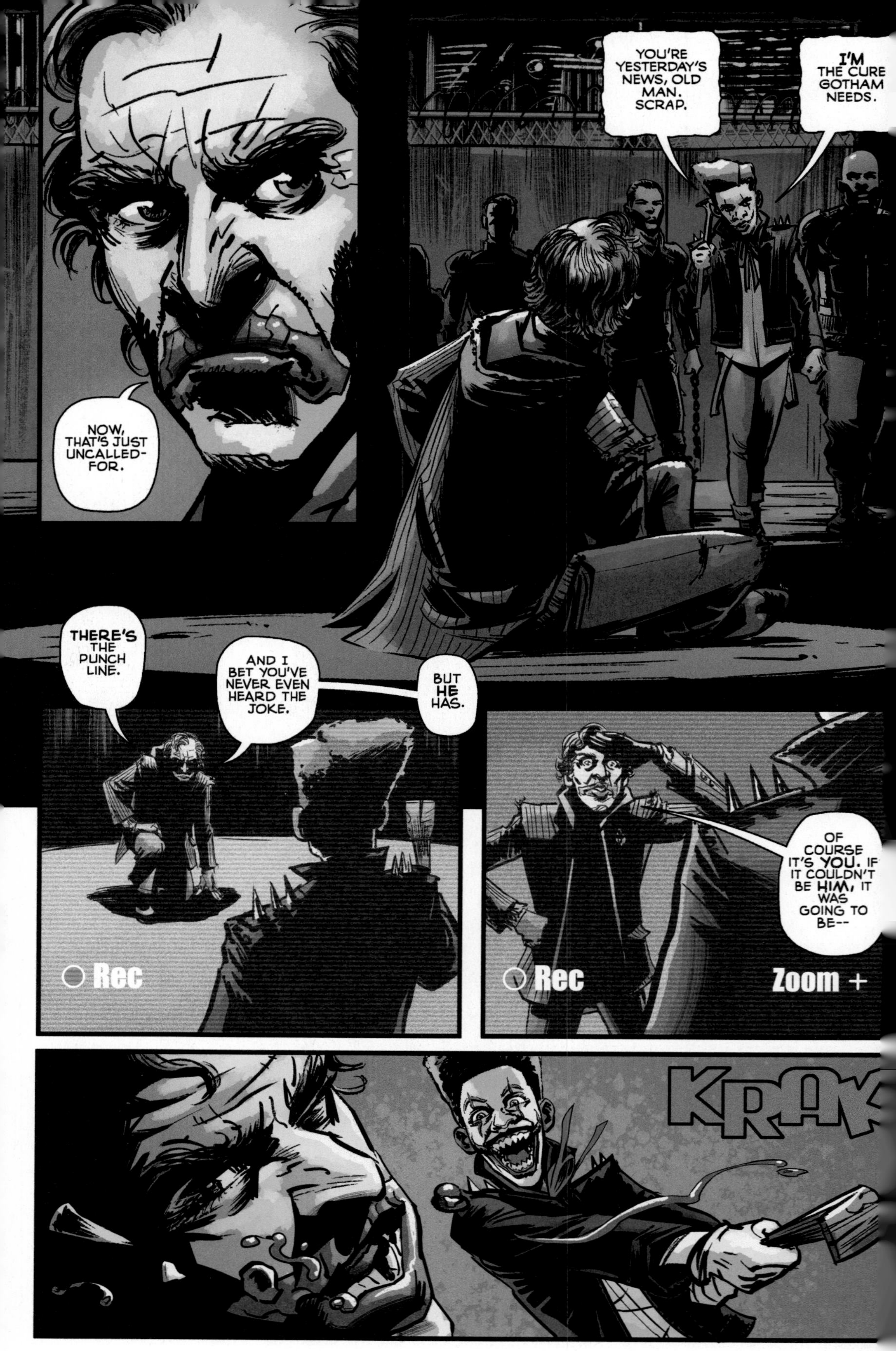

NOW, THAT'S JUST UNCALLED-FOR.
YOU'RE YESTERDAY'S NEWS, OLD MAN. SCRAP.
I'M THE CURE GOTHAM NEEDS.
THERE'S THE PUNCH LINE.
AND I BET YOU'VE NEVER EVEN HEARD THE JOKE.
BUT HE HAS.
Rec
Rec
Zoom +
OF COURSE IT'S YOU. IF IT COULDN'T BE HIM, IT WAS GOING TO BE--
KRAK

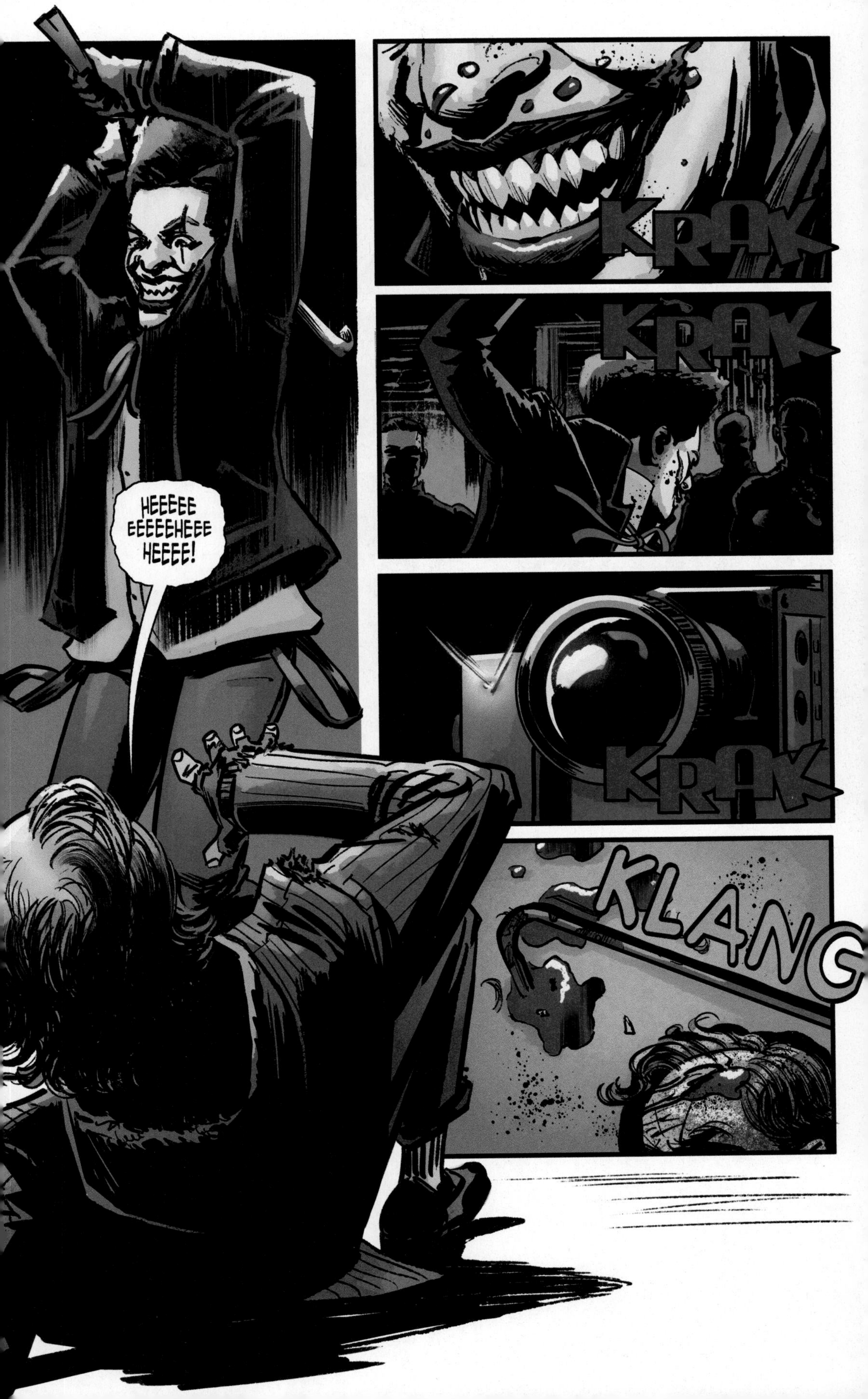
KRAK
KRAK
HEEEEE EEEEEHEEE HEEEE!
KRAK
KLANG

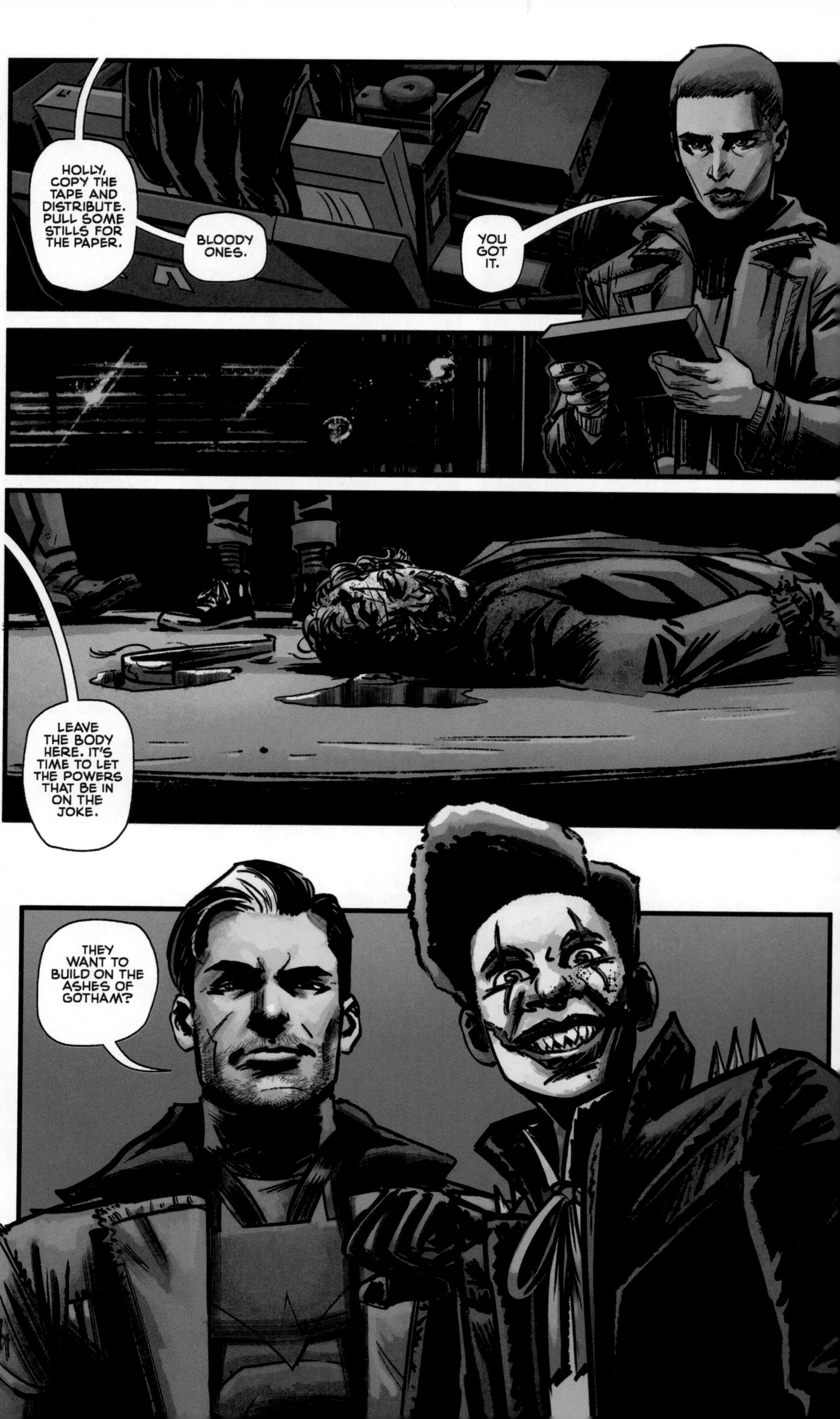

HOLLY, COPY THE TAPE AND DISTRIBUTE. PULL SOME STILLS FOR THE PAPER.
BLOODY ONES.
YOU GOT IT.
LEAVE THE BODY HERE. IT'S TIME TO LET THE POWERS THAT BE IN ON THE JOKE.
THEY WANT TO BUILD ON THE ASHES OF GOTHAM?

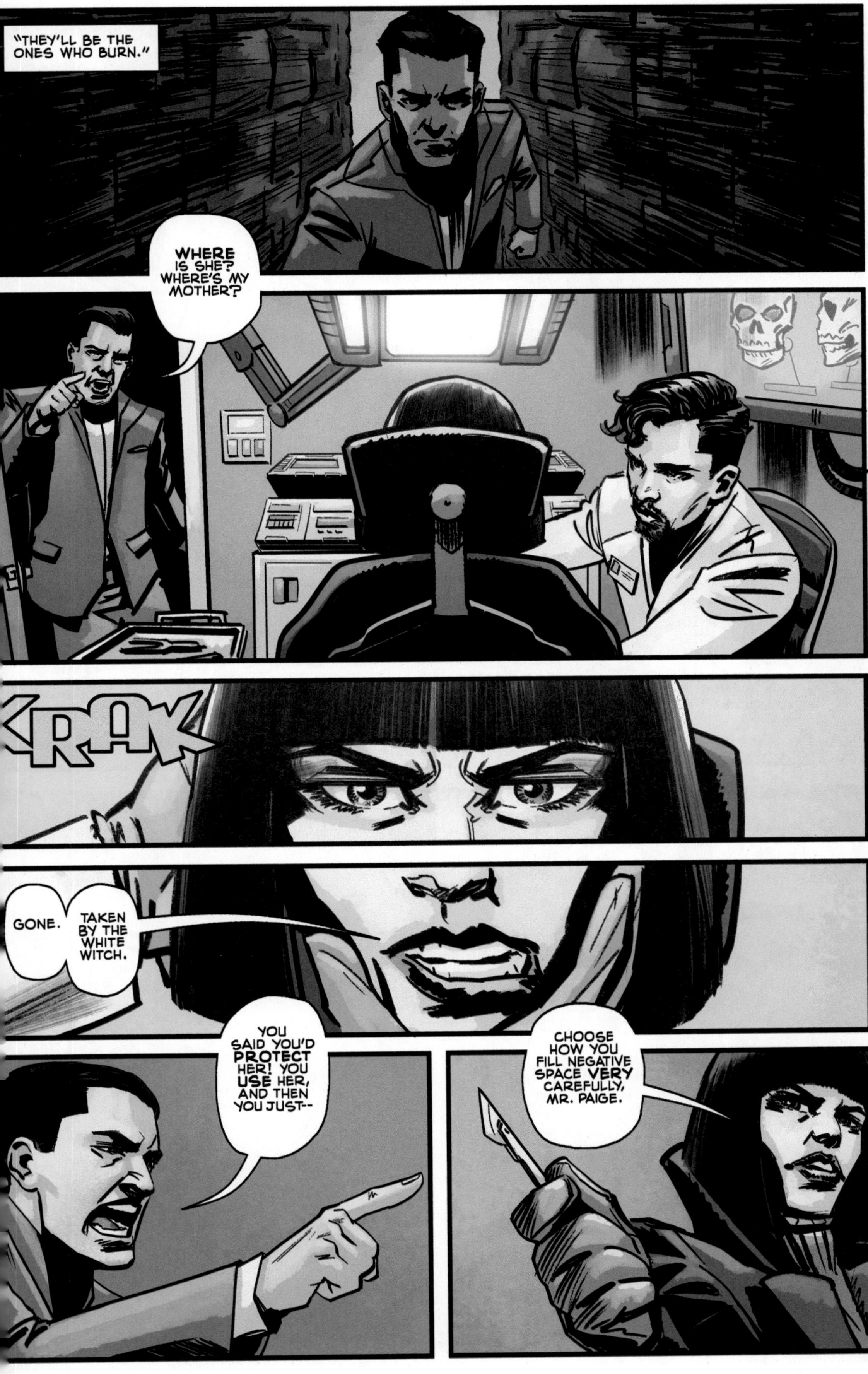
"THEY'LL BE THE ONES WHO BURN."
WHERE IS SHE? WHERE'S MY MOTHER?
KRAK
GONE.
TAKEN BY THE WHITE WITCH.
YOU SAID YOU'D PROTECT HER! YOU USE HER, AND THEN YOU JUST--
CHOOSE HOW YOU FILL NEGATIVE SPACE VERY CAREFULLY, MR. PAIGE.

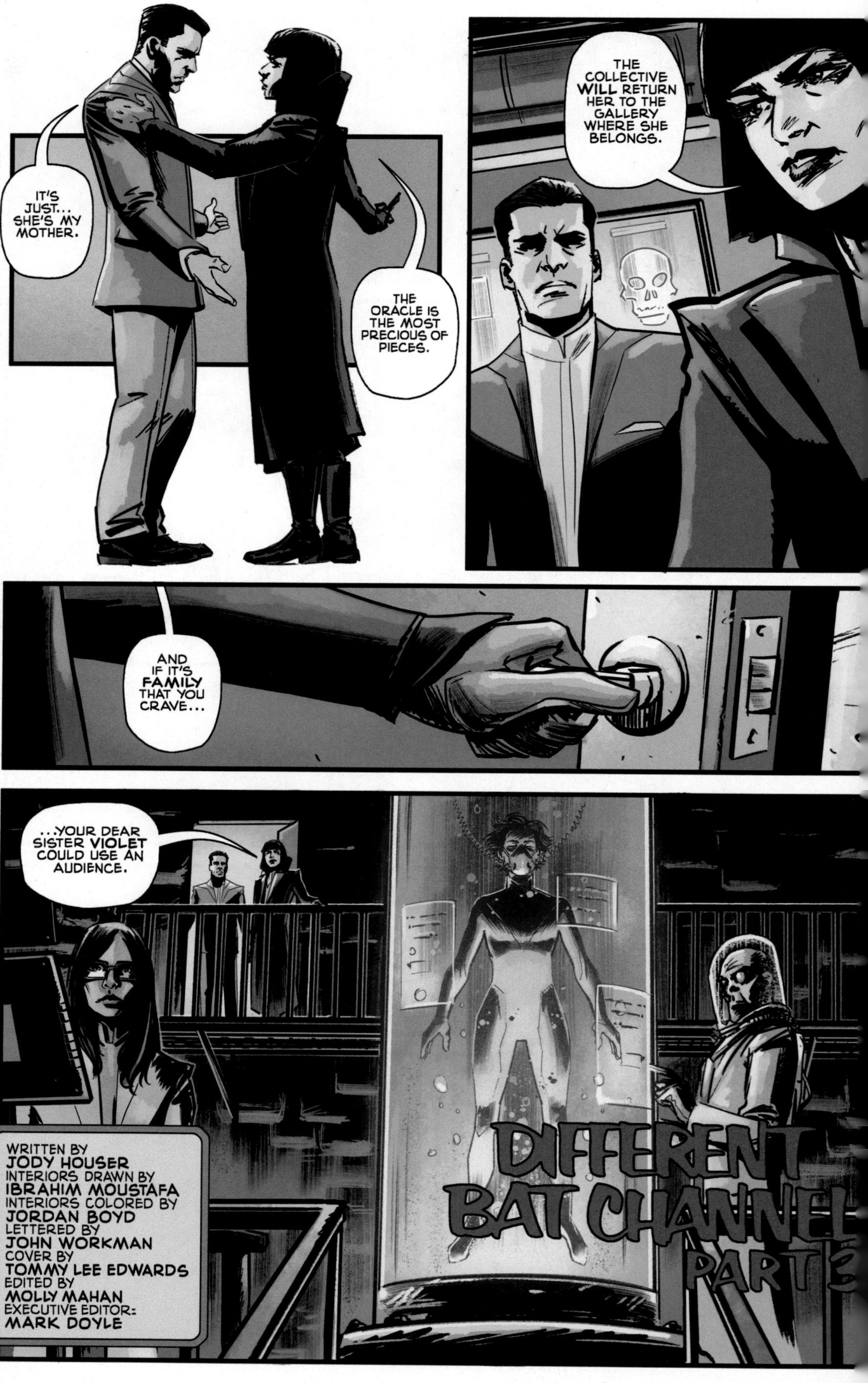
IT'S JUST... SHE'S MY MOTHER.
THE ORACLE IS THE MOST PRECIOUS OF PIECES.
THE COLLECTIVE WILL RETURN HER TO THE GALLERY WHERE SHE BELONGS.
AND IF IT'S FAMILY THAT YOU CRAVE...
...YOUR DEAR SISTER VIOLET COULD USE AN AUDIENCE.
DIFFERENT BAT CHANNEL PART 3
WRITTEN BY JODY HOUSER
INTERIORS DRAWN BY IBRAHIM MOUSTAFA
INTERIORS COLORED BY JORDAN BOYD
LETTERED BY JOHN WORKMAN
COVER BY TOMMY LEE EDWARDS
EDITED BY MOLLY MAHAN
EXECUTIVE EDITOR: MARK DOYLE

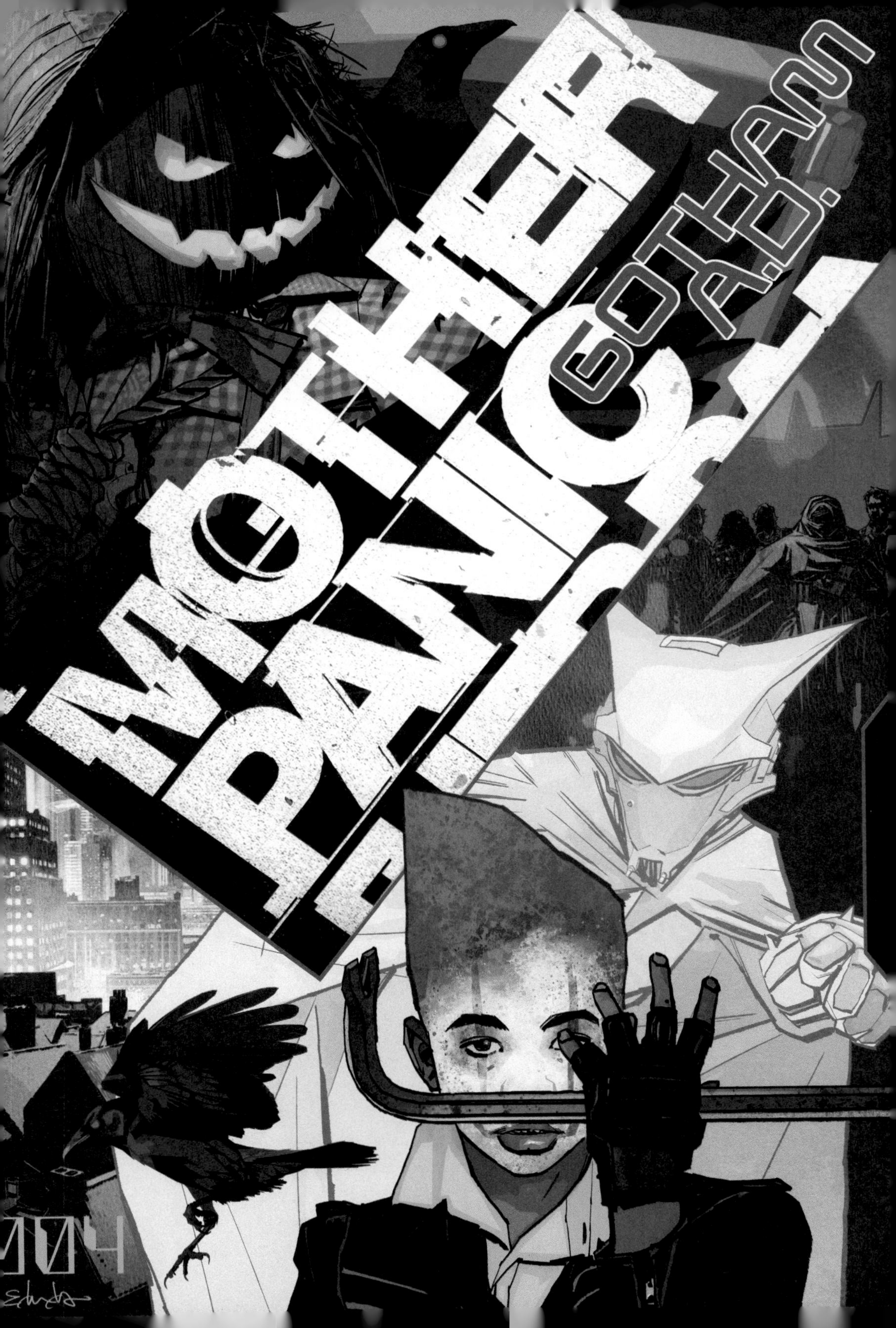
MOTHER PANIC
GOTHAM A.D.

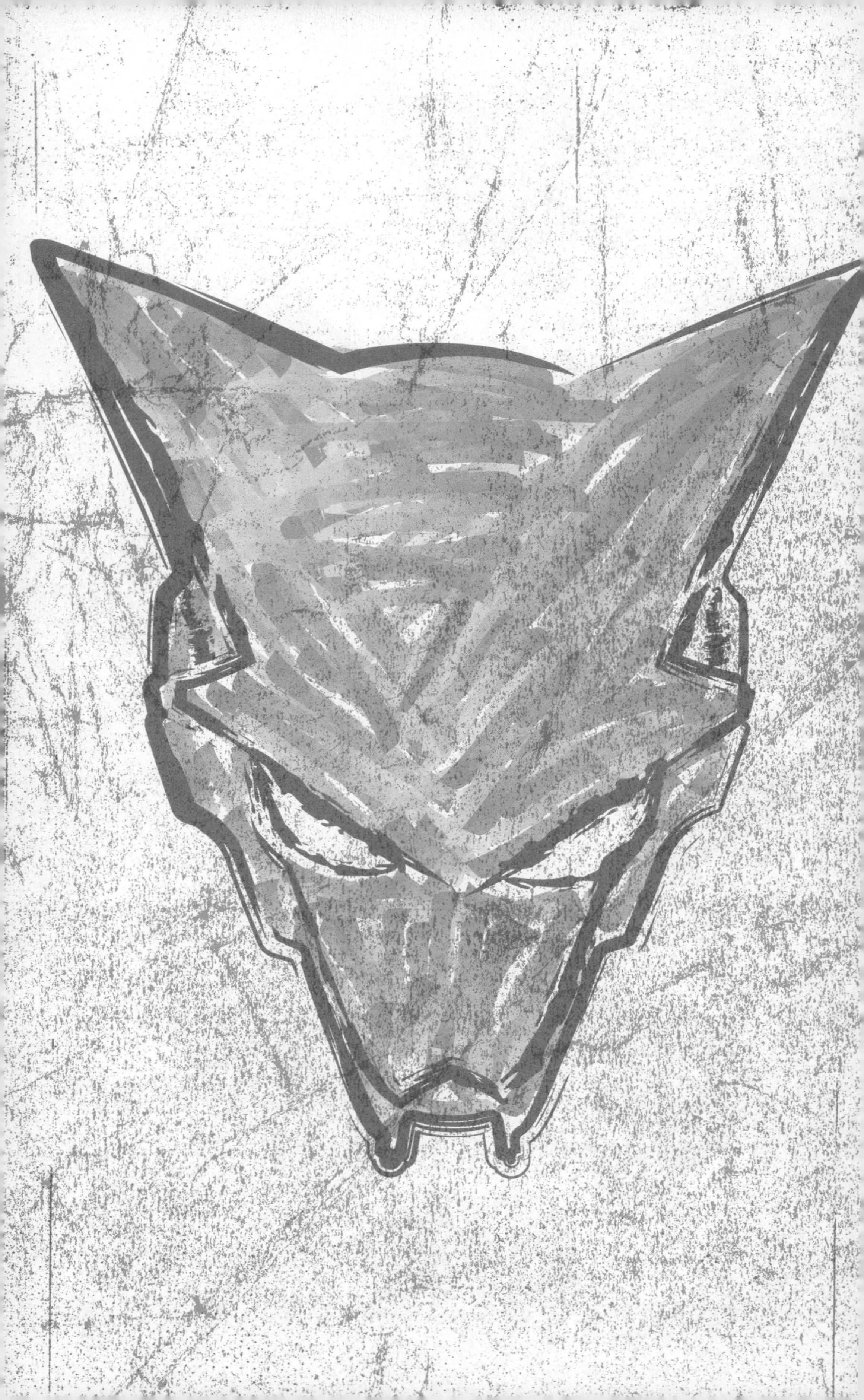

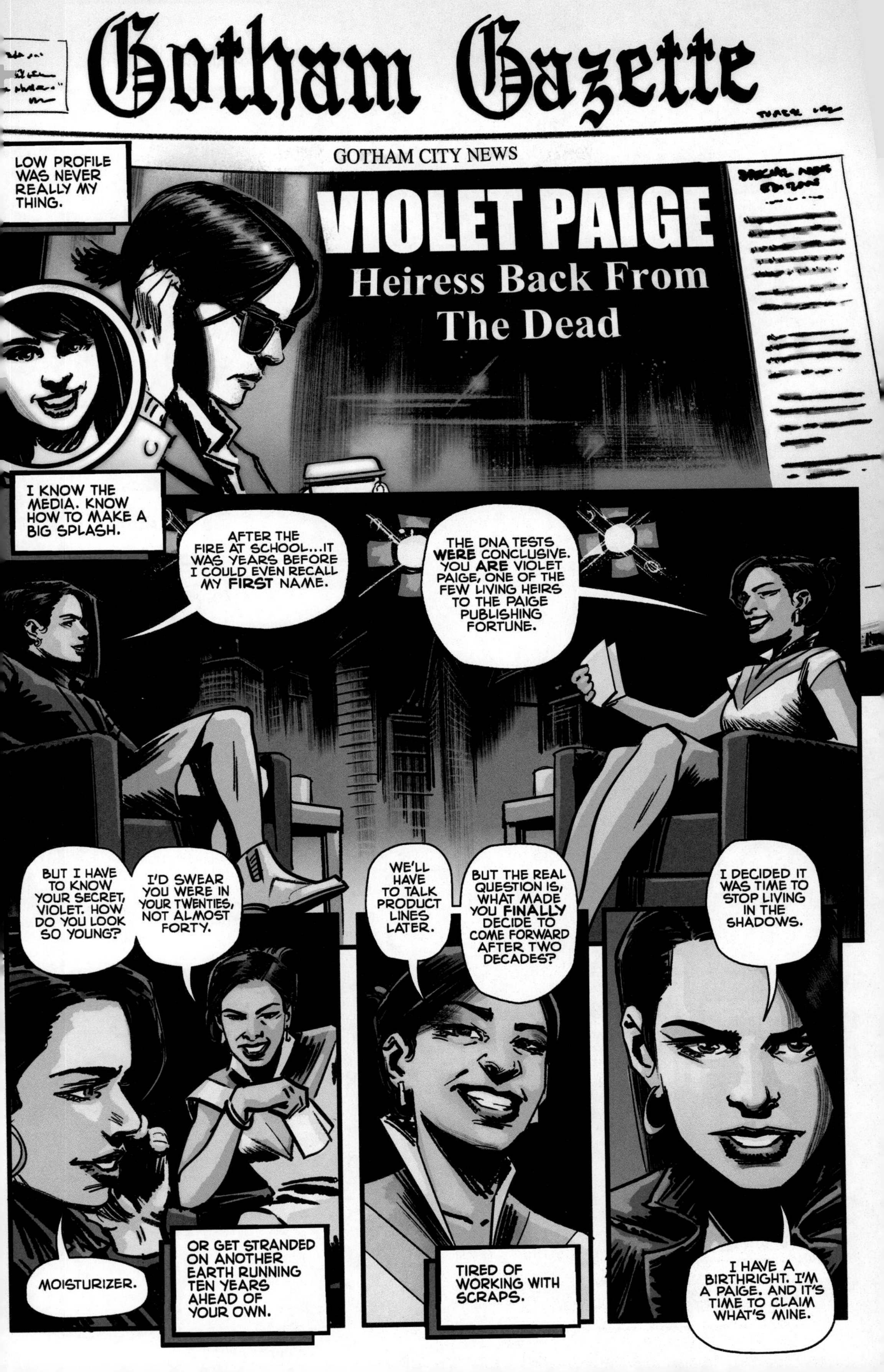
Gotham Gazette
GOTHAM CITY NEWS
LOW PROFILE WAS NEVER REALLY MY THING.
VIOLET PAIGE
Heiress Back From The Dead
I KNOW THE MEDIA. KNOW HOW TO MAKE A BIG SPLASH.
AFTER THE FIRE AT SCHOOL...IT WAS YEARS BEFORE I COULD EVEN RECALL MY **FIRST** NAME.
THE DNA TESTS **WERE** CONCLUSIVE. YOU **ARE** VIOLET PAIGE, ONE OF THE FEW LIVING HEIRS TO THE PAIGE PUBLISHING FORTUNE.
BUT I HAVE TO KNOW YOUR SECRET, VIOLET. HOW DO YOU LOOK SO YOUNG?
I'D SWEAR YOU WERE IN YOUR TWENTIES, NOT ALMOST FORTY.
MOISTURIZER.
OR GET STRANDED ON ANOTHER EARTH RUNNING TEN YEARS AHEAD OF YOUR OWN.
WE'LL HAVE TO TALK PRODUCT LINES LATER.
BUT THE REAL QUESTION IS, WHAT MADE YOU **FINALLY** DECIDE TO COME FORWARD AFTER TWO DECADES?
TIRED OF WORKING WITH SCRAPS.
I DECIDED IT WAS TIME TO STOP LIVING IN THE SHADOWS.
I HAVE A BIRTHRIGHT. I'M A PAIGE. AND IT'S TIME TO CLAIM WHAT'S MINE.

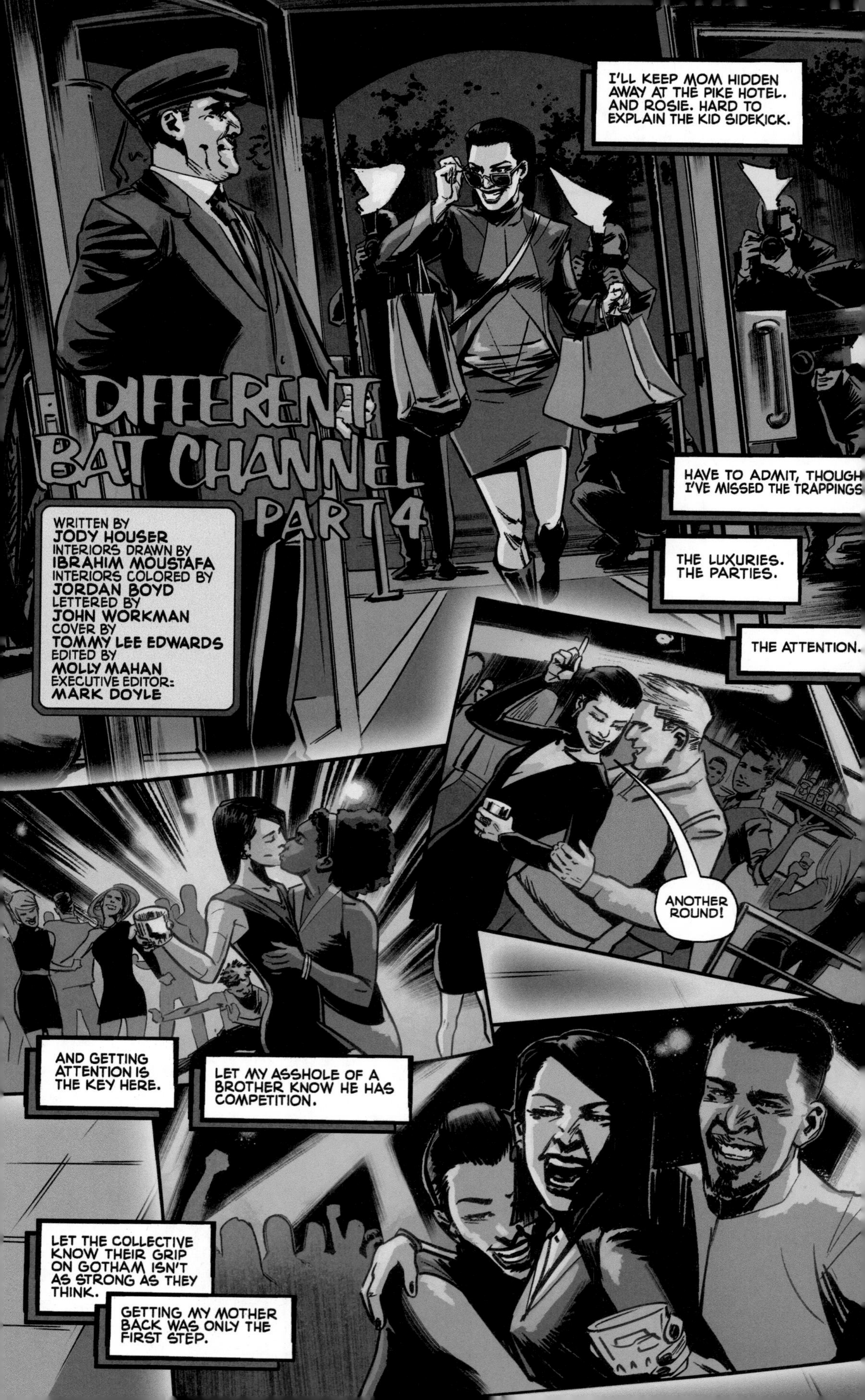
I'LL KEEP MOM HIDDEN AWAY AT THE PIKE HOTEL. AND ROSIE. HARD TO EXPLAIN THE KID SIDEKICK.
DIFFERENT BAT CHANNEL PART 4
WRITTEN BY JODY HOUSER INTERIORS DRAWN BY IBRAHIM MOUSTAFA INTERIORS COLORED BY JORDAN BOYD LETTERED BY JOHN WORKMAN COVER BY TOMMY LEE EDWARDS EDITED BY MOLLY MAHAN EXECUTIVE EDITOR: MARK DOYLE
HAVE TO ADMIT, THOUGH I'VE MISSED THE TRAPPINGS
THE LUXURIES. THE PARTIES.
THE ATTENTION.
ANOTHER ROUND!
AND GETTING ATTENTION IS THE KEY HERE.
LET MY ASSHOLE OF A BROTHER KNOW HE HAS COMPETITION.
LET THE COLLECTIVE KNOW THEIR GRIP ON GOTHAM ISN'T AS STRONG AS THEY THINK.
GETTING MY MOTHER BACK WAS ONLY THE FIRST STEP.

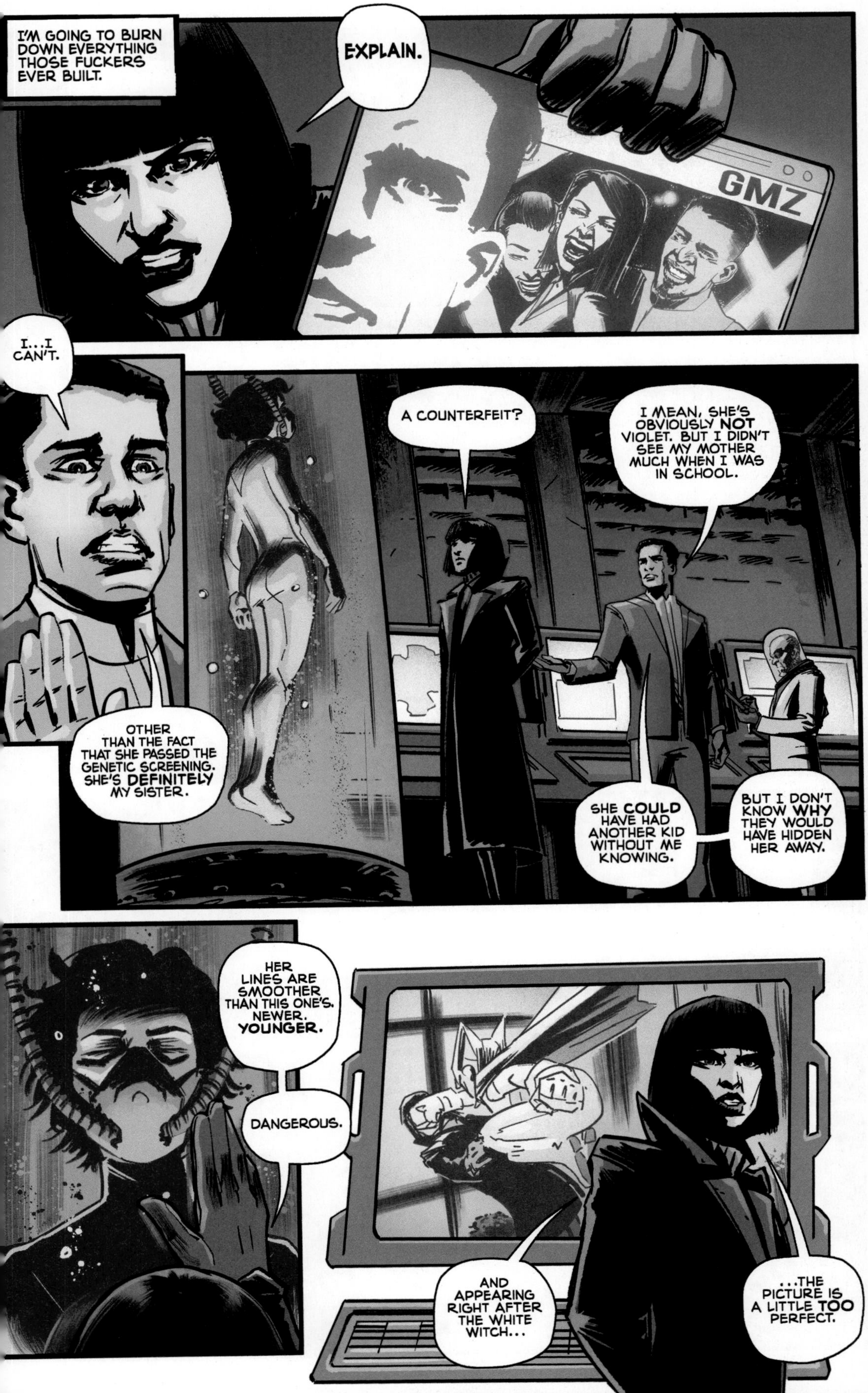

I'M GOING TO BURN DOWN EVERYTHING THOSE FUCKERS EVER BUILT.
EXPLAIN.
GMZ
I...I CAN'T.
A COUNTERFEIT?
I MEAN, SHE'S OBVIOUSLY NOT VIOLET. BUT I DIDN'T SEE MY MOTHER MUCH WHEN I WAS IN SCHOOL.
OTHER THAN THE FACT THAT SHE PASSED THE GENETIC SCREENING. SHE'S DEFINITELY MY SISTER.
SHE COULD HAVE HAD ANOTHER KID WITHOUT ME KNOWING.
BUT I DON'T KNOW WHY THEY WOULD HAVE HIDDEN HER AWAY.
HER LINES ARE SMOOTHER THAN THIS ONE'S. NEWER. YOUNGER.
DANGEROUS.
AND APPEARING RIGHT AFTER THE WHITE WITCH...
...THE PICTURE IS A LITTLE TOO PERFECT.

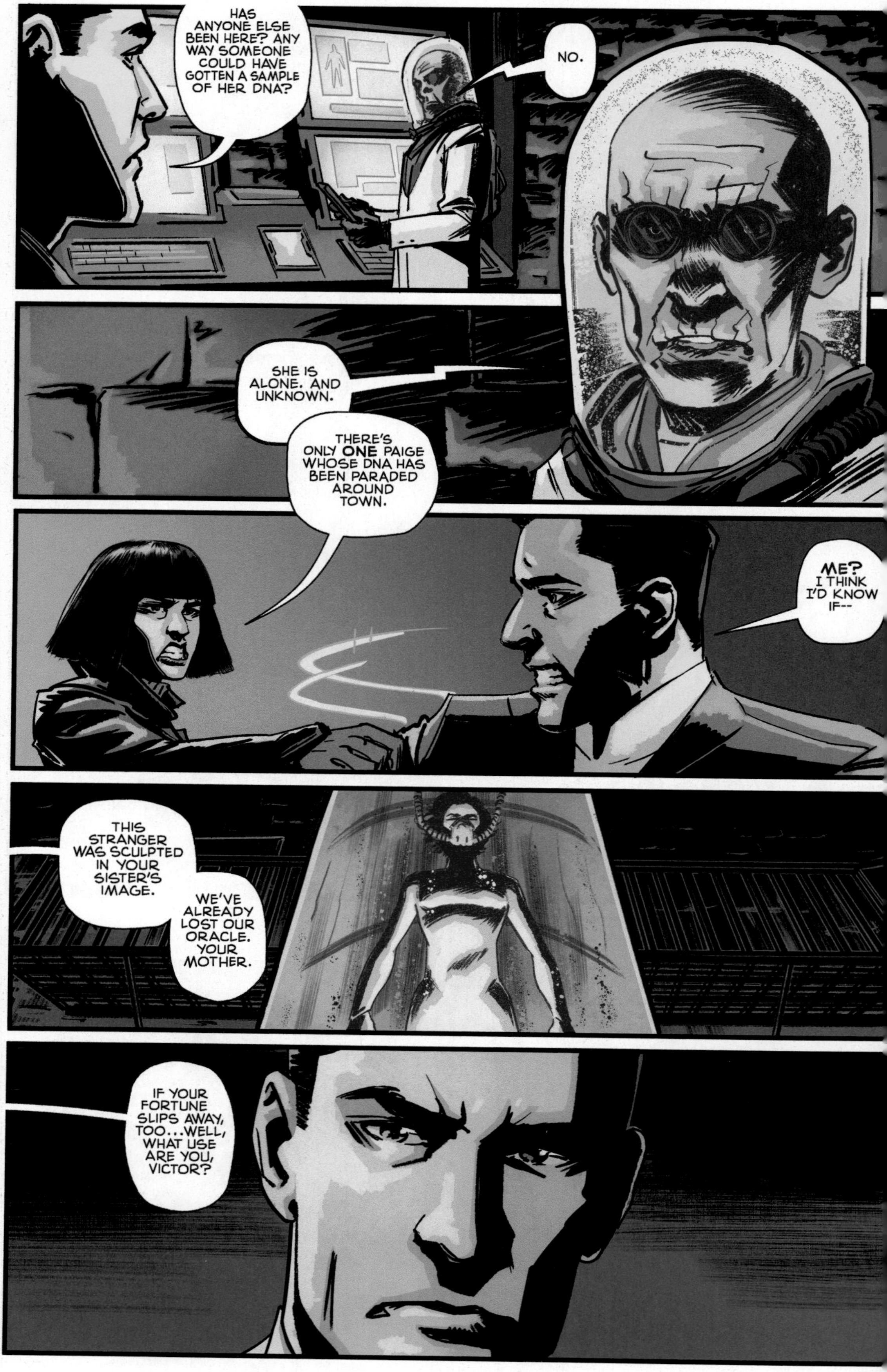
HAS ANYONE ELSE BEEN HERE? ANY WAY SOMEONE COULD HAVE GOTTEN A SAMPLE OF HER DNA?
NO.
SHE IS ALONE. AND UNKNOWN.
THERE'S ONLY ONE PAIGE WHOSE DNA HAS BEEN PARADED AROUND TOWN.
ME? I THINK I'D KNOW IF--
THIS STRANGER WAS SCULPTED IN YOUR SISTER'S IMAGE.
WE'VE ALREADY LOST OUR ORACLE. YOUR MOTHER.
IF YOUR FORTUNE SLIPS AWAY, TOO...WELL, WHAT USE ARE YOU, VICTOR?

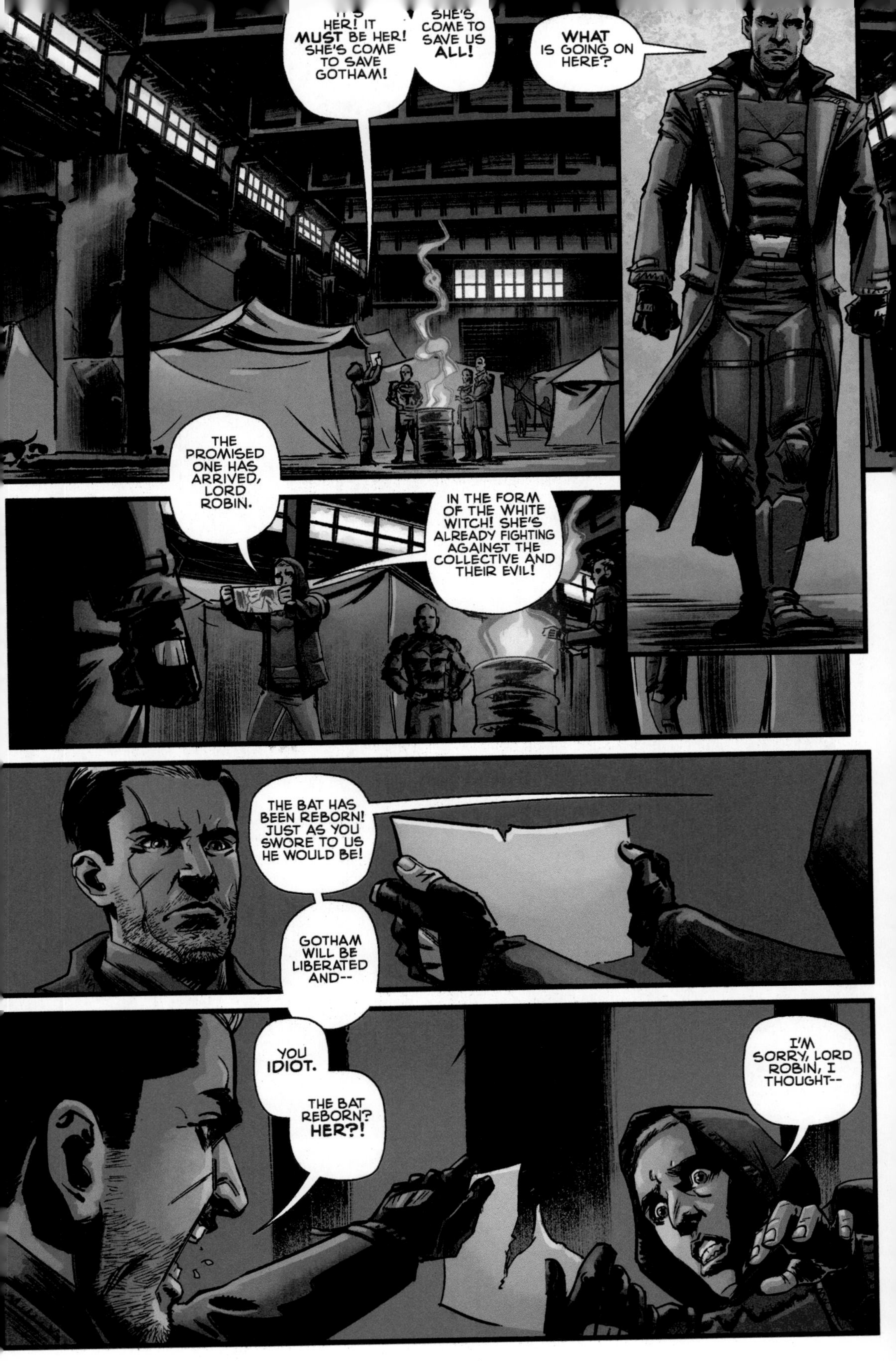
HER! IT MUST BE HER! SHE'S COME TO SAVE GOTHAM!
SHE'S COME TO SAVE US ALL!
WHAT IS GOING ON HERE?
THE PROMISED ONE HAS ARRIVED, LORD ROBIN.
IN THE FORM OF THE WHITE WITCH! SHE'S ALREADY FIGHTING AGAINST THE COLLECTIVE AND THEIR EVIL!
THE BAT HAS BEEN REBORN! JUST AS YOU SWORE TO US HE WOULD BE!
GOTHAM WILL BE LIBERATED AND--
YOU IDIOT.
THE BAT REBORN? HER?!
I'M SORRY, LORD ROBIN, I THOUGHT--

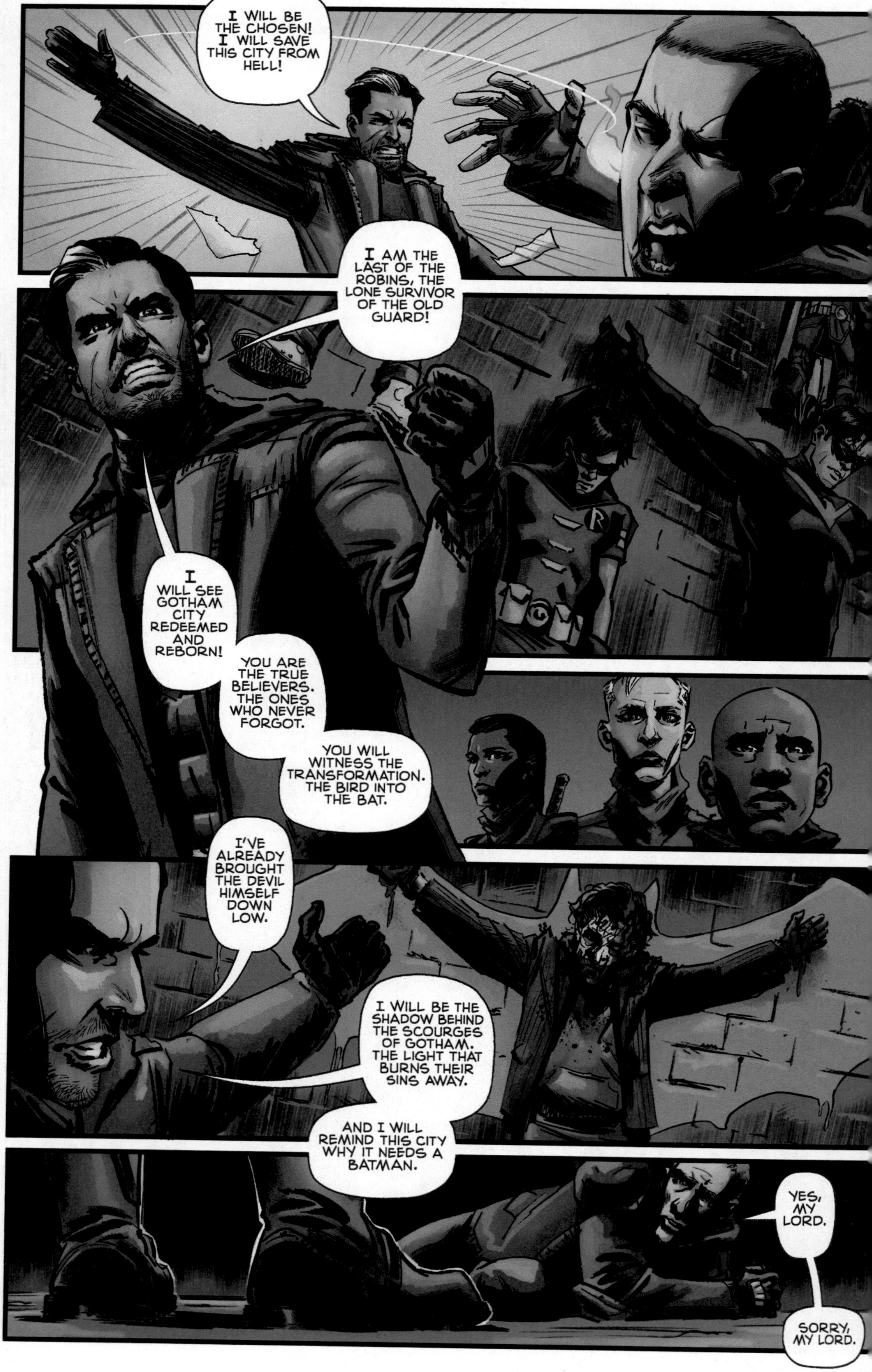
I WILL BE THE CHOSEN! I WILL SAVE THIS CITY FROM HELL!
I AM THE LAST OF THE ROBINS, THE LONE SURVIVOR OF THE OLD GUARD!
I WILL SEE GOTHAM CITY REDEEMED AND REBORN!
YOU ARE THE TRUE BELIEVERS. THE ONES WHO NEVER FORGOT.
YOU WILL WITNESS THE TRANSFORMATION. THE BIRD INTO THE BAT.
I'VE ALREADY BROUGHT THE DEVIL HIMSELF DOWN LOW.
I WILL BE THE SHADOW BEHIND THE SCOURGES OF GOTHAM. THE LIGHT THAT BURNS THEIR SINS AWAY.
AND I WILL REMIND THIS CITY WHY IT NEEDS A BATMAN.
YES, MY LORD.
SORRY, MY LORD.

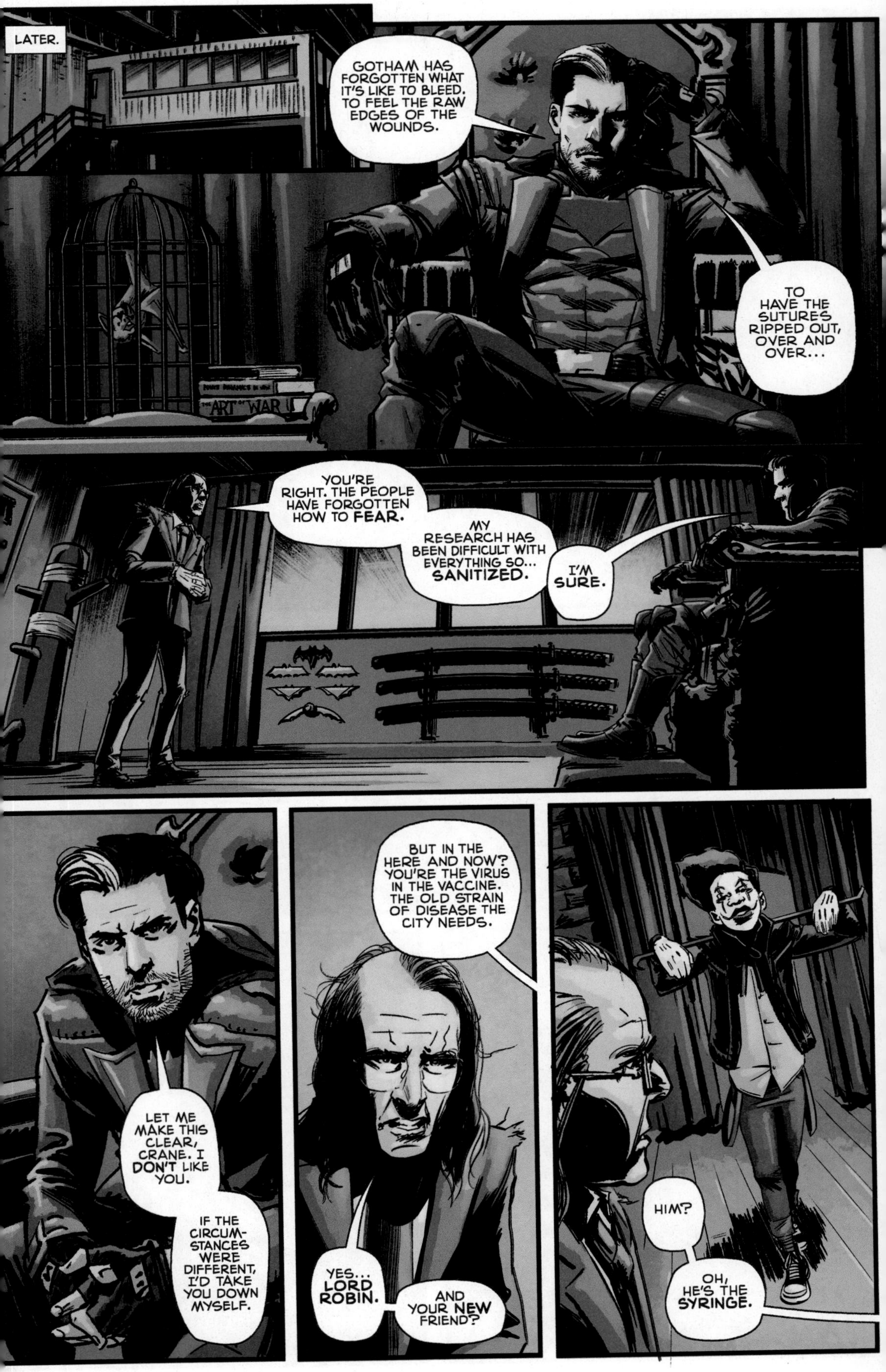
LATER.
GOTHAM HAS FORGOTTEN WHAT IT'S LIKE TO BLEED. TO FEEL THE RAW EDGES OF THE WOUNDS.
TO HAVE THE SUTURES RIPPED OUT, OVER AND OVER...
THE ART OF WAR
YOU'RE RIGHT. THE PEOPLE HAVE FORGOTTEN HOW TO FEAR.
MY RESEARCH HAS BEEN DIFFICULT WITH EVERYTHING SO... SANITIZED.
I'M SURE.
LET ME MAKE THIS CLEAR, CRANE. I DON'T LIKE YOU.
IF THE CIRCUMSTANCES WERE DIFFERENT, I'D TAKE YOU DOWN MYSELF.
BUT IN THE HERE AND NOW? YOU'RE THE VIRUS IN THE VACCINE. THE OLD STRAIN OF DISEASE THE CITY NEEDS.
YES... LORD ROBIN.
AND YOUR NEW FRIEND?
HIM?
OH, HE'S THE SYRINGE.

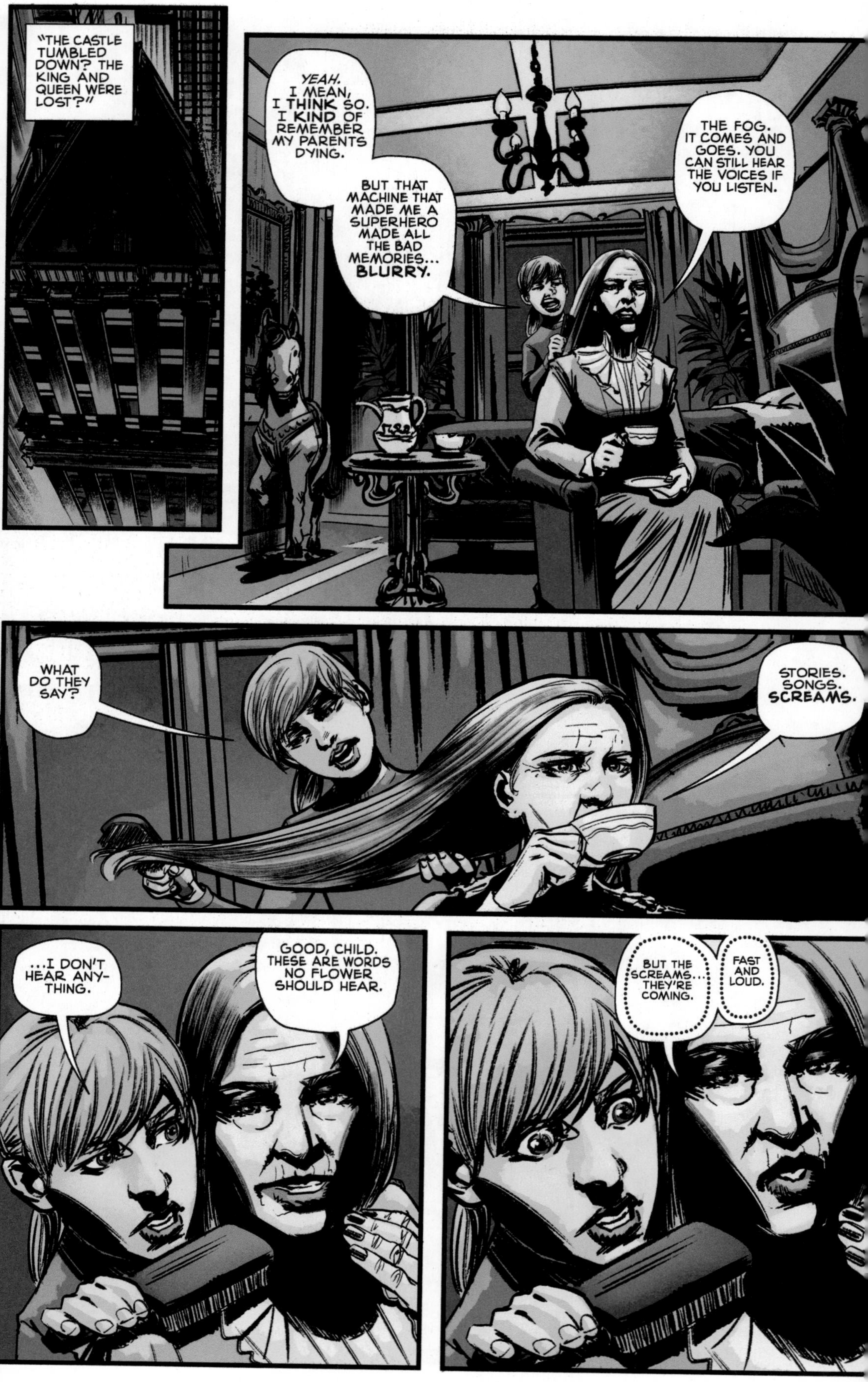
"THE CASTLE TUMBLED DOWN? THE KING AND QUEEN WERE LOST?"
YEAH. I MEAN, I THINK SO. I KIND OF REMEMBER MY PARENTS DYING.
BUT THAT MACHINE THAT MADE ME A SUPERHERO MADE ALL THE BAD MEMORIES... BLURRY.
THE FOG. IT COMES AND GOES. YOU CAN STILL HEAR THE VOICES IF YOU LISTEN.
WHAT DO THEY SAY?
STORIES. SONGS. SCREAMS.
...I DON'T HEAR ANY-THING.
GOOD, CHILD. THESE ARE WORDS NO FLOWER SHOULD HEAR.
BUT THE SCREAMS... THEY'RE COMING.
FAST AND LOUD.

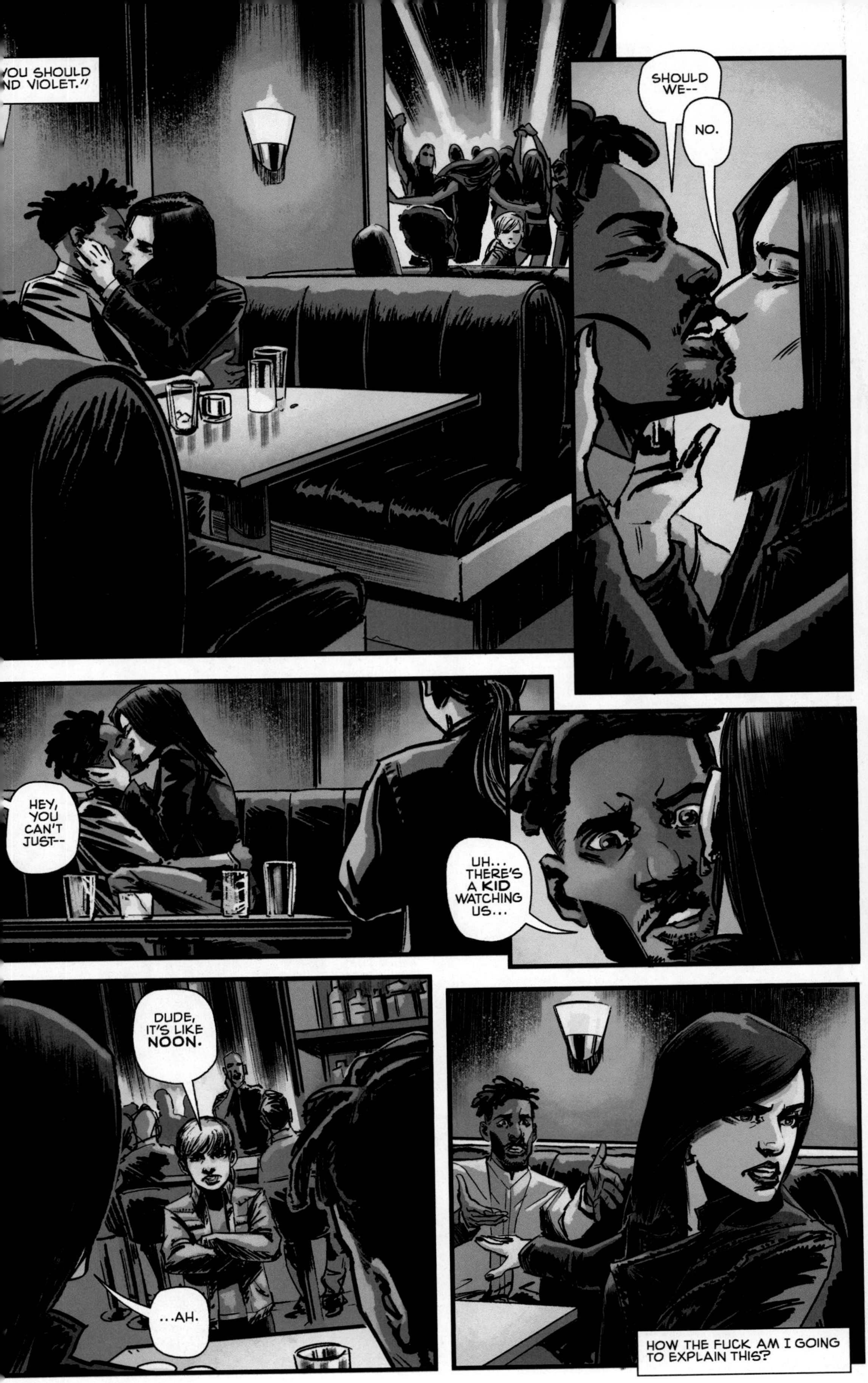

YOU SHOULD
ND VIOLET."
SHOULD WE--
NO.
HEY, YOU CAN'T JUST--
UH... THERE'S A **KID** WATCHING US...
DUDE, IT'S LIKE **NOON.**
...AH.
HOW THE FUCK AM I GOING TO EXPLAIN THIS?

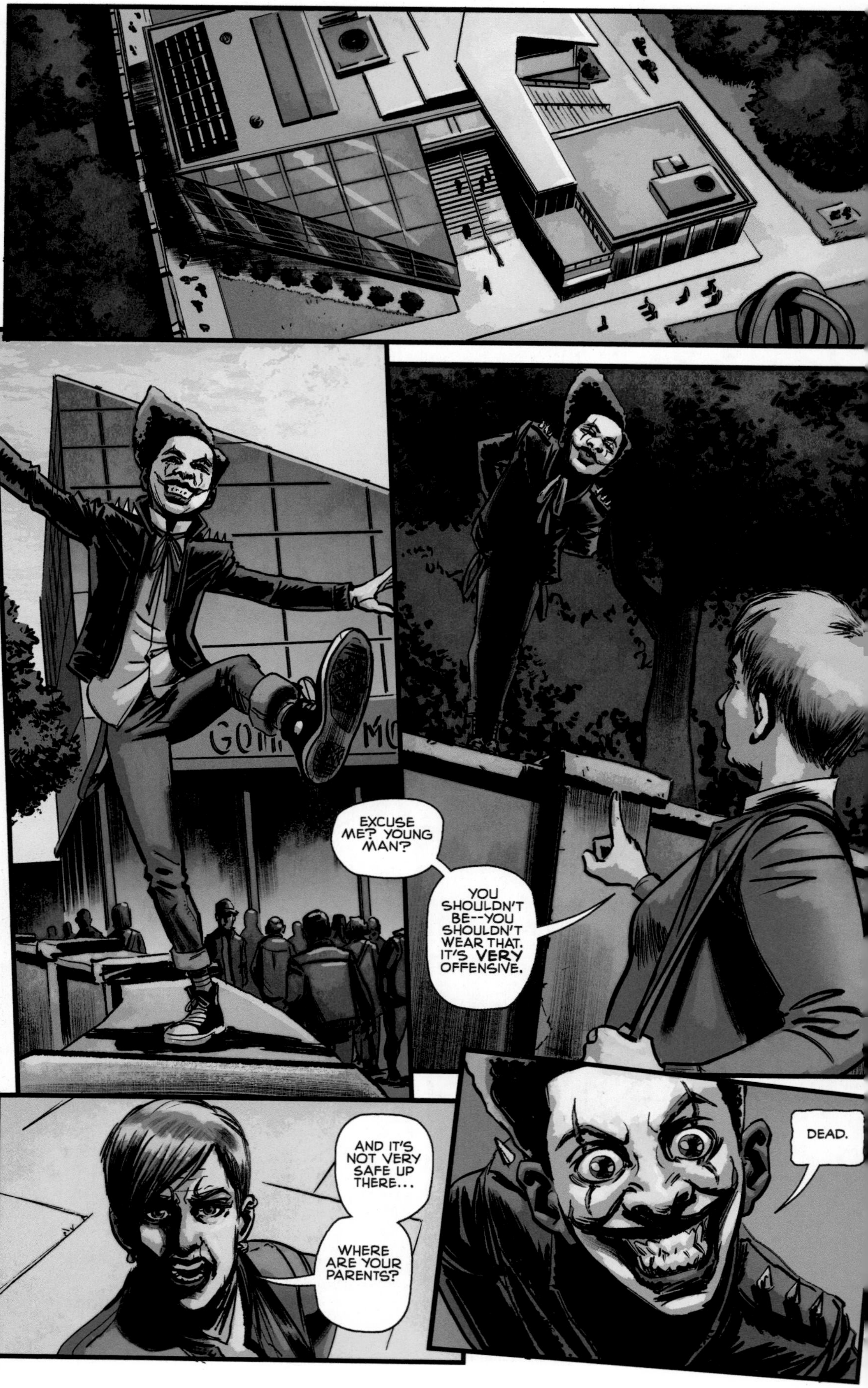
GOT
MO
EXCUSE ME? YOUNG MAN?
YOU SHOULDN'T BE--YOU SHOULDN'T WEAR THAT. IT'S VERY OFFENSIVE.
AND IT'S NOT VERY SAFE UP THERE...
WHERE ARE YOUR PARENTS?
DEAD.

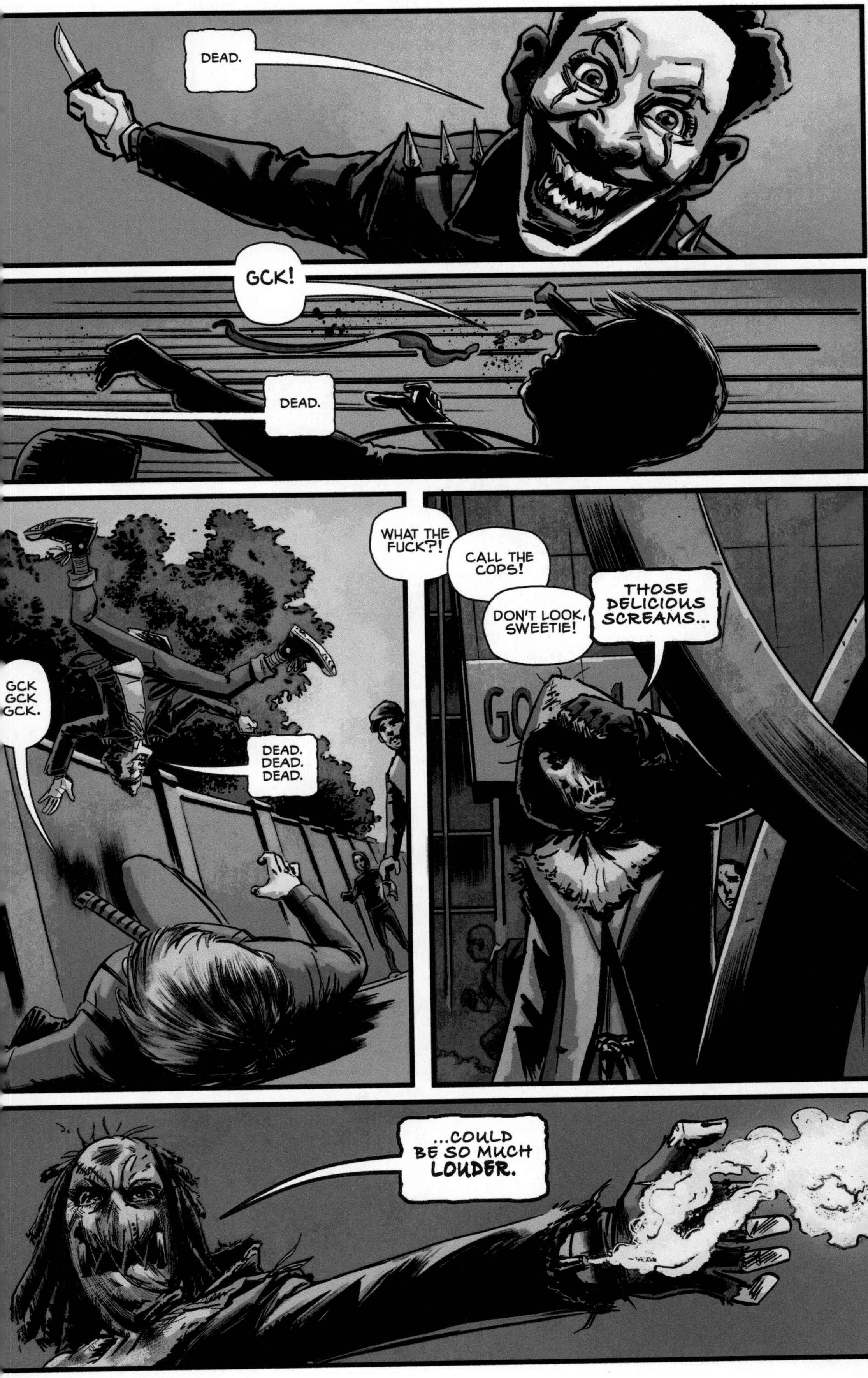
DEAD.
GCK!
DEAD.
GCK
GCK
GCK.
DEAD.
DEAD.
DEAD.
WHAT THE FUCK?!
CALL THE COPS!
DON'T LOOK, SWEETIE!
THOSE DELICIOUS SCREAMS...
GO
...COULD BE SO MUCH **LOUDER**.

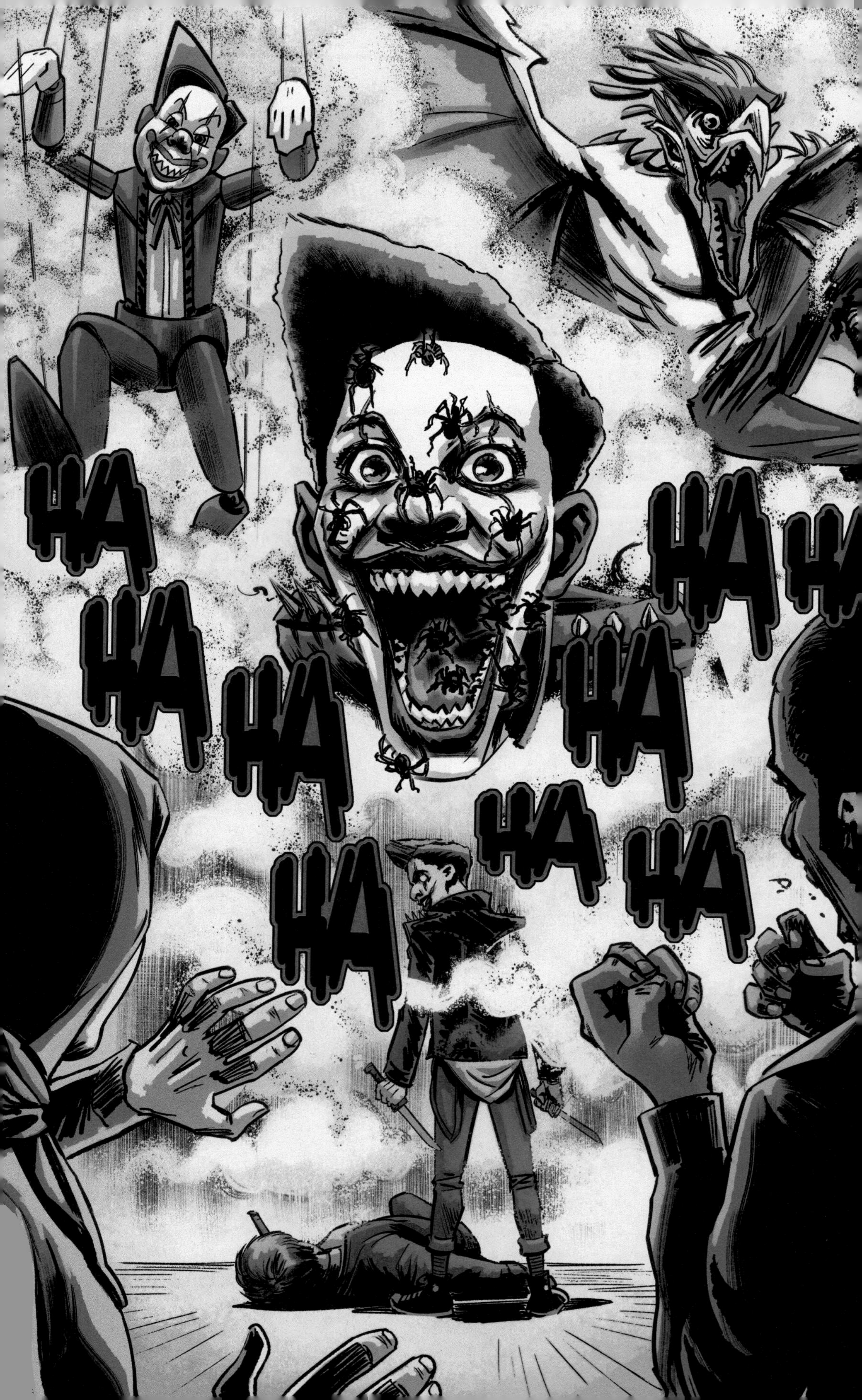
HA
HA
HA
HA
HA
HA
HA
HA

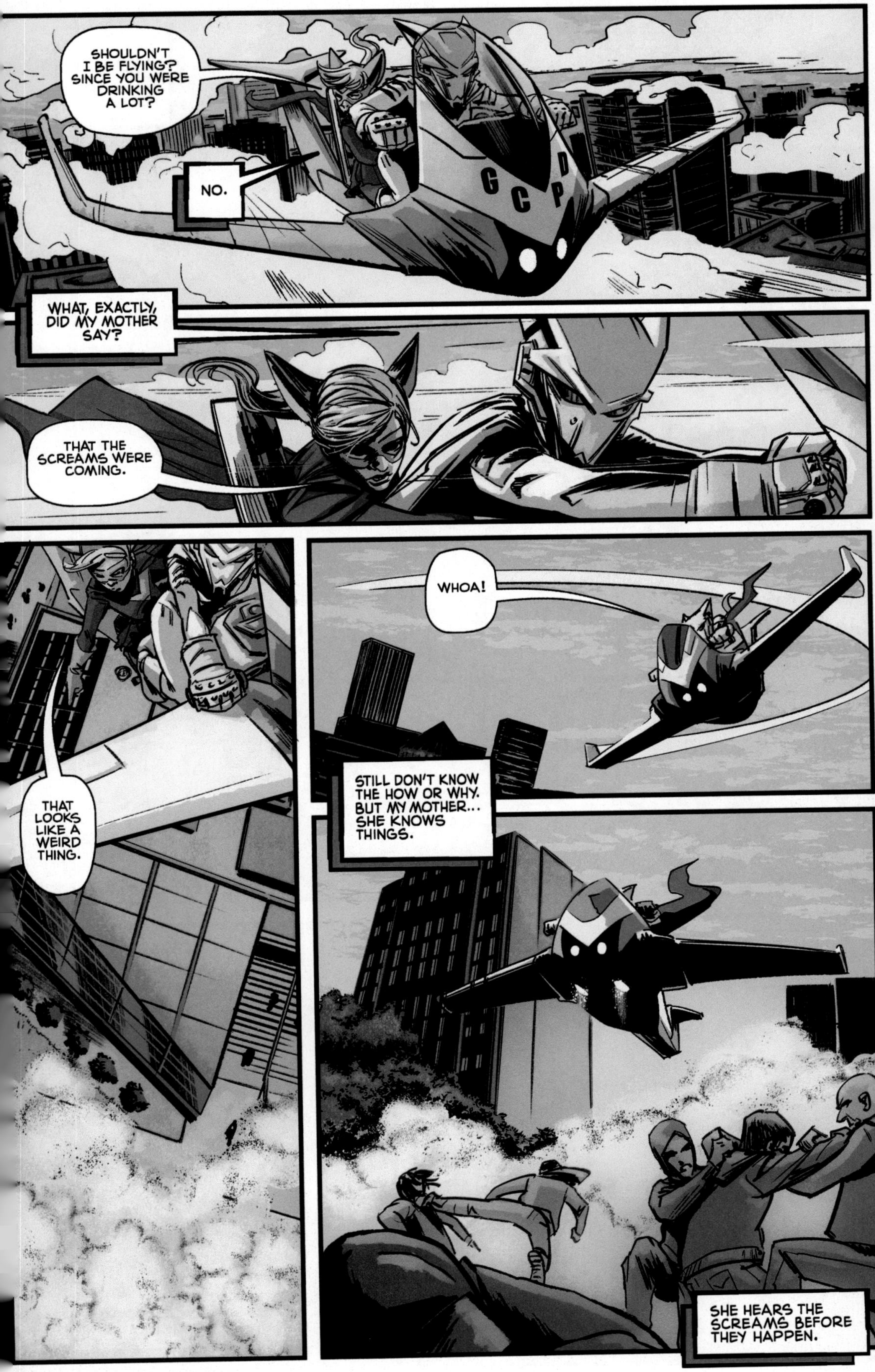
SHOULDN'T I BE FLYING? SINCE YOU WERE DRINKING A LOT?
NO.
GCPD
WHAT, EXACTLY, DID MY MOTHER SAY?
THAT THE SCREAMS WERE COMING.
THAT LOOKS LIKE A WEIRD THING.
WHOA!
STILL DON'T KNOW THE HOW OR WHY. BUT MY MOTHER... SHE KNOWS THINGS.
SHE HEARS THE SCREAMS BEFORE THEY HAPPEN.

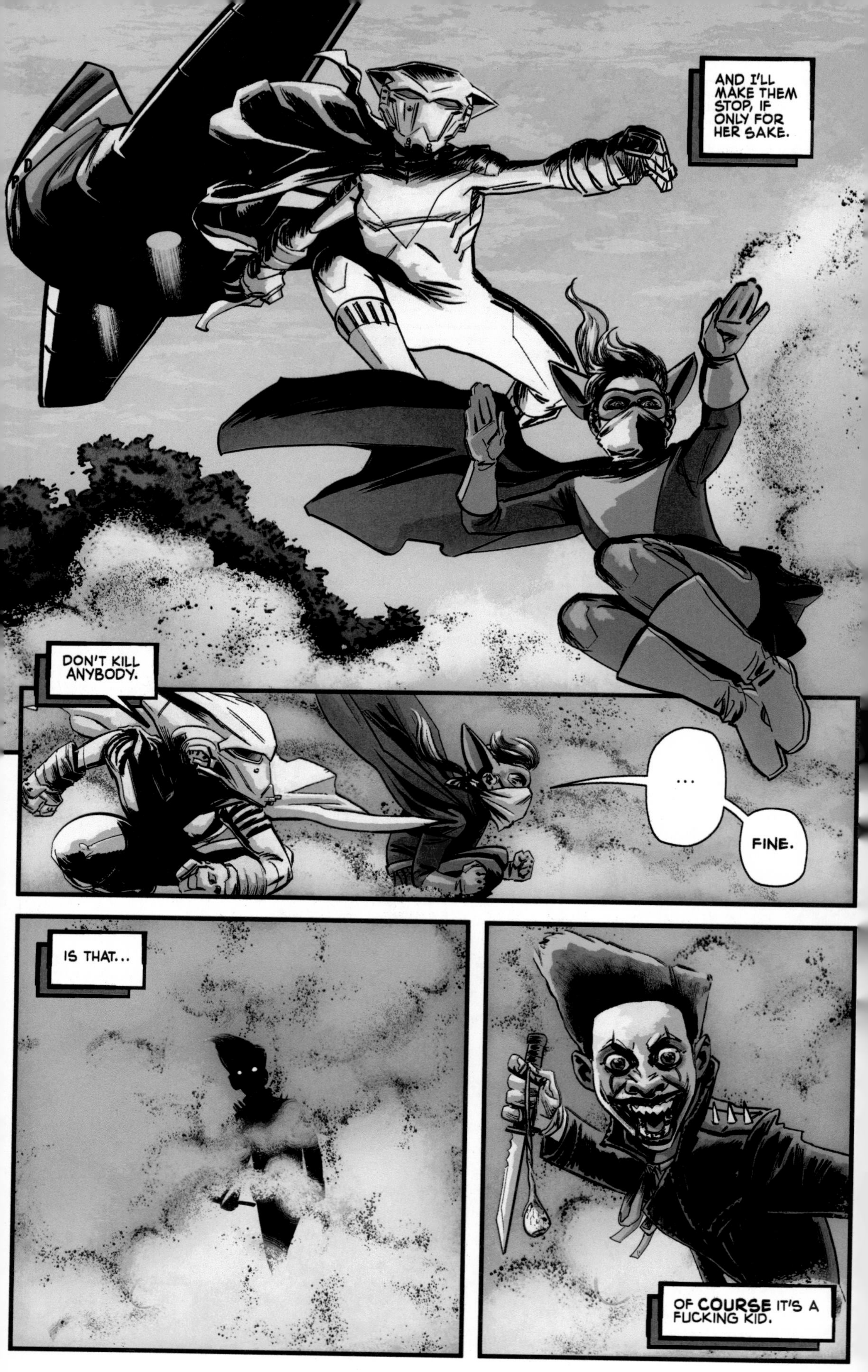
AND I'LL MAKE THEM STOP, IF ONLY FOR HER SAKE.
DON'T KILL ANYBODY.
...
FINE.
IS THAT...
OF COURSE IT'S A FUCKING KID.

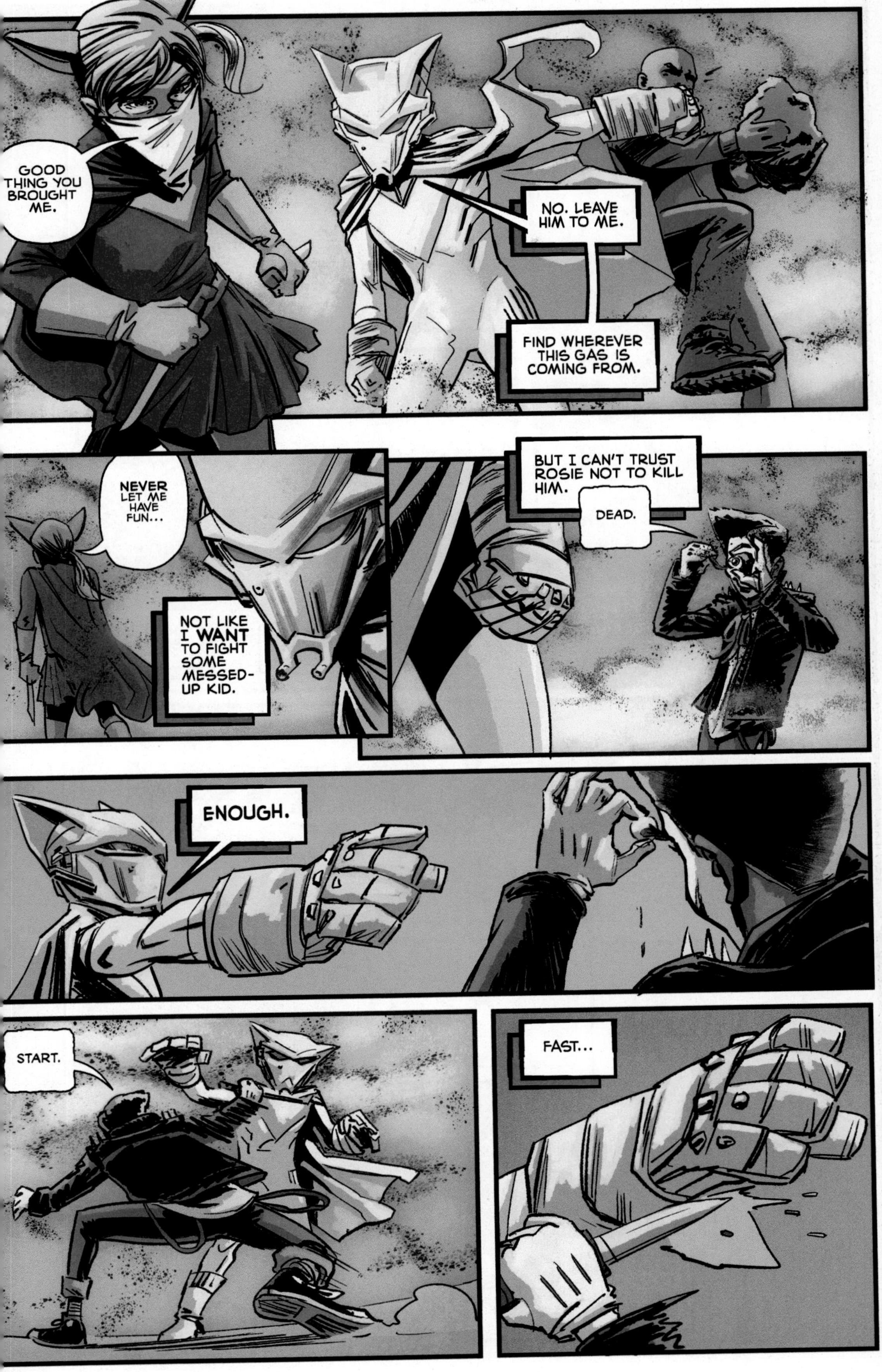
GOOD THING YOU BROUGHT ME.
NO. LEAVE HIM TO ME.
FIND WHEREVER THIS GAS IS COMING FROM.
NEVER LET ME HAVE FUN...
NOT LIKE I WANT TO FIGHT SOME MESSED-UP KID.
BUT I CAN'T TRUST ROSIE NOT TO KILL HIM.
DEAD.
ENOUGH.
START.
FAST...

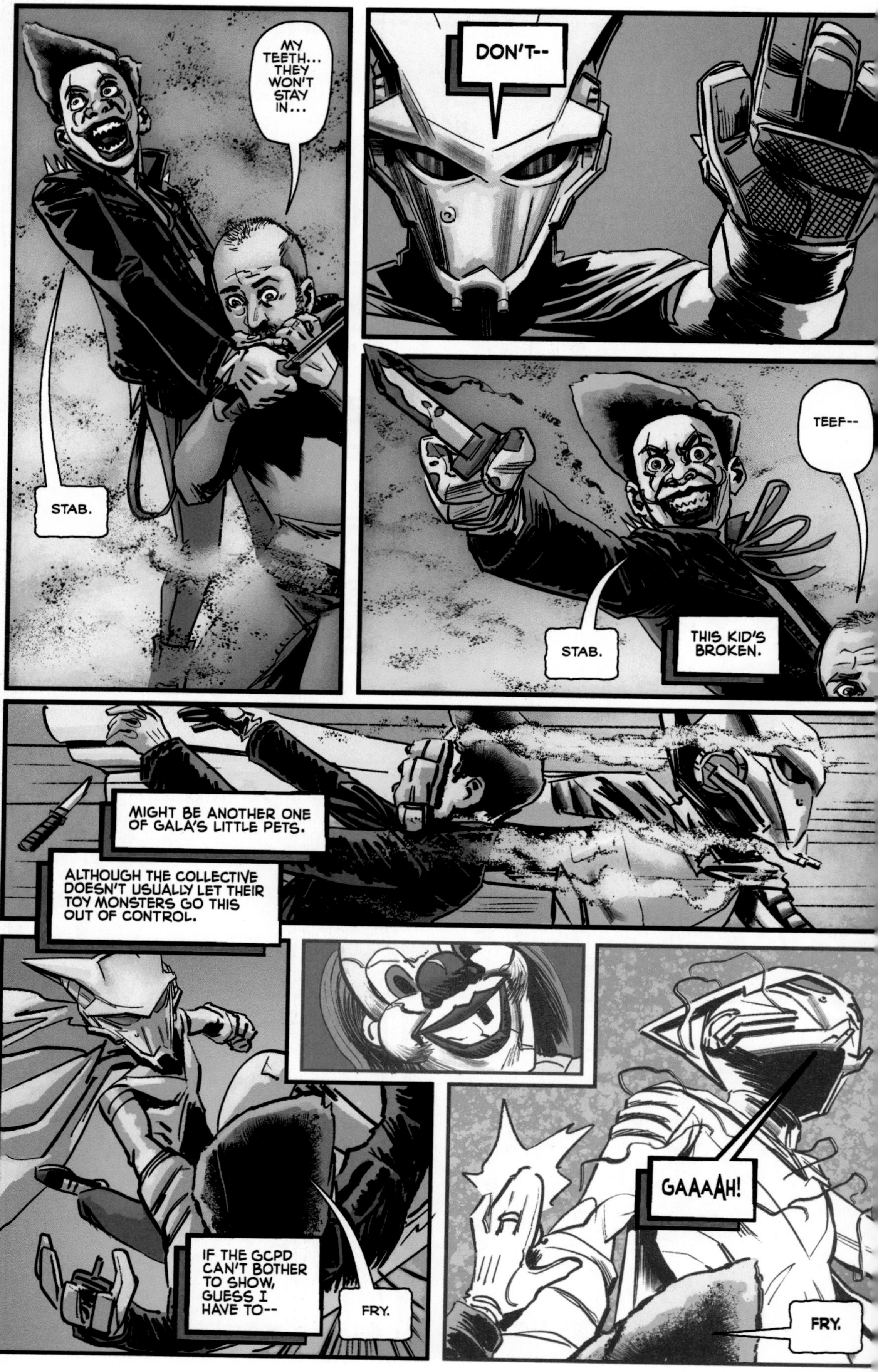
MY TEETH... THEY WON'T STAY IN...
STAB.
DON'T--
TEEF--
STAB.
THIS KID'S BROKEN.
MIGHT BE ANOTHER ONE OF GALA'S LITTLE PETS.
ALTHOUGH THE COLLECTIVE DOESN'T USUALLY LET THEIR TOY MONSTERS GO THIS OUT OF CONTROL.
IF THE GCPD CAN'T BOTHER TO SHOW, GUESS I HAVE TO--
FRY.
GAAAAH!
FRY.

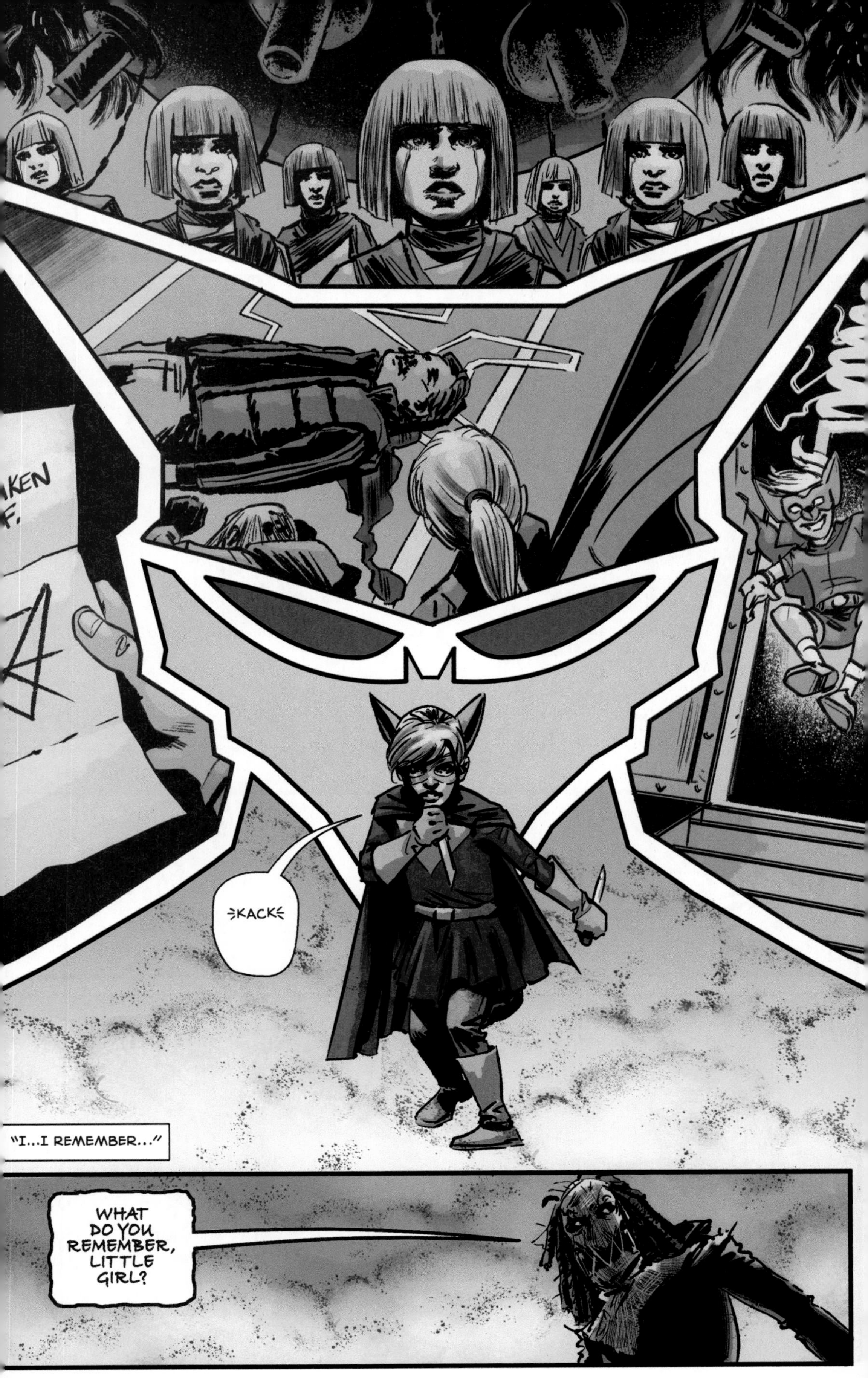

KAKEN
F.
≠KACK≠
"I...I REMEMBER..."
WHAT DO YOU REMEMBER, LITTLE GIRL?

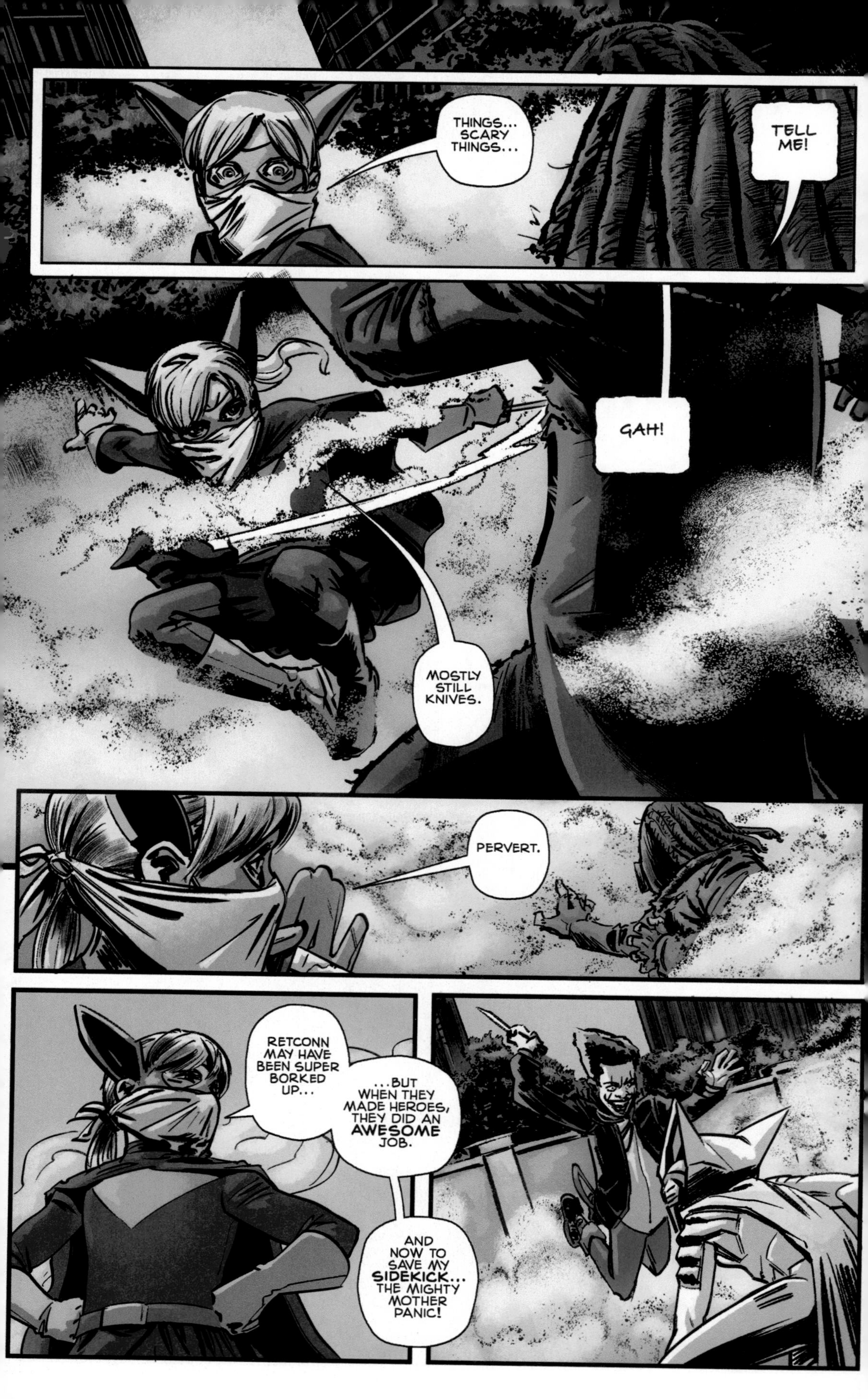

THINGS... SCARY THINGS...
TELL ME!
GAH!
MOSTLY STILL KNIVES.
PERVERT.
RETCONN MAY HAVE BEEN SUPER BORKED UP...
...BUT WHEN THEY MADE HEROES, THEY DID AN **AWESOME** JOB.
AND NOW TO SAVE MY **SIDEKICK**... THE MIGHTY MOTHER PANIC!

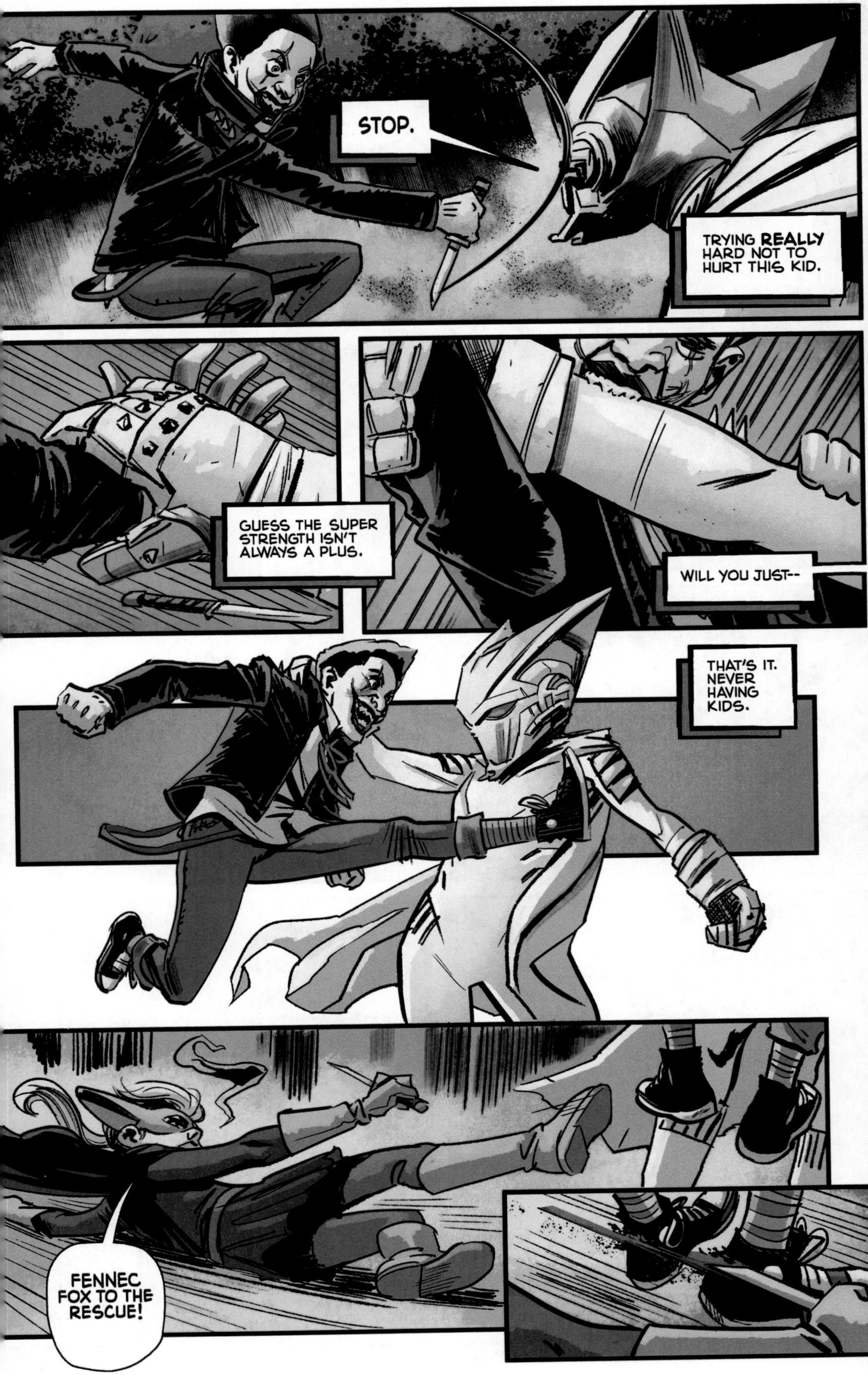
STOP.
TRYING REALLY HARD NOT TO HURT THIS KID.
GUESS THE SUPER STRENGTH ISN'T ALWAYS A PLUS.
WILL YOU JUST--
THAT'S IT. NEVER HAVING KIDS.
FENNEC FOX TO THE RESCUE!

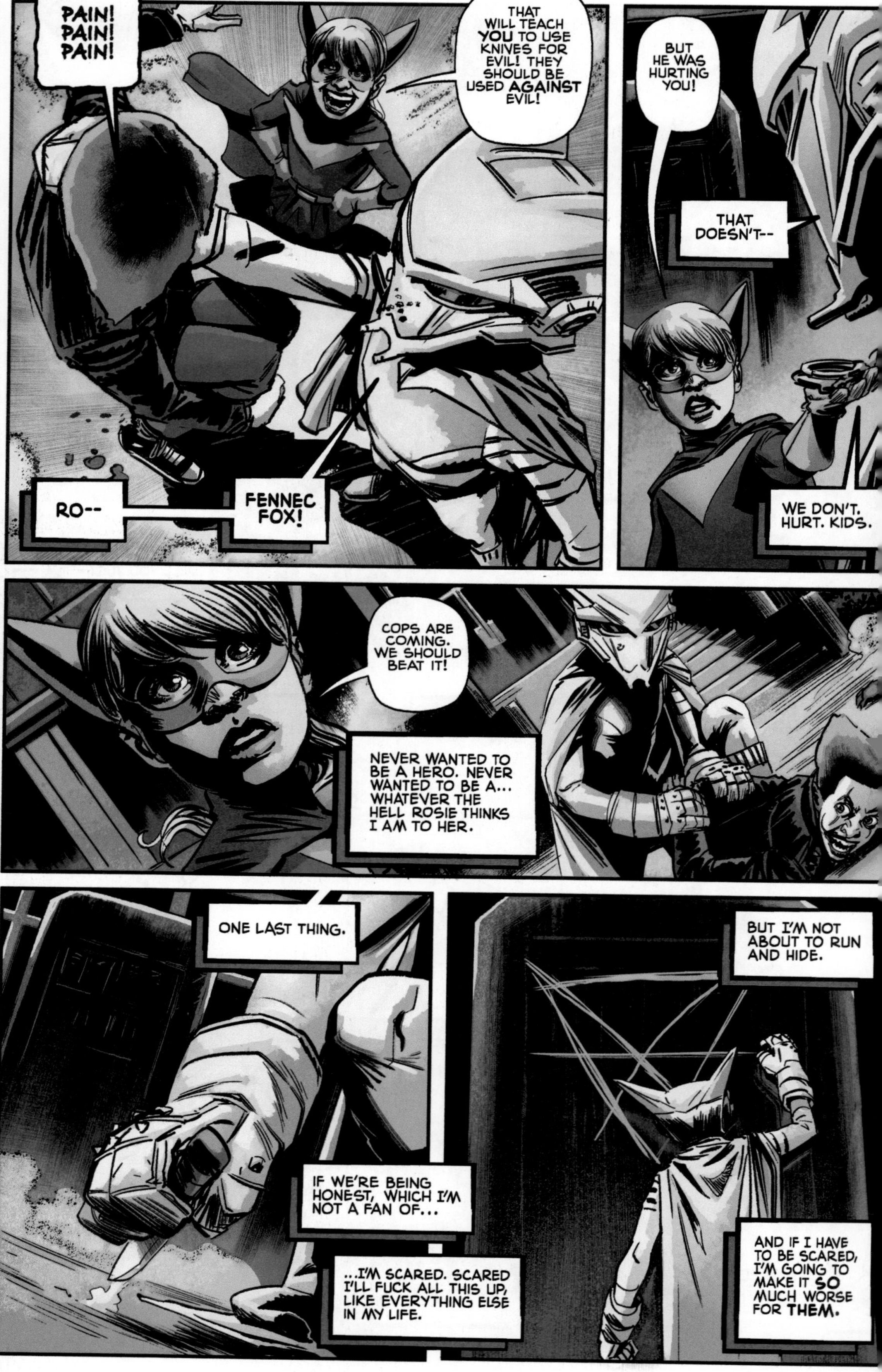
PAIN! PAIN! PAIN!
THAT WILL TEACH YOU TO USE KNIVES FOR EVIL! THEY SHOULD BE USED AGAINST EVIL!
RO--
FENNEC FOX!
BUT HE WAS HURTING YOU!
THAT DOESN'T--
WE DON'T. HURT. KIDS.
COPS ARE COMING. WE SHOULD BEAT IT!
NEVER WANTED TO BE A HERO. NEVER WANTED TO BE A... WHATEVER THE HELL ROSIE THINKS I AM TO HER.
ONE LAST THING.
IF WE'RE BEING HONEST, WHICH I'M NOT A FAN OF...
...I'M SCARED. SCARED I'LL FUCK ALL THIS UP, LIKE EVERYTHING ELSE IN MY LIFE.
BUT I'M NOT ABOUT TO RUN AND HIDE.
AND IF I HAVE TO BE SCARED, I'M GOING TO MAKE IT SO MUCH WORSE FOR THEM.

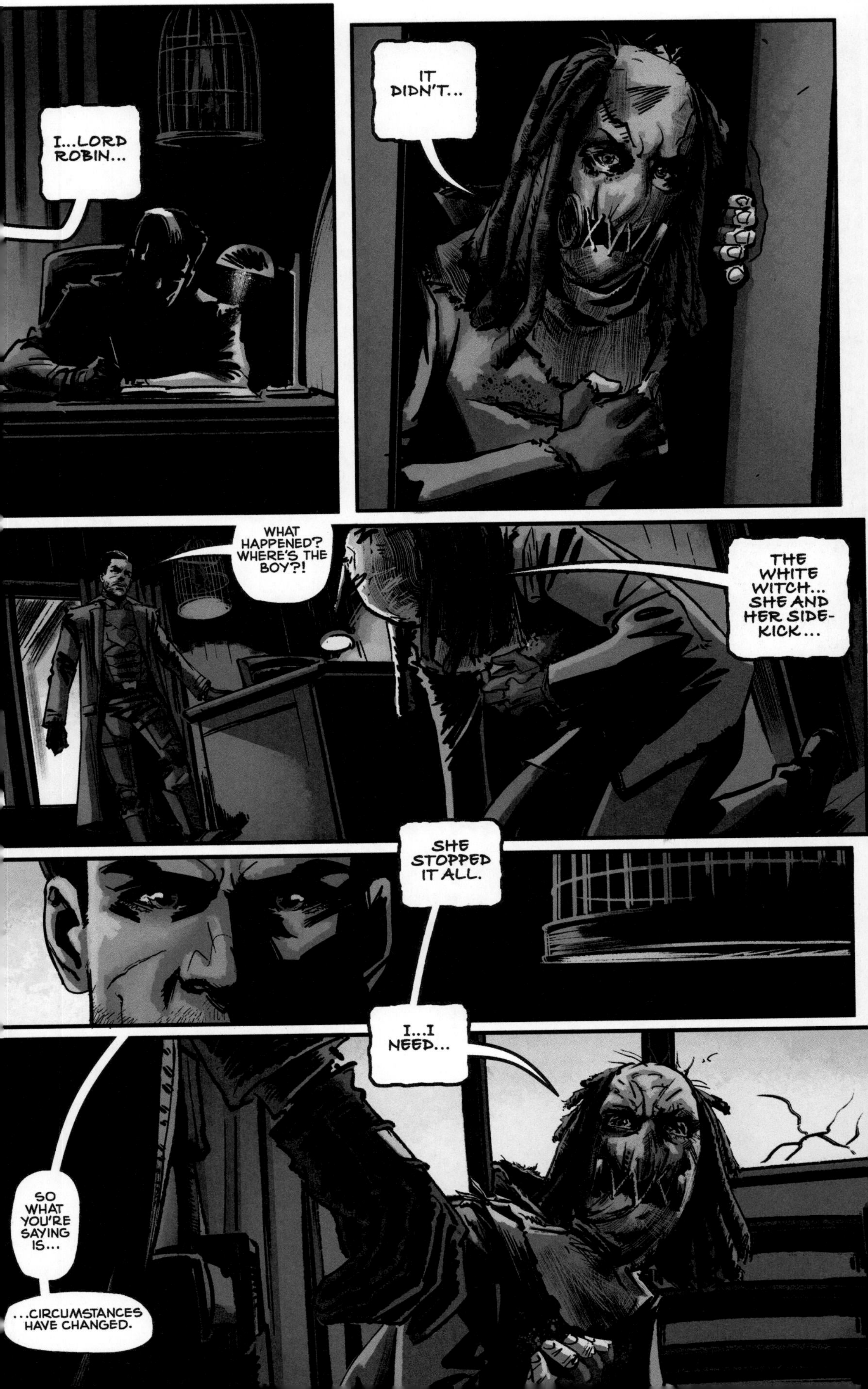
I...LORD ROBIN...
IT DIDN'T...
WHAT HAPPENED? WHERE'S THE BOY?!
THE WHITE WITCH... SHE AND HER SIDE-KICK...
SHE STOPPED IT ALL.
I...I NEED...
SO WHAT YOU'RE SAYING IS...
...CIRCUMSTANCES HAVE CHANGED.

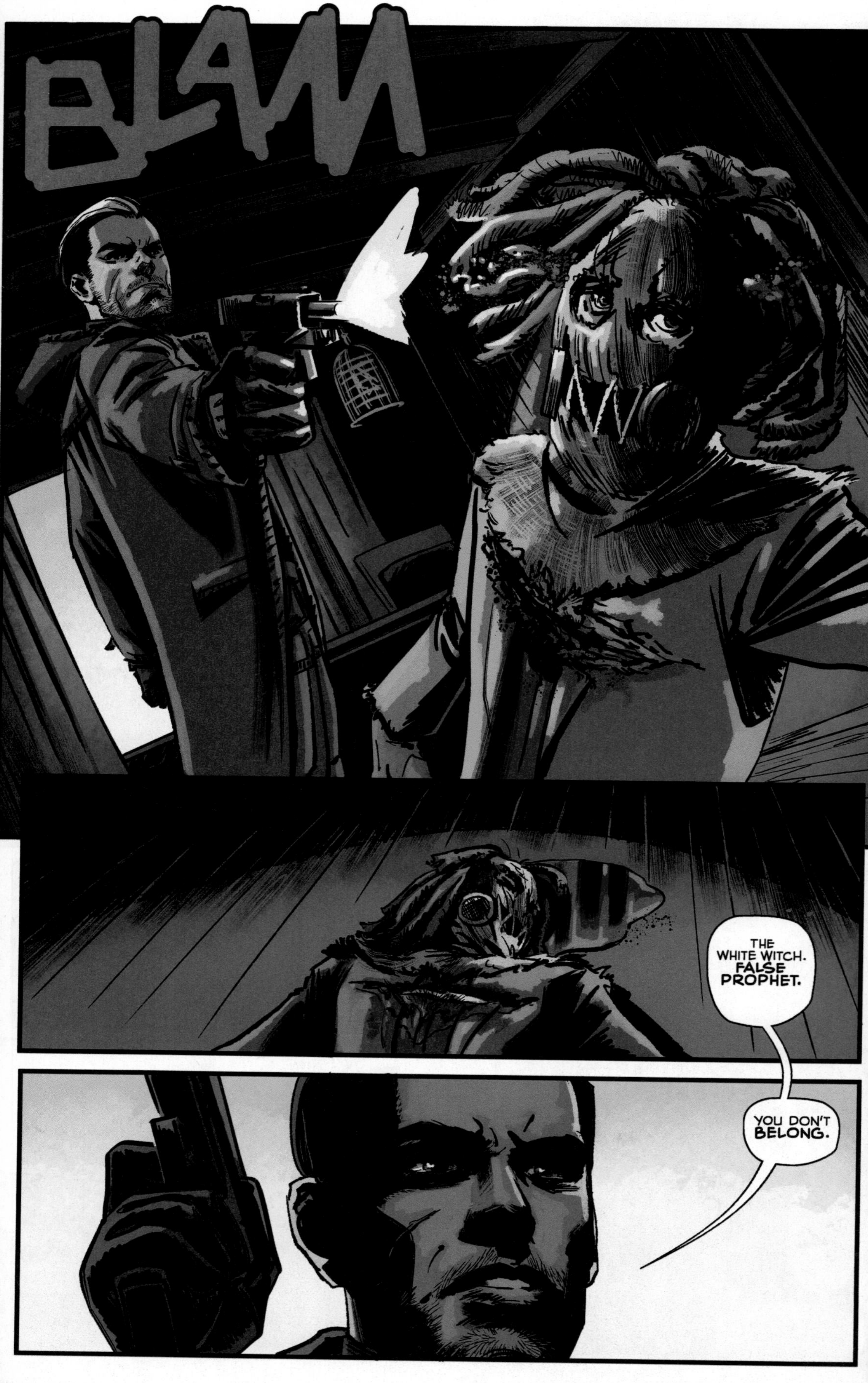
BLAM
THE WHITE WITCH. FALSE PROPHET.
YOU DON'T BELONG.

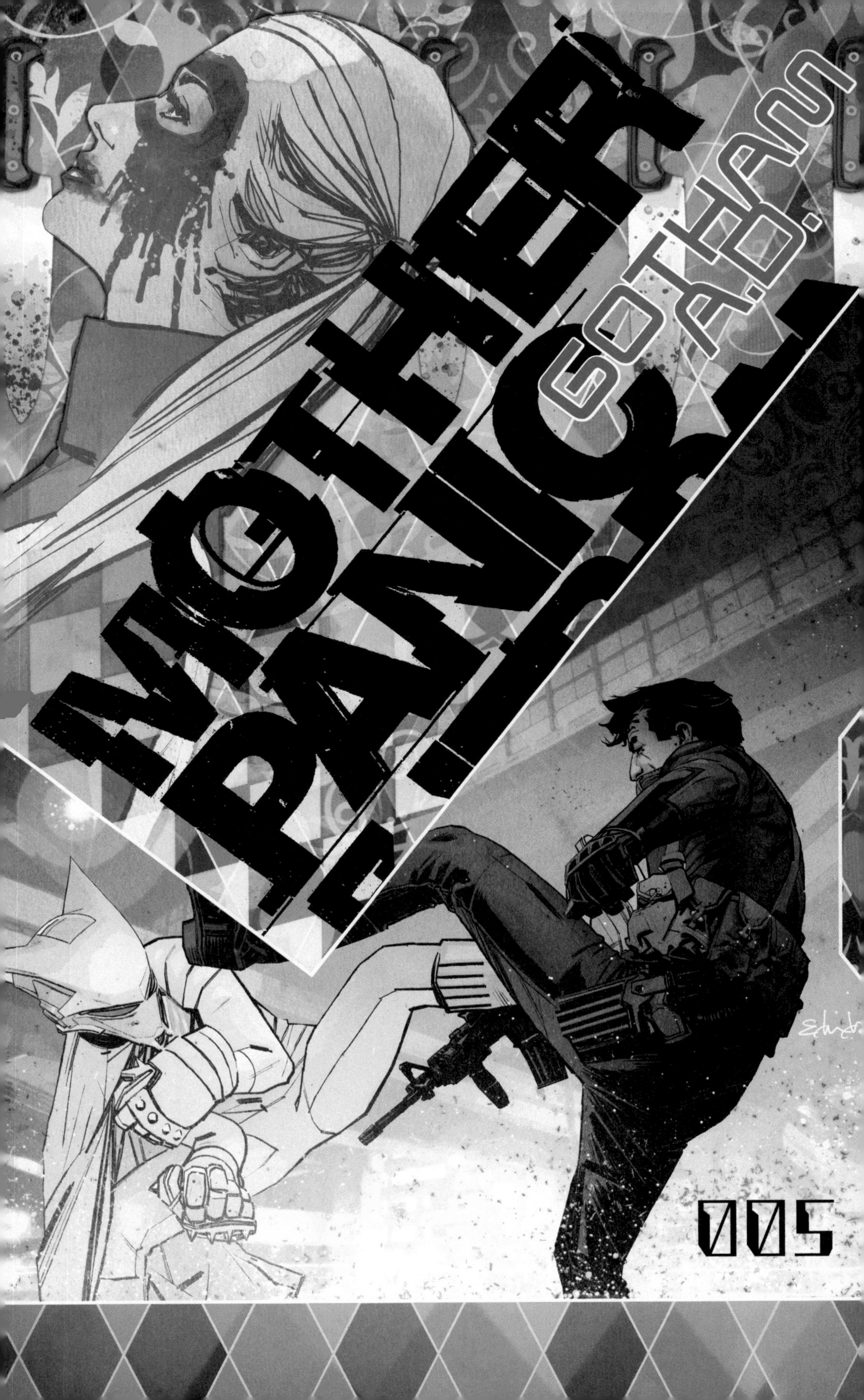

MOTHER PANIC
GOTHAM A.D.
005

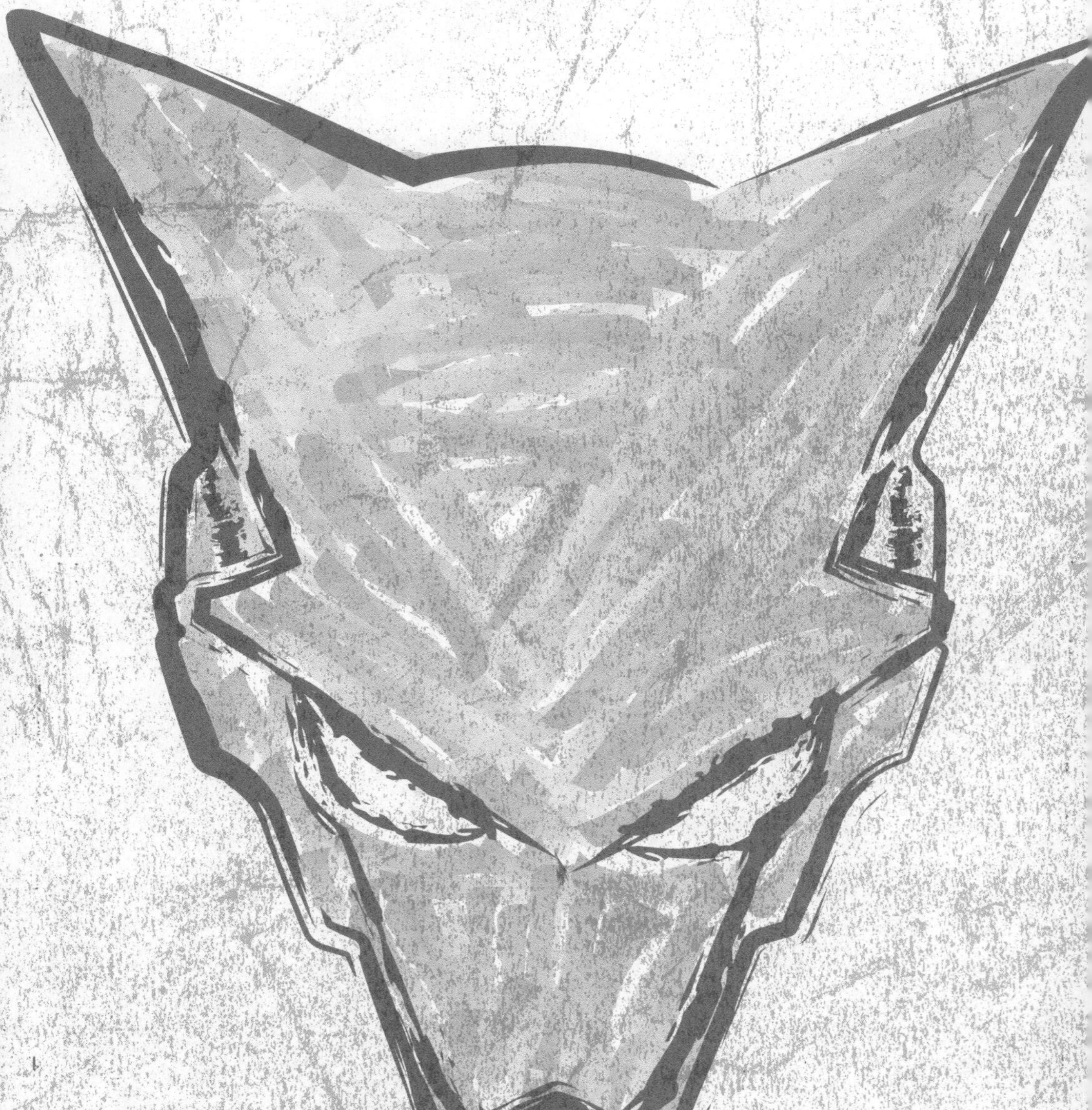

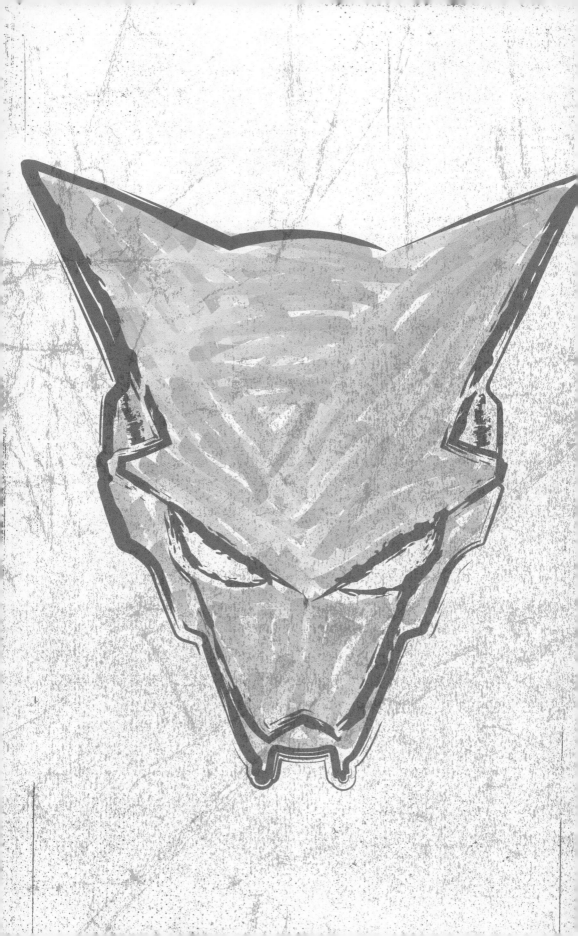

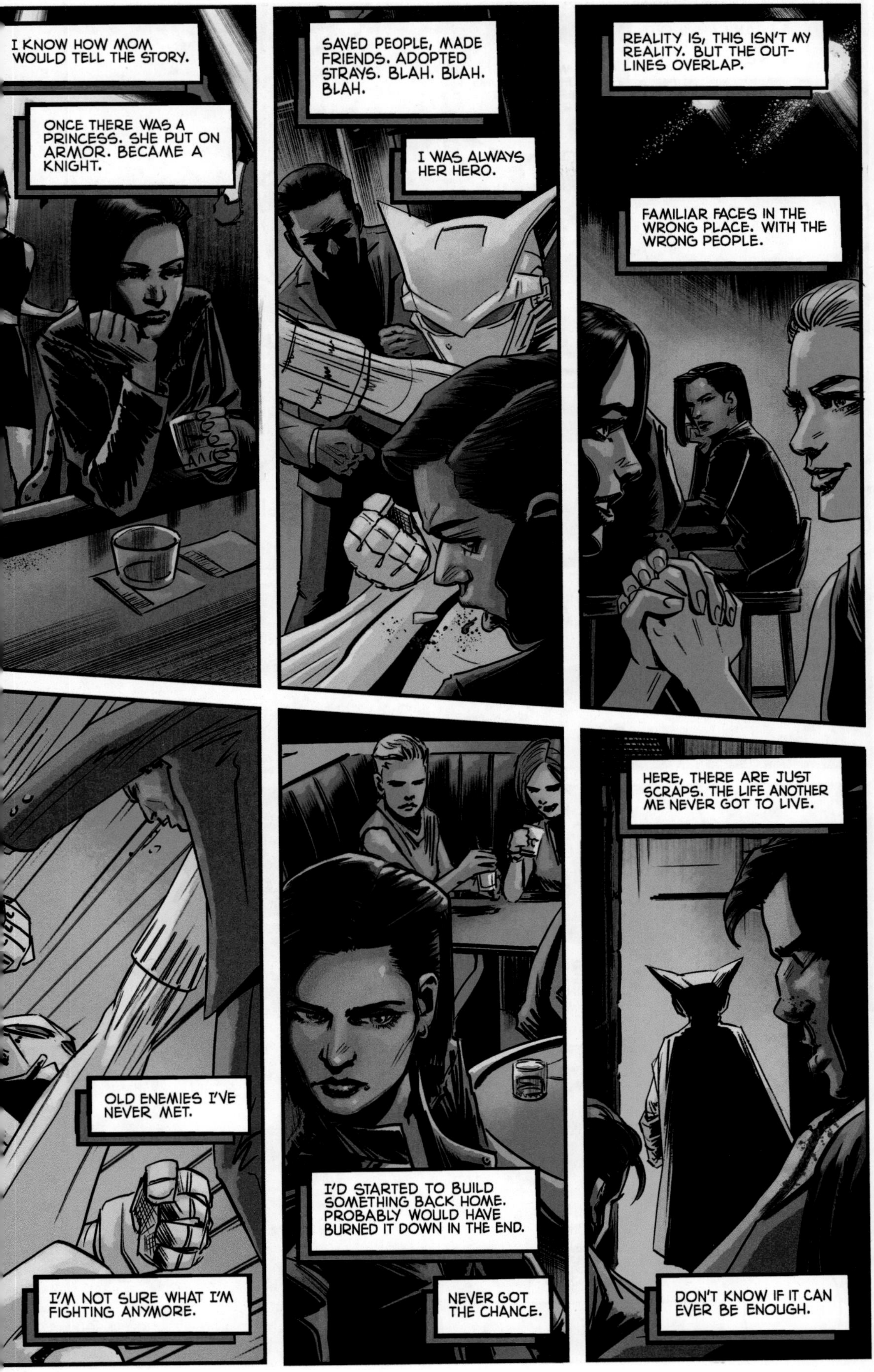

I KNOW HOW MOM WOULD TELL THE STORY.
ONCE THERE WAS A PRINCESS. SHE PUT ON ARMOR. BECAME A KNIGHT.
SAVED PEOPLE, MADE FRIENDS. ADOPTED STRAYS. BLAH. BLAH. BLAH.
I WAS ALWAYS HER HERO.
REALITY IS, THIS ISN'T MY REALITY. BUT THE OUTLINES OVERLAP.
FAMILIAR FACES IN THE WRONG PLACE. WITH THE WRONG PEOPLE.
OLD ENEMIES I'VE NEVER MET.
I'M NOT SURE WHAT I'M FIGHTING ANYMORE.
I'D STARTED TO BUILD SOMETHING BACK HOME. PROBABLY WOULD HAVE BURNED IT DOWN IN THE END.
NEVER GOT THE CHANCE.
HERE, THERE ARE JUST SCRAPS. THE LIFE ANOTHER ME NEVER GOT TO LIVE.
DON'T KNOW IF IT CAN EVER BE ENOUGH.

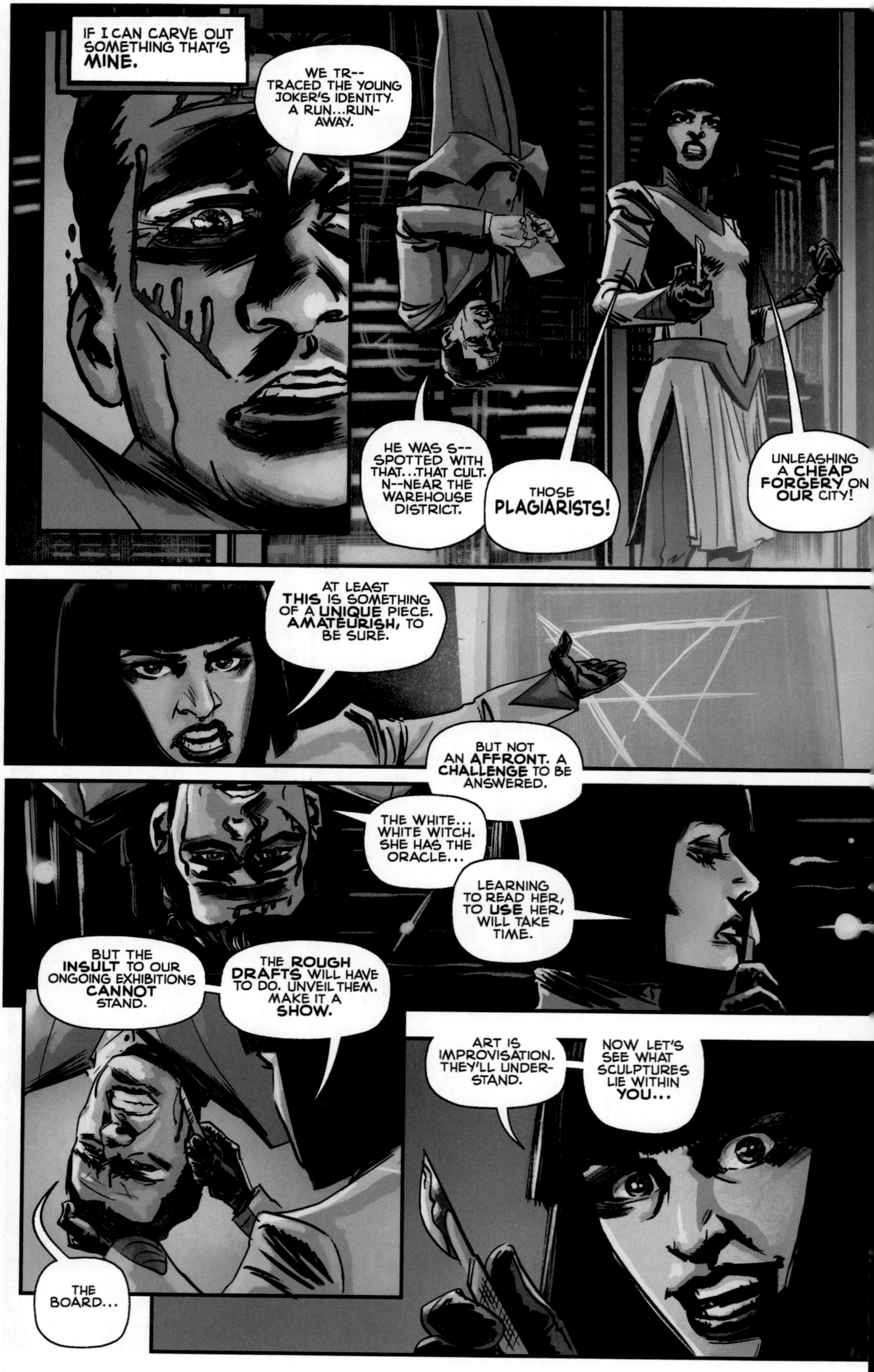
IF I CAN CARVE OUT SOMETHING THAT'S MINE.
WE TR-- TRACED THE YOUNG JOKER'S IDENTITY. A RUN...RUN-AWAY.
HE WAS S-- SPOTTED WITH THAT...THAT CULT. N--NEAR THE WAREHOUSE DISTRICT.
THOSE PLAGIARISTS!
UNLEASHING A CHEAP FORGERY ON OUR CITY!
AT LEAST THIS IS SOMETHING OF A UNIQUE PIECE. AMATEURISH, TO BE SURE.
BUT NOT AN AFFRONT. A CHALLENGE TO BE ANSWERED.
THE WHITE... WHITE WITCH. SHE HAS THE ORACLE...
LEARNING TO READ HER, TO USE HER, WILL TAKE TIME.
BUT THE INSULT TO OUR ONGOING EXHIBITIONS CANNOT STAND.
THE ROUGH DRAFTS WILL HAVE TO DO. UNVEIL THEM. MAKE IT A SHOW.
ART IS IMPROVISATION. THEY'LL UNDER-STAND.
NOW LET'S SEE WHAT SCULPTURES LIE WITHIN YOU...
THE BOARD...

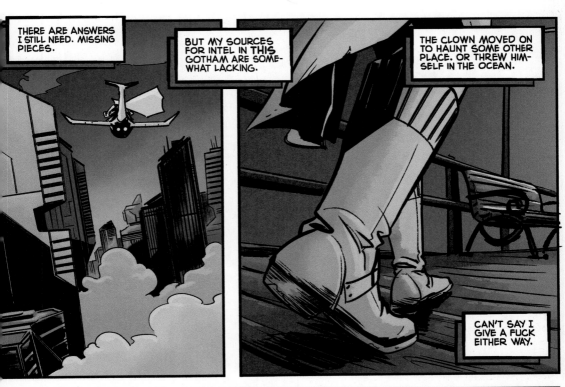

THERE ARE ANSWERS I STILL NEED. MISSING PIECES.

BUT MY SOURCES FOR INTEL IN **THIS** GOTHAM ARE SOMEWHAT LACKING.

THE CLOWN MOVED ON TO HAUNT SOME OTHER PLACE. OR THREW HIMSELF IN THE OCEAN.

CAN'T SAY I GIVE A FUCK EITHER WAY.

SO I'M RISKING THE PARK. THEY MADE IT CLEAR THAT THEY DIDN'T WANT ME COMING BACK.

BUT I'M LOW ON OPTIONS.

PREFER TO DO THIS ALONE.

DO THE TREES HERE **REALLY EAT** PEOPLE?

ONLY BAD ONES.

BUT SHE'D HAVE FOUND A WAY TO FOLLOW IF I'D LEFT HER BEHIND.

I'M NOT BAD.

I'M A HERO.

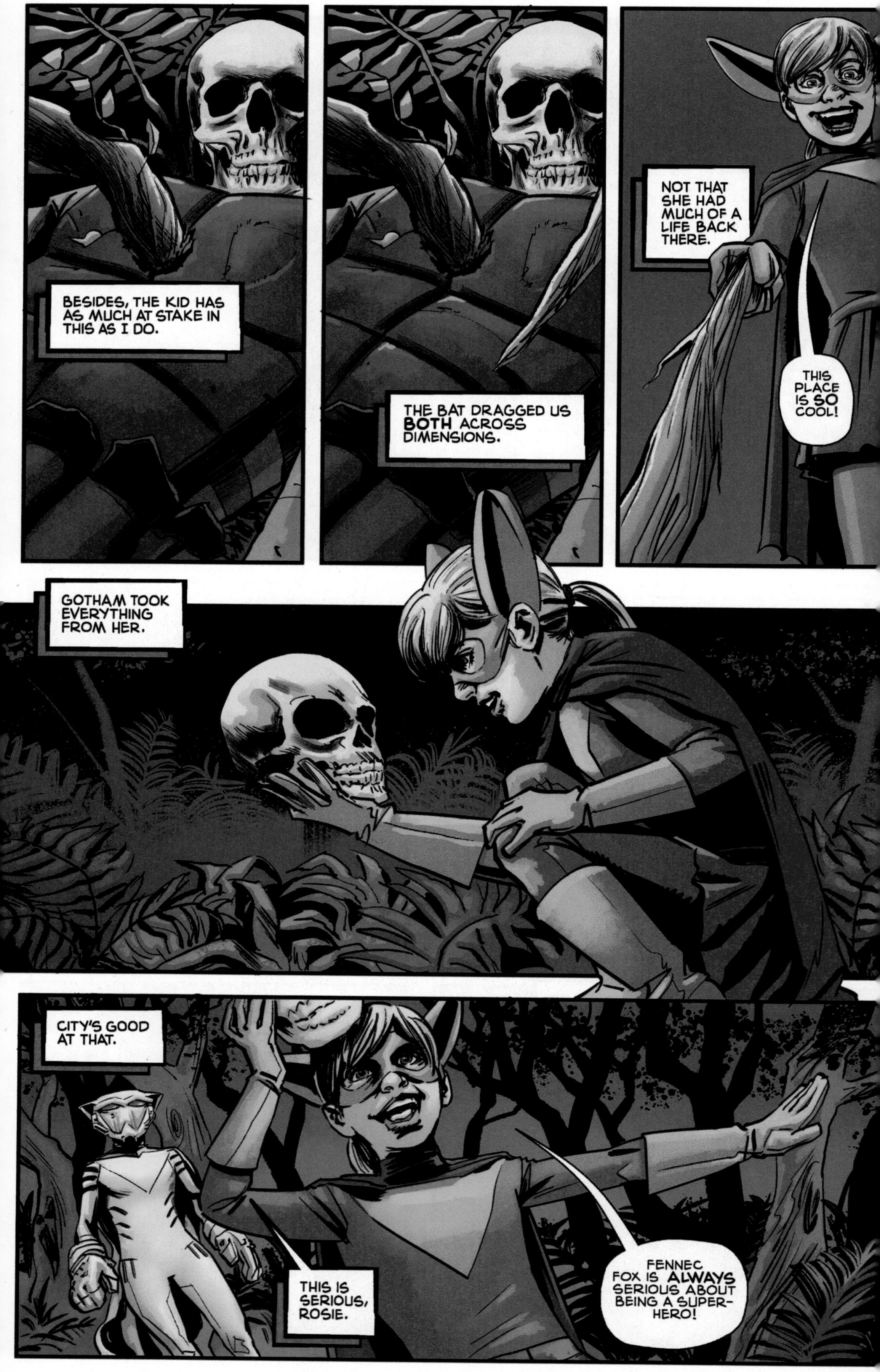

BESIDES, THE KID HAS AS MUCH AT STAKE IN THIS AS I DO.
THE BAT DRAGGED US BOTH ACROSS DIMENSIONS.
NOT THAT SHE HAD MUCH OF A LIFE BACK THERE.
THIS PLACE IS SO COOL!
GOTHAM TOOK EVERYTHING FROM HER.
CITY'S GOOD AT THAT.
THIS IS SERIOUS, ROSIE.
FENNEC FOX IS ALWAYS SERIOUS ABOUT BEING A SUPER-HERO!

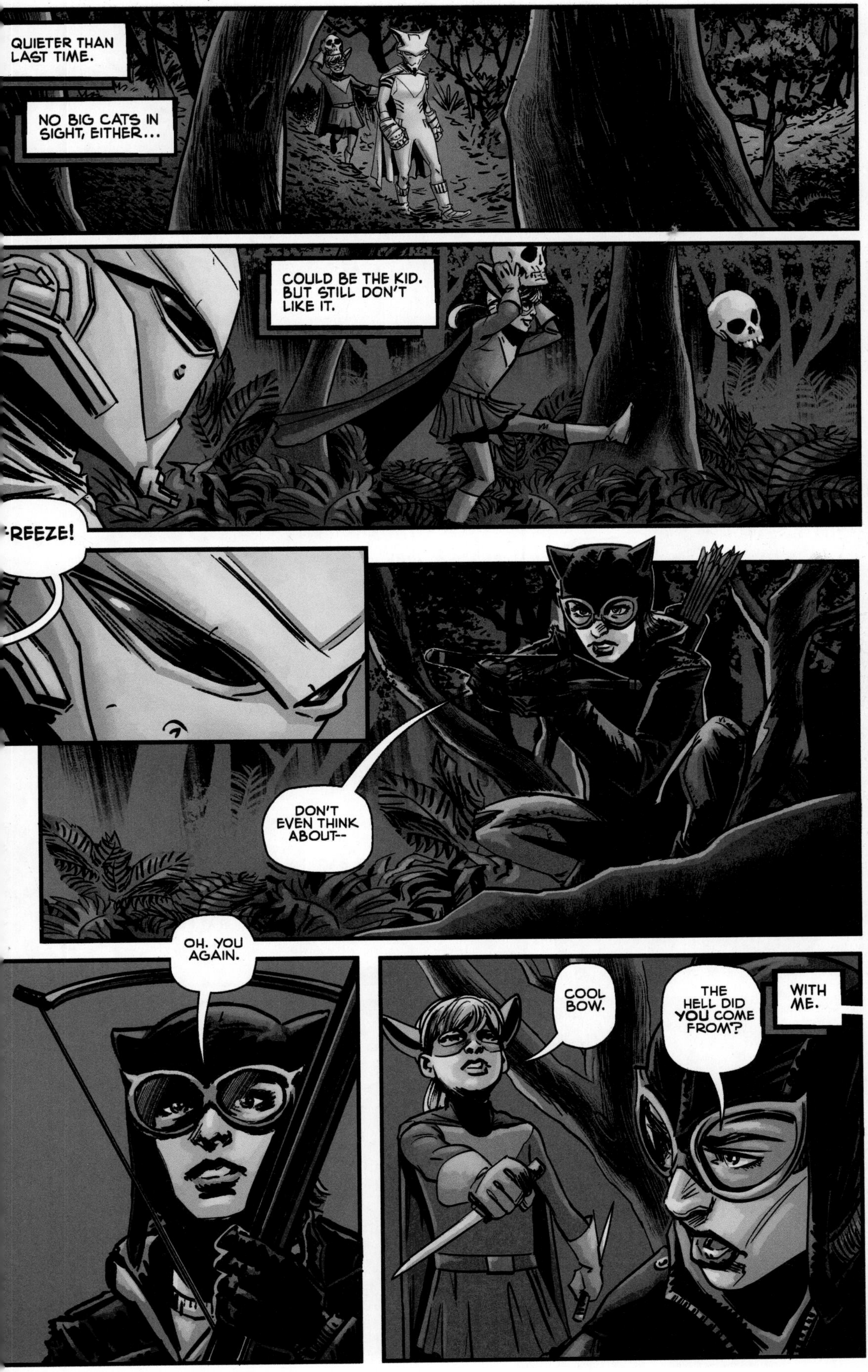

QUIETER THAN LAST TIME.
NO BIG CATS IN SIGHT, EITHER...
COULD BE THE KID. BUT STILL DON'T LIKE IT.
FREEZE!
DON'T EVEN THINK ABOUT--
OH. YOU AGAIN.
COOL BOW.
THE HELL DID YOU COME FROM?
WITH ME.

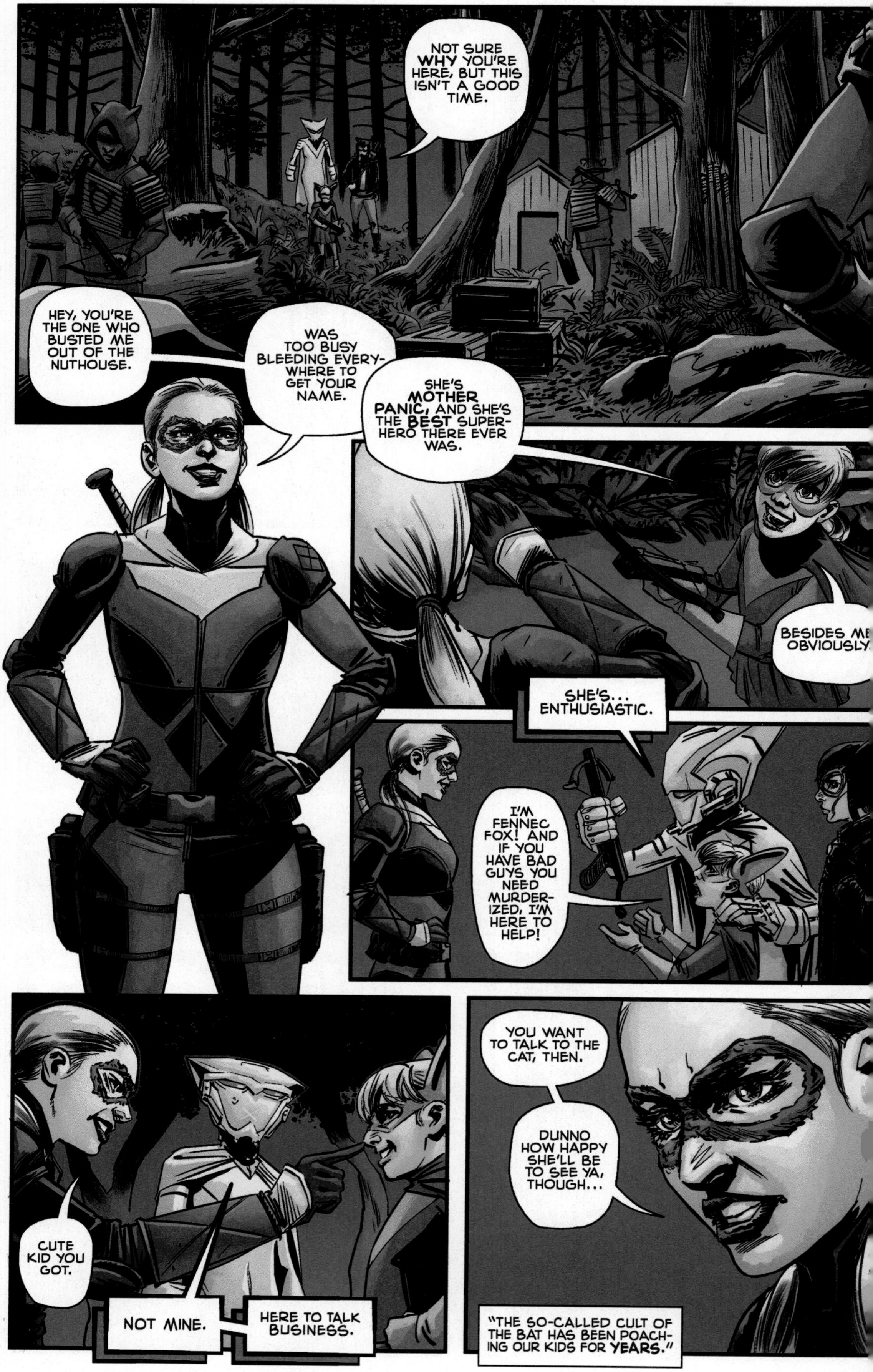
NOT SURE WHY YOU'RE HERE, BUT THIS ISN'T A GOOD TIME.
HEY, YOU'RE THE ONE WHO BUSTED ME OUT OF THE NUTHOUSE.
WAS TOO BUSY BLEEDING EVERYWHERE TO GET YOUR NAME.
SHE'S MOTHER PANIC, AND SHE'S THE BEST SUPERHERO THERE EVER WAS.
BESIDES ME OBVIOUSLY.
SHE'S... ENTHUSIASTIC.
I'M FENNEC FOX! AND IF YOU HAVE BAD GUYS YOU NEED MURDERIZED, I'M HERE TO HELP!
CUTE KID YOU GOT.
NOT MINE.
HERE TO TALK BUSINESS.
YOU WANT TO TALK TO THE CAT, THEN.
DUNNO HOW HAPPY SHE'LL BE TO SEE YA, THOUGH...
"THE SO-CALLED CULT OF THE BAT HAS BEEN POACHING OUR KIDS FOR YEARS."

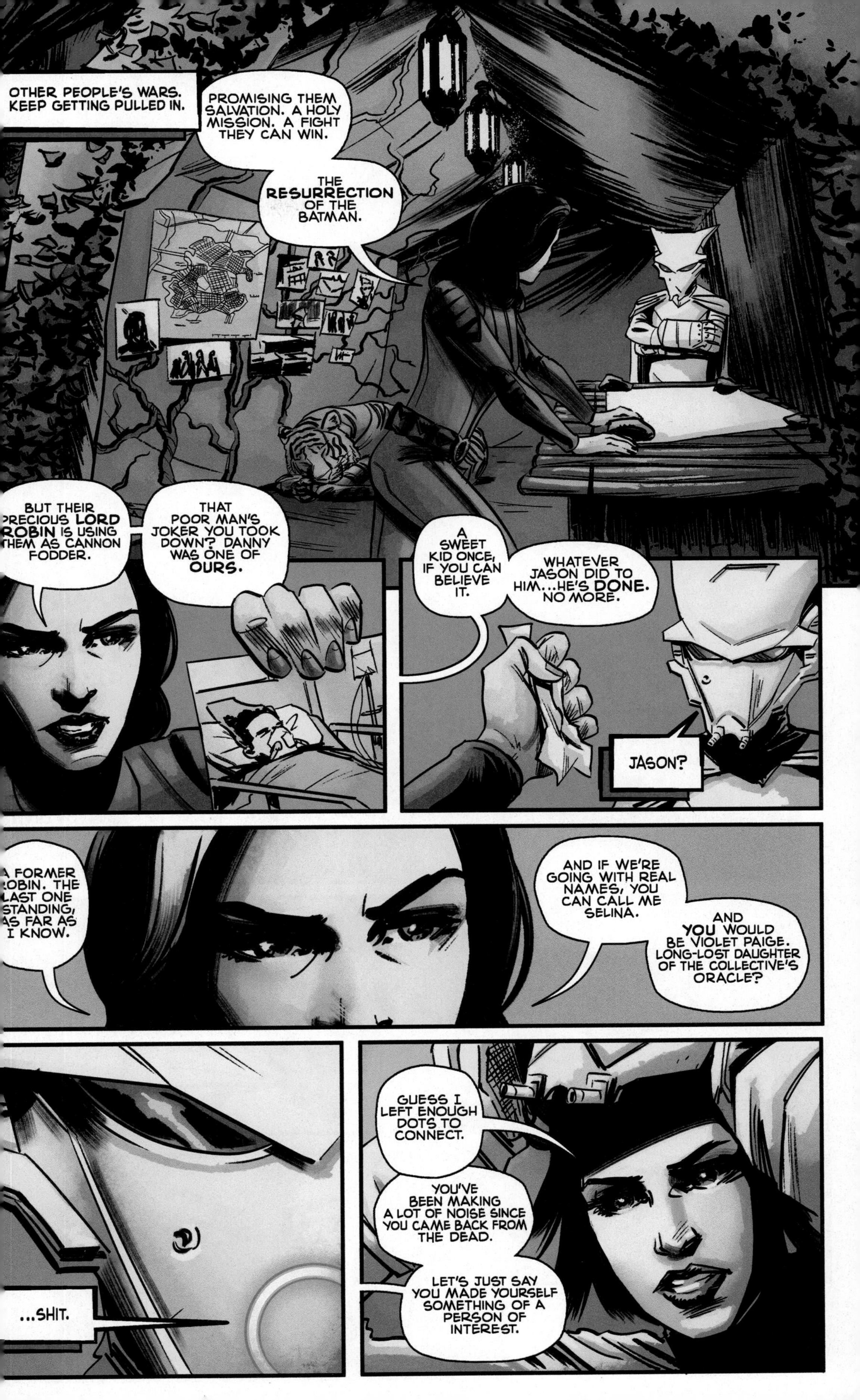

OTHER PEOPLE'S WARS. KEEP GETTING PULLED IN.
PROMISING THEM SALVATION. A HOLY MISSION. A FIGHT THEY CAN WIN.
THE RESURRECTION OF THE BATMAN.
BUT THEIR PRECIOUS LORD ROBIN IS USING THEM AS CANNON FODDER.
THAT POOR MAN'S JOKER YOU TOOK DOWN? DANNY WAS ONE OF OURS.
A SWEET KID ONCE, IF YOU CAN BELIEVE IT.
WHATEVER JASON DID TO HIM...HE'S DONE. NO MORE.
JASON?
A FORMER ROBIN. THE LAST ONE STANDING, AS FAR AS I KNOW.
AND IF WE'RE GOING WITH REAL NAMES, YOU CAN CALL ME SELINA.
AND YOU WOULD BE VIOLET PAIGE. LONG-LOST DAUGHTER OF THE COLLECTIVE'S ORACLE?
...SHIT.
GUESS I LEFT ENOUGH DOTS TO CONNECT.
YOU'VE BEEN MAKING A LOT OF NOISE SINCE YOU CAME BACK FROM THE DEAD.
LET'S JUST SAY YOU MADE YOURSELF SOMETHING OF A PERSON OF INTEREST.

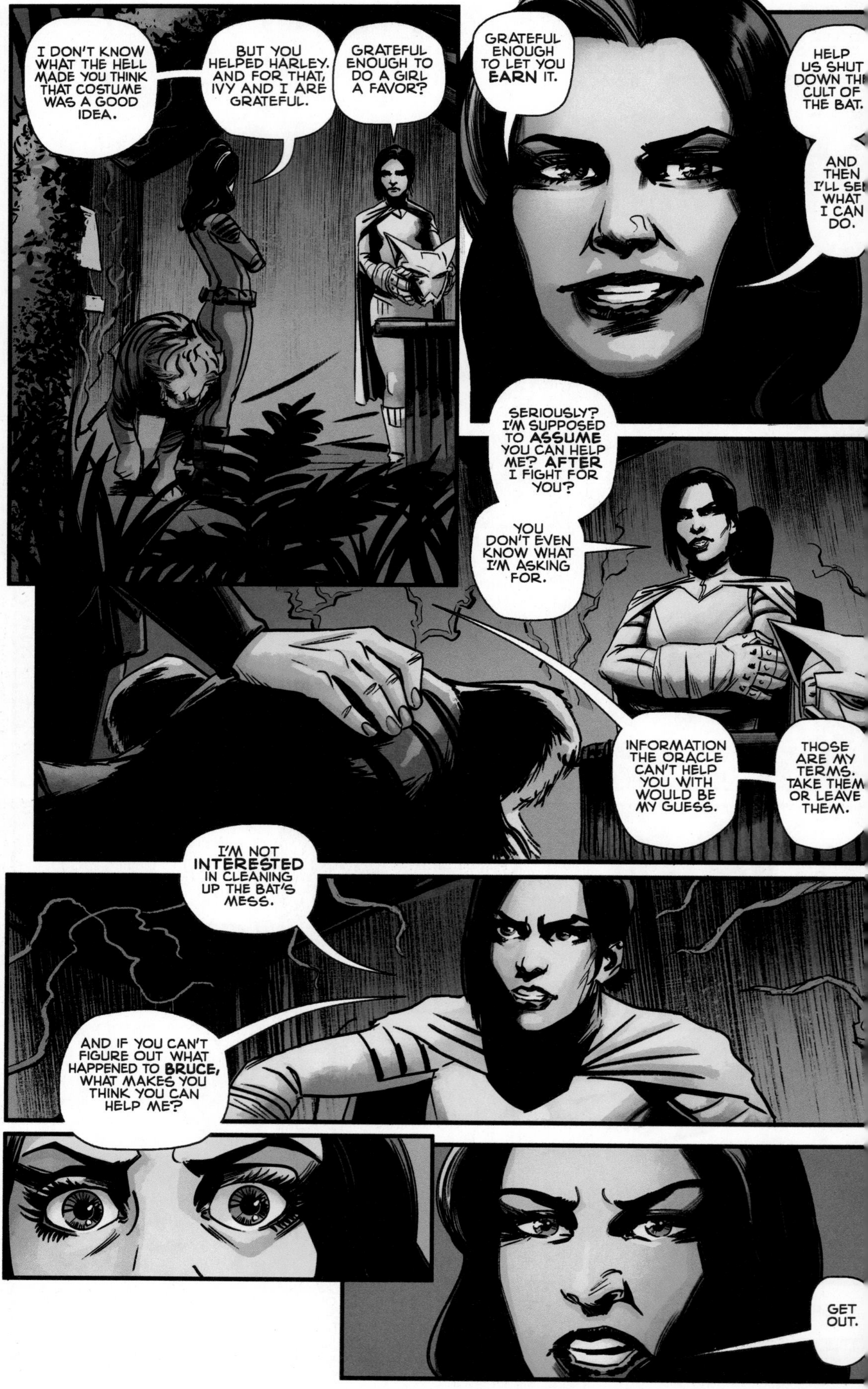
I DON'T KNOW WHAT THE HELL MADE YOU THINK THAT COSTUME WAS A GOOD IDEA.
BUT YOU HELPED HARLEY. AND FOR THAT, IVY AND I ARE GRATEFUL.
GRATEFUL ENOUGH TO DO A GIRL A FAVOR?
GRATEFUL ENOUGH TO LET YOU EARN IT.
HELP US SHUT DOWN TH CULT OF THE BAT.
AND THEN I'LL SE WHAT I CAN DO.
SERIOUSLY? I'M SUPPOSED TO ASSUME YOU CAN HELP ME? AFTER I FIGHT FOR YOU?
YOU DON'T EVEN KNOW WHAT I'M ASKING FOR.
INFORMATION THE ORACLE CAN'T HELP YOU WITH WOULD BE MY GUESS.
THOSE ARE MY TERMS. TAKE THEM OR LEAVE THEM.
I'M NOT INTERESTED IN CLEANING UP THE BAT'S MESS.
AND IF YOU CAN'T FIGURE OUT WHAT HAPPENED TO BRUCE, WHAT MAKES YOU THINK YOU CAN HELP ME?
GET OUT.

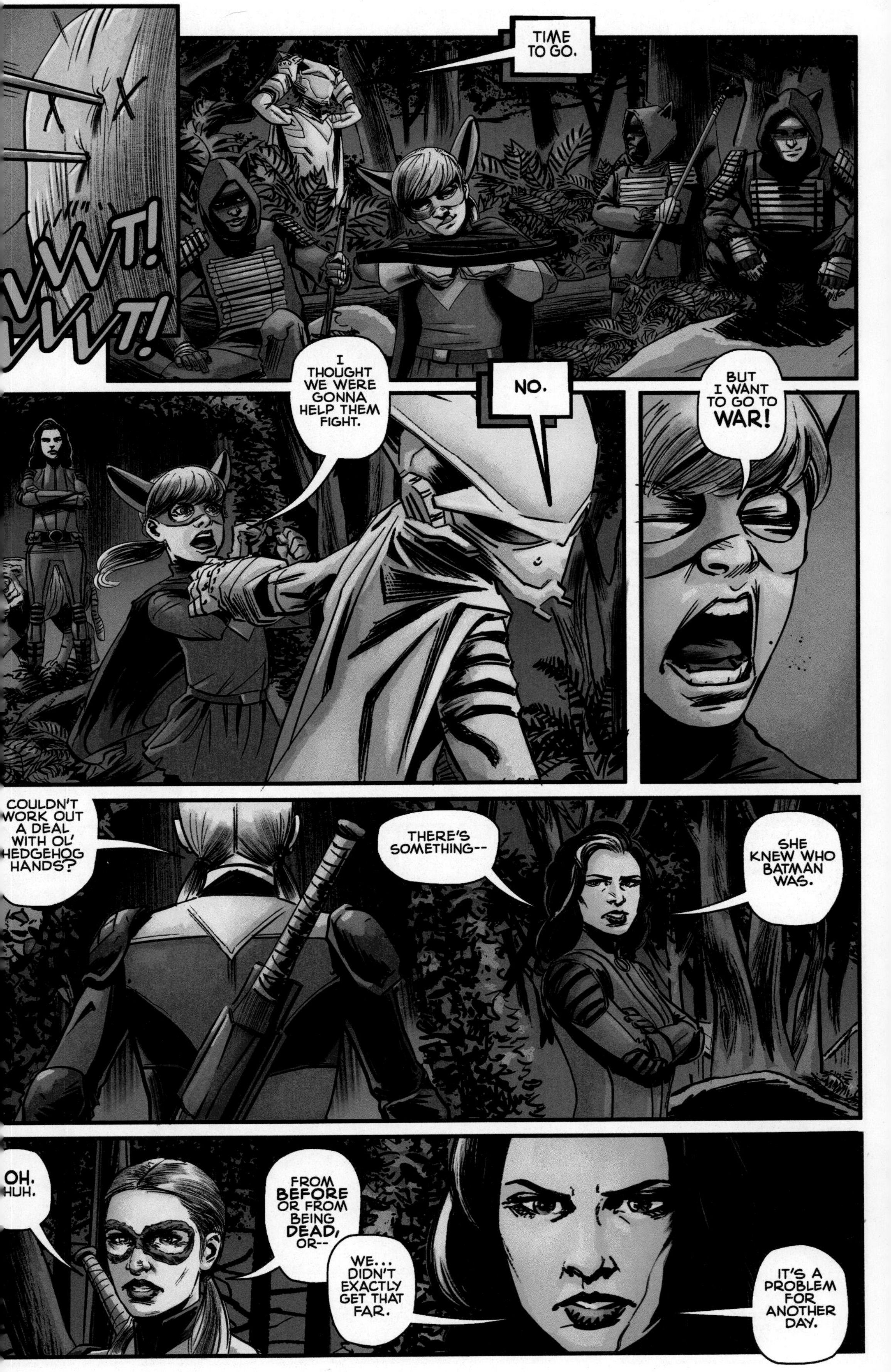
VVVT!
VVVT!
TIME TO GO.
I THOUGHT WE WERE GONNA HELP THEM FIGHT.
NO.
BUT I WANT TO GO TO WAR!
COULDN'T WORK OUT A DEAL WITH OL' HEDGEHOG HANDS?
THERE'S SOMETHING--
SHE KNEW WHO BATMAN WAS.
OH. HUH.
FROM BEFORE OR FROM BEING DEAD, OR--
WE... DIDN'T EXACTLY GET THAT FAR.
IT'S A PROBLEM FOR ANOTHER DAY.

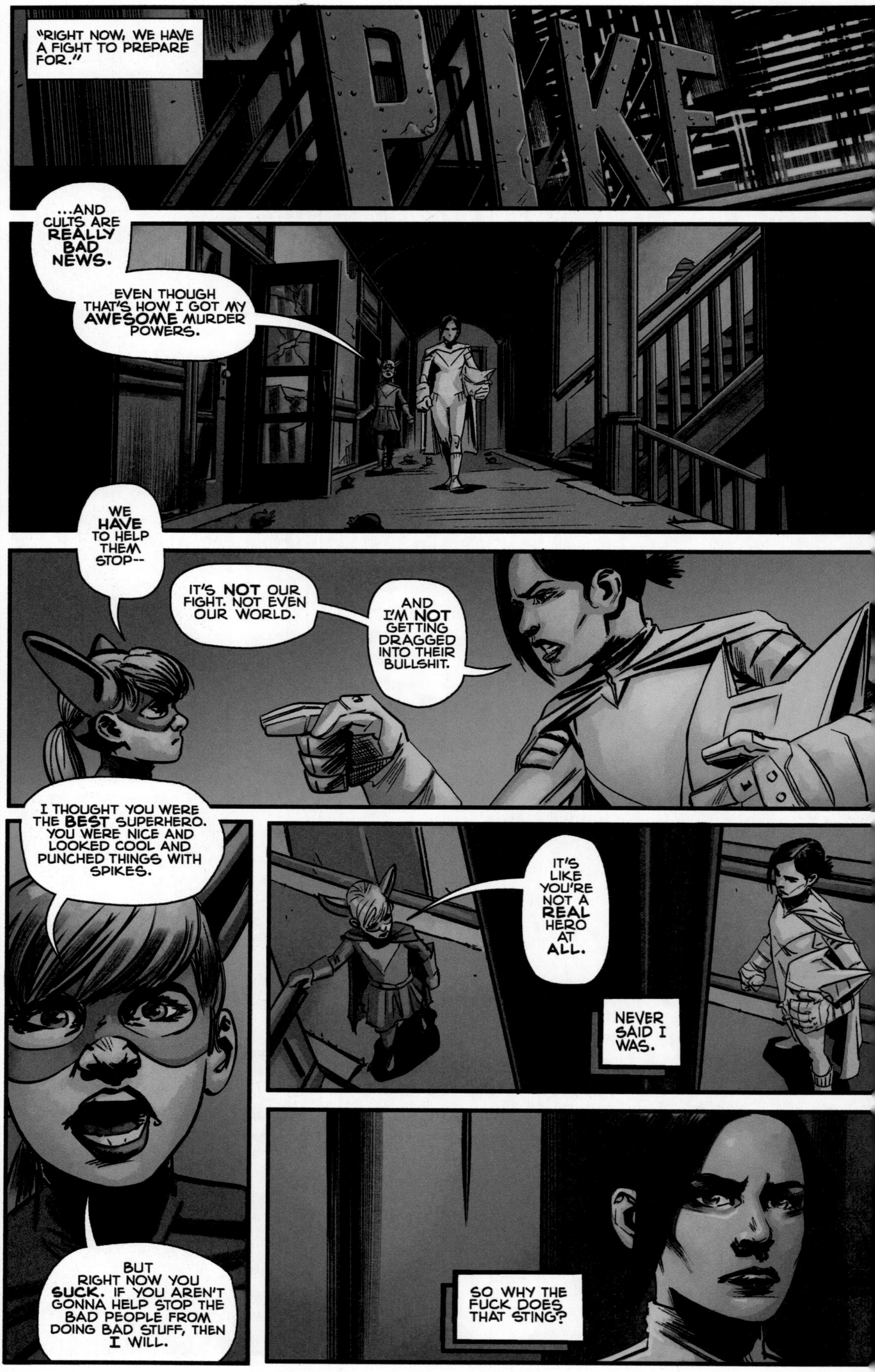

"RIGHT NOW, WE HAVE A FIGHT TO PREPARE FOR."
PIKE
...AND CULTS ARE REALLY BAD NEWS.
EVEN THOUGH THAT'S HOW I GOT MY AWESOME MURDER POWERS.
WE HAVE TO HELP THEM STOP--
IT'S NOT OUR FIGHT. NOT EVEN OUR WORLD.
AND I'M NOT GETTING DRAGGED INTO THEIR BULLSHIT.
I THOUGHT YOU WERE THE BEST SUPERHERO. YOU WERE NICE AND LOOKED COOL AND PUNCHED THINGS WITH SPIKES.
BUT RIGHT NOW YOU SUCK. IF YOU AREN'T GONNA HELP STOP THE BAD PEOPLE FROM DOING BAD STUFF, THEN I WILL.
IT'S LIKE YOU'RE NOT A REAL HERO AT ALL.
NEVER SAID I WAS.
SO WHY THE FUCK DOES THAT STING?

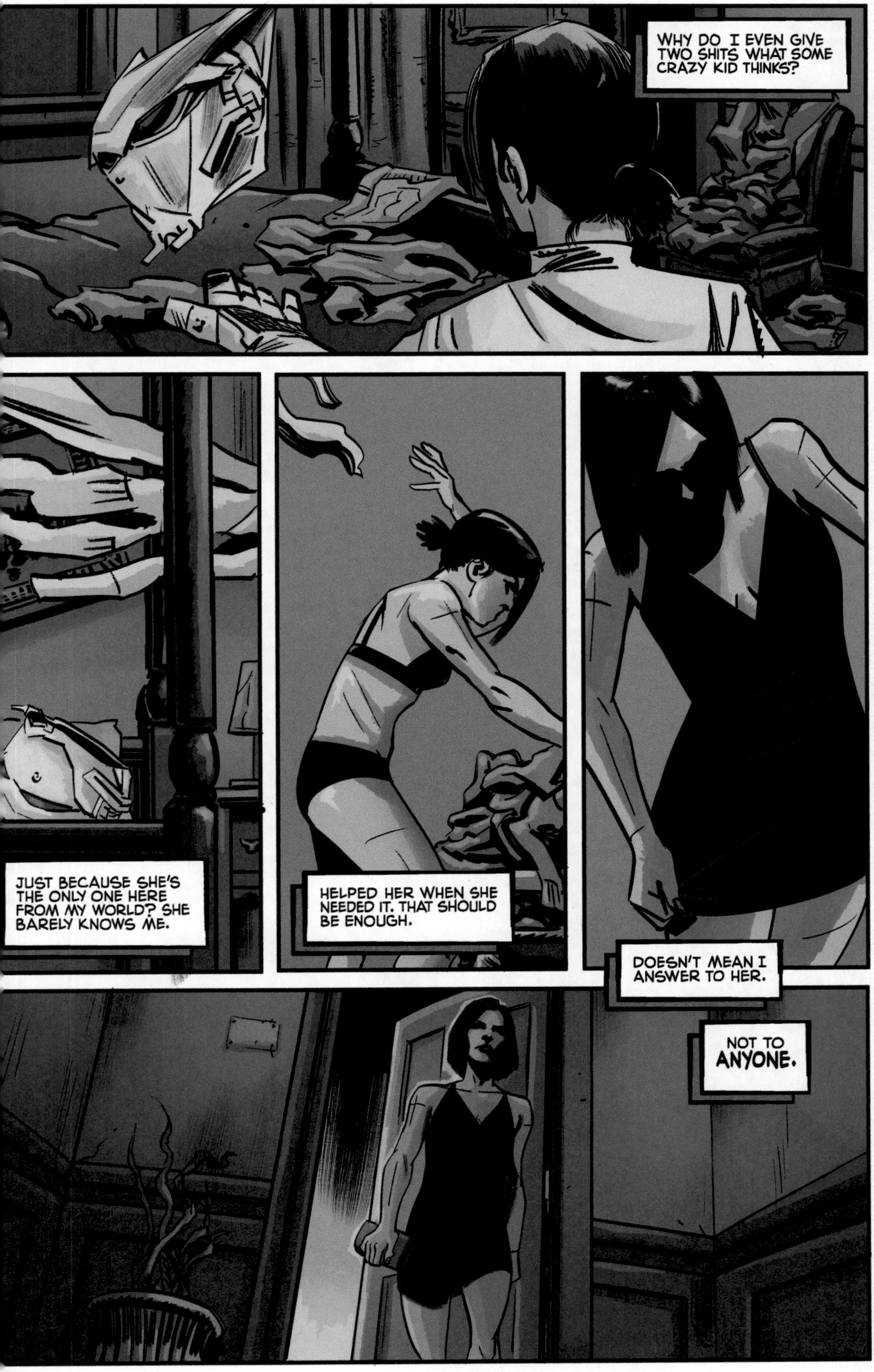
WHY DO I EVEN GIVE TWO SHITS WHAT SOME CRAZY KID THINKS?
JUST BECAUSE SHE'S THE ONLY ONE HERE FROM MY WORLD? SHE BARELY KNOWS ME.
HELPED HER WHEN SHE NEEDED IT. THAT SHOULD BE ENOUGH.
DOESN'T MEAN I ANSWER TO HER.
NOT TO ANYONE.

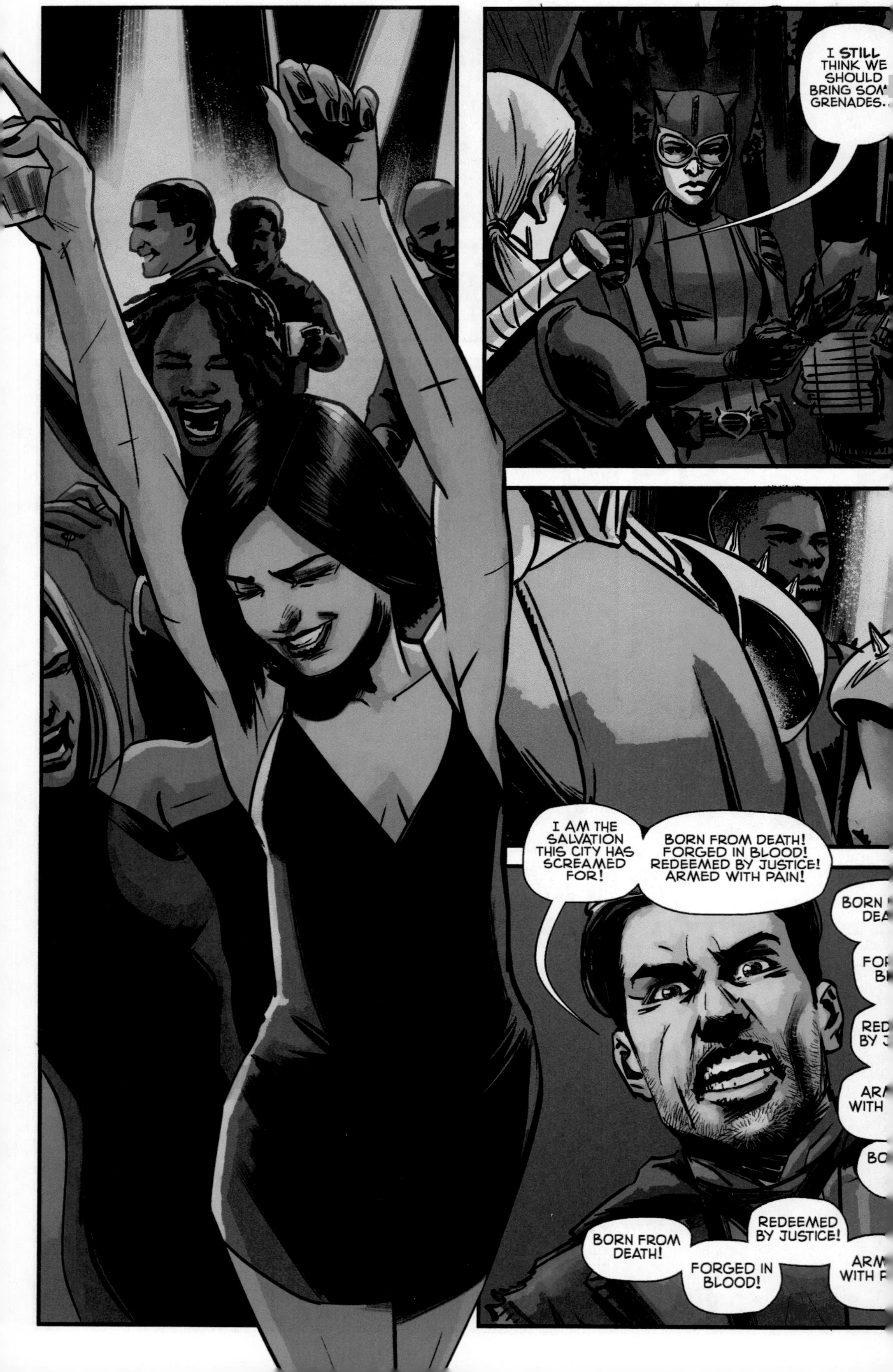

I STILL THINK WE SHOULD BRING SOM GRENADES...
I AM THE SALVATION THIS CITY HAS SCREAMED FOR!
BORN FROM DEATH! FORGED IN BLOOD! REDEEMED BY JUSTICE! ARMED WITH PAIN!
BORN FROM DEATH!
FORGED IN BLOOD!
REDEEMED BY JUSTICE!

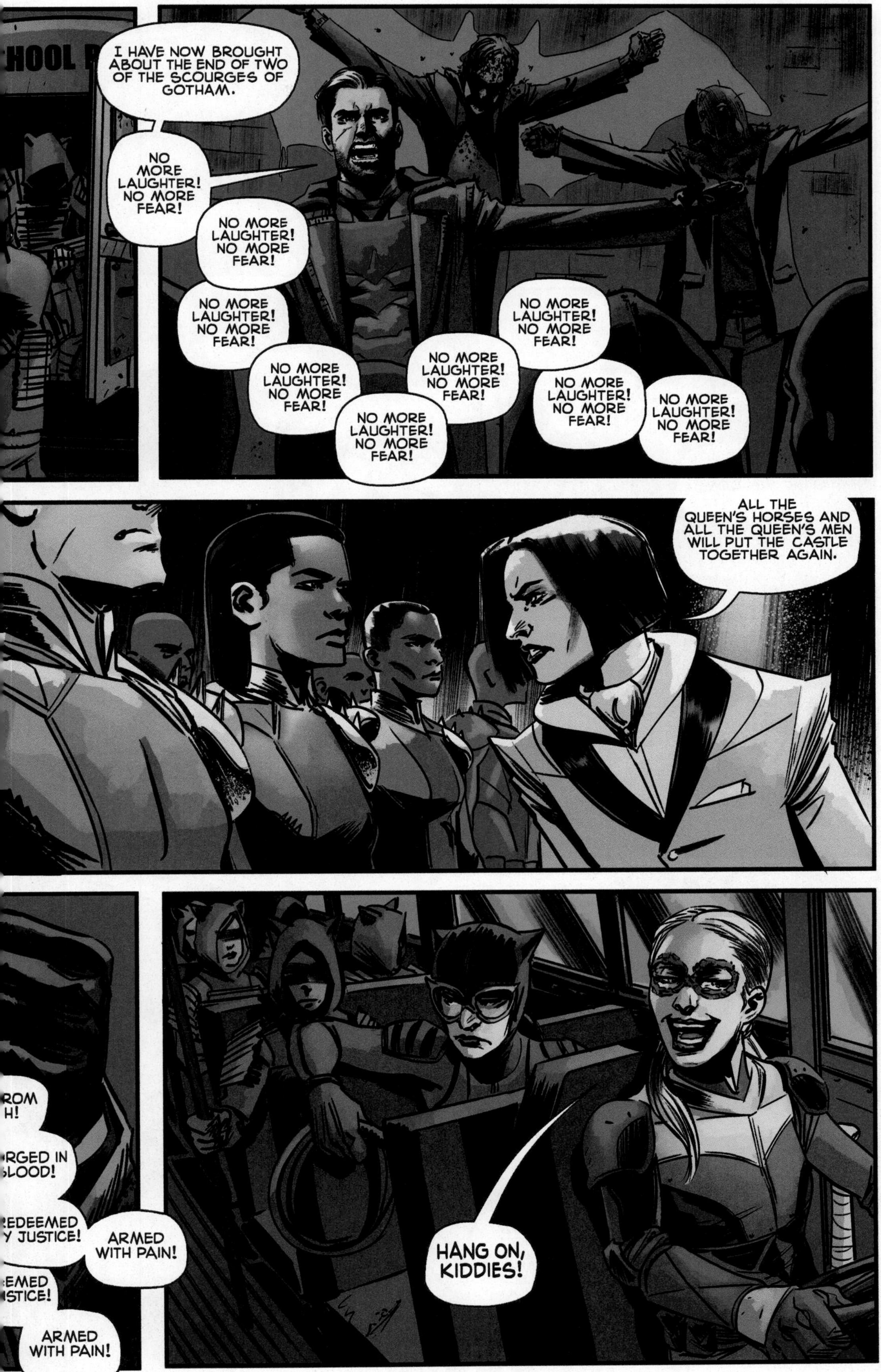

I HAVE NOW BROUGHT ABOUT THE END OF TWO OF THE SCOURGES OF GOTHAM.
NO MORE LAUGHTER! NO MORE FEAR!
NO MORE LAUGHTER! NO MORE FEAR!
NO MORE LAUGHTER! NO MORE FEAR!
NO MORE LAUGHTER! NO MORE FEAR!
NO MORE LAUGHTER! NO MORE FEAR!
NO MORE LAUGHTER! NO MORE FEAR!
NO MORE LAUGHTER! NO MORE FEAR!
NO MORE LAUGHTER! NO MORE FEAR!
NO MORE LAUGHTER! NO MORE FEAR!
ALL THE QUEEN'S HORSES AND ALL THE QUEEN'S MEN WILL PUT THE CASTLE TOGETHER AGAIN.
ARMED WITH PAIN!
ARMED WITH PAIN!
HANG ON, KIDDIES!

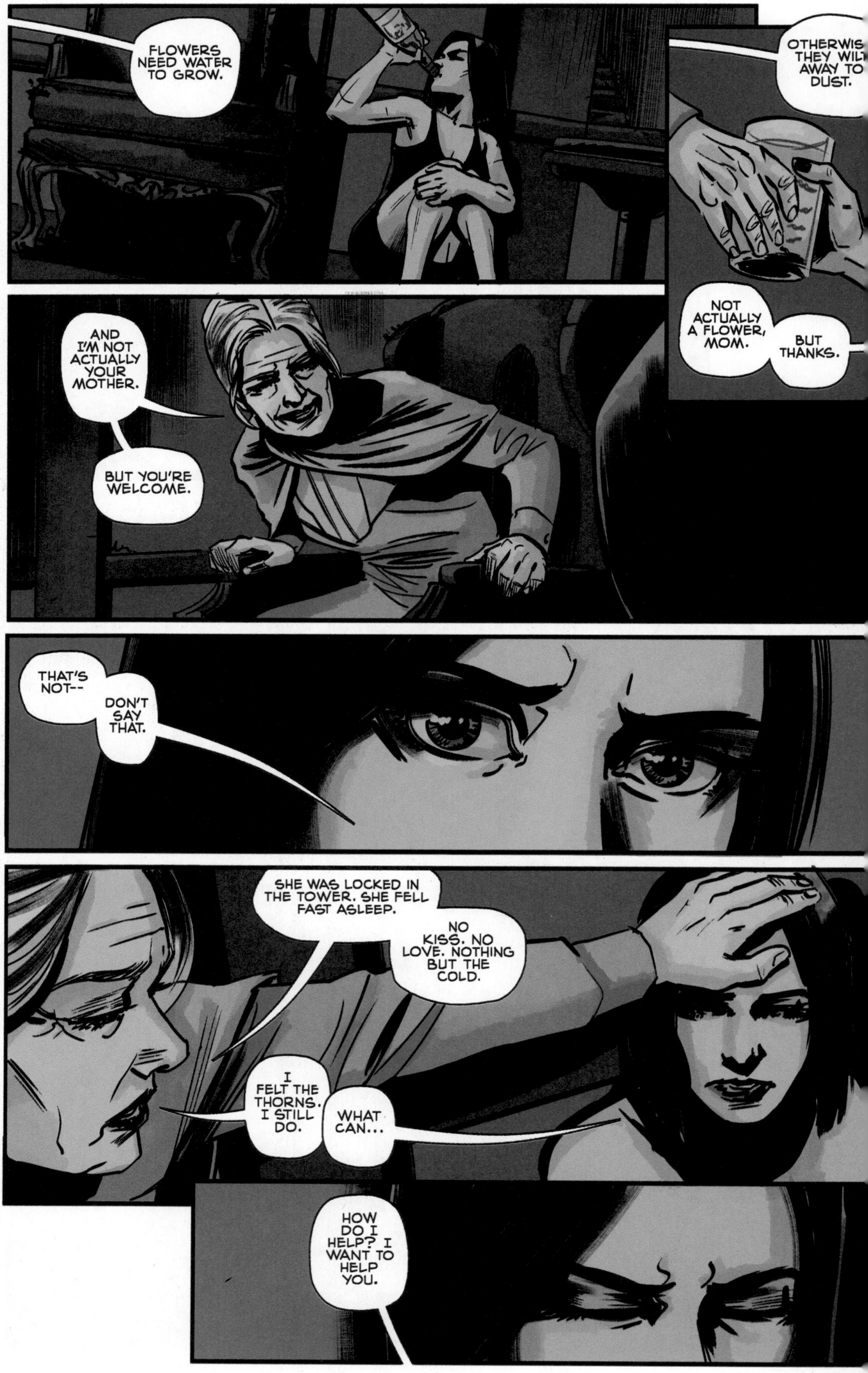
FLOWERS NEED WATER TO GROW.
OTHERWIS THEY WIL AWAY TO DUST.
NOT ACTUALLY A FLOWER, MOM.
BUT THANKS.
AND I'M NOT ACTUALLY YOUR MOTHER.
BUT YOU'RE WELCOME.
THAT'S NOT--
DON'T SAY THAT.
SHE WAS LOCKED IN THE TOWER. SHE FELL FAST ASLEEP.
NO KISS. NO LOVE. NOTHING BUT THE COLD.
I FELT THE THORNS. I STILL DO.
WHAT CAN...
HOW DO I HELP? I WANT TO HELP YOU.

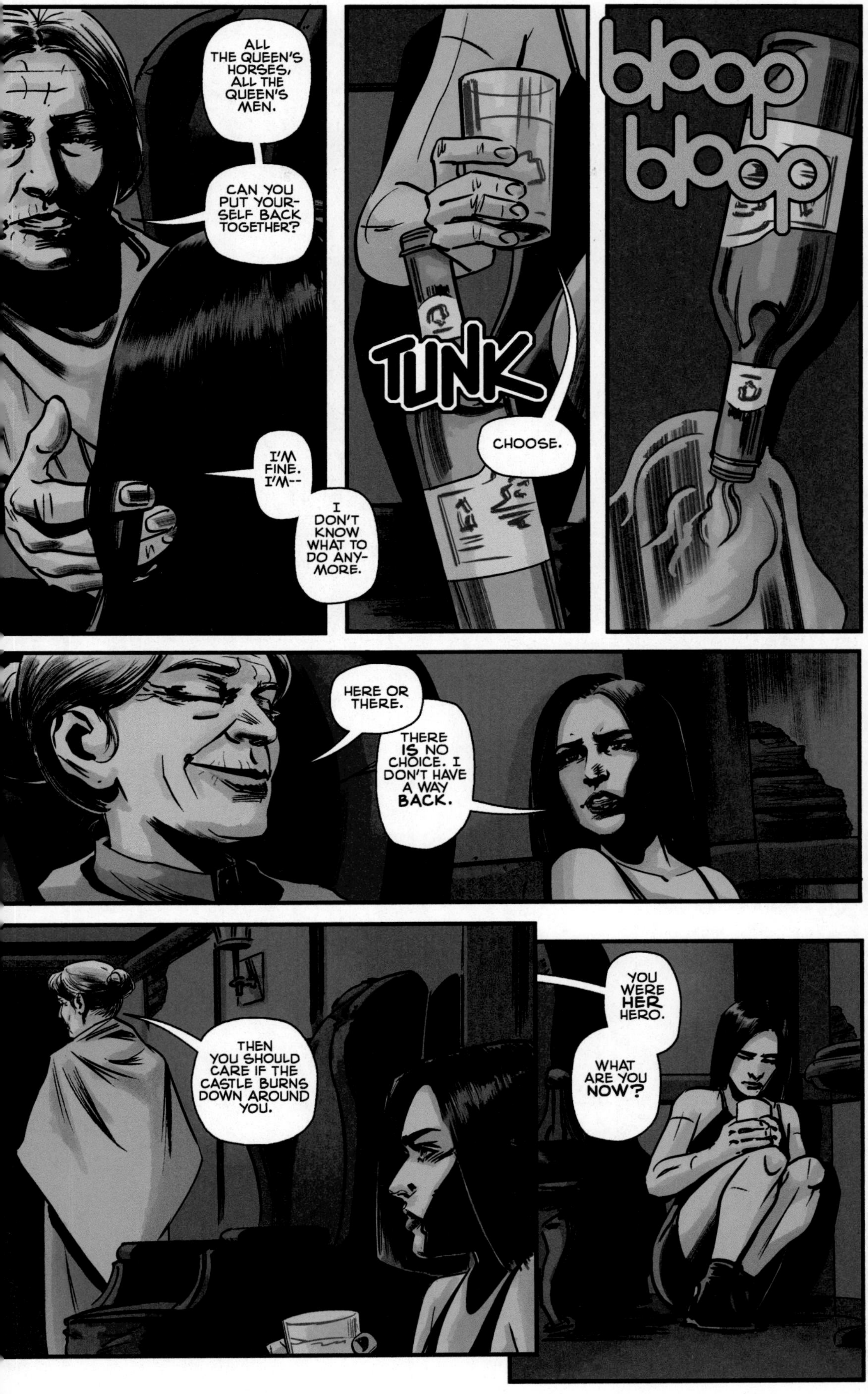
ALL THE QUEEN'S HORSES, ALL THE QUEEN'S MEN.
CAN YOU PUT YOURSELF BACK TOGETHER?
I'M FINE. I'M--
I DON'T KNOW WHAT TO DO ANYMORE.
TUNK
CHOOSE.
bloop bloop
HERE OR THERE.
THERE IS NO CHOICE. I DON'T HAVE A WAY BACK.
THEN YOU SHOULD CARE IF THE CASTLE BURNS DOWN AROUND YOU.
YOU WERE HER HERO.
WHAT ARE YOU NOW?

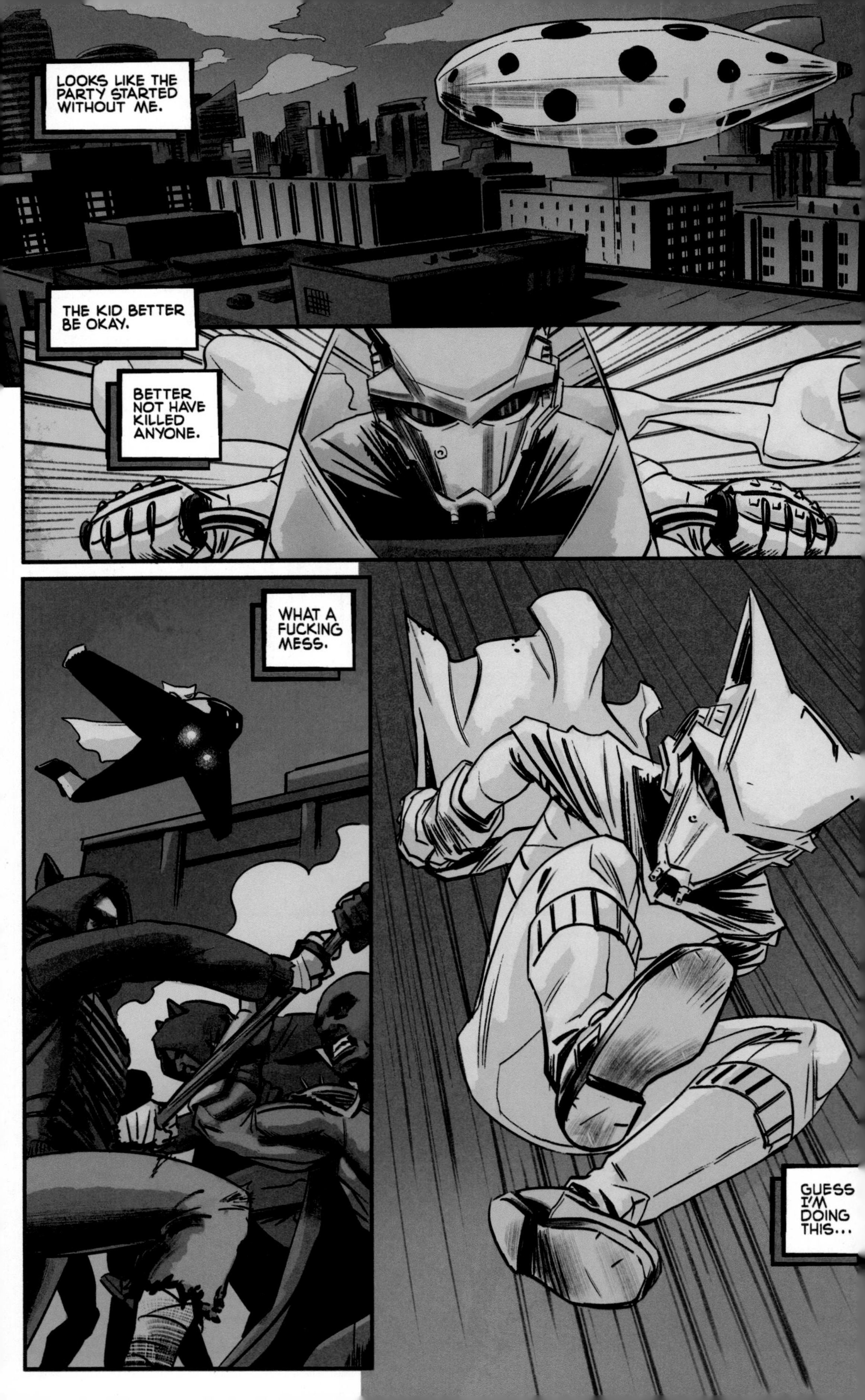
LOOKS LIKE THE PARTY STARTED WITHOUT ME.
THE KID BETTER BE OKAY.
BETTER NOT HAVE KILLED ANYONE.
WHAT A FUCKING MESS.
GUESS I'M DOING THIS...

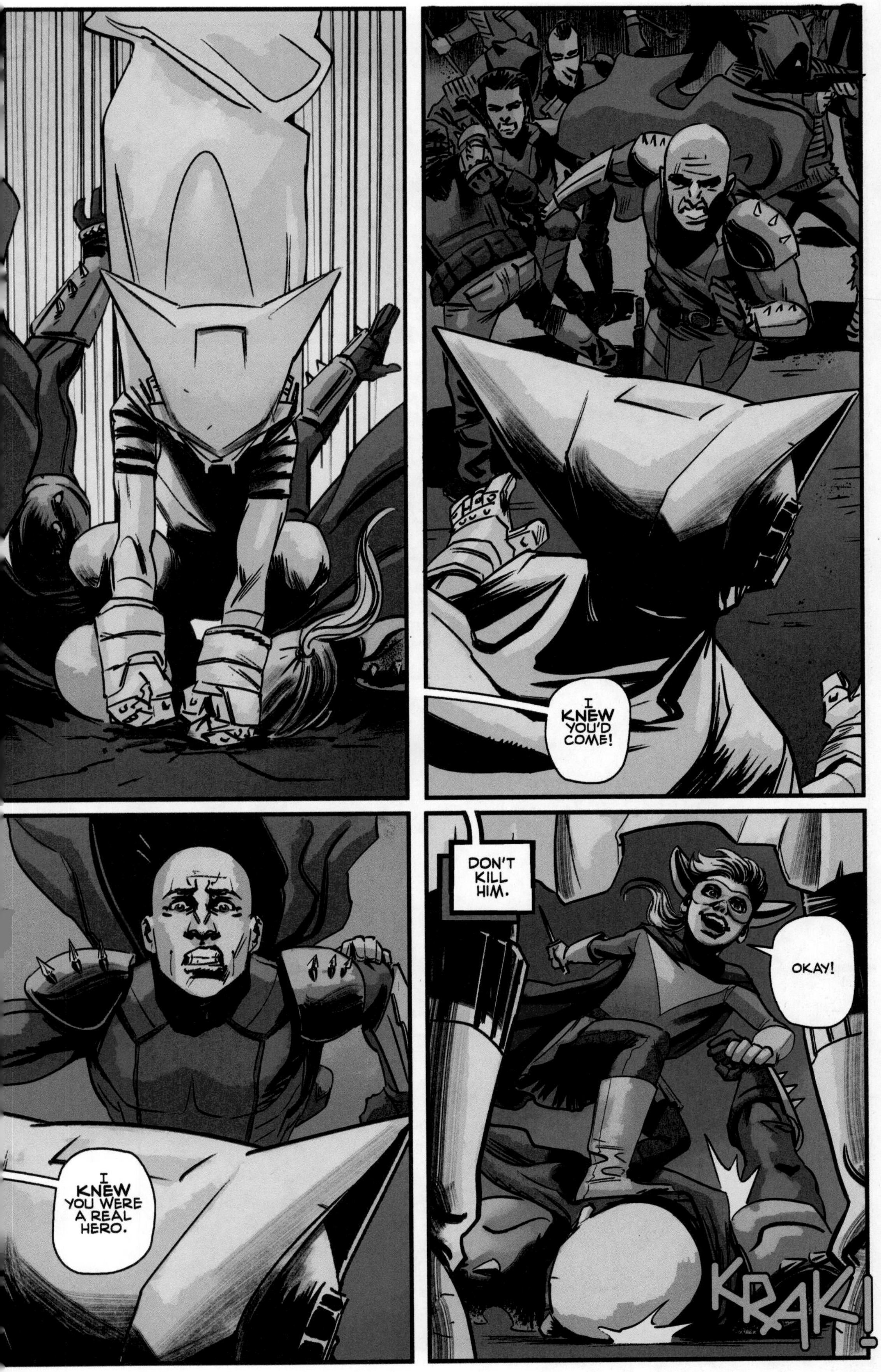
I KNEW YOU'D COME!
I KNEW YOU WERE A REAL HERO.
DON'T KILL HIM.
OKAY!
KRAK!

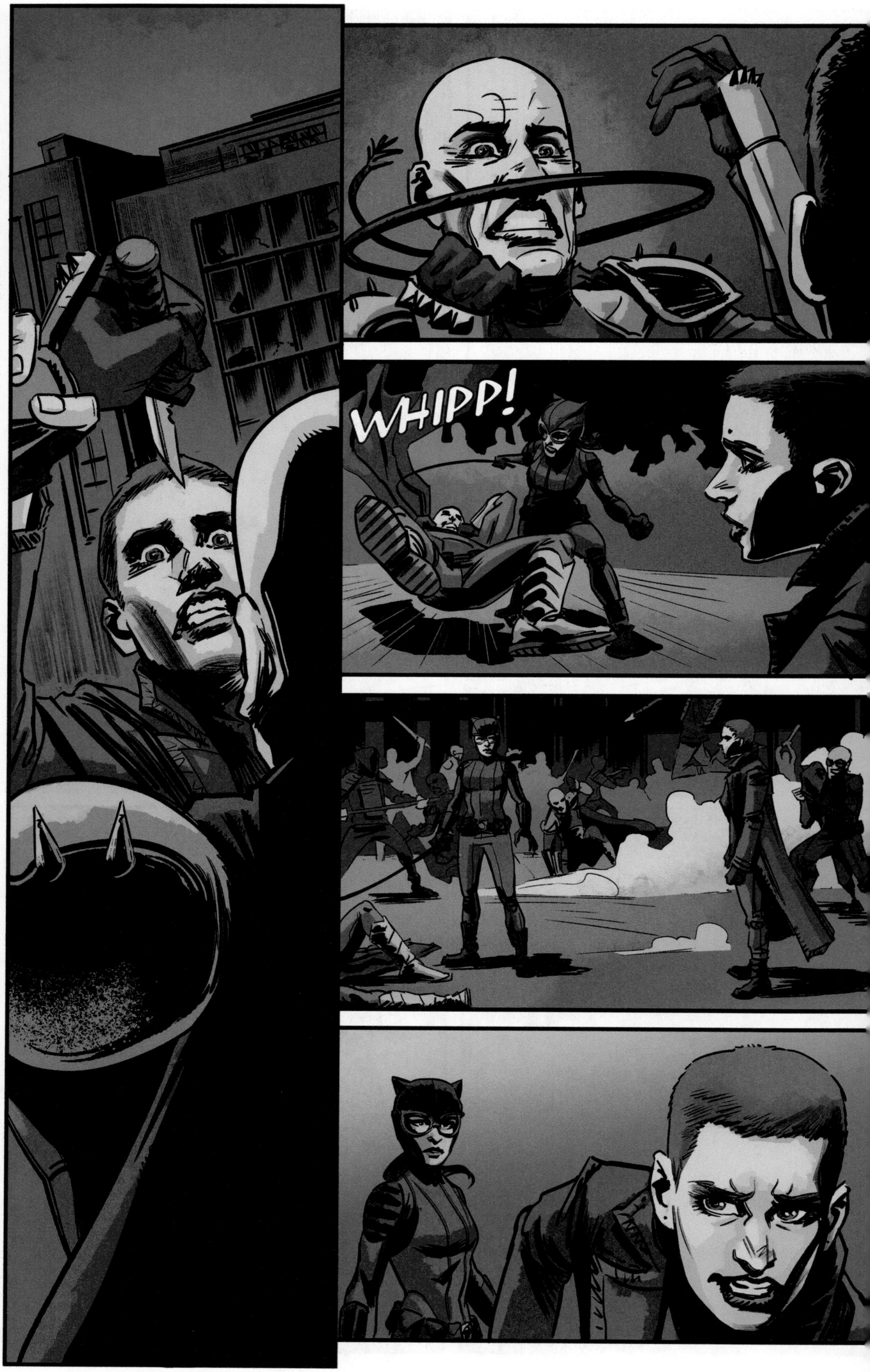
WHIPP!

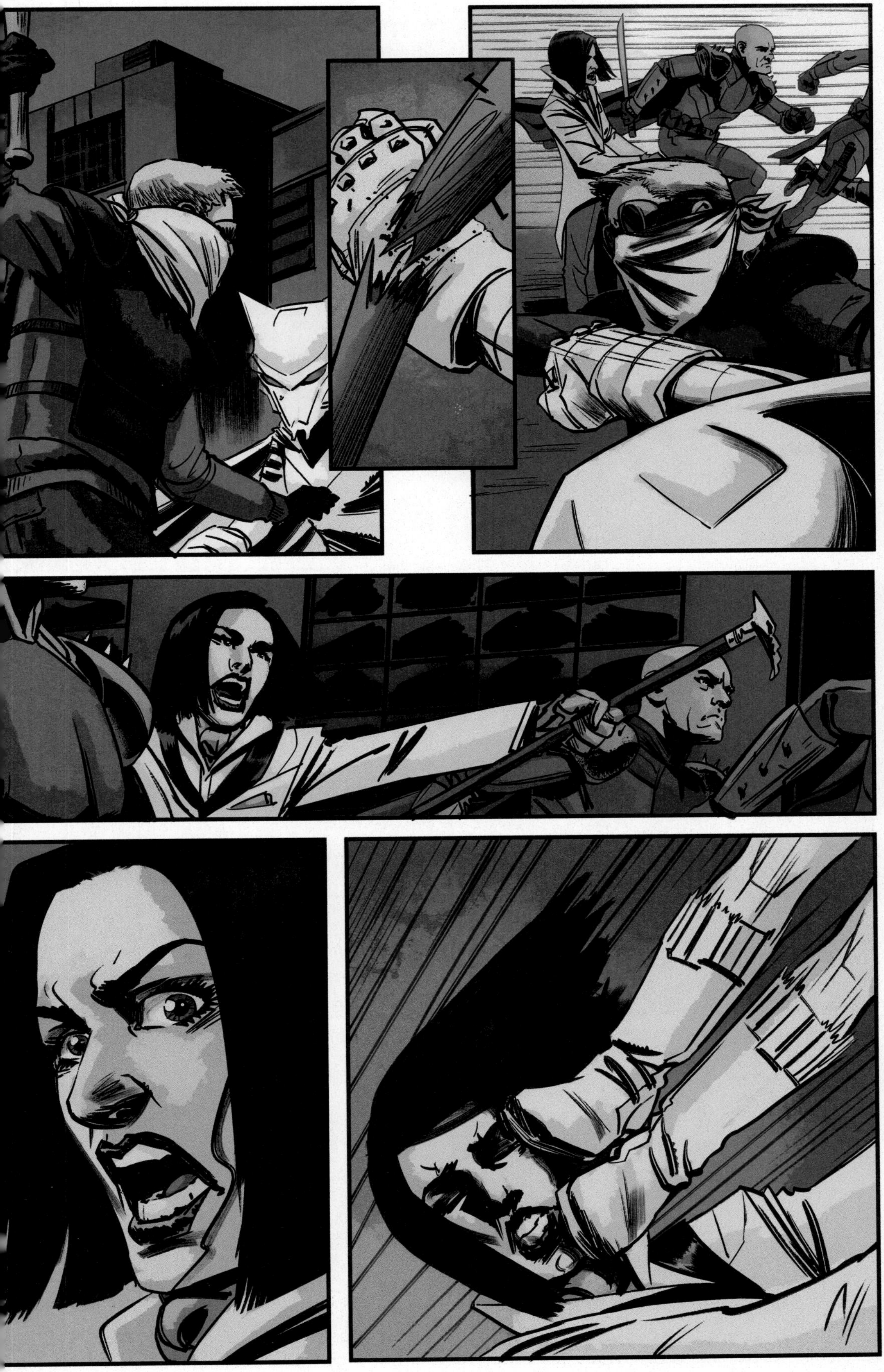

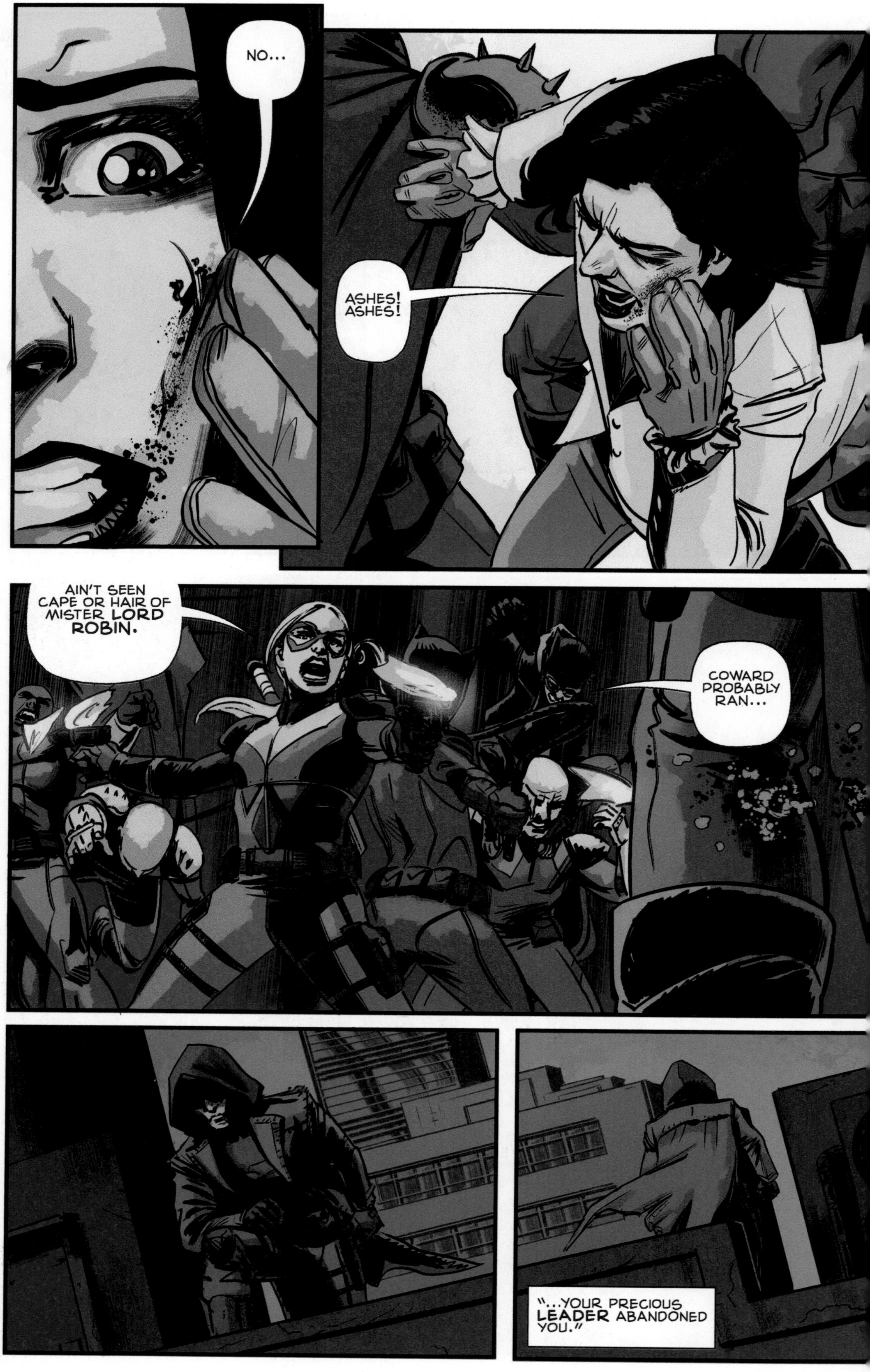
NO...
ASHES! ASHES!
AIN'T SEEN CAPE OR HAIR OF MISTER LORD ROBIN.
COWARD PROBABLY RAN...
"...YOUR PRECIOUS LEADER ABANDONED YOU."

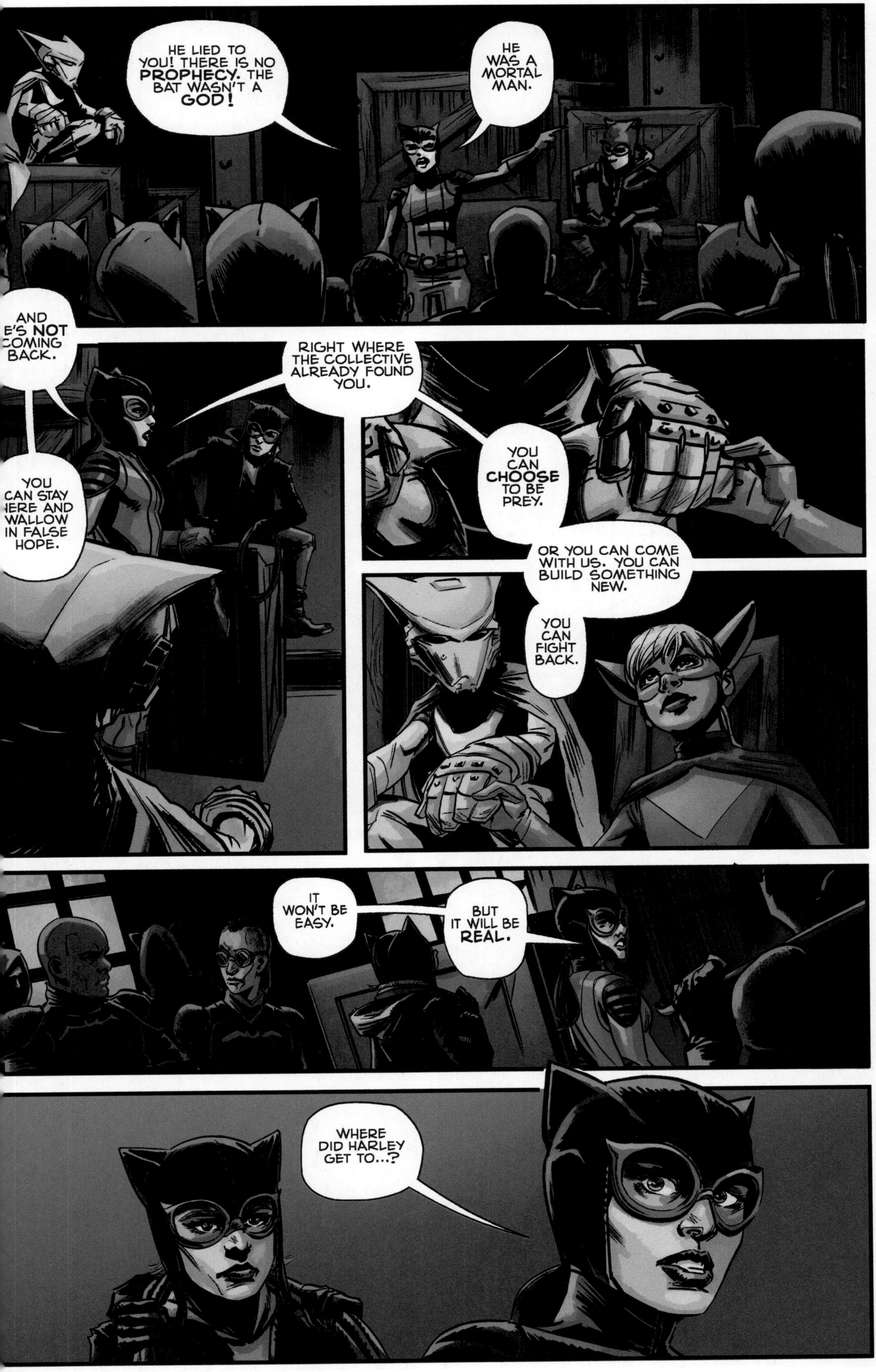
HE LIED TO YOU! THERE IS NO PROPHECY. THE BAT WASN'T A GOD!
HE WAS A MORTAL MAN.
AND E'S NOT COMING BACK.
YOU CAN STAY HERE AND WALLOW IN FALSE HOPE.
RIGHT WHERE THE COLLECTIVE ALREADY FOUND YOU.
YOU CAN CHOOSE TO BE PREY.
OR YOU CAN COME WITH US. YOU CAN BUILD SOMETHING NEW.
YOU CAN FIGHT BACK.
IT WON'T BE EASY.
BUT IT WILL BE REAL.
WHERE DID HARLEY GET TO...?

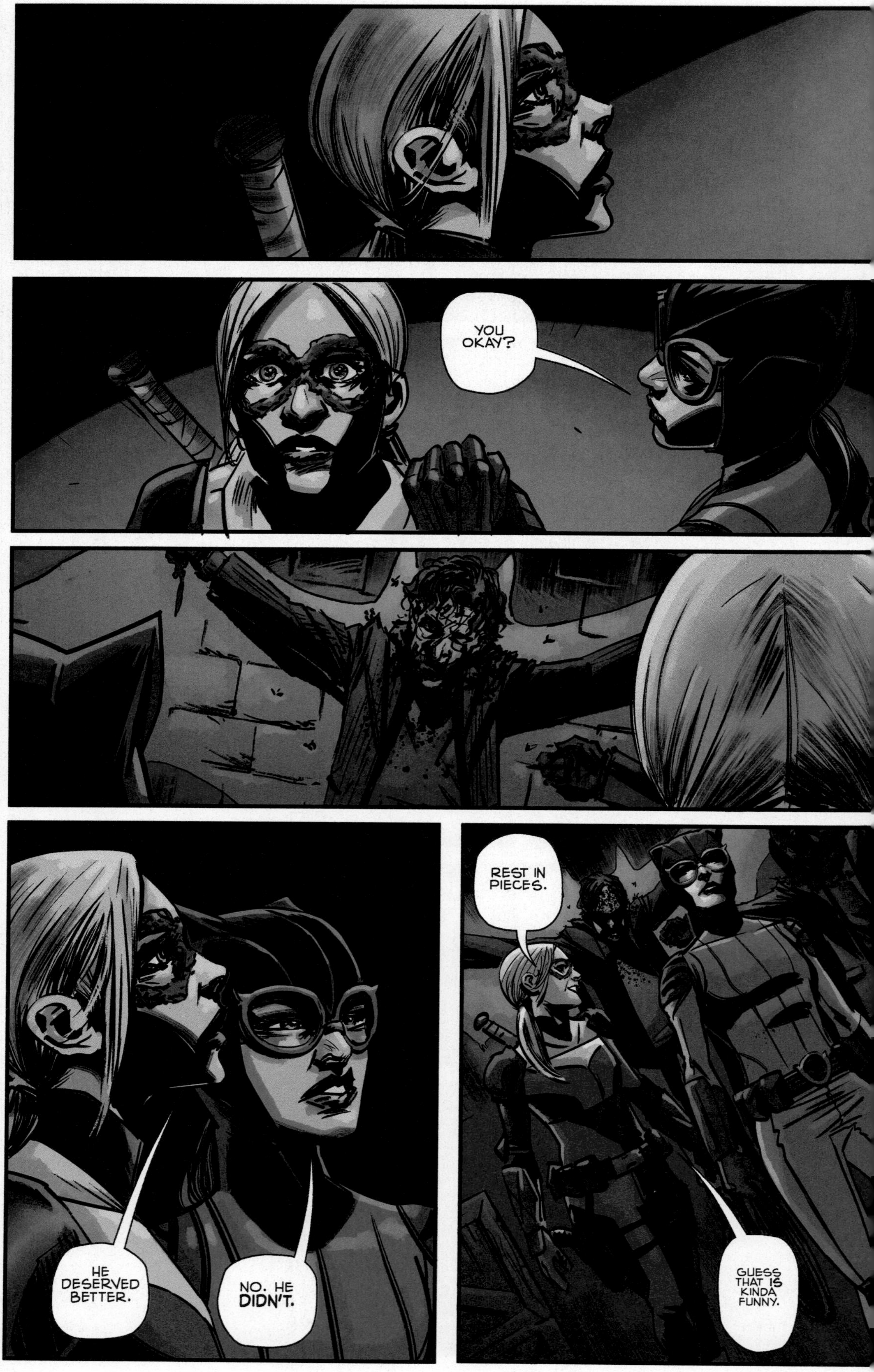
YOU OKAY?
HE DESERVED BETTER.
NO. HE DIDN'T.
REST IN PIECES.
GUESS THAT IS KINDA FUNNY.

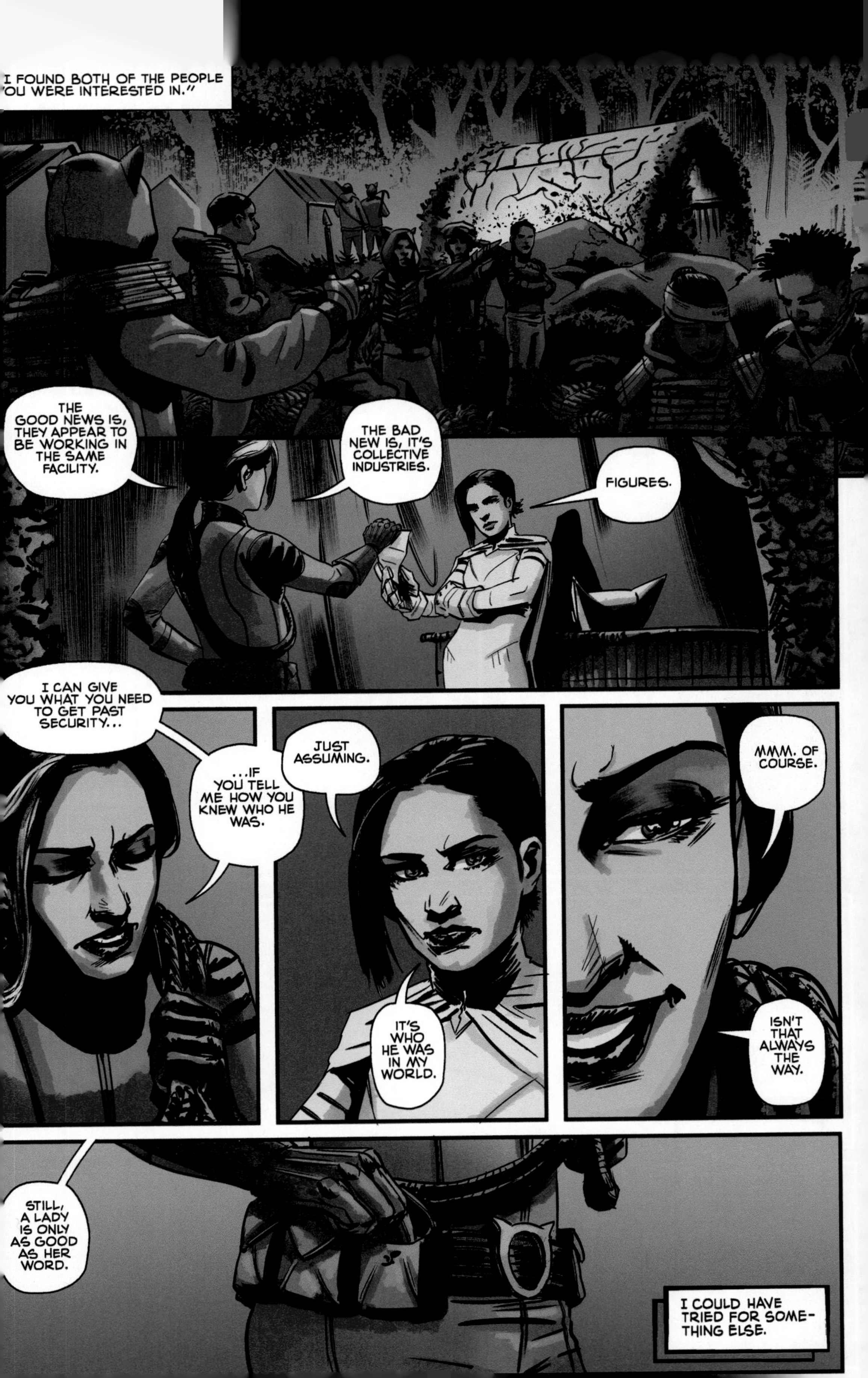
I FOUND BOTH OF THE PEOPLE
'OU WERE INTERESTED IN."
THE GOOD NEWS IS, THEY APPEAR TO BE WORKING IN THE SAME FACILITY.
THE BAD NEW IS, IT'S COLLECTIVE INDUSTRIES.
FIGURES.
I CAN GIVE YOU WHAT YOU NEED TO GET PAST SECURITY...
...IF YOU TELL ME HOW YOU KNEW WHO HE WAS.
JUST ASSUMING.
IT'S WHO HE WAS IN MY WORLD.
MMM. OF COURSE.
ISN'T THAT ALWAYS THE WAY.
STILL, A LADY IS ONLY AS GOOD AS HER WORD.
I COULD HAVE TRIED FOR SOME-THING ELSE.

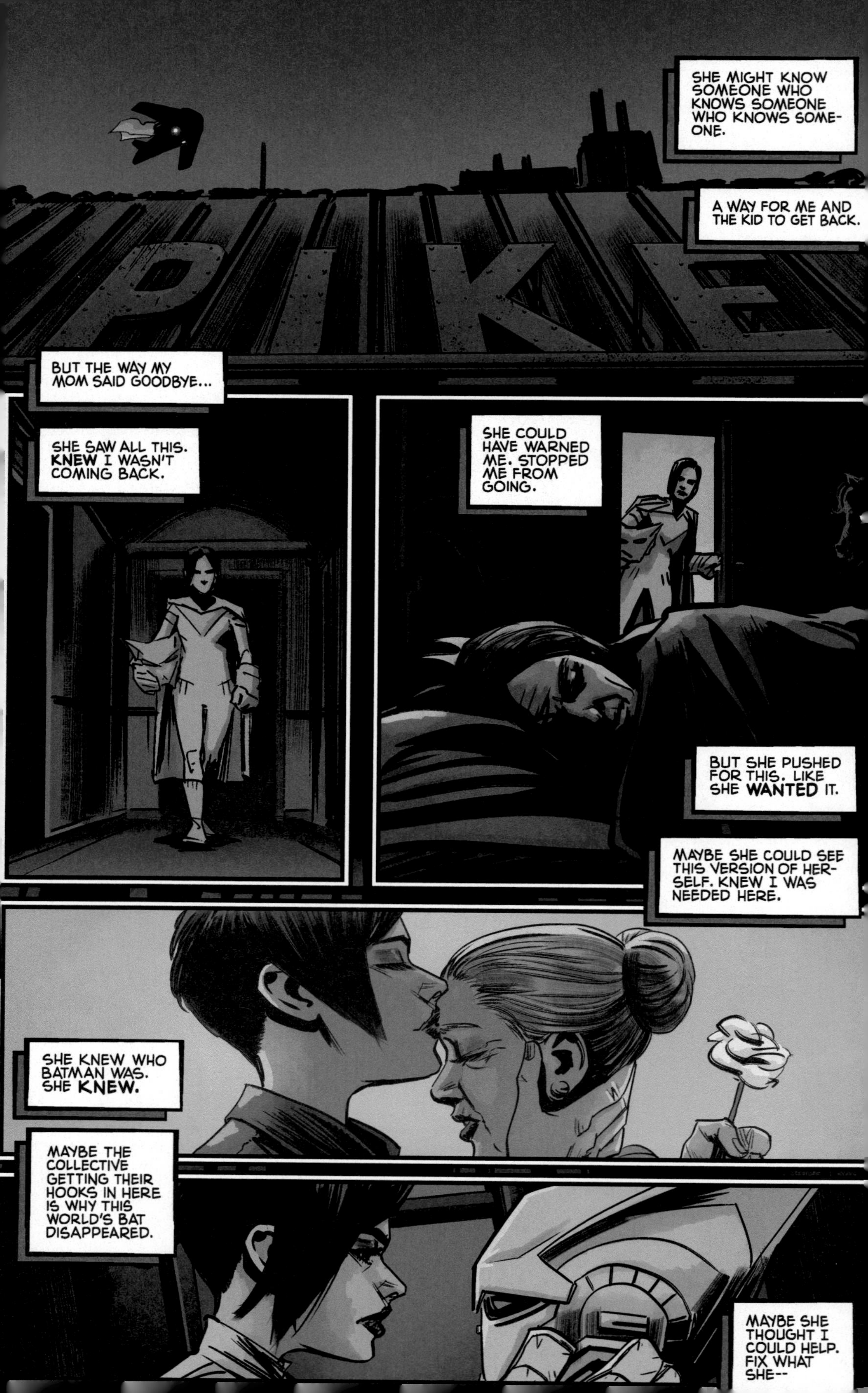
SHE MIGHT KNOW SOMEONE WHO KNOWS SOMEONE WHO KNOWS SOME-ONE.
A WAY FOR ME AND THE KID TO GET BACK.
BUT THE WAY MY MOM SAID GOODBYE...
SHE SAW ALL THIS. KNEW I WASN'T COMING BACK.
SHE COULD HAVE WARNED ME. STOPPED ME FROM GOING.
BUT SHE PUSHED FOR THIS. LIKE SHE WANTED IT.
MAYBE SHE COULD SEE THIS VERSION OF HER-SELF. KNEW I WAS NEEDED HERE.
SHE KNEW WHO BATMAN WAS. SHE KNEW.
MAYBE THE COLLECTIVE GETTING THEIR HOOKS IN HERE IS WHY THIS WORLD'S BAT DISAPPEARED.
MAYBE SHE THOUGHT I COULD HELP. FIX WHAT SHE--

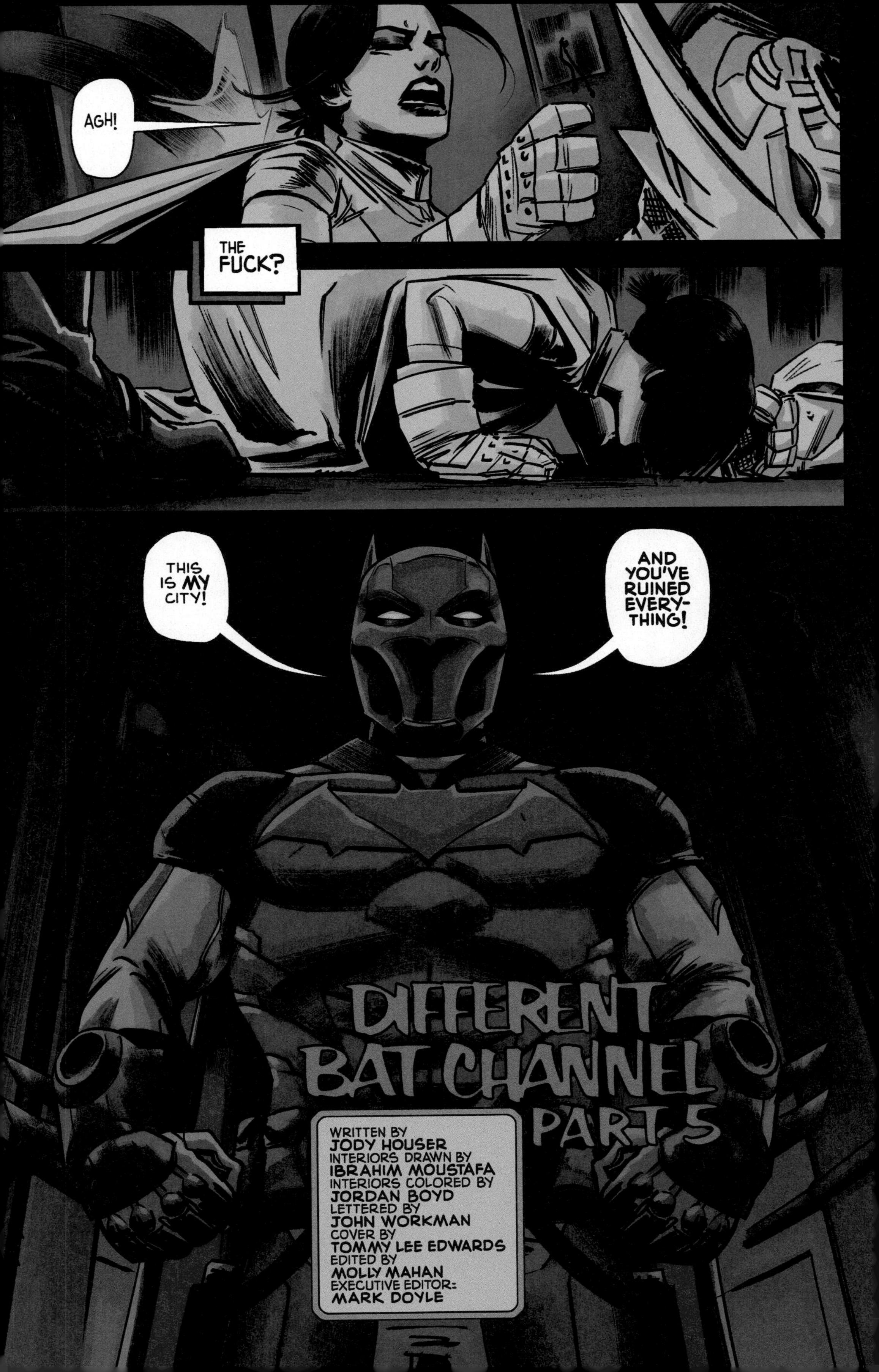
AGH!
THE FUCK?
THIS IS MY CITY!
AND YOU'VE RUINED EVERY-THING!
DIFFERENT BAT CHANNEL PART 5
WRITTEN BY JODY HOUSER
INTERIORS DRAWN BY IBRAHIM MOUSTAFA
INTERIORS COLORED BY JORDAN BOYD
LETTERED BY JOHN WORKMAN
COVER BY TOMMY LEE EDWARDS
EDITED BY MOLLY MAHAN
EXECUTIVE EDITOR: MARK DOYLE

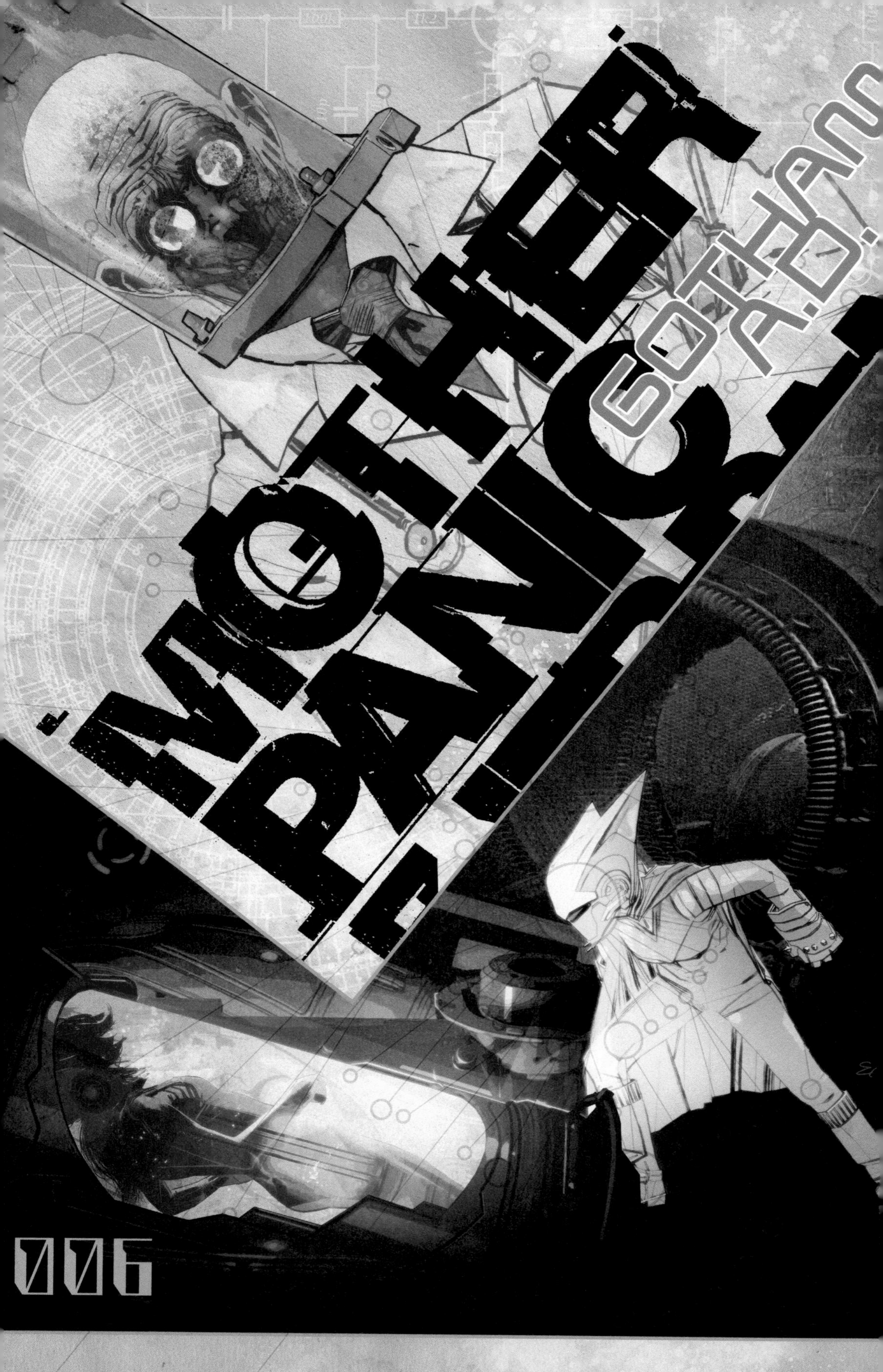
MOTHER PANIC
GOTHAM A.D.
006

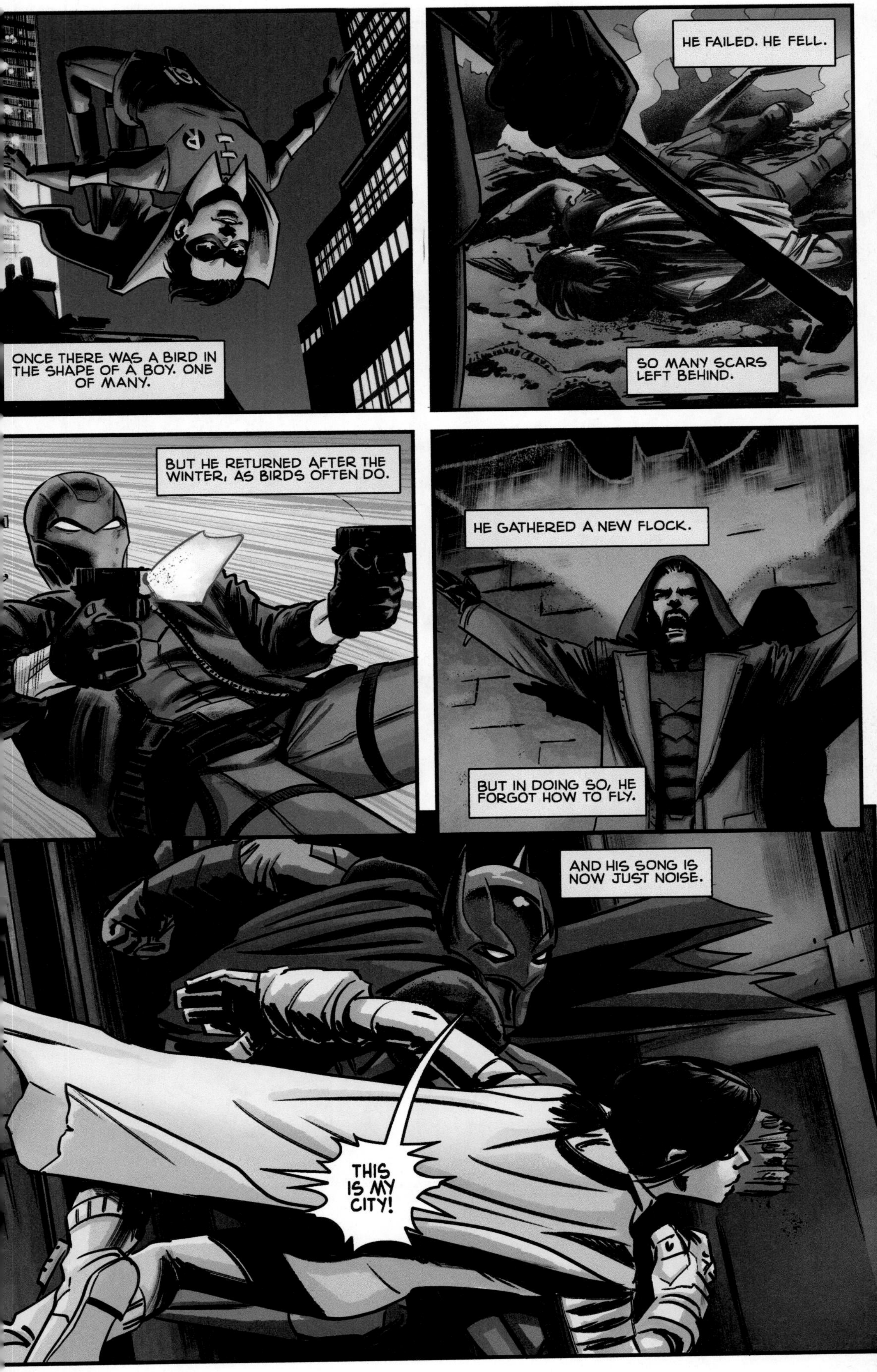
ONCE THERE WAS A BIRD IN THE SHAPE OF A BOY. ONE OF MANY.
HE FAILED. HE FELL.
SO MANY SCARS LEFT BEHIND.
BUT HE RETURNED AFTER THE WINTER, AS BIRDS OFTEN DO.
HE GATHERED A NEW FLOCK.
BUT IN DOING SO, HE FORGOT HOW TO FLY.
AND HIS SONG IS NOW JUST NOISE.
THIS IS MY CITY!

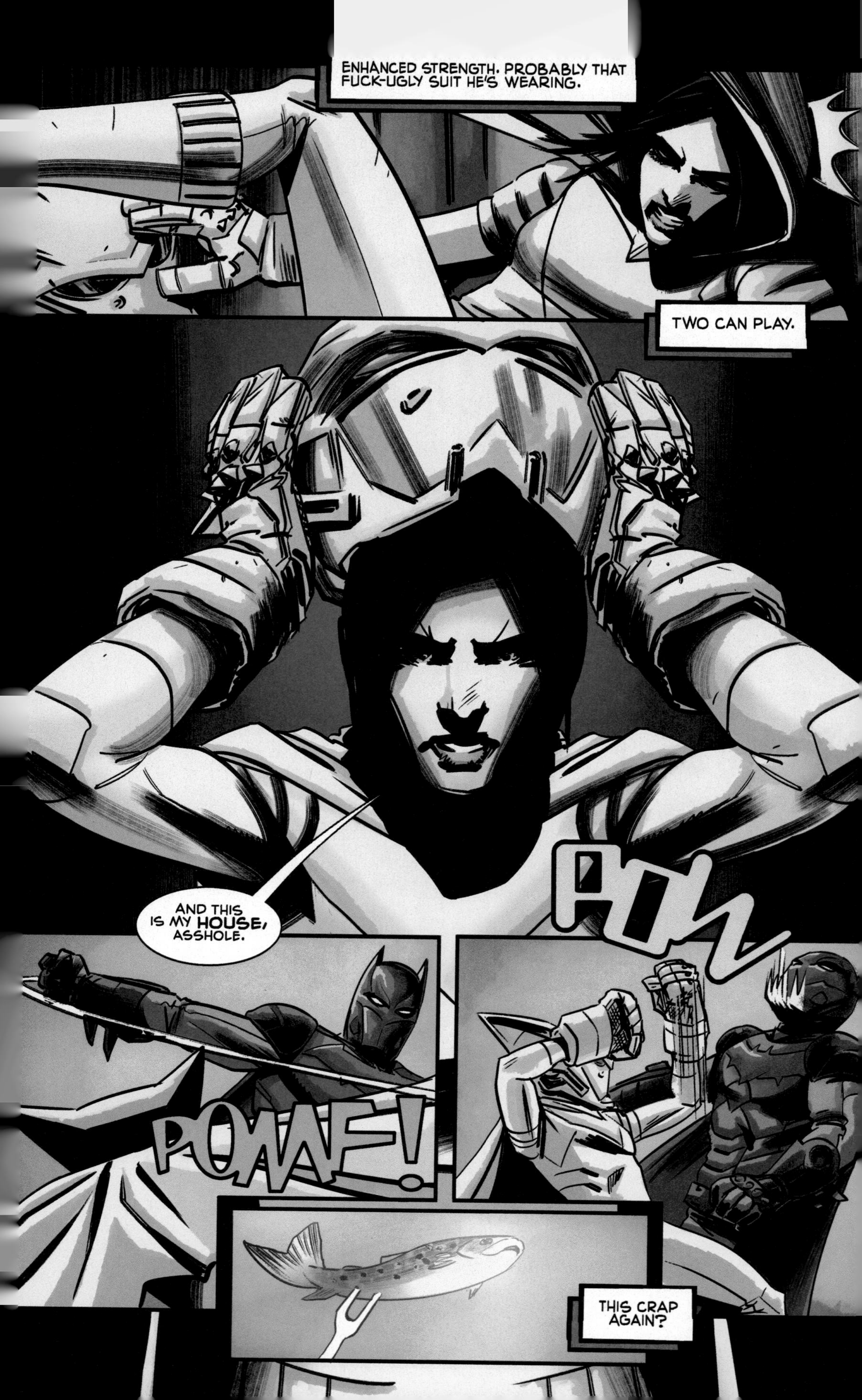
ENHANCED STRENGTH. PROBABLY THAT FUCK-UGLY SUIT HE'S WEARING.
TWO CAN PLAY.
AND THIS IS MY HOUSE, ASSHOLE.
POWAF!
THIS CRAP AGAIN?

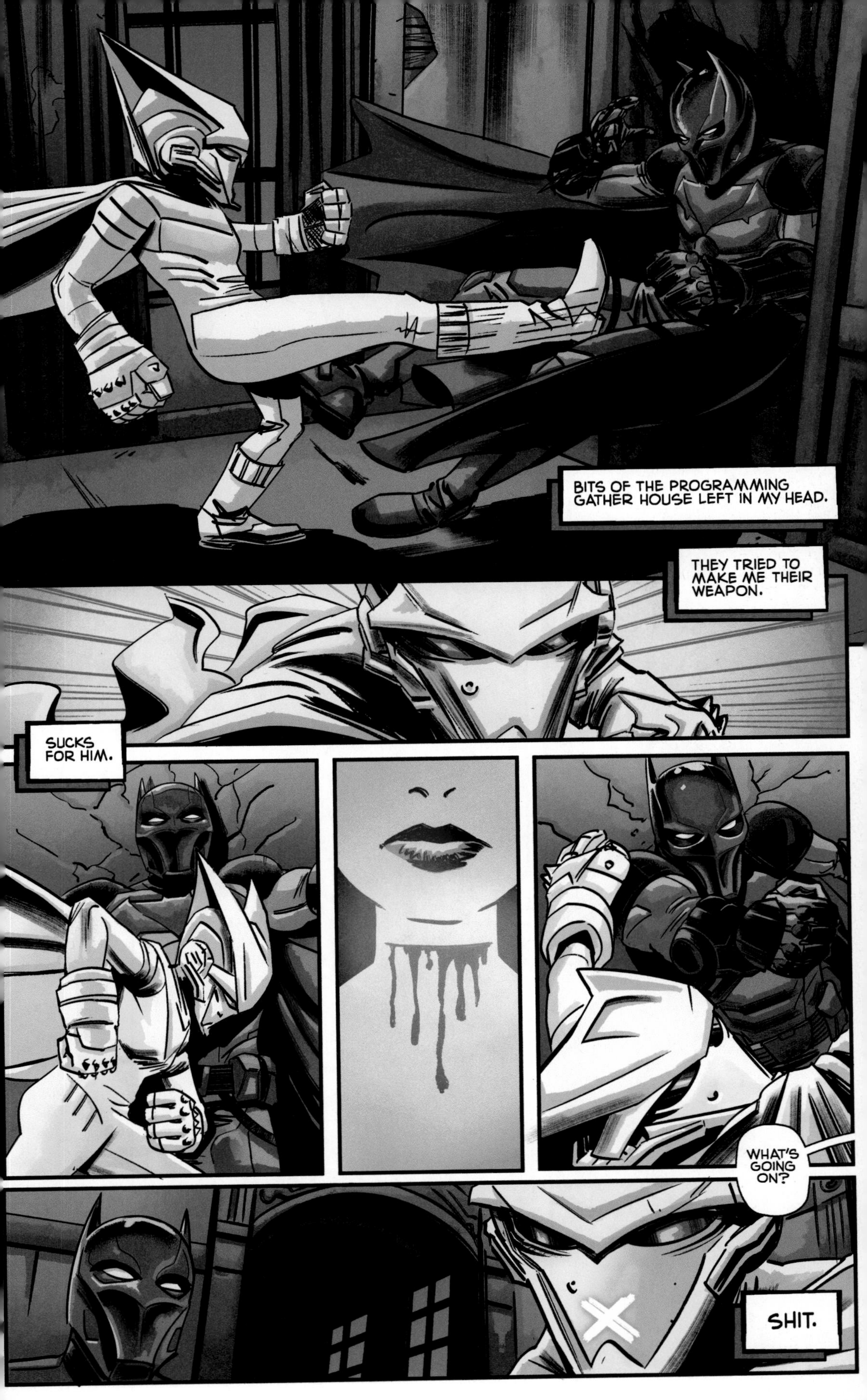
BITS OF THE PROGRAMMING GATHER HOUSE LEFT IN MY HEAD.
THEY TRIED TO MAKE ME THEIR WEAPON.
SUCKS FOR HIM.
WHAT'S GOING ON?
SHIT.

I HEARD FIGHTING...

NO...

HEY! YOU'RE THAT **JERK** WE WERE LOOKING FOR BEFORE!

DID YOU STOP BEING A STUPID COWARD BABY?

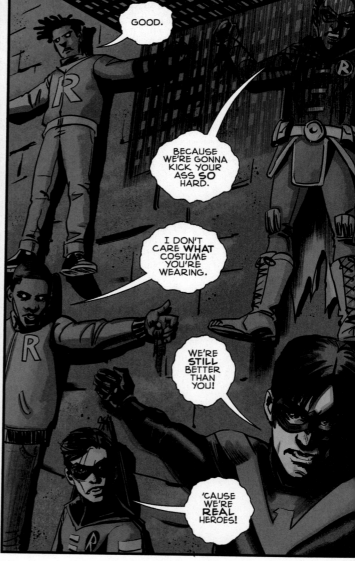

GOOD.

BECAUSE WE'RE GONNA KICK YOUR ASS **SO** HARD.

I DON'T CARE **WHAT** COSTUME YOU'RE WEARING.

WE'RE **STILL** BETTER THAN YOU!

'CAUSE WE'RE **REAL** HEROES!

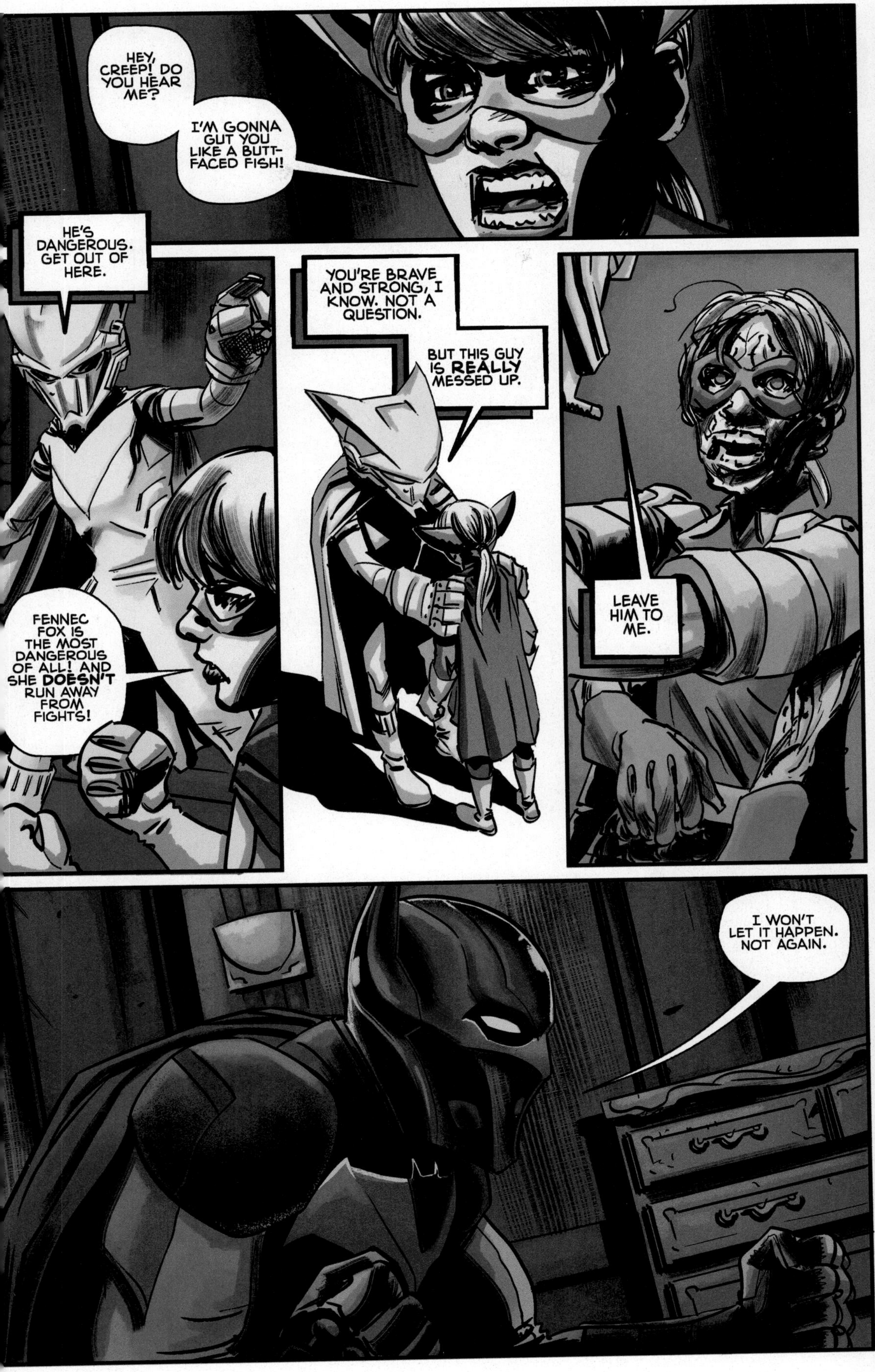
HEY, CREEP! DO YOU HEAR ME?
I'M GONNA GUT YOU LIKE A BUTT-FACED FISH!
HE'S DANGEROUS. GET OUT OF HERE.
FENNEC FOX IS THE MOST DANGEROUS OF ALL! AND SHE **DOESN'T** RUN AWAY FROM FIGHTS!
YOU'RE BRAVE AND STRONG, I KNOW. NOT A QUESTION.
BUT THIS GUY IS **REALLY** MESSED UP.
LEAVE HIM TO ME.
I WON'T LET IT HAPPEN. NOT AGAIN.

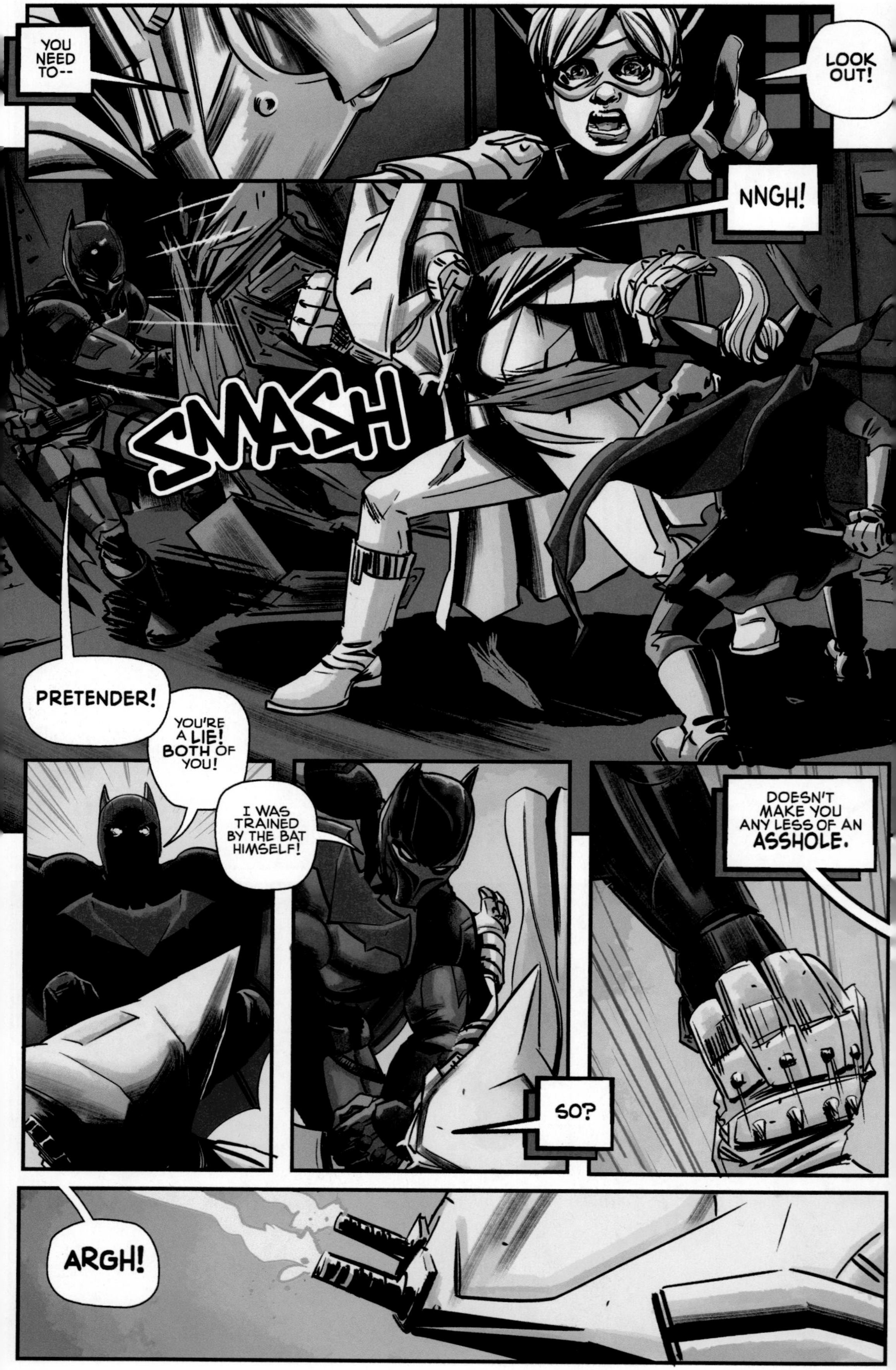
YOU NEED TO--
LOOK OUT!
NNGH!
SMASH
PRETENDER!
YOU'RE A LIE! BOTH OF YOU!
I WAS TRAINED BY THE BAT HIMSELF!
SO?
DOESN'T MAKE YOU ANY LESS OF AN ASSHOLE.
ARGH!

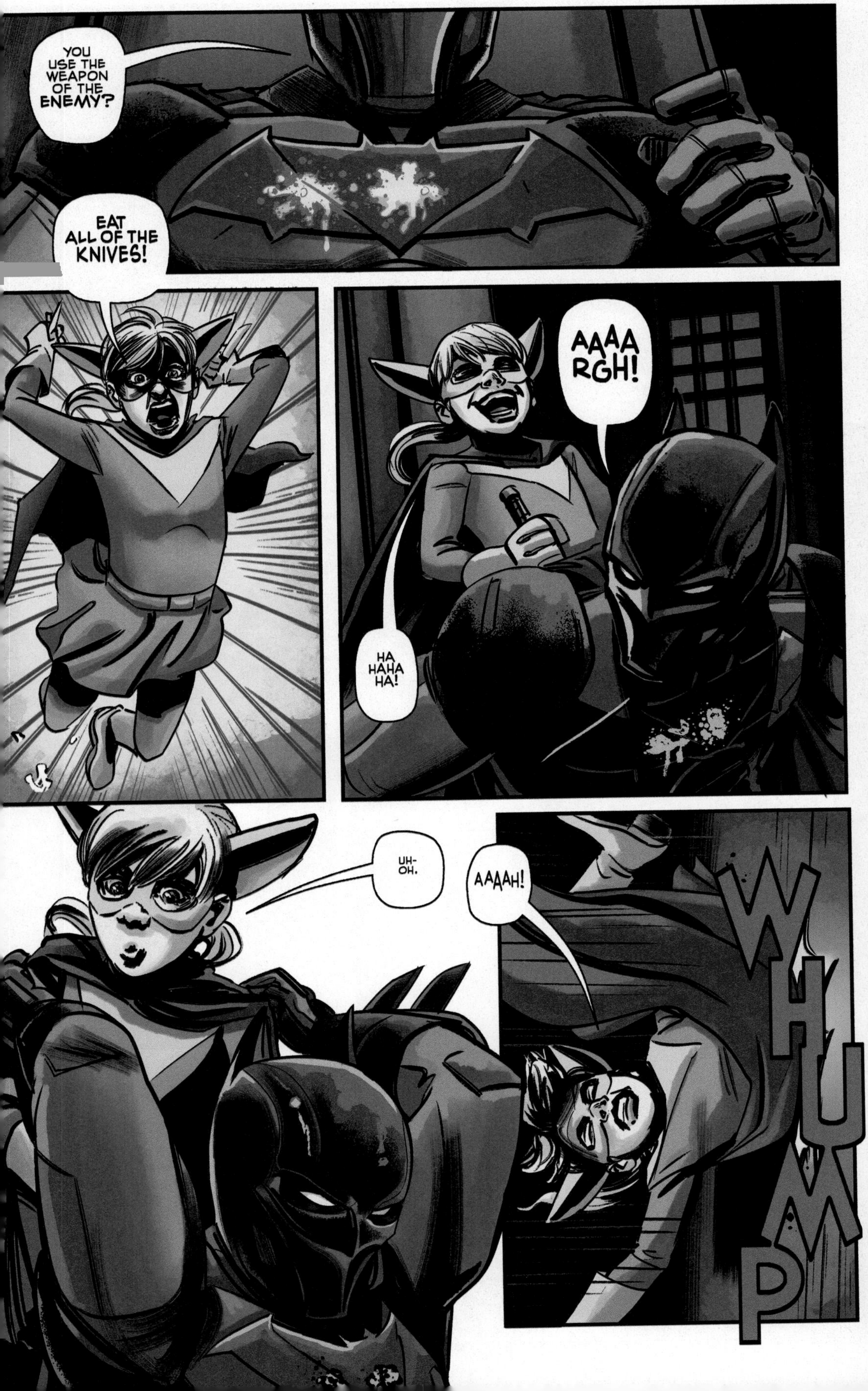
YOU USE THE WEAPON OF THE ENEMY?
EAT ALL OF THE KNIVES!
AAAA RGH!
HA HAHAHA HA!
UH-OH.
AAAAH!
WHUMP

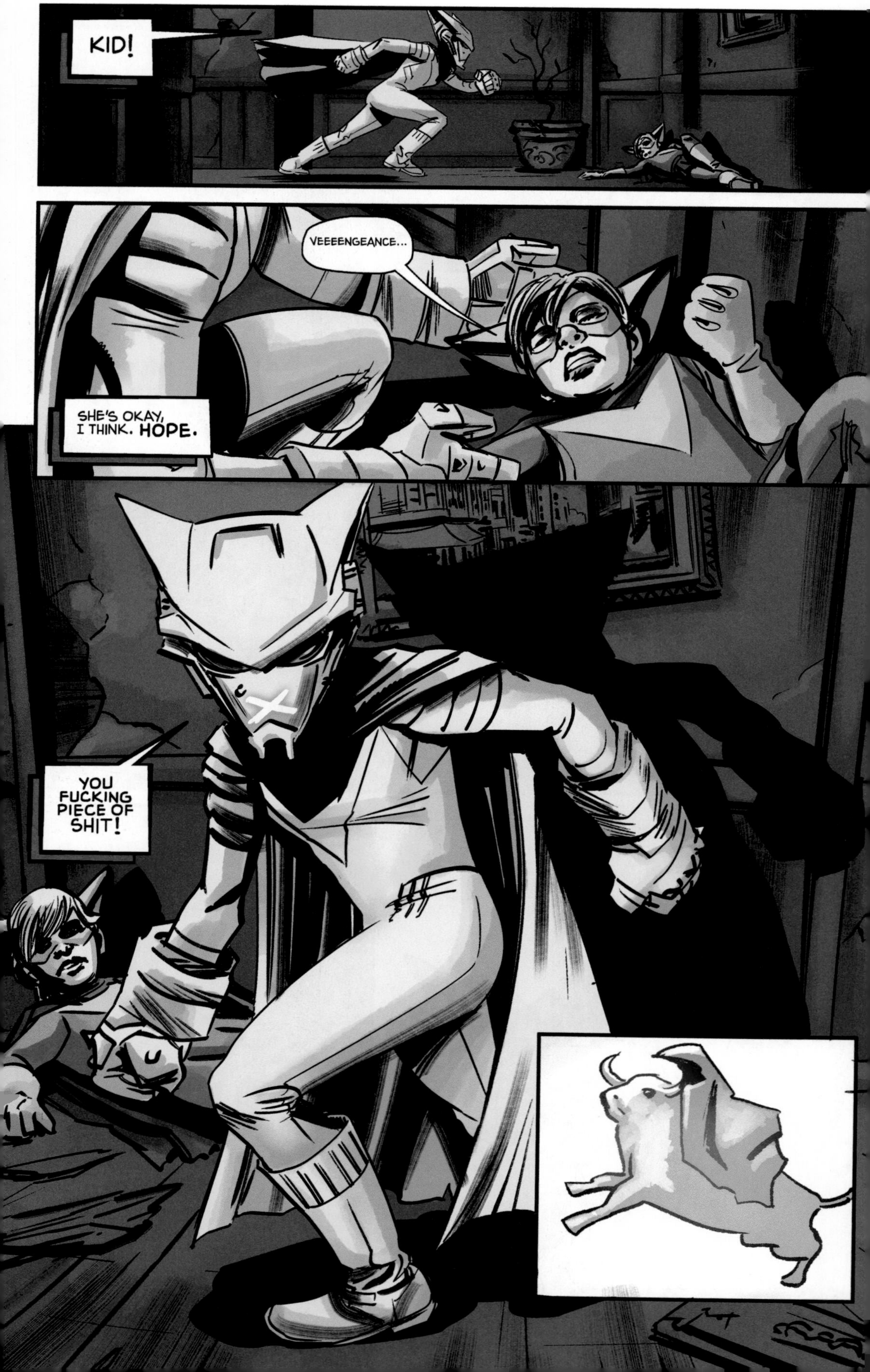
KID!
VEEEENGEANCE...
SHE'S OKAY, I THINK. HOPE.
YOU FUCKING PIECE OF SHIT!

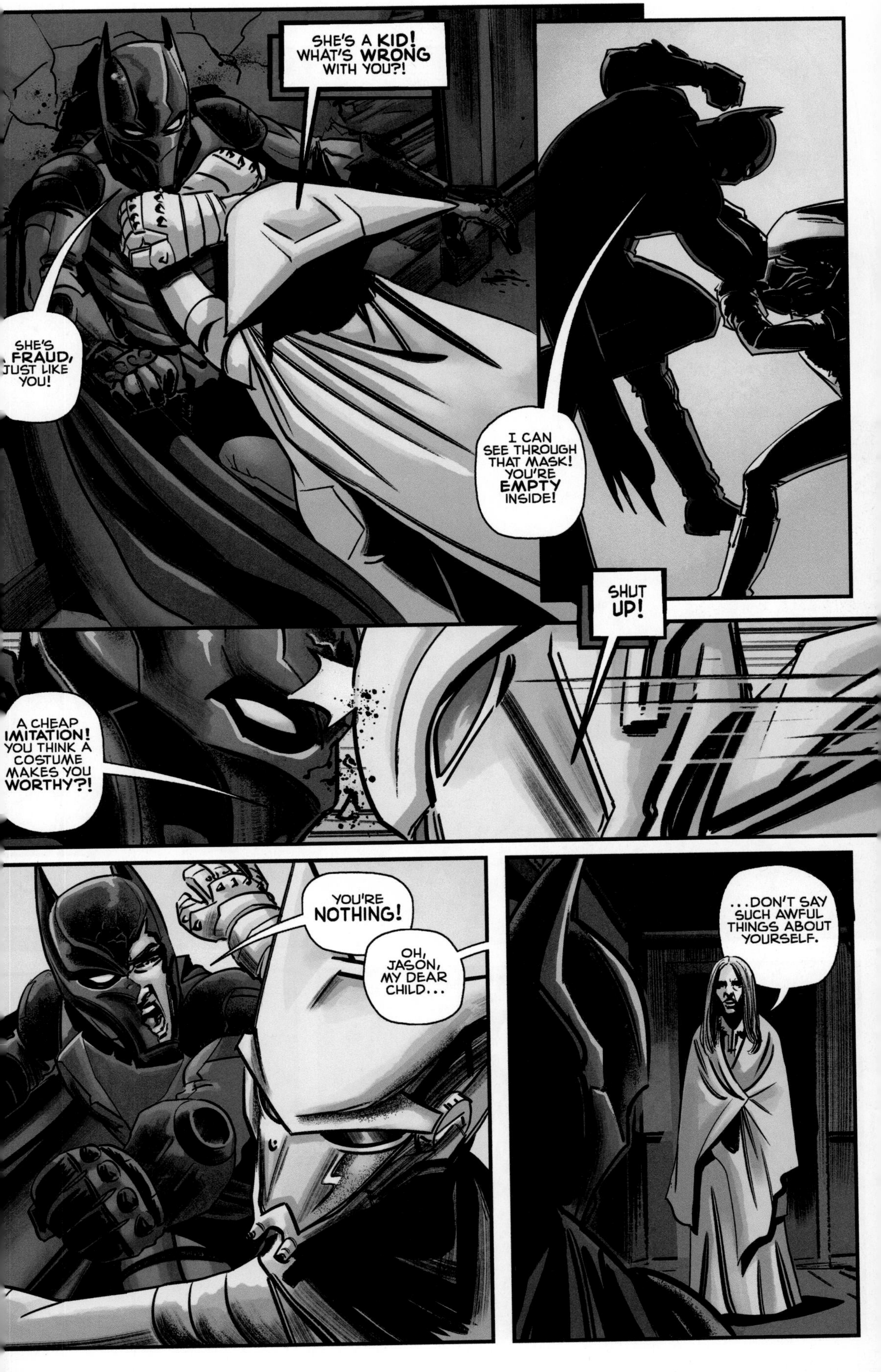

SHE'S A KID! WHAT'S WRONG WITH YOU?!
SHE'S A FRAUD, JUST LIKE YOU!
I CAN SEE THROUGH THAT MASK! YOU'RE EMPTY INSIDE!
SHUT UP!
A CHEAP IMITATION! YOU THINK A COSTUME MAKES YOU WORTHY?!
YOU'RE NOTHING!
OH, JASON, MY DEAR CHILD...
...DON'T SAY SUCH AWFUL THINGS ABOUT YOURSELF.

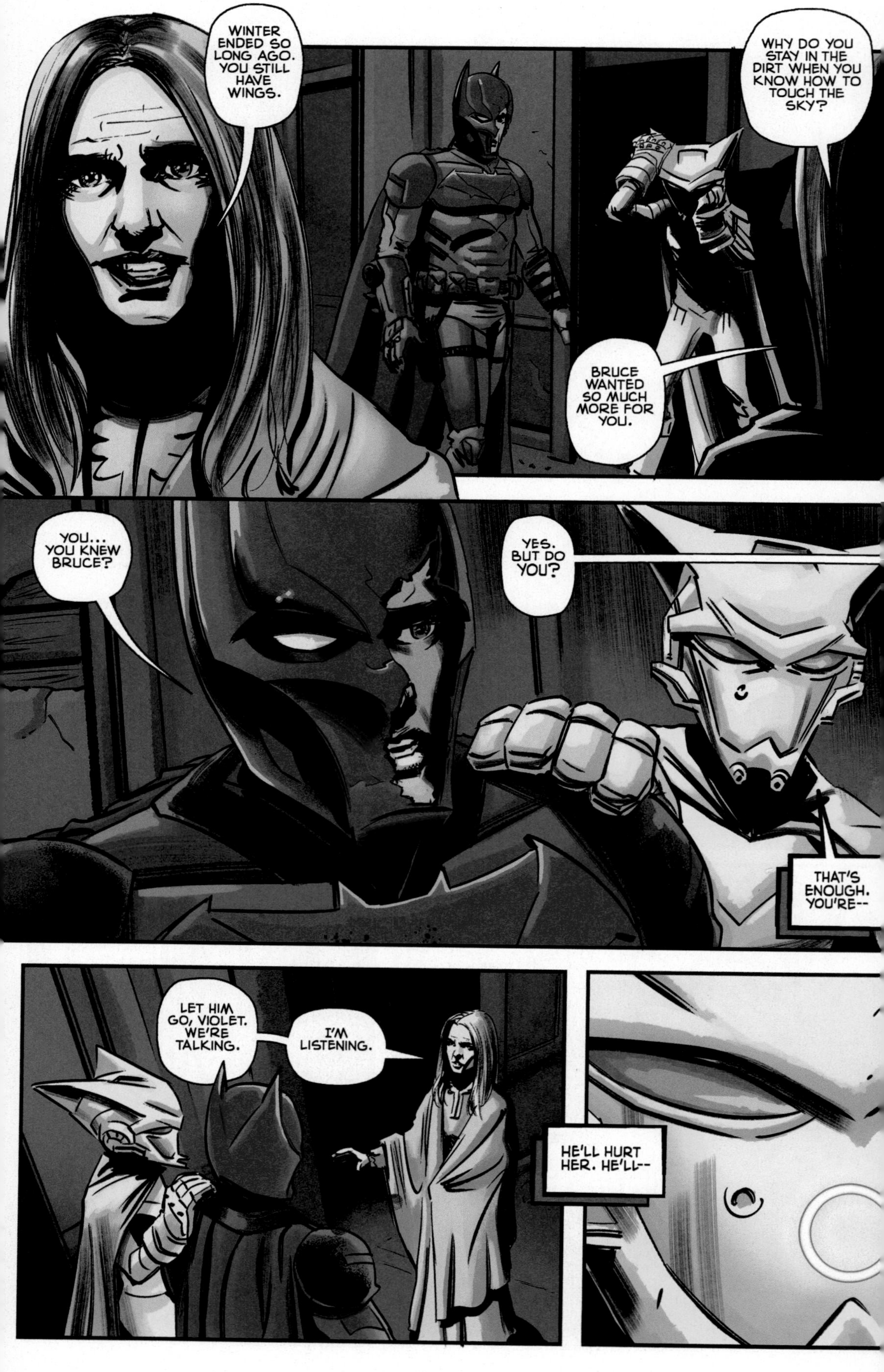
WINTER ENDED SO LONG AGO. YOU STILL HAVE WINGS.
WHY DO YOU STAY IN THE DIRT WHEN YOU KNOW HOW TO TOUCH THE SKY?
BRUCE WANTED SO MUCH MORE FOR YOU.
YOU... YOU KNEW BRUCE?
YES. BUT DO YOU?
THAT'S ENOUGH. YOU'RE--
LET HIM GO, VIOLET. WE'RE TALKING.
I'M LISTENING.
HE'LL HURT HER. HE'LL--

THAT'S ALL WE EVER WANT. SOMEONE TO HEAR US.

SOMEONE TO UNDER-STAND.

I CAN HEAR YOU. CAN YOU HEAR ME?

SHE BETTER BE RIGHT ABOUT THIS.

HE'S GONE. BUT I'M STILL HERE.

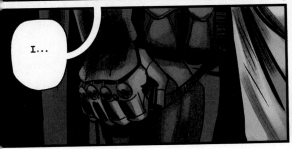

I...

...I HEAR YOU.

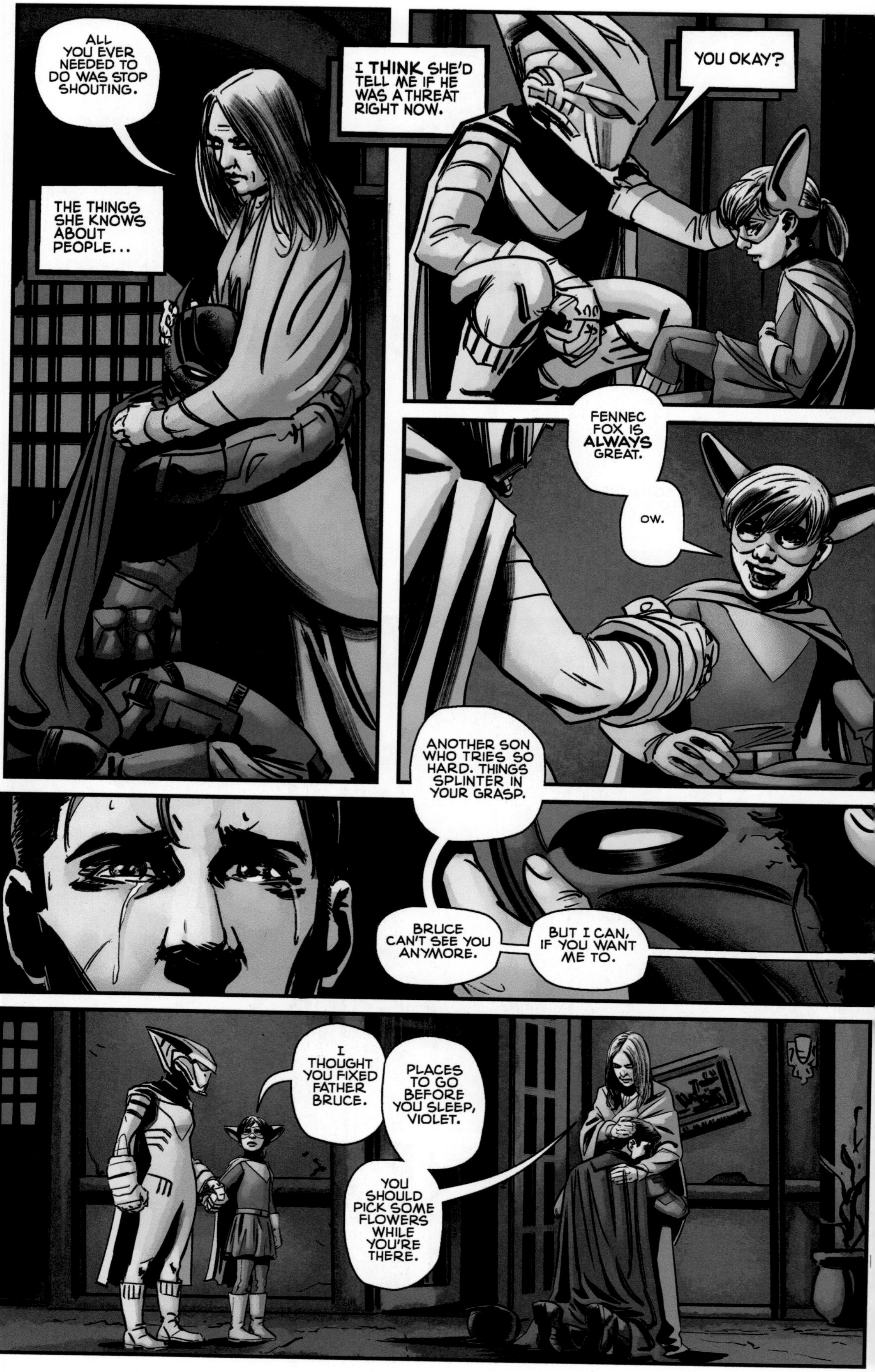

ALL YOU EVER NEEDED TO DO WAS STOP SHOUTING.
THE THINGS SHE KNOWS ABOUT PEOPLE...
I THINK SHE'D TELL ME IF HE WAS A THREAT RIGHT NOW.
YOU OKAY?
FENNEC FOX IS ALWAYS GREAT.
OW.
ANOTHER SON WHO TRIES SO HARD. THINGS SPLINTER IN YOUR GRASP.
BRUCE CAN'T SEE YOU ANYMORE.
BUT I CAN, IF YOU WANT ME TO.
I THOUGHT YOU FIXED FATHER BRUCE.
PLACES TO GO BEFORE YOU SLEEP, VIOLET.
YOU SHOULD PICK SOME FLOWERS WHILE YOU'RE THERE.

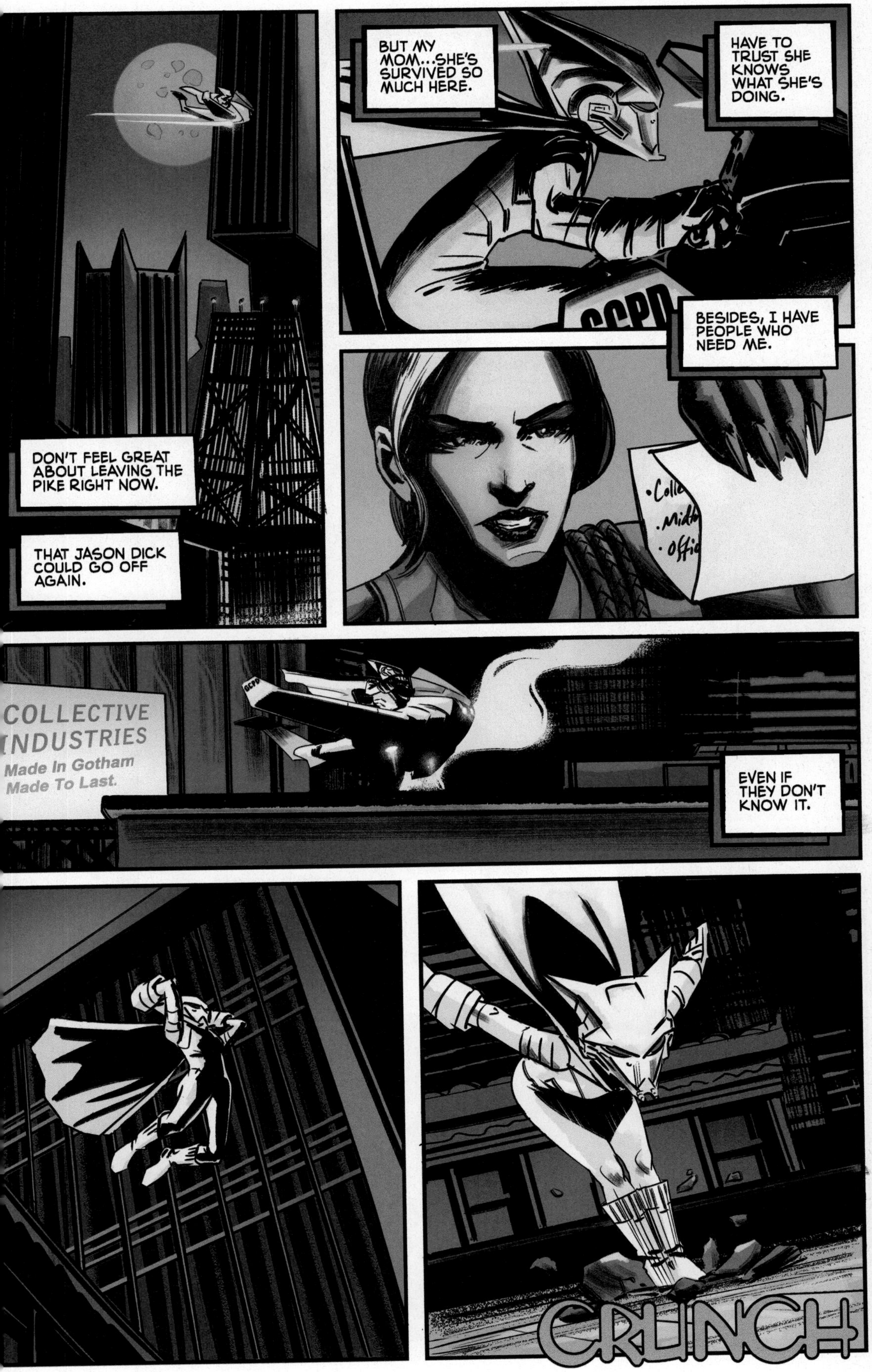
DON'T FEEL GREAT ABOUT LEAVING THE PIKE RIGHT NOW.
THAT JASON DICK COULD GO OFF AGAIN.
BUT MY MOM...SHE'S SURVIVED SO MUCH HERE.
HAVE TO TRUST SHE KNOWS WHAT SHE'S DOING.
GCPD
BESIDES, I HAVE PEOPLE WHO NEED ME.
COLLECTIVE INDUSTRIES
Made In Gotham
Made To Last.
GCPD
EVEN IF THEY DON'T KNOW IT.
CRUNCH

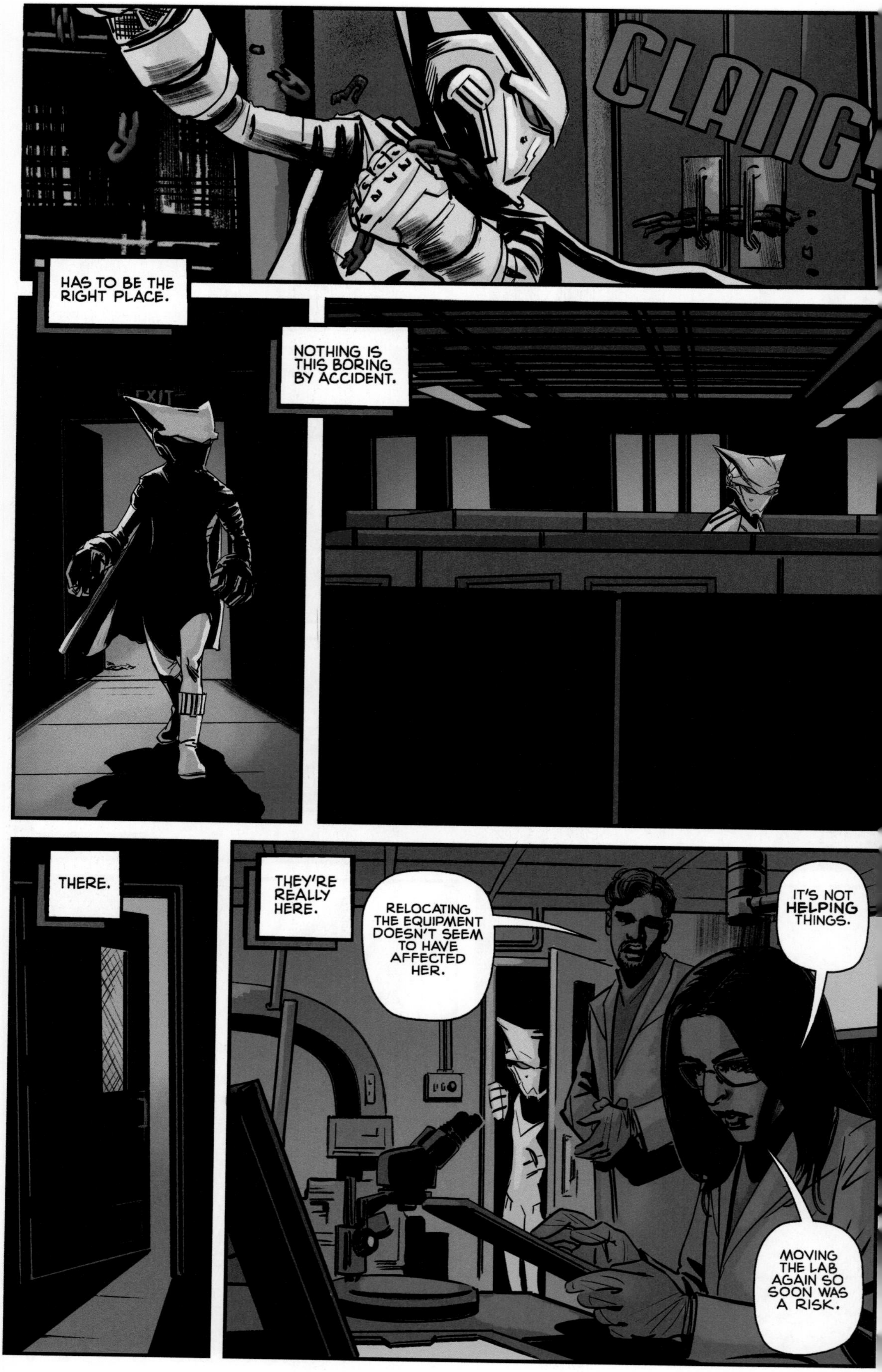
CLANG!
HAS TO BE THE RIGHT PLACE.
EXIT
NOTHING IS THIS BORING BY ACCIDENT.
THERE.
THEY'RE REALLY HERE.
RELOCATING THE EQUIPMENT DOESN'T SEEM TO HAVE AFFECTED HER.
IT'S NOT **HELPING** THINGS.
MOVING THE LAB AGAIN SO SOON WAS A RISK.

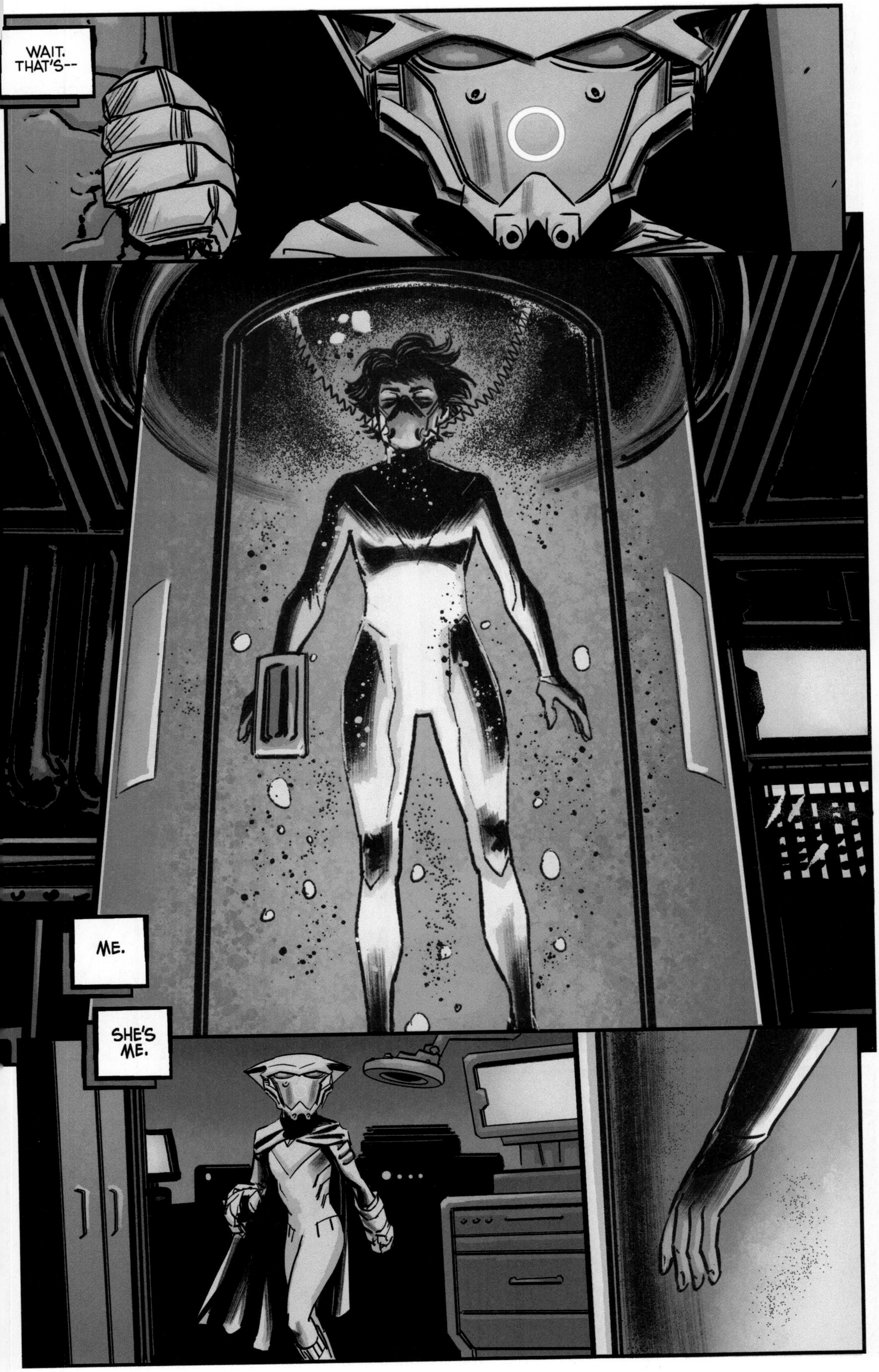
WAIT. THAT'S--
ME.
SHE'S ME.

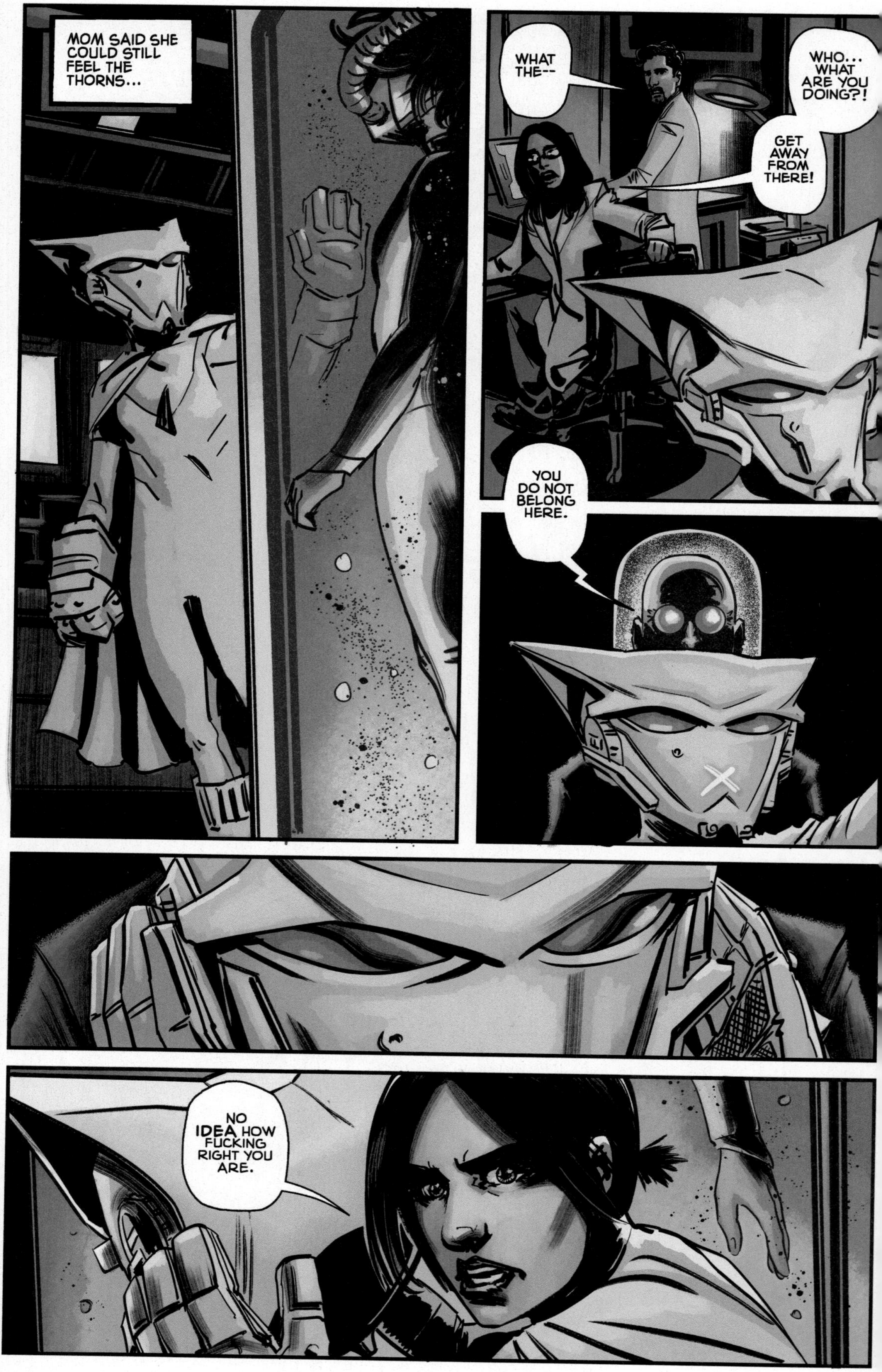
MOM SAID SHE COULD STILL FEEL THE THORNS...
WHAT THE--
WHO... WHAT ARE YOU DOING?!
GET AWAY FROM THERE!
YOU DO NOT BELONG HERE.
NO IDEA HOW FUCKING RIGHT YOU ARE.

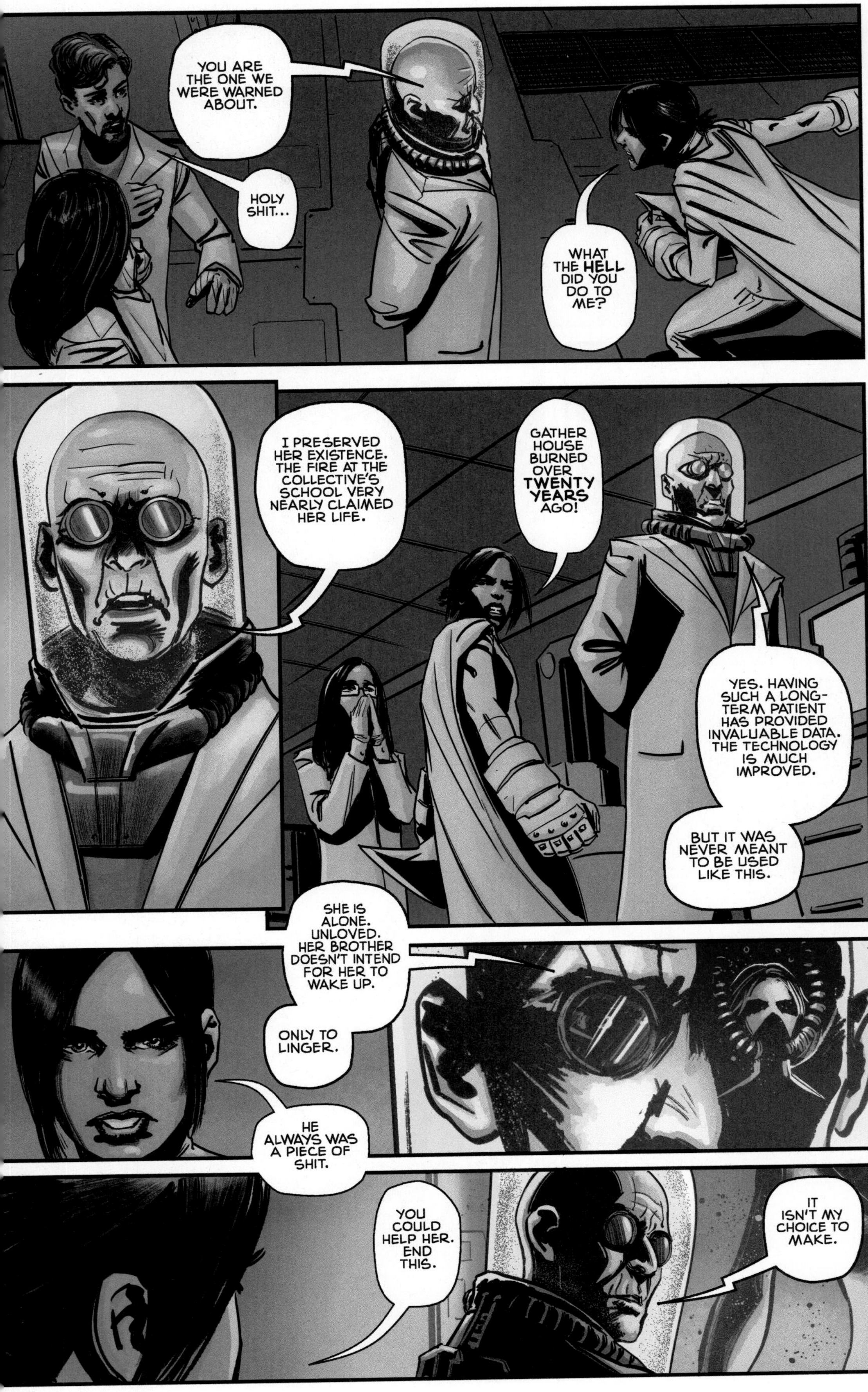
YOU ARE THE ONE WE WERE WARNED ABOUT.
HOLY SHIT...
WHAT THE HELL DID YOU DO TO ME?
I PRESERVED HER EXISTENCE. THE FIRE AT THE COLLECTIVE'S SCHOOL VERY NEARLY CLAIMED HER LIFE.
GATHER HOUSE BURNED OVER TWENTY YEARS AGO!
YES. HAVING SUCH A LONG-TERM PATIENT HAS PROVIDED INVALUABLE DATA. THE TECHNOLOGY IS MUCH IMPROVED.
BUT IT WAS NEVER MEANT TO BE USED LIKE THIS.
SHE IS ALONE. UNLOVED. HER BROTHER DOESN'T INTEND FOR HER TO WAKE UP.
ONLY TO LINGER.
HE ALWAYS WAS A PIECE OF SHIT.
YOU COULD HELP HER. END THIS.
IT ISN'T MY CHOICE TO MAKE.

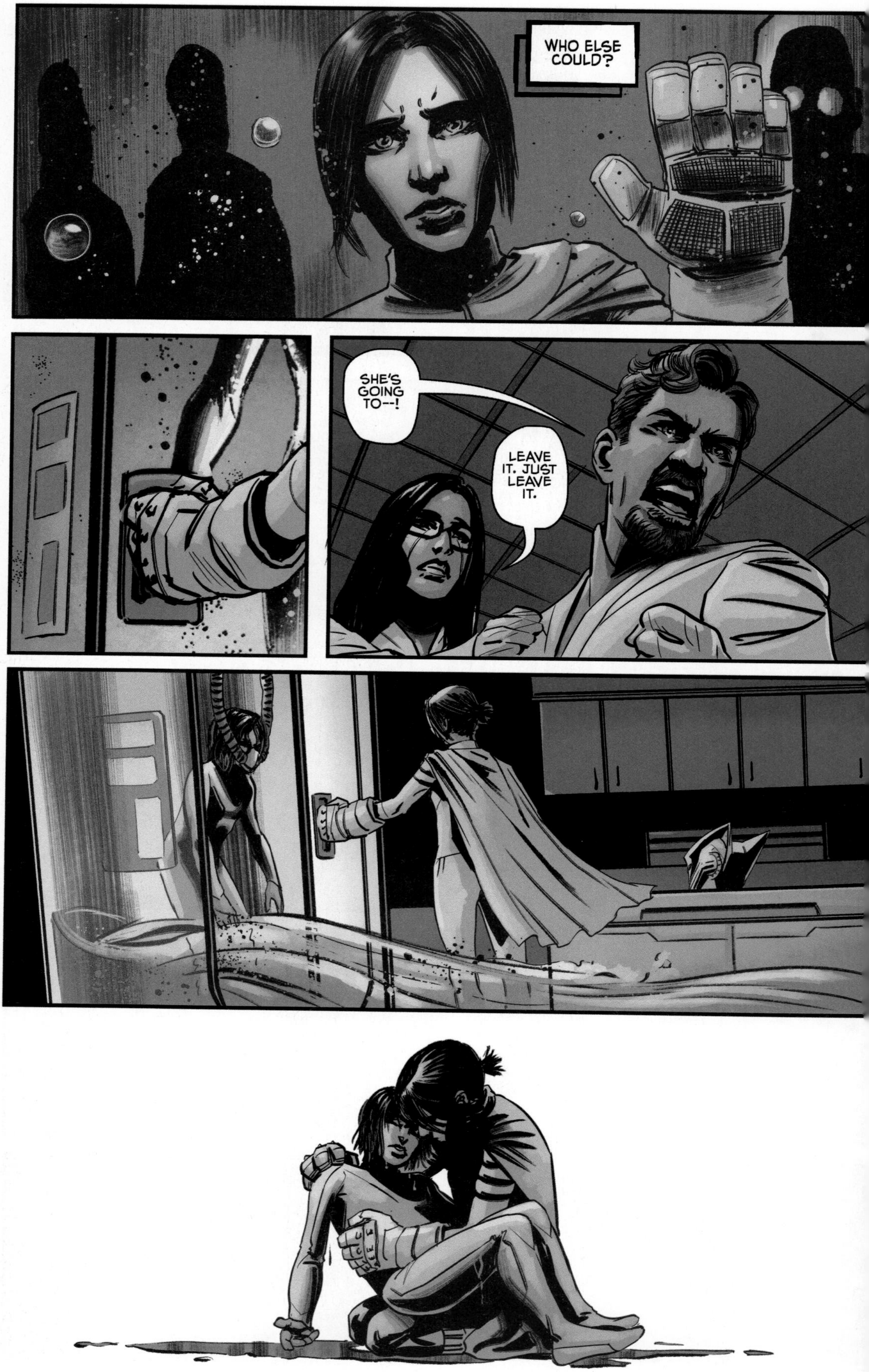
WHO ELSE COULD?
SHE'S GOING TO--!
LEAVE IT. JUST LEAVE IT.

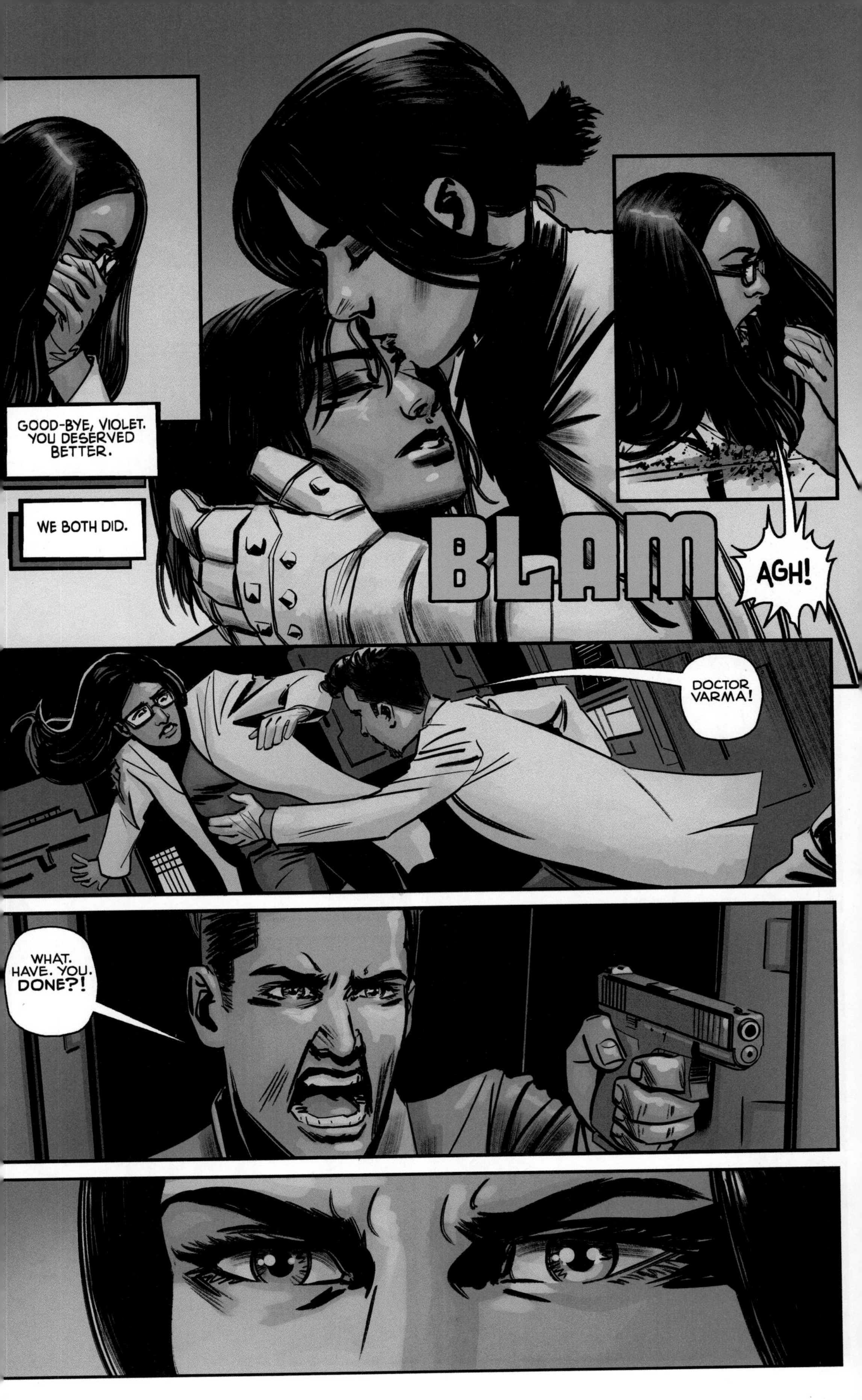
GOOD-BYE, VIOLET. YOU DESERVED BETTER.
WE BOTH DID.
BLAM
AGH!
DOCTOR VARMA!
WHAT. HAVE. YOU. DONE?!

VICTOR PAIGE. MY OWN BROTHER.

THE ONE WHO GAVE ME UP TO BE CUT UP. REMADE.

WHO WANTED ME TO BE TORTURED.

WHO TURNED ME INTO THIS.

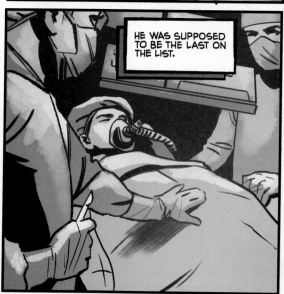

HE WAS SUPPOSED TO BE THE LAST ON THE LIST.

BUT NOW...

...HE'S STANDING RIGHT HERE.

WHAT ARE YOU?

GAAH! KRAK

WHAT YOU MADE ME.

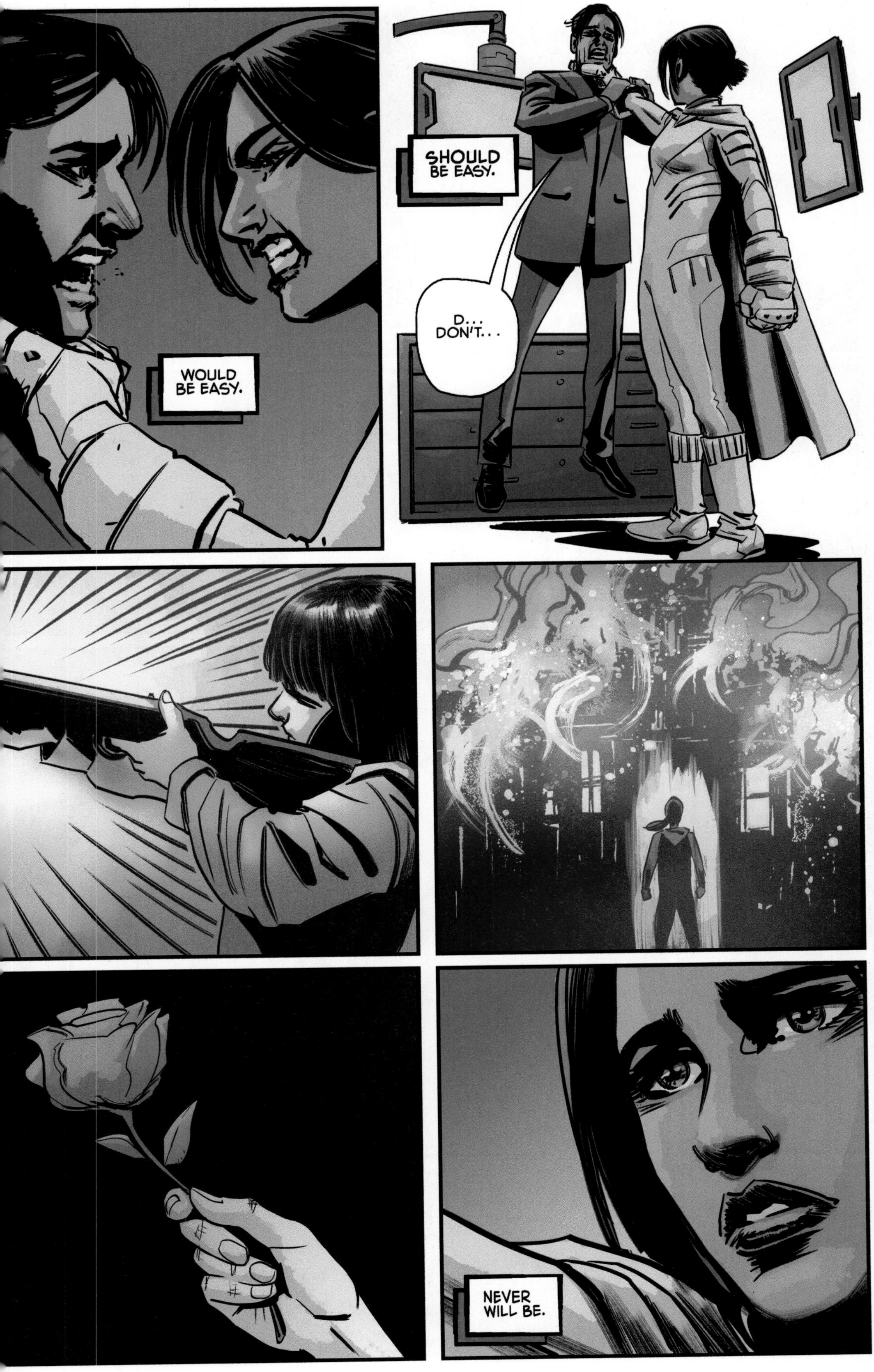
WOULD BE EASY.
SHOULD BE EASY.
D... DON'T...
NEVER WILL BE.

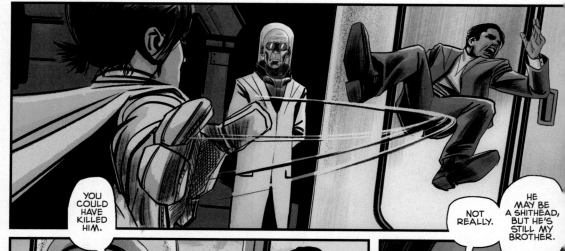

YOU COULD HAVE KILLED HIM.

NOT REALLY.

HE MAY BE A SHITHEAD, BUT HE'S STILL MY BROTHER.

A SORT OF LOVE. OR SOMETHING AKIN TO IT.

I WILL TAKE CARE OF HIM.

I CAN'T PRETEND TO UNDERSTAND WHO OR WHAT YOU ARE.

BUT THE COLLECTIVE WON'T BE HAPPY ABOUT THIS.

ANOTHER WHAT?

IT'S... COMPLICATED. BUT I KNEW YOU IN ANOTHER REALITY.

YOU BOTH WORKED FOR ME THERE. HOPED TO CONVINCE YOU TO DO THE SAME HERE.

IF YOU HAVE AN OUT FOR US, THAT'S ALL THE CONVINCING I NEED.

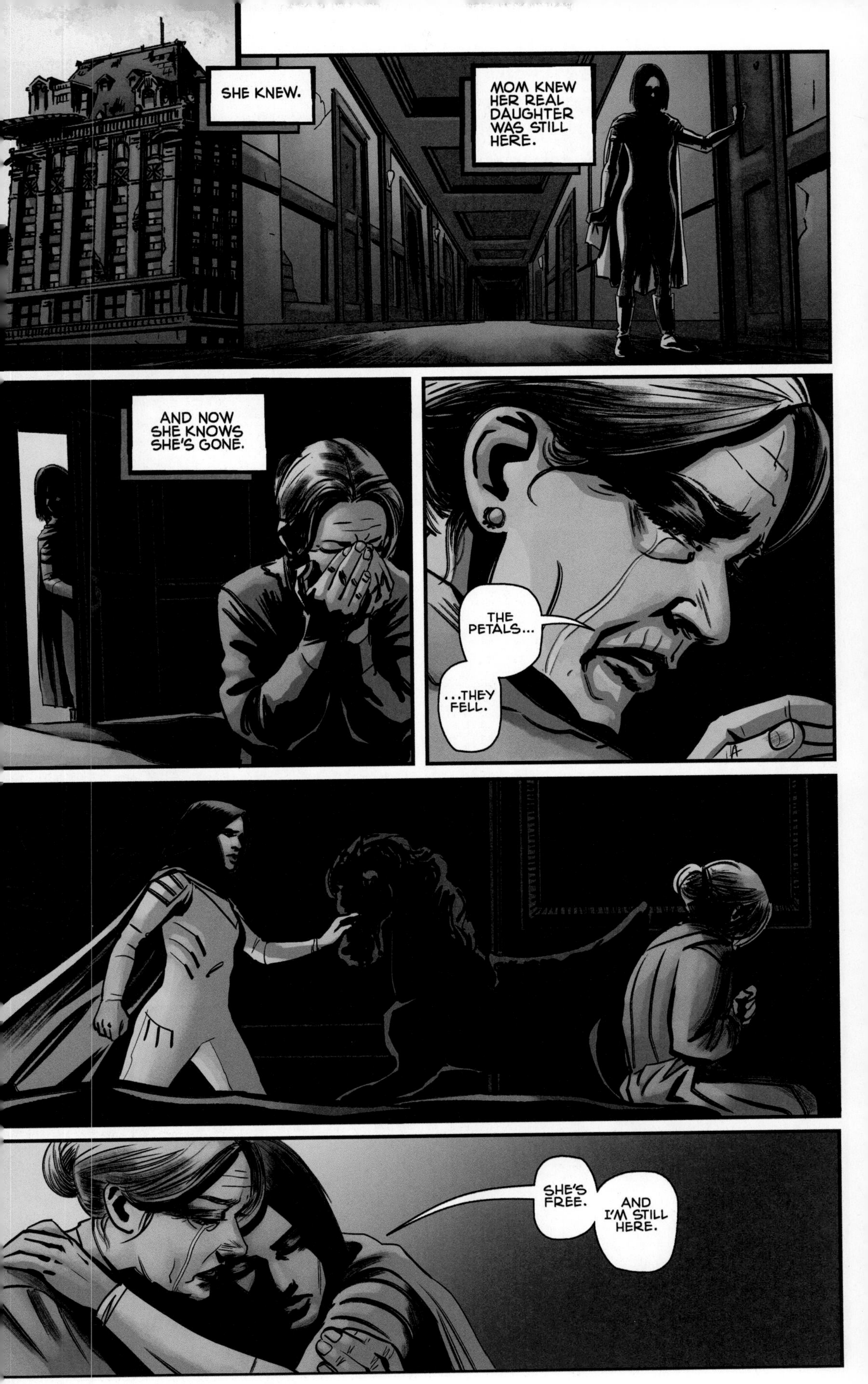
SHE KNEW.
MOM KNEW HER REAL DAUGHTER WAS STILL HERE.
AND NOW SHE KNOWS SHE'S GONE.
THE PETALS...
...THEY FELL.
SHE'S FREE.
AND I'M STILL HERE.

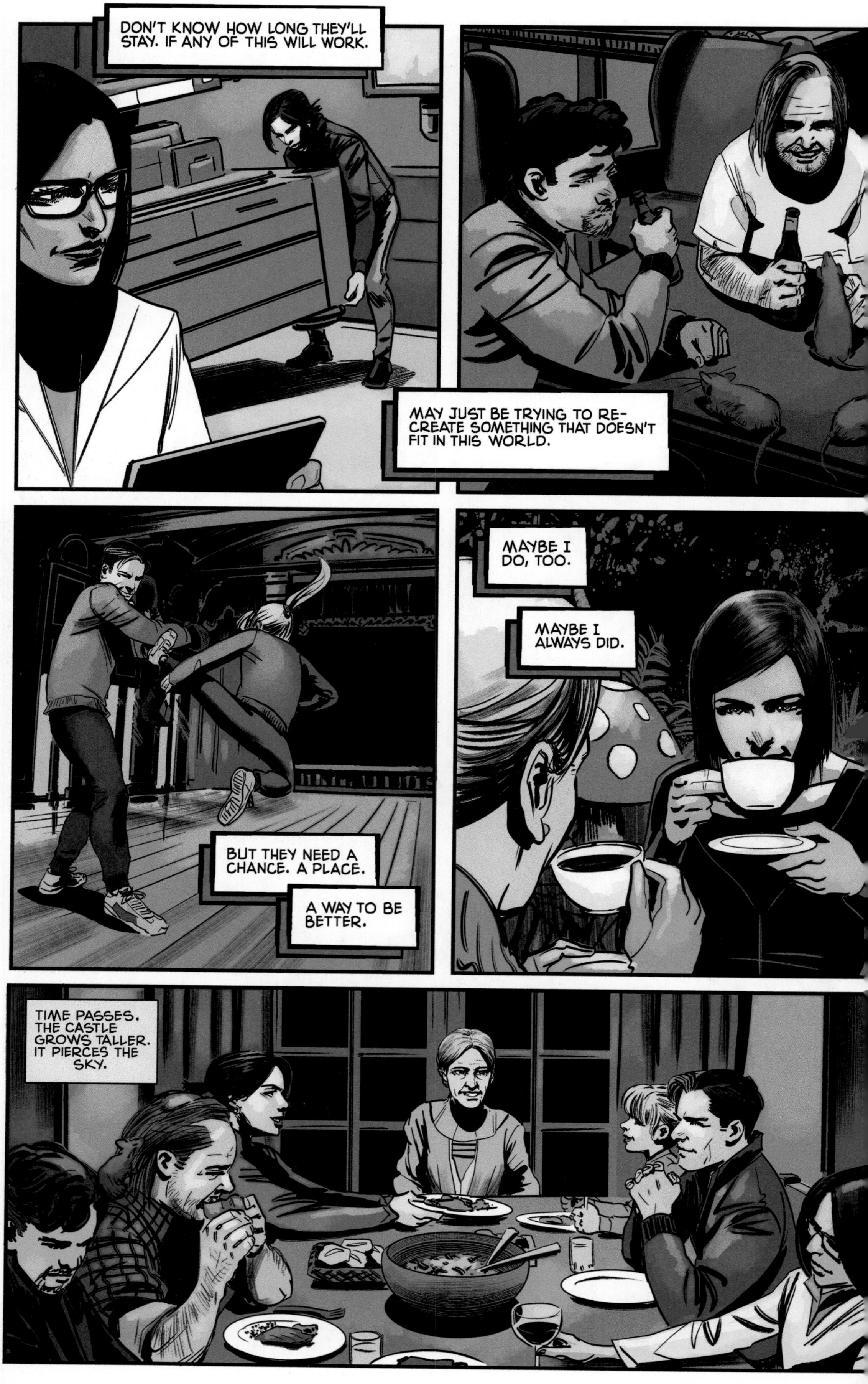
DON'T KNOW HOW LONG THEY'LL STAY. IF ANY OF THIS WILL WORK.
MAY JUST BE TRYING TO RE-CREATE SOMETHING THAT DOESN'T FIT IN THIS WORLD.
BUT THEY NEED A CHANCE. A PLACE.
A WAY TO BE BETTER.
MAYBE I DO, TOO.
MAYBE I ALWAYS DID.
TIME PASSES. THE CASTLE GROWS TALLER. IT PIERCES THE SKY.

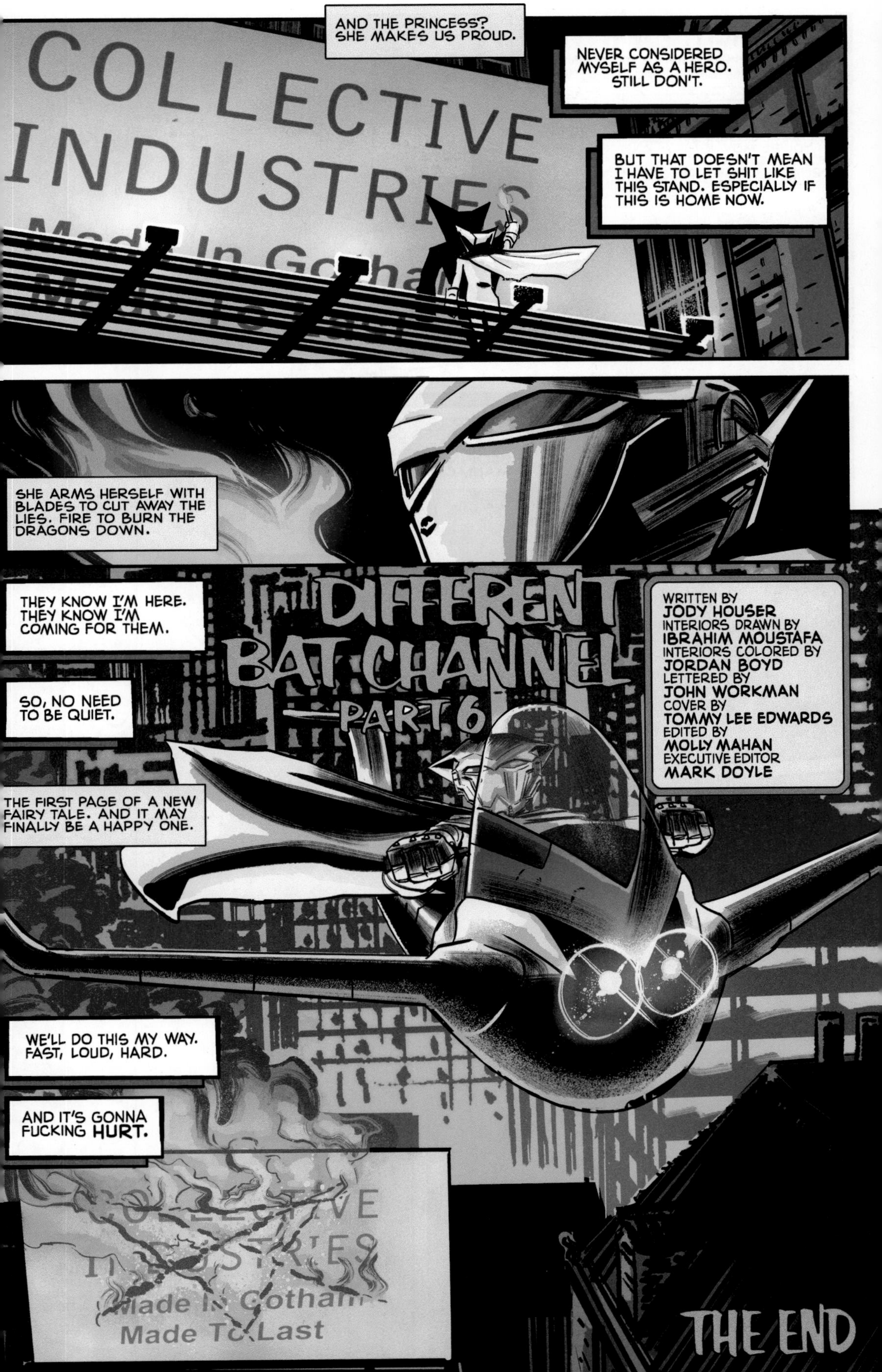

COLLECTIVE INDUSTRIES
AND THE PRINCESS? SHE MAKES US PROUD.
NEVER CONSIDERED MYSELF AS A HERO. STILL DON'T.
BUT THAT DOESN'T MEAN I HAVE TO LET SHIT LIKE THIS STAND. ESPECIALLY IF THIS IS HOME NOW.
SHE ARMS HERSELF WITH BLADES TO CUT AWAY THE LIES. FIRE TO BURN THE DRAGONS DOWN.
THEY KNOW I'M HERE. THEY KNOW I'M COMING FOR THEM.
DIFFERENT BAT CHANNEL
PART 6
WRITTEN BY JODY HOUSER
INTERIORS DRAWN BY IBRAHIM MOUSTAFA
INTERIORS COLORED BY JORDAN BOYD
LETTERED BY JOHN WORKMAN
COVER BY TOMMY LEE EDWARDS
EDITED BY MOLLY MAHAN
EXECUTIVE EDITOR MARK DOYLE
SO, NO NEED TO BE QUIET.
THE FIRST PAGE OF A NEW FAIRY TALE. AND IT MAY FINALLY BE A HAPPY ONE.
WE'LL DO THIS MY WAY. FAST, LOUD, HARD.
AND IT'S GONNA FUCKING HURT.
Made To Last
THE END

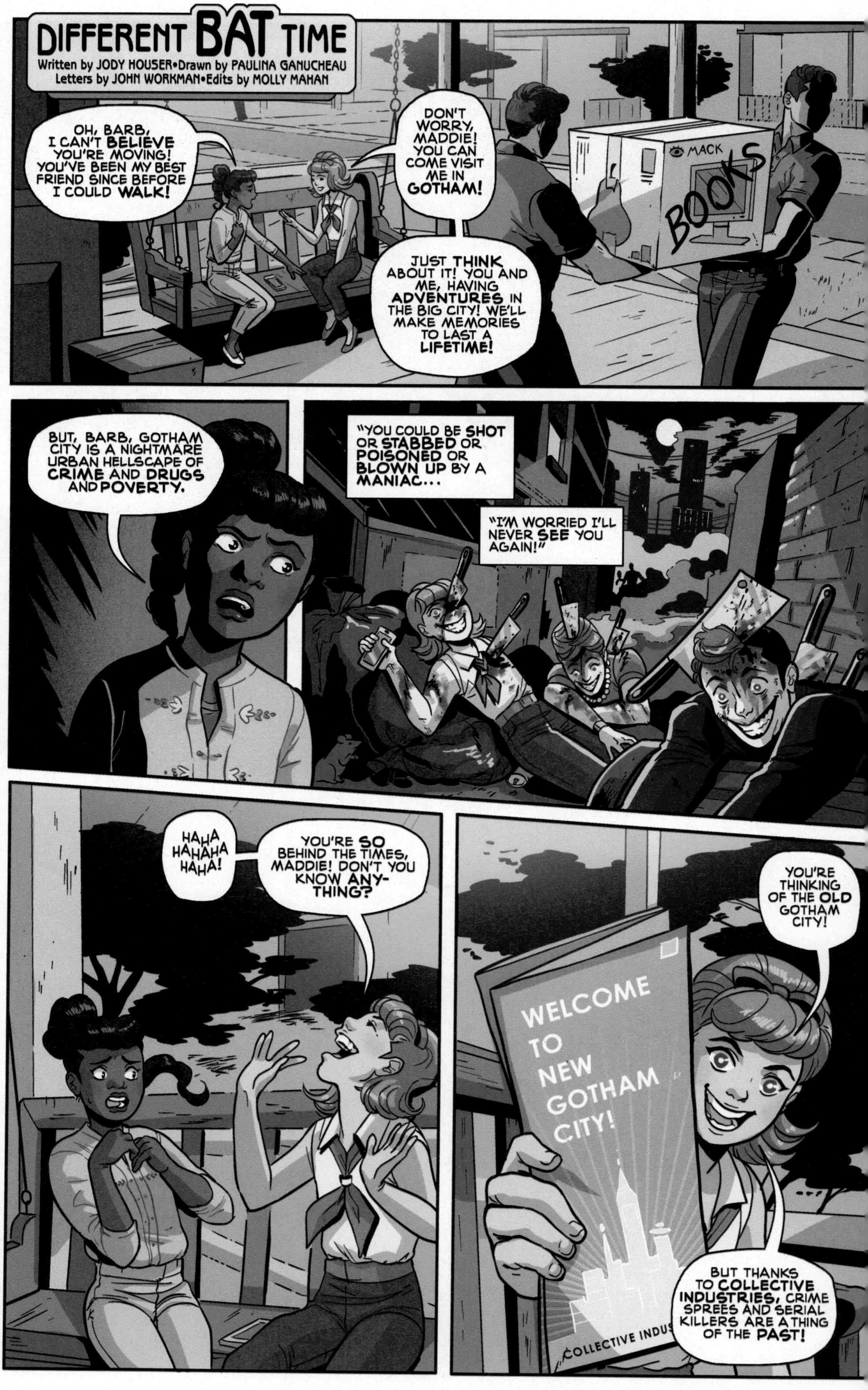
DIFFERENT BAT TIME
Written by JODY HOUSER•Drawn by PAULINA GANUCHEAU
Letters by JOHN WORKMAN•Edits by MOLLY MAHAN
OH, BARB, I CAN'T BELIEVE YOU'RE MOVING! YOU'VE BEEN MY BEST FRIEND SINCE BEFORE I COULD WALK!
DON'T WORRY, MADDIE! YOU CAN COME VISIT ME IN GOTHAM!
JUST THINK ABOUT IT! YOU AND ME, HAVING ADVENTURES IN THE BIG CITY! WE'LL MAKE MEMORIES TO LAST A LIFETIME!
MACK
BOOKS
BUT, BARB, GOTHAM CITY IS A NIGHTMARE URBAN HELLSCAPE OF CRIME AND DRUGS AND POVERTY.
"YOU COULD BE SHOT OR STABBED OR POISONED OR BLOWN UP BY A MANIAC...
"I'M WORRIED I'LL NEVER SEE YOU AGAIN!"
HAHA HAHAHA HAHA!
YOU'RE SO BEHIND THE TIMES, MADDIE! DON'T YOU KNOW ANY-THING?
YOU'RE THINKING OF THE OLD GOTHAM CITY!
WELCOME TO NEW GOTHAM CITY!
COLLECTIVE INDUS
BUT THANKS TO COLLECTIVE INDUSTRIES, CRIME SPREES AND SERIAL KILLERS ARE A THING OF THE PAST!

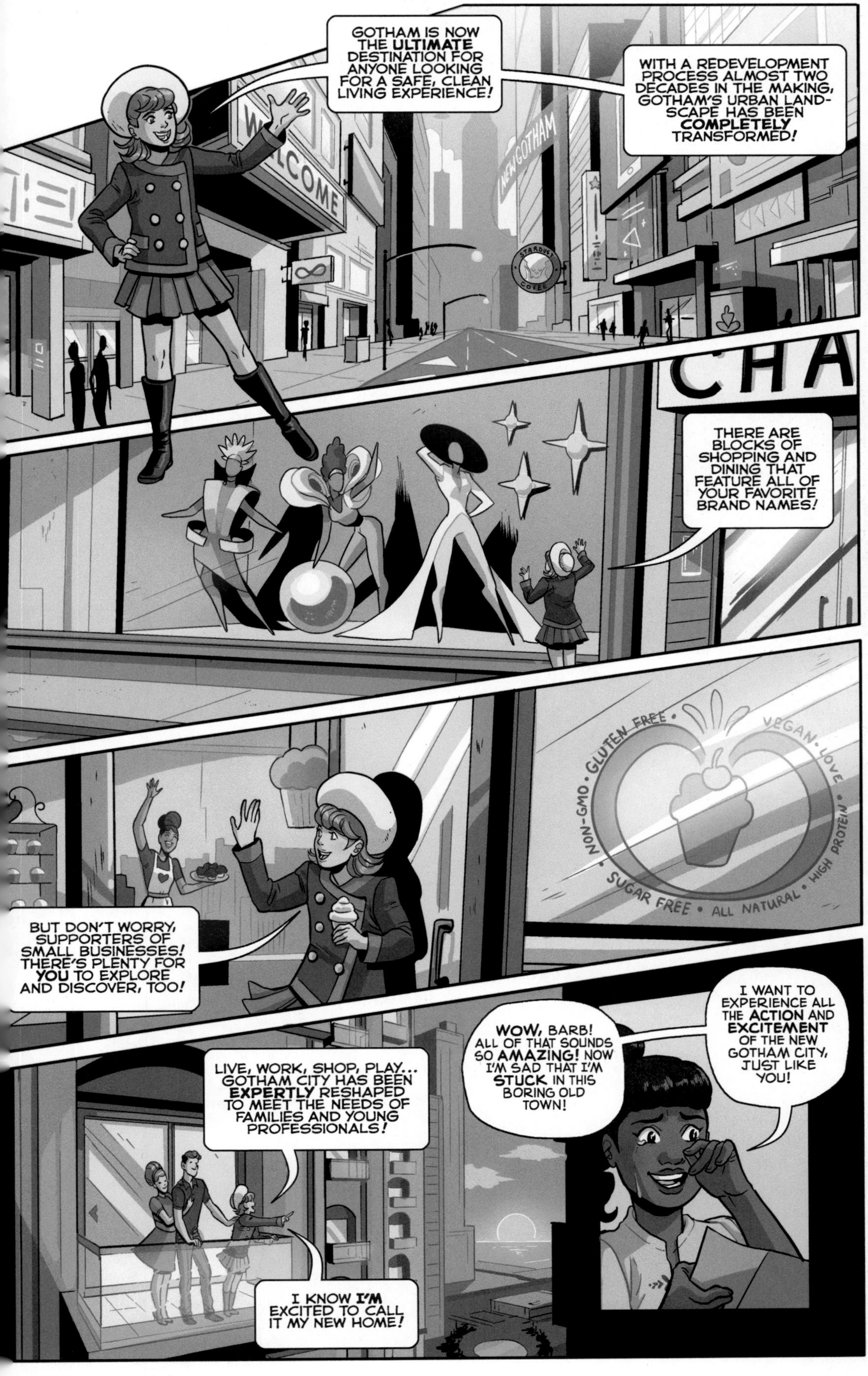
GOTHAM IS NOW THE ULTIMATE DESTINATION FOR ANYONE LOOKING FOR A SAFE, CLEAN LIVING EXPERIENCE!
WITH A REDEVELOPMENT PROCESS ALMOST TWO DECADES IN THE MAKING, GOTHAM'S URBAN LAND-SCAPE HAS BEEN COMPLETELY TRANSFORMED!
WELCOME
NEW GOTHAM
STARDUST COFFEE
CHA
THERE ARE BLOCKS OF SHOPPING AND DINING THAT FEATURE ALL OF YOUR FAVORITE BRAND NAMES!
GLUTEN FREE • VEGAN • LOVE • HIGH PROTEIN • ALL NATURAL • SUGAR FREE • NON-GMO
BUT DON'T WORRY, SUPPORTERS OF SMALL BUSINESSES! THERE'S PLENTY FOR YOU TO EXPLORE AND DISCOVER, TOO!
LIVE, WORK, SHOP, PLAY... GOTHAM CITY HAS BEEN EXPERTLY RESHAPED TO MEET THE NEEDS OF FAMILIES AND YOUNG PROFESSIONALS!
I KNOW I'M EXCITED TO CALL IT MY NEW HOME!
WOW, BARB! ALL OF THAT SOUNDS SO AMAZING! NOW I'M SAD THAT I'M STUCK IN THIS BORING OLD TOWN!
I WANT TO EXPERIENCE ALL THE ACTION AND EXCITEMENT OF THE NEW GOTHAM CITY, JUST LIKE YOU!

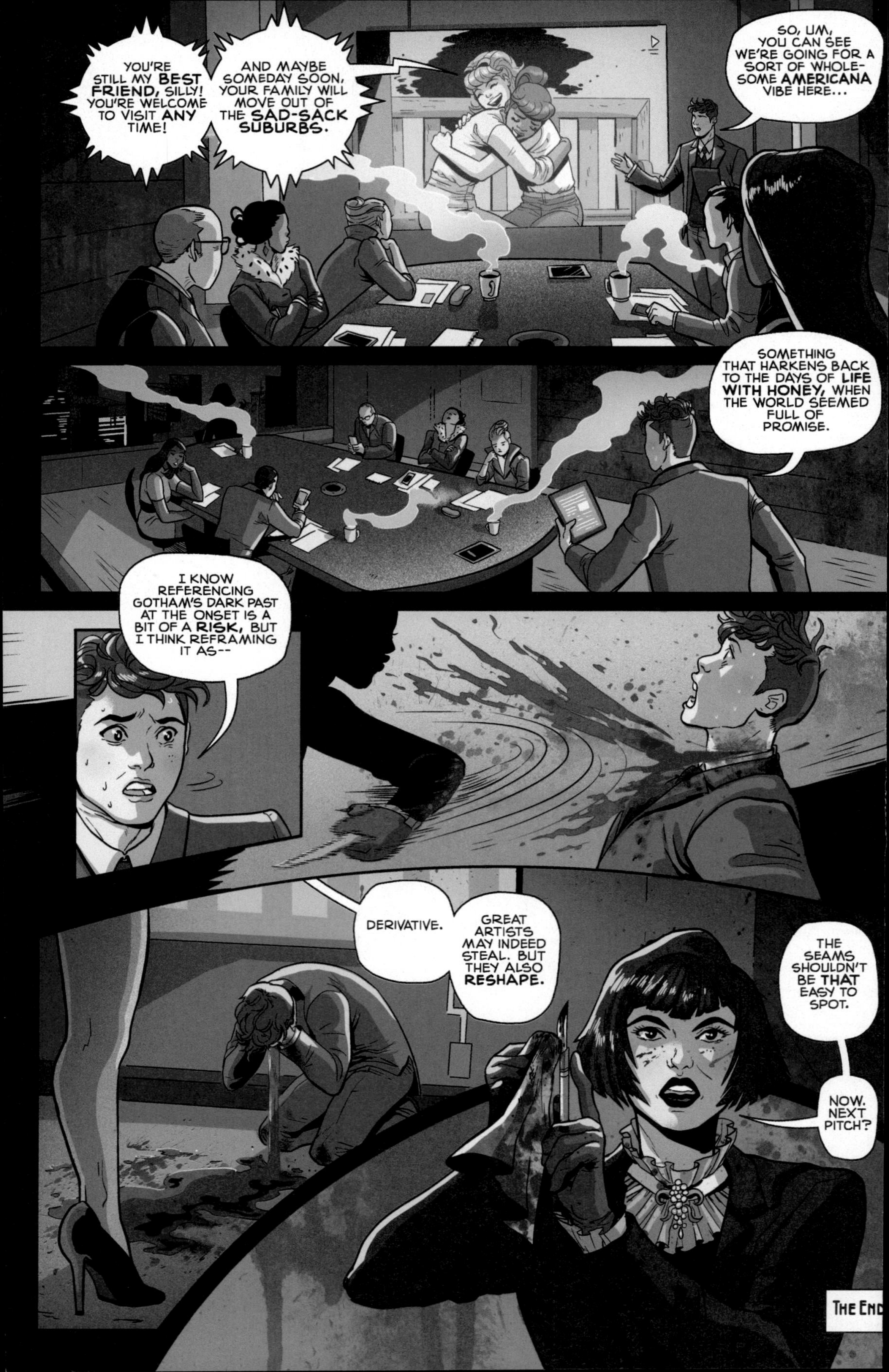
YOU'RE STILL MY BEST FRIEND, SILLY! YOU'RE WELCOME TO VISIT ANY TIME!
AND MAYBE SOMEDAY SOON, YOUR FAMILY WILL MOVE OUT OF THE SAD-SACK SUBURBS.
SO, UM, YOU CAN SEE WE'RE GOING FOR A SORT OF WHOLE-SOME AMERICANA VIBE HERE...
SOMETHING THAT HARKENS BACK TO THE DAYS OF LIFE WITH HONEY, WHEN THE WORLD SEEMED FULL OF PROMISE.
I KNOW REFERENCING GOTHAM'S DARK PAST AT THE ONSET IS A BIT OF A RISK, BUT I THINK REFRAMING IT AS--
DERIVATIVE.
GREAT ARTISTS MAY INDEED STEAL. BUT THEY ALSO RESHAPE.
THE SEAMS SHOULDN'T BE THAT EASY TO SPOT.
NOW. NEXT PITCH?
THE END

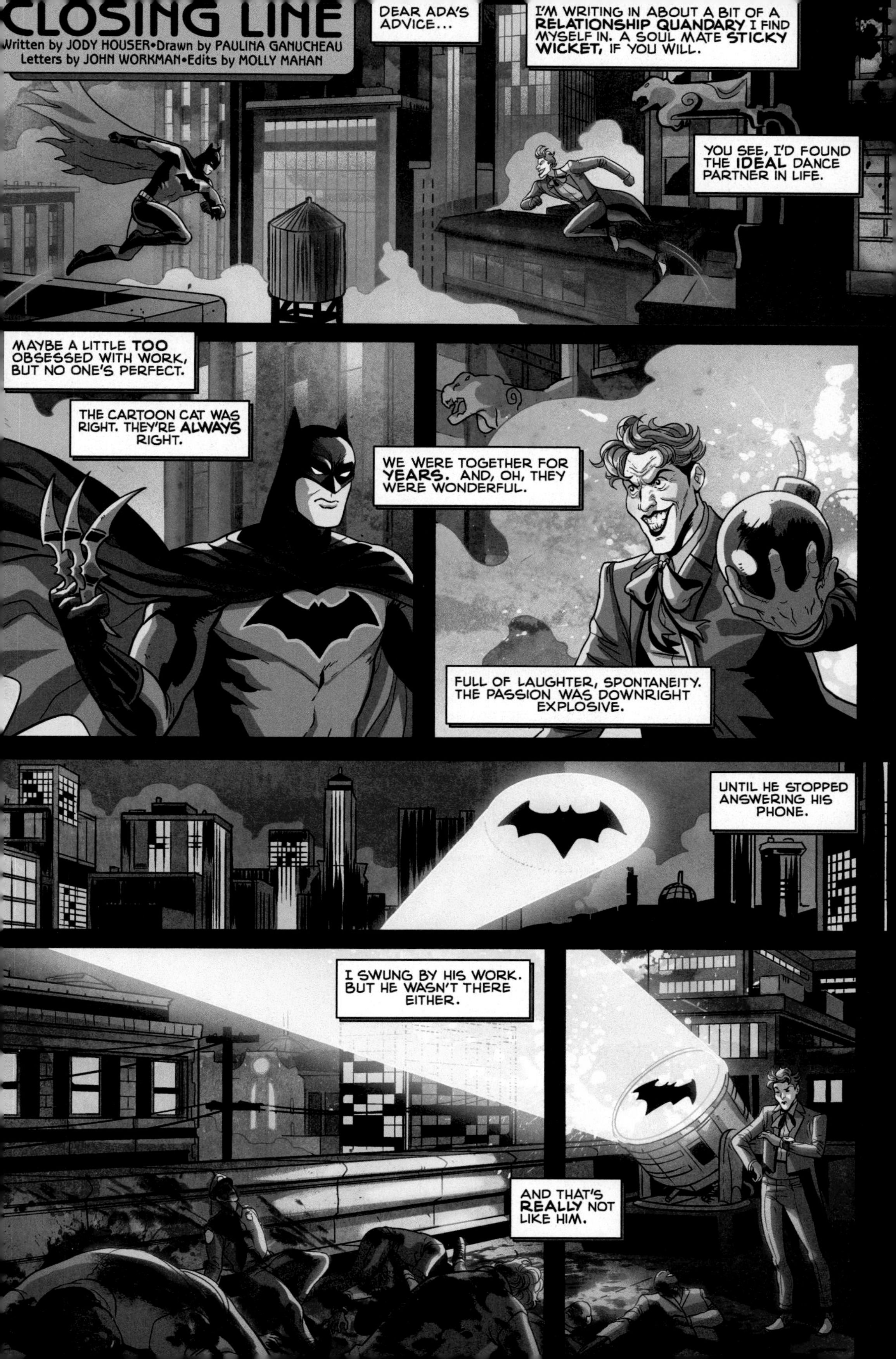
CLOSING LINE
Written by JODY HOUSER•Drawn by PAULINA GANUCHEAU
Letters by JOHN WORKMAN•Edits by MOLLY MAHAN
DEAR ADA'S ADVICE...
I'M WRITING IN ABOUT A BIT OF A RELATIONSHIP QUANDARY I FIND MYSELF IN. A SOUL MATE STICKY WICKET, IF YOU WILL.
YOU SEE, I'D FOUND THE IDEAL DANCE PARTNER IN LIFE.
MAYBE A LITTLE TOO OBSESSED WITH WORK, BUT NO ONE'S PERFECT.
THE CARTOON CAT WAS RIGHT. THEY'RE ALWAYS RIGHT.
WE WERE TOGETHER FOR YEARS. AND, OH, THEY WERE WONDERFUL.
FULL OF LAUGHTER, SPONTANEITY. THE PASSION WAS DOWNRIGHT EXPLOSIVE.
UNTIL HE STOPPED ANSWERING HIS PHONE.
I SWUNG BY HIS WORK. BUT HE WASN'T THERE EITHER.
AND THAT'S REALLY NOT LIKE HIM.

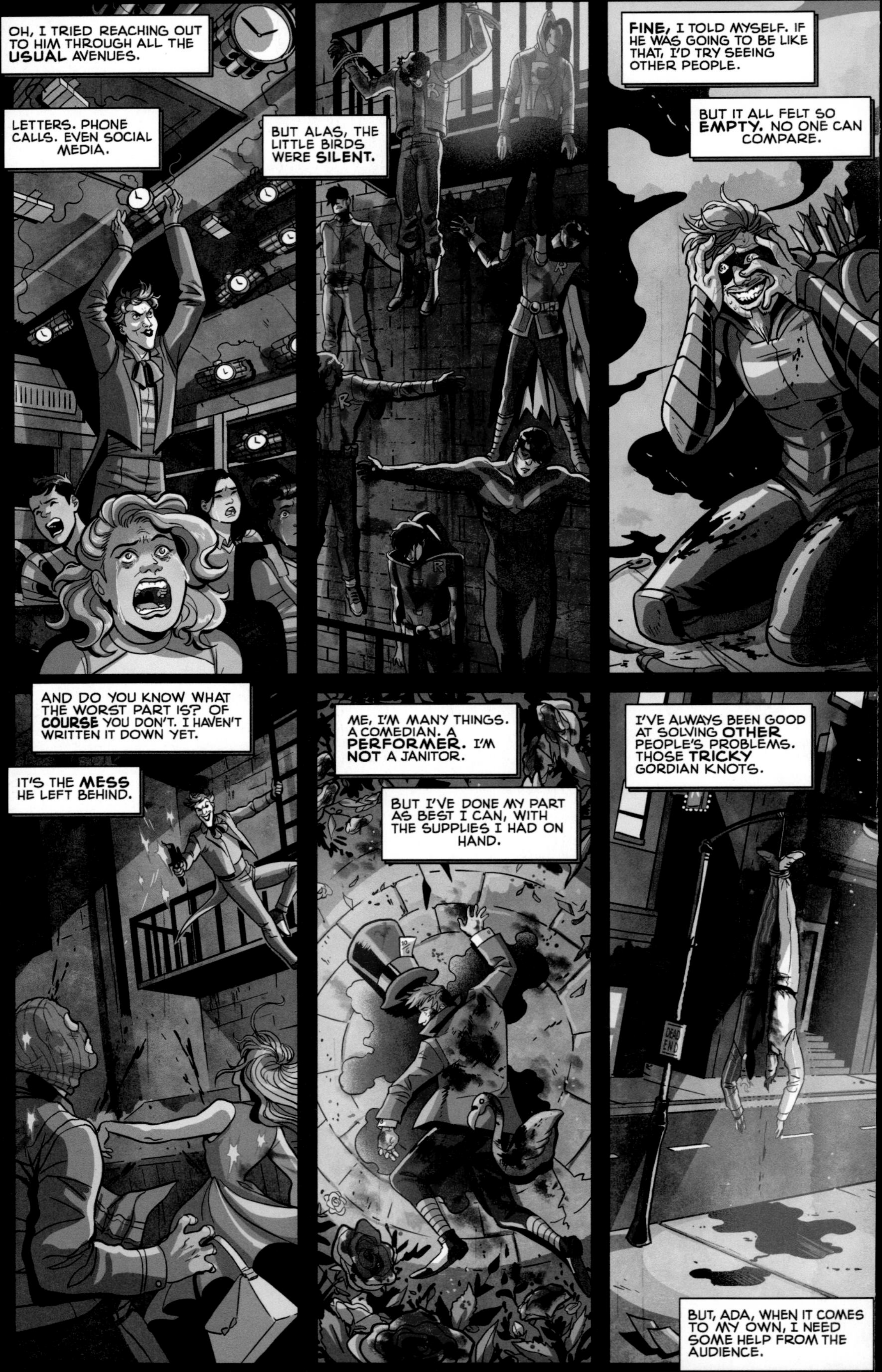
OH, I TRIED REACHING OUT TO HIM THROUGH ALL THE USUAL AVENUES.
LETTERS. PHONE CALLS. EVEN SOCIAL MEDIA.
BUT ALAS, THE LITTLE BIRDS WERE SILENT.
FINE, I TOLD MYSELF. IF HE WAS GOING TO BE LIKE THAT, I'D TRY SEEING OTHER PEOPLE.
BUT IT ALL FELT SO EMPTY. NO ONE CAN COMPARE.
AND DO YOU KNOW WHAT THE WORST PART IS? OF COURSE YOU DON'T. I HAVEN'T WRITTEN IT DOWN YET.
IT'S THE MESS HE LEFT BEHIND.
ME, I'M MANY THINGS. A COMEDIAN. A PERFORMER. I'M NOT A JANITOR.
BUT I'VE DONE MY PART AS BEST I CAN, WITH THE SUPPLIES I HAD ON HAND.
I'VE ALWAYS BEEN GOOD AT SOLVING OTHER PEOPLE'S PROBLEMS. THOSE TRICKY GORDIAN KNOTS.
DEAD END
BUT, ADA, WHEN IT COMES TO MY OWN, I NEED SOME HELP FROM THE AUDIENCE.

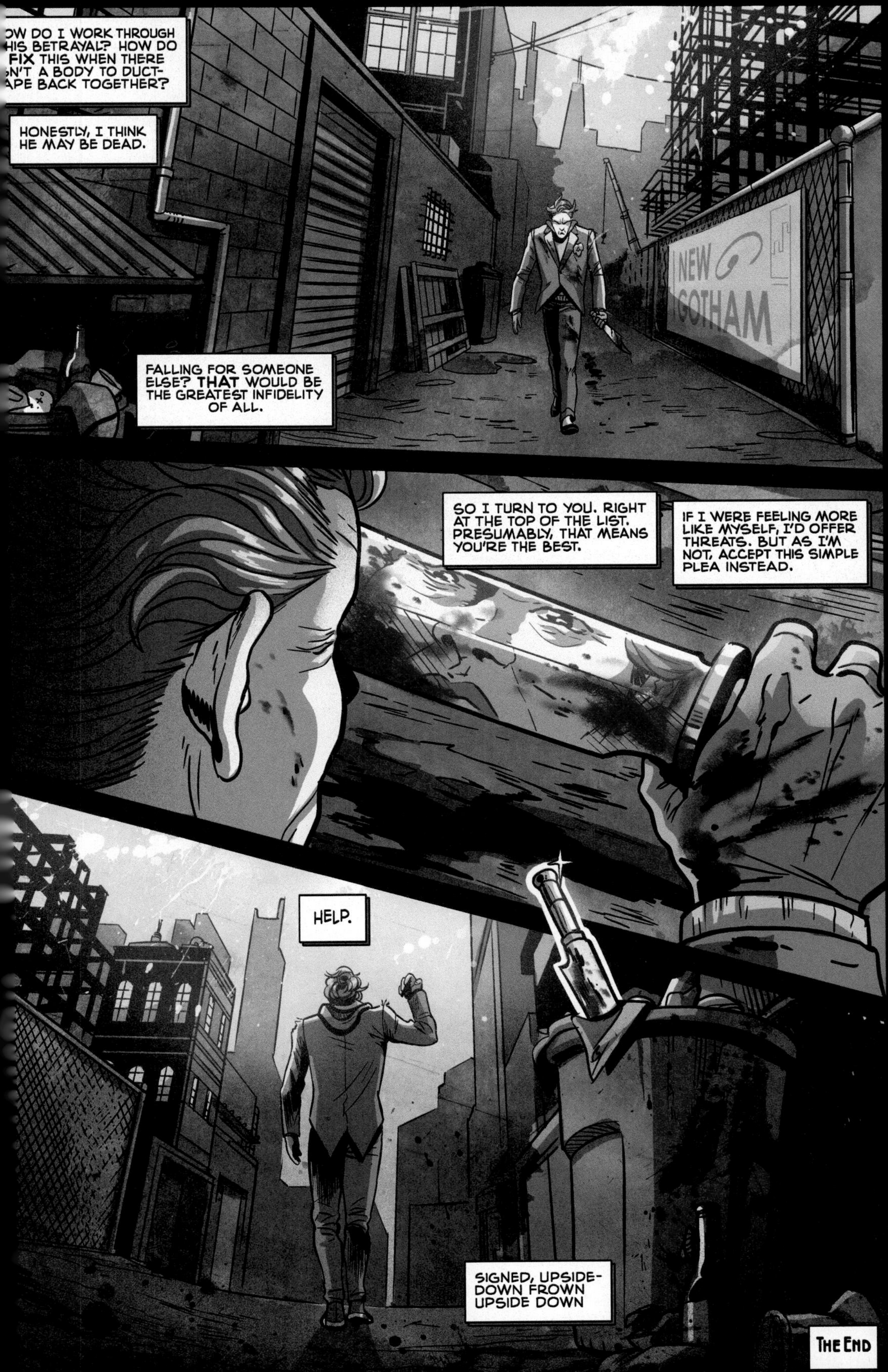
OW DO I WORK THROUGH HIS BETRAYAL? HOW DO FIX THIS WHEN THERE N'T A BODY TO DUCT-APE BACK TOGETHER?
HONESTLY, I THINK HE MAY BE DEAD.
NEW GOTHAM
FALLING FOR SOMEONE ELSE? THAT WOULD BE THE GREATEST INFIDELITY OF ALL.
SO I TURN TO YOU. RIGHT AT THE TOP OF THE LIST. PRESUMABLY, THAT MEANS YOU'RE THE BEST.
IF I WERE FEELING MORE LIKE MYSELF, I'D OFFER THREATS. BUT AS I'M NOT, ACCEPT THIS SIMPLE PLEA INSTEAD.
HELP.
SIGNED, UPSIDE-DOWN FROWN UPSIDE DOWN
THE END

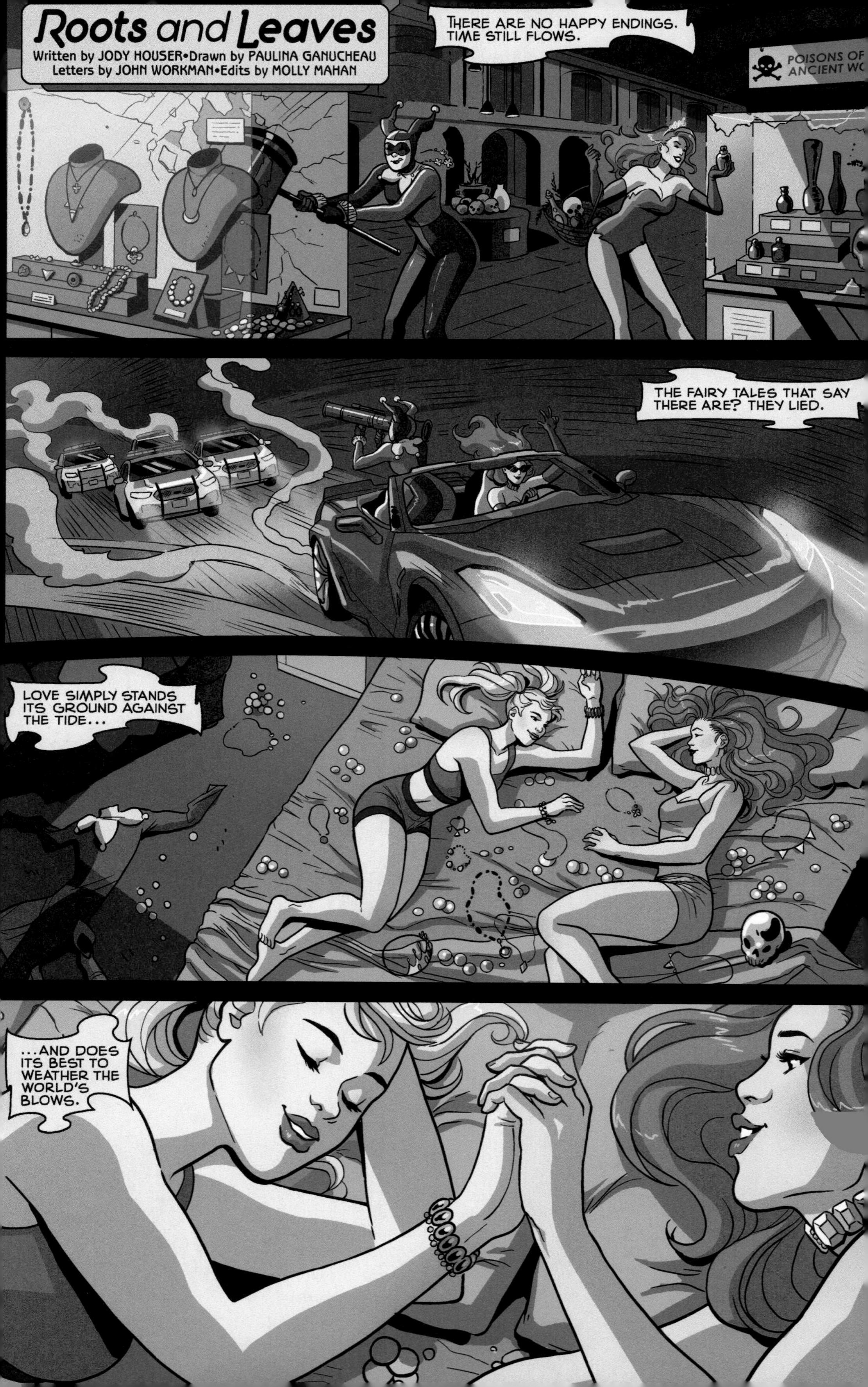
Roots and Leaves
Written by JODY HOUSER•Drawn by PAULINA GANUCHEAU
Letters by JOHN WORKMAN•Edits by MOLLY MAHAN
THERE ARE NO HAPPY ENDINGS. TIME STILL FLOWS.
POISONS OF ANCIENT WO
THE FAIRY TALES THAT SAY THERE ARE? THEY LIED.
LOVE SIMPLY STANDS ITS GROUND AGAINST THE TIDE...
...AND DOES ITS BEST TO WEATHER THE WORLD'S BLOWS.

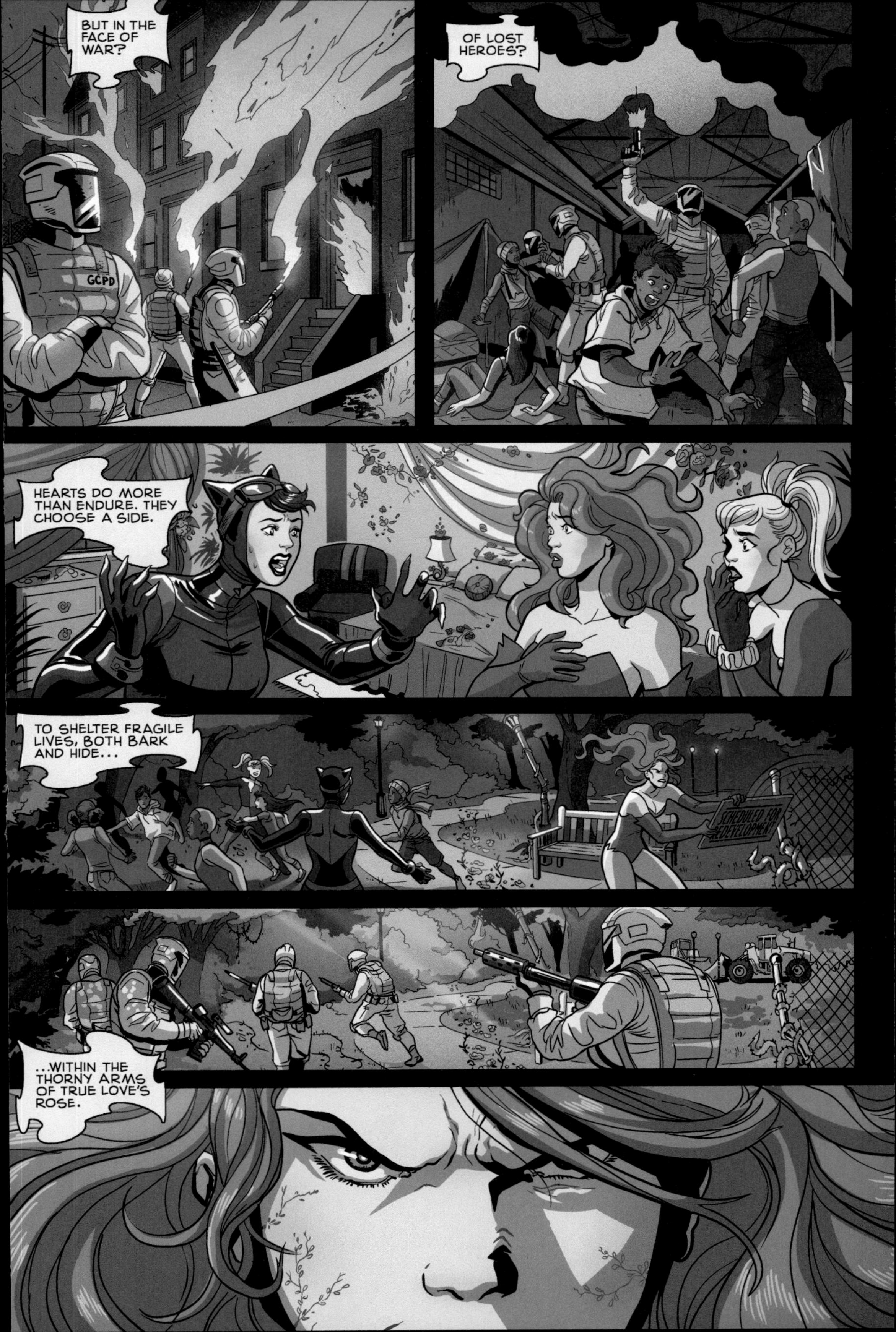
BUT IN THE FACE OF WAR?
OF LOST HEROES?
GCPD
HEARTS DO MORE THAN ENDURE. THEY CHOOSE A SIDE.
TO SHELTER FRAGILE LIVES, BOTH BARK AND HIDE...
SCHEDULED FOR REDEVELOPMENT
...WITHIN THE THORNY ARMS OF TRUE LOVE'S ROSE.

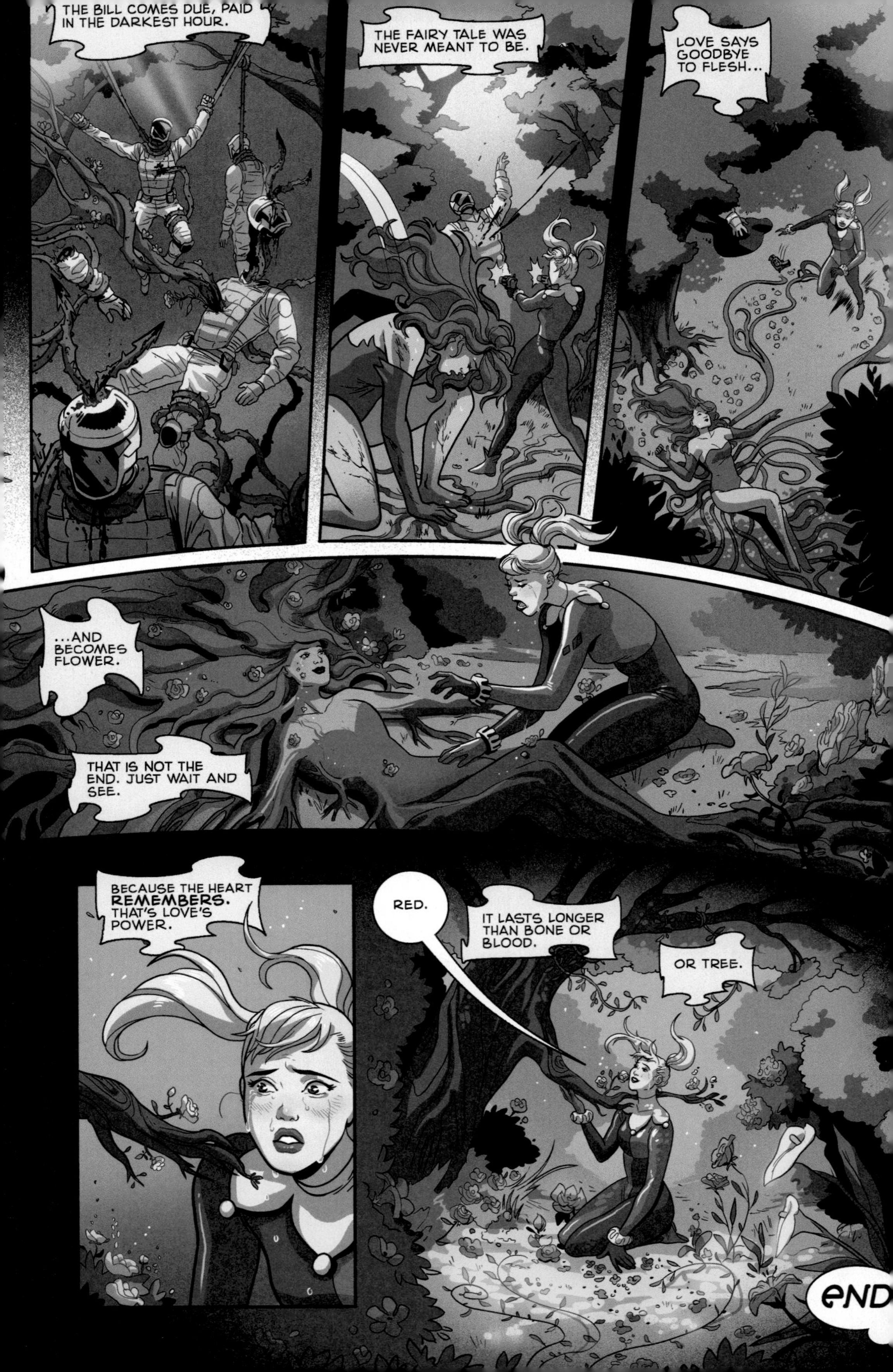
THE BILL COMES DUE, PAID IN THE DARKEST HOUR.
THE FAIRY TALE WAS NEVER MEANT TO BE.
LOVE SAYS GOODBYE TO FLESH...
...AND BECOMES FLOWER.
THAT IS NOT THE END. JUST WAIT AND SEE.
BECAUSE THE HEART REMEMBERS. THAT'S LOVE'S POWER.
RED.
IT LASTS LONGER THAN BONE OR BLOOD.
OR TREE.
END

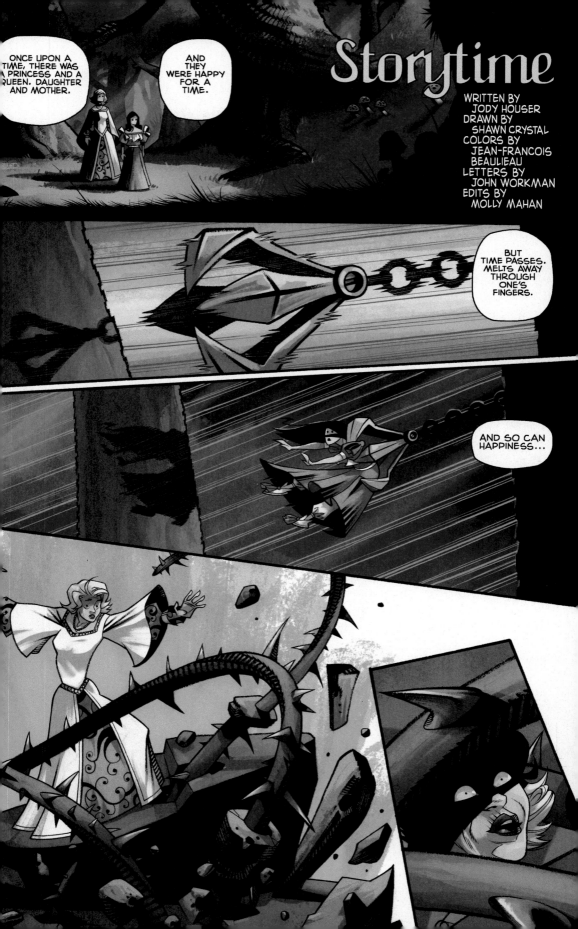

Storytime

WRITTEN BY
JODY HOUSER
DRAWN BY
SHAWN CRYSTAL
COLORS BY
JEAN-FRANCOIS
BEAULIEAU
LETTERS BY
JOHN WORKMAN
EDITS BY
MOLLY MAHAN

ONCE UPON A TIME, THERE WAS A PRINCESS AND A QUEEN. DAUGHTER AND MOTHER.

AND THEY WERE HAPPY FOR A TIME.

BUT TIME PASSES. MELTS AWAY THROUGH ONE'S FINGERS.

AND SO CAN HAPPINESS...

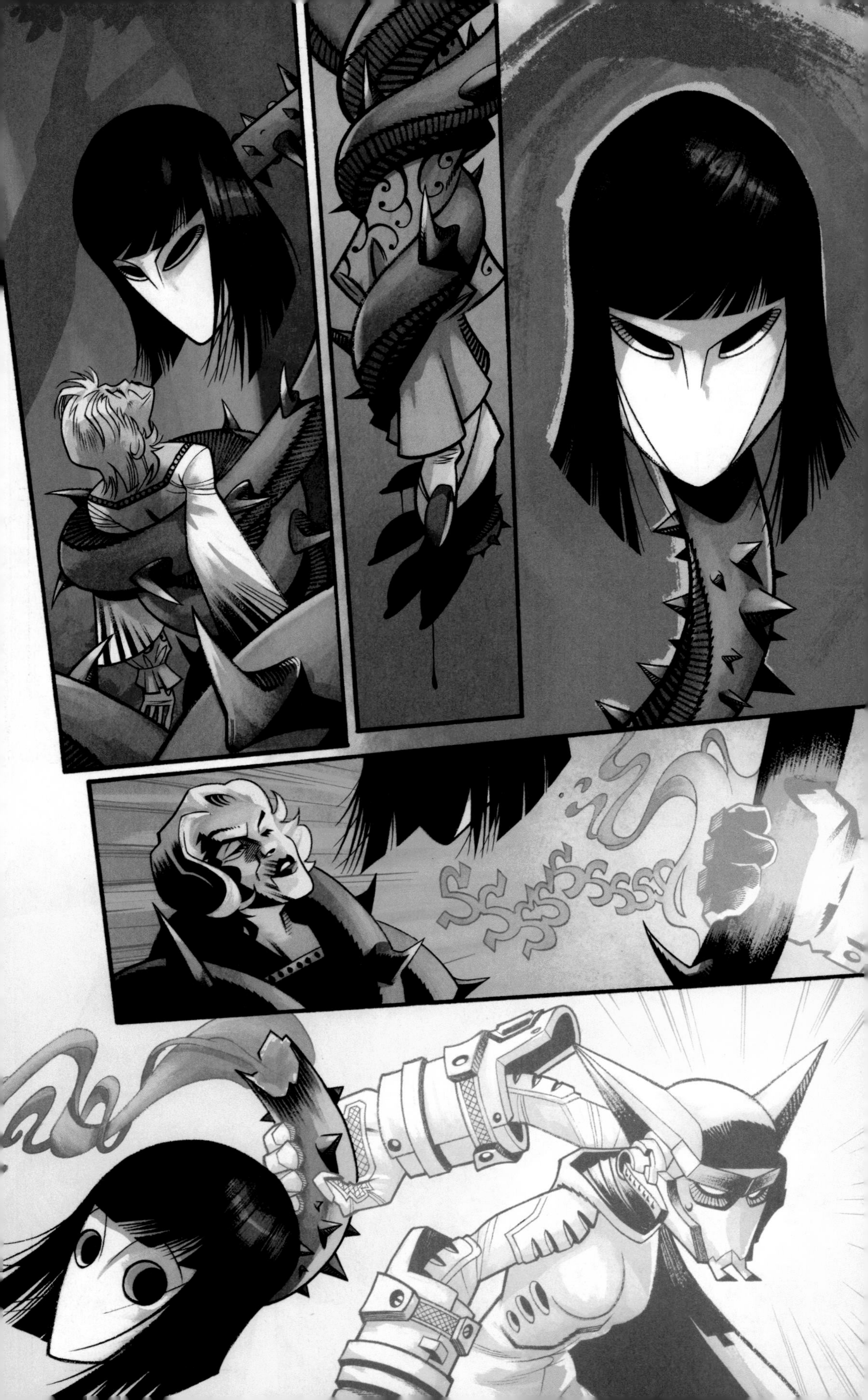
SSSSSSSSS

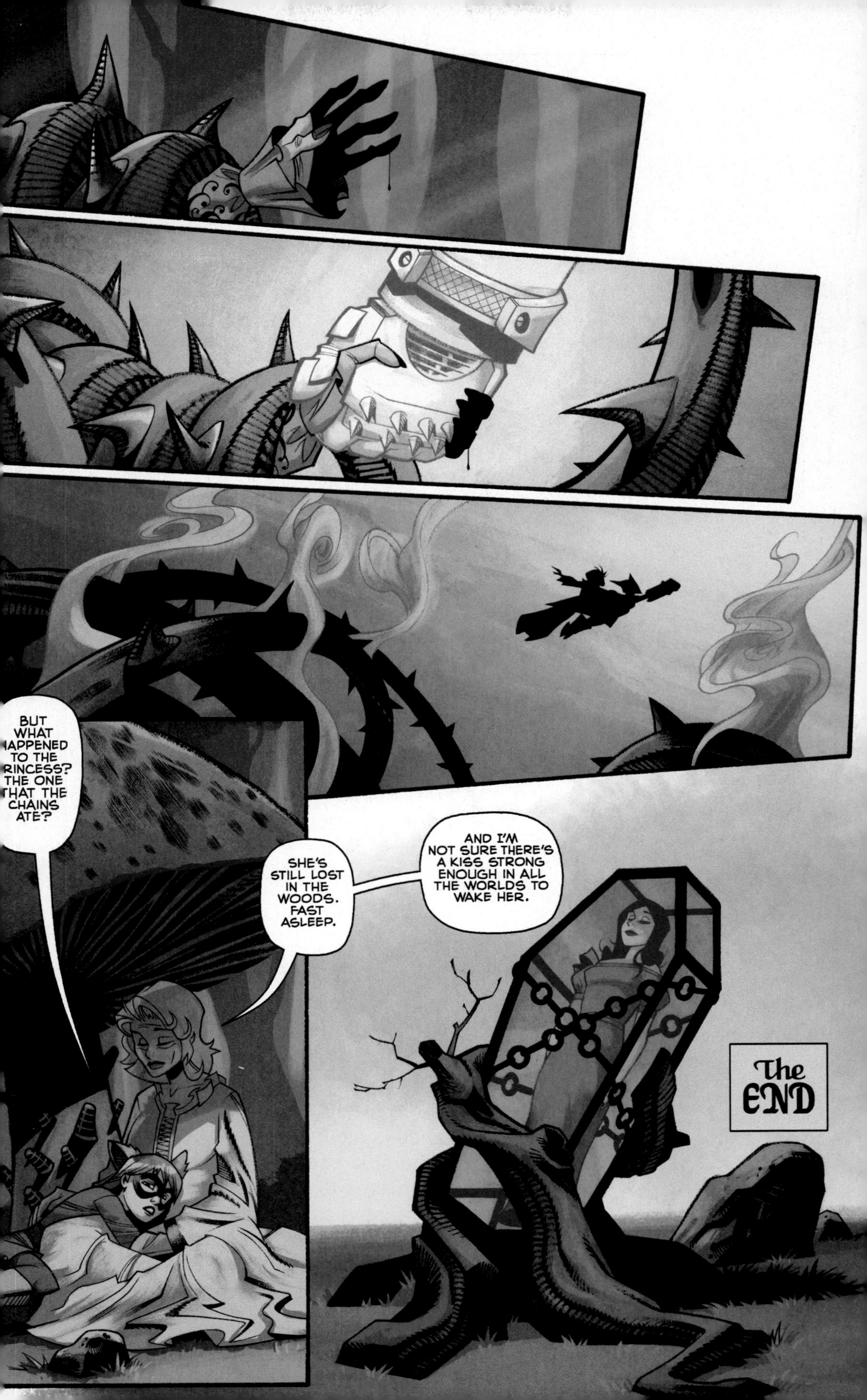
BUT WHAT HAPPENED TO THE PRINCESS? THE ONE THAT THE CHAINS ATE?
SHE'S STILL LOST IN THE WOODS. FAST ASLEEP.
AND I'M NOT SURE THERE'S A KISS STRONG ENOUGH IN ALL THE WORLDS TO WAKE HER.
The END

Creating Gotham Without Batman

Ibrahim Moustafa

One of my favorite things to do is draw reimagined versions of established characters. With MOTHER PANIC: GOTHAM A.D. I'm getting to do exactly that. In addition to our sad old clown version of The Joker, Jody and I have been able to put our spin on this new Gotham's version of Selina Kyle's protégé, Catgirl, as well as Gotham's own resident green thumb, Poison Ivy.

Our villains, "The Collective," are the corporate-types, and like any establishment villains, a good ol' underground resistance is the key to taking them down. With Selina overseeing an Ivy-possessed vegetated stronghold in the heart of the city, we needed one of her young wayward familiars to don the pointy ears. The cowl and goggles were essential for this to read as a cat character. We also wanted to update her with a more youthful sensibility that reflected the harsh times that an underground resistance would endure in this future Gotham. She sports a frayed leather jacket with jeans and sensible boots (which I added cat-claws to for a bit of flair--this IS Gotham City, after all).

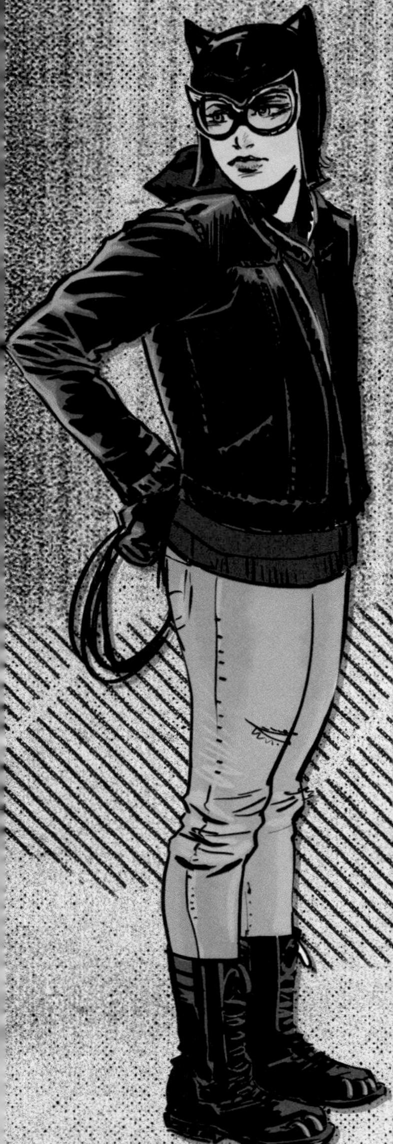

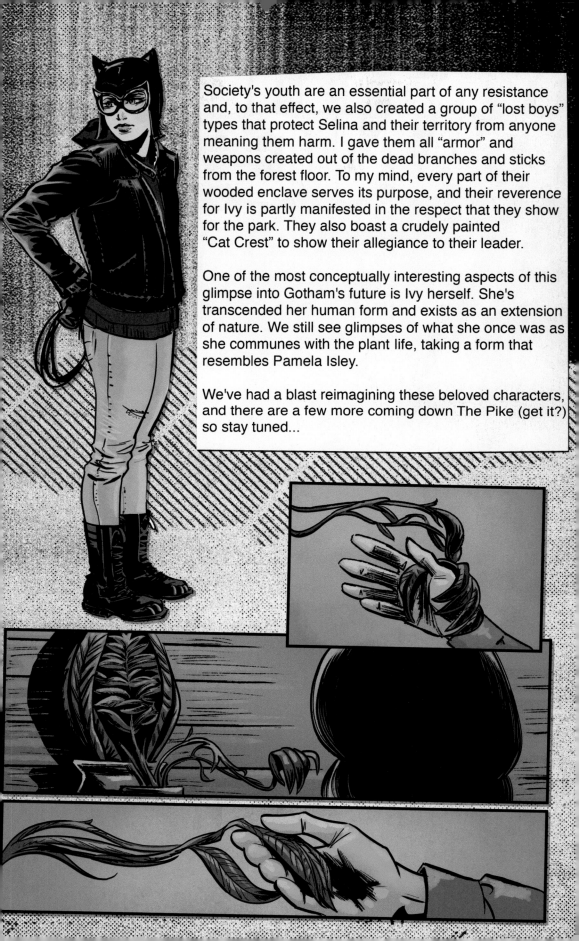

Society's youth are an essential part of any resistance and, to that effect, we also created a group of "lost boys" types that protect Selina and their territory from anyone meaning them harm. I gave them all "armor" and weapons created out of the dead branches and sticks from the forest floor. To my mind, every part of their wooded enclave serves its purpose, and their reverence for Ivy is partly manifested in the respect that they show for the park. They also boast a crudely painted "Cat Crest" to show their allegiance to their leader.

One of the most conceptually interesting aspects of this glimpse into Gotham's future is Ivy herself. She's transcended her human form and exists as an extension of nature. We still see glimpses of what she once was as she communes with the plant life, taking a form that resembles Pamela Isley.

We've had a blast reimagining these beloved characters, and there are a few more coming down The Pike (get it?) so stay tuned...

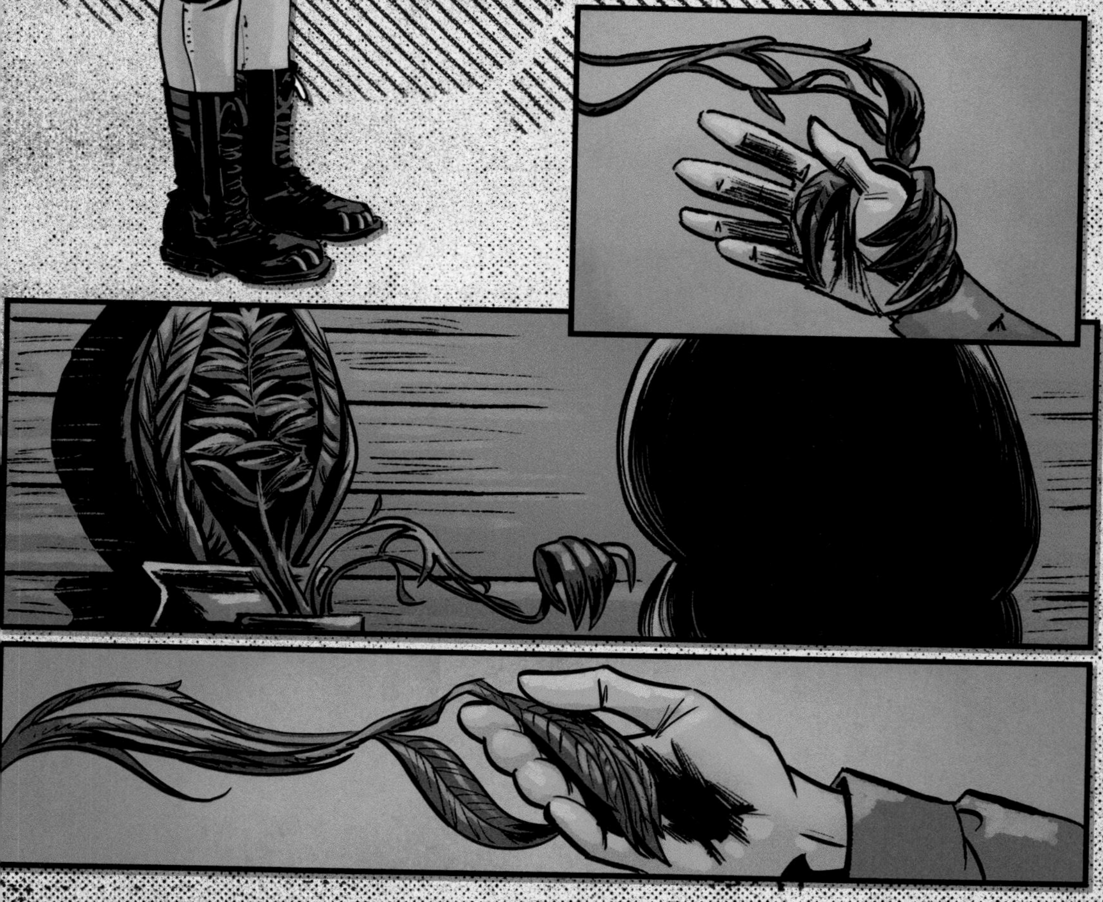

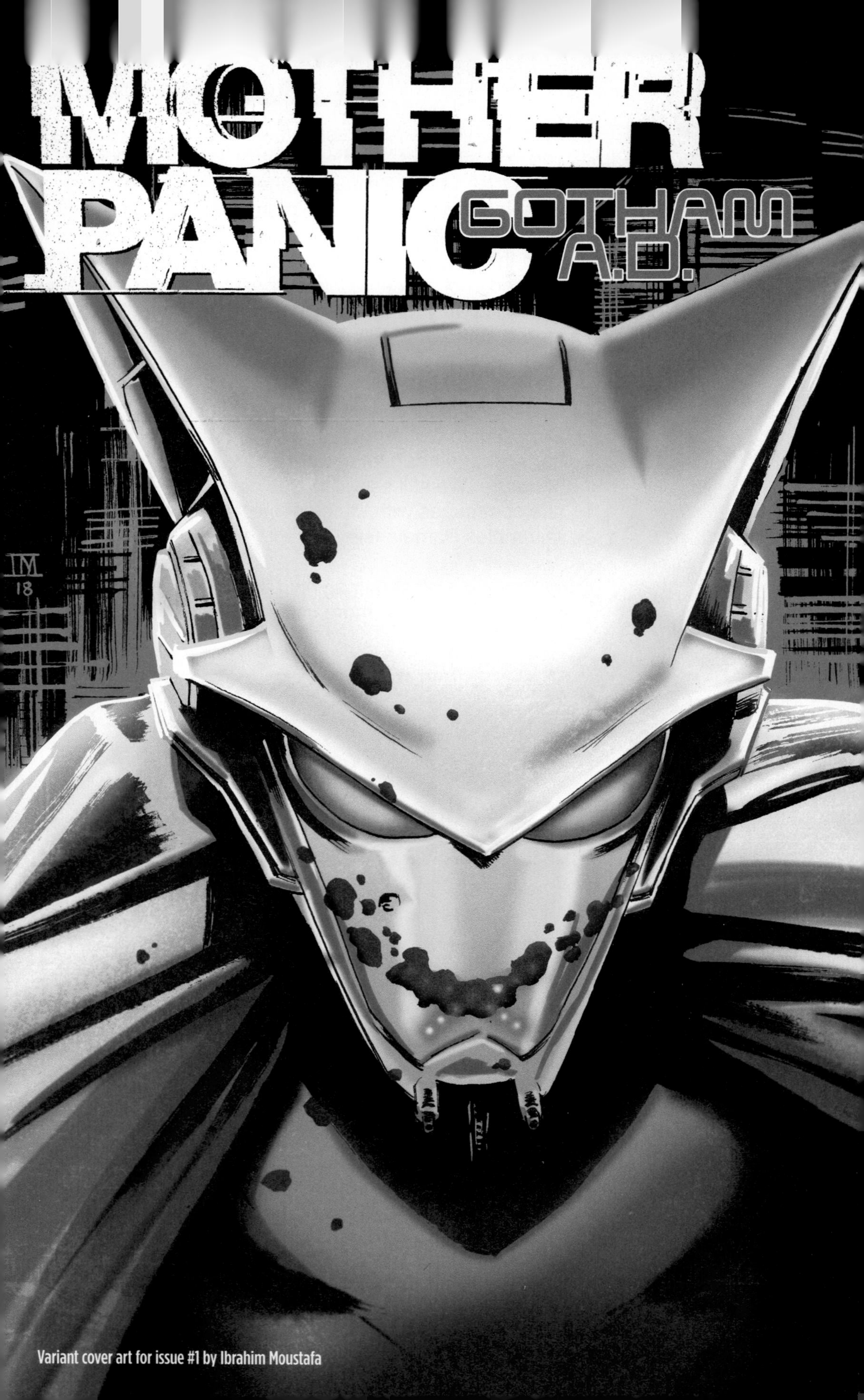
MOTHER PANIC
GOTHAM A.D.
IM 18

Variant cover art for issue #1 by Ibrahim Moustafa